Parting Knowledge

Parting Knowledge

Essays after Augustine

James Wetzel

CASCADE Books • Eugene, Oregon

PARTING KNOWLEDGE
Essays after Augustine

Copyright © 2013 James Wetzel. All rights reserved. Except for brief quotations in critical publications or reviews, no part of this book may be reproduced in any manner without prior written permission from the publisher. Write: Permissions, Wipf and Stock Publishers, 199 W. 8th Ave., Suite 3, Eugene, OR 97401.

Cascade Books
An Imprint of Wipf and Stock Publishers
199 W. 8th Ave., Suite 3
Eugene, OR 97401

www.wipfandstock.com

ISBN 13: 978-1-60899-945-3

Cataloging-in-Publication data:

Wetzel, James.

    Parting knowledge : essays after Augustine / James Wetzel.

    xiv + 290 p. ; 23 cm. —Includes bibliographical references and index.

    ISBN 13: 978-1-60899-945-3

    1. Augustine, Saint, Bishop of Hippo. 2. Augustine, Saint, Bishop of Hippo—Influence. I. Title.

B655.Z7 W466 2013

Manufactured in the U.S.A.

For Nathalie, Anna, and Rowan
interior intimo meo

Contents

Provenance of the Essays and Abstracts   ix
Abbreviations   xiii

Introduction: Philosophy's Birthmark   1

Groundwork
1   Agony in the Garden: Augustine's Myth of Will   9
2   Crisis Mentalities: Augustine after Descartes   28
3   The Alleged Importance of Free Choice: Augustine on *Liberum Arbitrium*   45
4   Trappings of Woe: Augustine's Confession of Grief   58
5   Prodigal Heart: Augustine's Theology of the Emotions   81
6   Life in Unlikeness: The Materiality of Augustine's Conversion   97
7   A Short History of Philosophy: Augustine's Platonism   117

Cultivation
8   Some Thoughts on the Anachronism of Forgiveness   133
9   A Meditation on Hell: Lessons from Dante   155
10 Myth and Moral Philosophy   178
11 The Original Sin: Sex and Christian Ethics   199
    ... and a Dialogical Postscript   209
12 From Aphrodite to God the Father: A Question of Beauty   213
13 Wittgenstein's Augustine: The Inauguration of the Later Philosophy   225
14 What the Saints Know: Quasi-Epistemological Reflections   248

Works Cited   263
Index   269

Provenance of the Essays and Abstracts

ALL OF THE ESSAYS that appear in this volume have, with the exception of the essay on sex and original sin (chapter 11), appeared elsewhere. I have made corrections and revised some of the prose, but the essays remain fundamentally as they were. They are used here with permission.

1. Published as "Augustine on the Will," in *A Companion to Augustine*, ed. Mark Vessey (Oxford: Wiley-Blackwell, 2012) 339–52.

    Here I look at the illusion of autonomy in a will to sin and watch it give way in Augustine to a story of original innocence and willful forgetting. I argue that Augustine is a better mythologist of will than he is a theorist.

2. Published in *American Catholic Philosophical Quarterly*, Special Issue on St. Augustine, ed. Roland J. Teske 64.1 (2000) 115–33.

    Augustine transforms the inward turn of Plotinus—his favorite Platonist—into psychological self-awareness, but inwardness is not for him a privileged precinct of knowledge. I explicate Augustinian interiority and contrast it to the inwardness of the Cartesian *res cogitans*.

3. Published as "The Alleged Importance of *liberum arbitrium*," in *Spiritus et Littera: Beiträge zur Augustinus-Forschung*, ed. Guntram Förster, Andreas Grote, and Christof Müller (Würzburg: Echter, 2009) 405–19.

    Augustine speaks of *liberum arbitrium*—free choice—as a middling good, pitched between an ineluctable will to sin and angelic stability in virtue. I argue Augustine against Augustine in this essay. His deeper insight into freedom, the one that connects freedom to love, renders freedom a form of acknowledgment, a life lived out of gratitude. Once the middling good of freedom is exposed for the illusion that it is, it becomes clear that Christ, not Adam, recalls us to the original bone of our humanity.

4. Published as chapter 4 of *A Reader's Companion to Augustine's Confessions*, ed. Kim Paffenroth and Robert P. Kennedy (Louisville: Westminster John Knox, 2003) 53–69.

To some ancient luminaries—the Stoics especially—grief signaled a lack of wisdom: in a rational order everything is as it should be, and the sage, being fully attuned to reason, should be able to *feel* that it is. In book 4 of the *Confessions*, Augustine recounts his grief over the death of a childhood friend and chides himself, not for grieving, but for not grieving very well. Augustine's reconciliation of wisdom with grief marks his profoundest break from the philosophical culture of autarky.

5. Published as "Augustine," in *The Oxford Handbook of Religion and Emotion*, ed. John Corrigan (Oxford: Oxford University Press, 2008) 349–63.

Here I set out Augustine's appropriation and critique, via Cicero, of a Stoic conception of emotion. It is Augustine's critique of Stoic *apatheia*, particularly as he develops it in *City of God*, that gives me a window into his theology of the heart. For much of the essay, I detail the striking ways in which the realities of sin and grace render the Augustinian will into something more akin to a passion than a faculty of choice.

6. Published in *Journal of Religion* 91.1 (2011) 43–63.

The conversion that Augustine famously describes in book 8 of the *Confessions* is less a resolution of will than an acceptance of divinely mothered humanity. I look at the notion of materiality in Augustine, remaining mindful of its connection to "mater" (mother), and I explicate his fretful acceptance of God's material grace.

7. Published as "Augustine's Short History of Philosophy," in *Theology and Philosophy*, vol. 1: *Faith and Reason*, ed. Oliver Crisp, Gavin D'Costa, Mervyn Davies, and Peter Hampson (London: T. & T. Clark, 2011) 89–101. Reprinted by kind permission of Continuum International Publishing Group.

In the story of philosophy that Augustine tells in book 8 of *City of God*, the Platonists are the moral. They are the philosophers with the greatest

Provenance of the Essays and Abstracts

insight into God, but they lack the humility to reject the gods and revere Christ. I discuss Augustine's greatest debt to these Platonists, their conception of divine simplicity, and consider what force there is in his critique of their piety.

8. Published in *Journal of Religious Ethics* 27.1 (1999) 83–102.

   Forgiveness outside of a theistic context is fundamentally reactive. The sin comes first, then (if at all) the grace. With Anselm as my primary interlocutor, I argue for the truth of the inverse perspective. Forgiveness is what we begin with.

9. Published in *Modern Theology* 18.3 (2002) 375–94.

   Hell as a place where souls are wholly absented from divine love is a seductive but also corrupting fiction. The truth is that God, as the Lord of Hell, is present (even if unnoticed) in human despair. Dante's fiction of hell is attentive to this truth. I explicate how.

10. Published in *Thinking Through Myths: Philosophical Perspectives*, ed. Kevin Schilbrack (London: Routledge, 2002) 123–41.

    I look at Kant's attempt to rationalize the doctrine of original sin. His theory ends in mythology, and the mythology, despite his intentions, ends up being better than the theory. (This essay can be read as the counterpart to chapter 1.)

11. Given as the Belk Endowed Lecture in Christian Ethics, Wesleyan College, October 23, 2007; the dialogical postscript is an excerpt from a personal exchange between Kathleen Skerrett and myself.

    If original knowledge has something to do with being able to take in the image of God as both male and female (Gen 1:27), then sexuality is arguably both a path and an impediment to this end. I discuss the uneasy relationship between the natural and spiritual sides of sex in this essay, with some attention to Augustine's theology of marriage. The dialogical postscript offers a further reflection on the intimacy of male and female in God.

12. Published in *Theology Today* 64.1 (2007) 25–35.

    The move in mindset from Aphrodite to God the Father seems to involve a loss of beauty (not to mention a sublimation of sex). In this essay, I attempt to reimagine beauty within the paradigm of a divine

Provenance of the Essays and Abstracts

father figure. Freud notoriously dismissed such a paradigm as infantile and pathetically needy. In the Christian mythos, the suffering son offers to release his father from having to avenge his son's suffering and death: "Father, forgive them, for they know not what they do" (Luke 23:34). There is beauty in the trust that transcends neediness, and infants can grow up to find it in their fathers.

13. Published in *Augustine and Philosophy*, ed. Phillip Cary, John Doody, and Kim Paffenroth (Lanham, MD: Rowman & Littlefield, 2010) 219–42.

I begin with a careful look at Wittgenstein's use of *Confessions* 1.8.13 to kick off the *Philosophical Investigations*. I go on to explore the nature and necessity of confessional philosophy.

14. Published in *A Companion to Christian Mysticism*, ed. Julia Lamm (Oxford: Wiley-Blackwell, 2012) 550–61.

When Anselm meditates on his mantra for God—the being greater than which none can be conceived—he realizes that such a being would be have to be both conceivable and not. The conjunction issues in an apparent dilemma: if his God is too conceivable, then his God is not God; if his God is beyond conceiving, then his God is not his. In this essay I think through Anselm's dilemma in an attempt to get at what either the saint or the mystic can know of God.

Abbreviations

Augustine's titles:

c. Acad.	Contra Academicos	Against the Skeptics (CCL 29)
b. conjug.	De bono conjugali	On the good of marriage (CSEL 41)
c. ep. Pel.	Contra duas epistolas Pelagianorum	Against two letters of the Pelagians (CSEL 60)
c. Jul. imp.	Contra Julianum opus imperfectum	Against Julian—the unfinished work (CSEL 85.1)
civ. Dei	De civitate Dei	City of God (CCSL 47–48)
conf.	Confessionum libri XIII	Confessions (CCSL 27)
corrept.	De correptione et gratia	On correction and grace (BA 24)
duab. an.	De duabus animabus	On the two souls (CSEL 25)
ex. prop. Rm.	Expositio quarundam propositionum ex epistula Apostoli ad Romanos	Commentary on Romans—select verses (CSEL 84)
Gn. adv. Man.	De Genesi adversus Manicheos	On Genesis—the anti-Manichean commentary (CSEL 91)

Abbreviations

Gn. litt.	*De Genesi ad litteram*	*On Genesis—the literal commentary* (CSEL 28.1)
lib. arb.	*De libero arbitrio*	*On free choice* (CCSL 29)
mag.	*De magistro*	*On the teacher* (CCSL 29)
nupt. et conc.	*De nuptiis et concupiscentia*	*Marriage and sex* (CSEL 42)
persev.	*De dono perseverantiae*	*On the gift of perseverance* (BA 24)
praed. sanct.	*De praedestinatione sanctorum*	*On the predestination of saints* (BA 24)
retr.	*Retractationes*	*Reconsiderations* (CCSL 57)
Simpl.	*Ad Simplicianum de diversis quaestionibus*	*To Simplician—on various questions* (CCSL 44)
spir. et. litt.	*De spiritu et littera*	*On the sprit and the letter* (CSEL 60)
Trin.	*De Trinitate*	*The Trinity* (CCSL 50)

Latin source collections:

BA	*Bibliothèque Augustinienne*	Paris: Institut d'Études Augustiniennes
CCSL	*Corpus Christianorum Series Latina*	Turnhout: Brepols
CSEL	*Corpus Scriptorum Ecclesiasticorum Latinorum*	Vienna: Österreichische Akademie der Wissenschaften

Introduction
Philosophy's Birthmark

"Why do you call me good? No one is good but God alone."
—MARK 10:18

I THINK OF MYSELF as philosopher—a thought, no doubt, that pleases me too much—but what I mean by philosophy is mostly mundane and hardly exceptional. Like any other thinking animal, I desire many things and devise the means, more or less thoughtfully, to get what I want. There is nothing directly philosophical in all of this desire-mongering, even granting that the expenditure of my intelligence here may be considerable. It is only when I wed my desires to thoughts about the good that my dormant desire for wisdom begins to budge. Is it good for me to want the things that I want? What makes a thing good to want? Am I myself good, or am I wanting? These can be perfectly ordinary questions, and in one form or another, a thinking animal, such as myself, falls into the business of posing them. And yet the desire that such questions delimit—a desire for the good—is no ordinary desire. It is its own order of desire, and although I sometimes like to think that desire for the good orders, from its lofty perch, my workaday desires for particular goods, I don't have much of a picture for how it would do this, and, to the extent that I do have one, I suspect that the picture misleads.

When I have a desire for a particular good—such as wanting, say, to revive my spoken French—often I have a clear idea of what it would mean for me to have that good, if not perfectly, then proximately at least. (Being able to order a meal in French or to open a bank account is a step along the way toward the good of francophone life; being able to express humor or irony in French or to befriend a native speaker, who knows no English, is a step further along.) But when I seek to have the good itself, and not some particular good, I am at a loss to say what "having" would mean. Minimally I find myself committed to the idea, though not without reason, that having the good cannot be a matter of having a collection of particular goods, however well-ordered or comprehensive that collection may turn out to be.

That is enough of a commitment to make me out as a Platonist in one of the grand disjunctions of philosophical self-identification. My Aristotelian counterpart (who would here be most any one of my teachers) reminds me that it is of course impossible to speak intelligibly of goodness apart from some implied or specified context of application. What is the good? Well, what sort of goodness is at issue? A knife or a mind is good when it is sharp; a pain when sharp is not so good, or at least worrisome. While it can sometimes be useful to put a particular context of application into question—is it, say, ever really good to be a good liar?—it seems self-defeating to put all the contexts into question at once. I risk sounding like the toddler who asks the "why" question once too often and elicits the exasperated parental response: "because it just is." The good, when it just is, comes off as less than informative. (As even the toddler surely senses.)

I respect the Aristotelian complaint. I feel its force. But I persist in my Platonism. If I lose the idea of the good, of the goodness that transcends the sum of goods, I lose the idea that gaining ground in goodness, taking root in the knowledge of it, is essentially a feat of recognition. Goodness, when I recognize it, confirms me in an undatable prior knowledge that I am now getting in altered form, exteriorized—the difference that beauty makes. When I come to know that I know, I am less intent on consuming a good than on acknowledging one. I become more open to inspiration. The problem of not knowing how to characterize what it means to "have the good" starts to speak less to some impossible conundrum of knowing, ripe for dissolution, than to a gripping illusion: that goods, more than goodness, can be readily possessed. For the all the sophisticated ways we find to invent and acquire new consumer goods, it strikes me that, apart from a path of recognition, we travel the road of blind appetite.

But like the interlocutor to whom I owe the most—Saint Augustine of Hippo—I am not at ease in my Platonism. A recollected knowledge implies an original, and I certainly cannot tell you what original knowing is, how it was lost, or what it looks like when it is finally and fully regained.

Introduction

I am not even sure that it makes sense to look for a *perfected* recollection, as if it were really possible to compare something out of time and space to a thing of this world and arrive at an equivalence. Augustine is of two minds about the Platonism I have been sketching. As a teacher of sacred doctrine, he offers confident answers to the questions I am going to leave unresolved. He tells us that original knowledge is what the first human beings, Adam and Eve in Eden, naturally know of God; that such knowledge gets lost when they covet greater knowledge and thereby deregulate their minds; that the knowledge returns, in securer form, when some of their descendents, the graced ones, rediscover God in Christ, the obedient Adam, and finally come to know that there is nothing more to be known. As a student of sacred doctrine, still about the business of fathoming the dark truths of divinity, Augustine is helpfully less confident. He is alive to the oddness of two genuinely content beings willfully opting for discontent, this being basically the spectacle of a self-blinding reason, and so he brings less conviction to his belief that human willfulness can account for the breach between God (eternal wisdom) and humankind (time-tested affection). The willfulness expresses, but does not explain, the oddness.

It is the student more than the teacher who puts me in mind of Christianity's most radical claim: that Christ is no mere means to God, but is the one God incarnate. As a mere means, he would be veiling the mysteries of original knowledge and tempting us to imagine that a knowledge, once outgrown, could still be made out to be sustaining in its original form (a boon of resurrection; blink twice). As God incarnate, Christ is Jesus of Nazareth, a particular man of a particular time, a mortal and no superman; his humanity, however admirable, is not his leg up to a divine life. The divinity that forms such an intimate part of his incarnation leaves his native humanity intact—more intact, indeed, than would otherwise have been the case. And so there may be no need, here or in other cases, for terms of equivalence between a divine and a human form of life, terms that would doubtless, in the end, force a choice.

I owe to Augustine my sense that Platonism's greatest puzzle—the secret unity of two disparate realities, high and low—is better dissolved than solved. The set-up of the puzzle may itself be the product of misdirection. I also owe to him my sense that I know too little about misdirection to discount my discontent with unities and settle into a peaceful dissolution. (As Saint Paul says at Philippians 4:7, the peace of God surpasses all understanding, but I wonder whether I *resist* understanding it. Perhaps I still have to work toward an honest incomprehension.) The essays that

Parting Knowledge

I have written over the course of the past decade or so, some fourteen of which I have modestly reworked and gathered together for this volume, find me in the space of the reluctant teacher. I am always self-consciously writing ahead of my wisdom, taking on the persona of someone who can make pronouncements about divine things. I would, if this would work, continue to study within the sanctuary of uncertainty, but I have discovered that I cannot move forward in "divine" knowledge, the sort that made Adam both great and miserable, unless I am first willing to test a conviction. And of course I cannot test what I do not have.

Augustine has been abundantly helpful to me here. I have come to many of my convictions by testing his, and by "testing" I mean less an attempt to refute than a resolve to understand. I do not assume that I can readily know what he means when he makes his pronouncements about divine things. And as I enter into his theological ingenuity, mainly as his student, I begin to notice what has become stably convincing for me from one reading of him to the next. One conviction in particular has profoundly shaped my readings of Augustine over the period of time that covers these essays, and it is internal to what I have been describing as my Platonism. I do not believe that alienation from the good, or what Augustine calls sin, is fundamentally a matter of what a rational being—such as an angel or an Adam—wills to bring about. On the face of it, this may seem that I am flatly convinced of the falsity of Augustine's doctrine of original sin. My view is more complex than that, as I trust will become evident in the seven essays that I have grouped under the rubric "groundwork." There I work out and test the implications of my negative conviction about alienation in my engagements with Augustine on perversity of will, free choice, the mythology of sin, interior life, the propriety of grief, emotional intelligence, conversion, and the aspiration for transcendence.

In the remaining set of seven essays, the grouping that promises "cultivation," my focus is more Augustinian than on Augustine, though in some of the essays he continues to make an explicit appearance. The part of his thinking that I most want to export to other philosophical climes—where I find myself engaged with thinkers as diverse as Anselm, Dante, Kant, Freud, and Wittgenstein—is his doctrine of grace. At the heart of his doctrine is this idea: that goodness exhausts the possibilities of being. Or in language more theologically hued: conversion is not the emergence of good out of evil, but the meeting up of the God without with the God within; it is incarnation. Grace, thus construed, is not a denial of evil; it is a denial of evil's pretense of defining a personality, of establishing a

Introduction

counter-incarnation. Apart from God, there is nothing to be. The tease of apotheosis here has dramatic implications for moral reasoning, forgiveness, the existence of hell, sexual piety, confessional philosophy, and saintly knowledge—topics covered, in varying degrees of depth, under "cultivation."

Augustine never claims that sin, in its original form, is willed in direct defiance of God. His Satan is not Milton's Satan, not the demon who proclaims, with tragic relish, "Evil, be thou my good." Augustine's Satan is a typical, if terrifying, self-aggrandizer, one who exalts the good of self over God. The irony of this is that sin, here the cause of self-alienated goodness, is what makes the choice between God and self, or God and *any* other kind of good, possible. A selfish desire may be said to be sinful, but it is necessarily too belated a desire to be sin's beginning. Augustine concedes that no desire for a good, small *g*, can be other than "a deficient cause" (*causa deficiens*; *civ. Dei* 12.7) of sin. The question that dogs his theology is whether a deficient cause is still a cause. If it is, then deficiency will serve to underscore creaturely independence and a God-forsaken trade of goodness for freedom. If it is not, then deficiency speaks to a cause that is essentially unintelligible—a cause beyond being. Obviously, no one can be expected to account for how such a cause could be, but I believe that its originality is implied in God's love for creatures who are, mysteriously, not God.

I suggest the metaphor of a birthmark for thinking about the dually interpretable deficiency that prefigures both sin and grace. A birthmark is not considered a "normal" part of a newborn's physiognomy, and in that regard it can seem either disfiguring or a bringer of distinctiveness. Perhaps it is hard to have the one thought without the other. But know that in this collection of essays I have worked to bend my thoughts toward the more benign possibility.

James Wetzel
Villanova, Pennsylvania
2012

Groundwork

1

Agony in the Garden
Augustine's Myth of Will

AUGUSTINE HAS OFTEN BEEN thought to emphasize the will over other features of human psychology, principally reason and appetite. This is not surprising given his insistence not only on a soul's absolute responsibility for its fallen condition but also on God's absolute sovereignty over the choice and course of a soul's redemption. Set within the context of a metaphysical tug-of-war between deficiently motivated perversity and mysteriously bestowed grace, the will tends to emerge in relief.

In this chapter, I am going to consider the genesis of this peculiar tug-of-war in Augustine (that is the task of section one), but mainly with the aim of downplaying its significance. Augustine's offering of will comes less in his disposition to absolutize will than his willingness to trade in the absolutism for a good story about the complexity of desire—and desire for the flesh, in particular. I chart this shift of focus in two contexts: his confessional struggle with his own carnality (largely the theme of section two) and his reading of the Adamic struggle with carnality in Genesis (largely the theme of section three). Since Augustine's confessional sensibilities are always exegetically informed, I never treat his personal confession as nakedly "existential." I allow him, throughout the inquiry, to be a reader of texts. In my short conclusion, I suggest why his offering of will is best read as a story, still to be determined, about desire.

I. Absolute Resolution

When Augustine describes his moment of crisis in book 8 of the *Confessions*, where we find him agonizing in a garden over his inability to part himself from already discredited lusts, he casts his internal struggle as a conflict of two wills, one carnal, the other spiritual (*conf.* 8.5.10). More precisely he speaks of one will split into alienated personae (*conf.* 8.11.21); their mysterious original unity, now lost, leaves each side partial, diminished in strength, and vainly desirous for either a reconciliation or a final parting. The two sides of his split will—allies and enemies—wrangle to a stalemate, rendering their passive host momentously unresolved.

It is common enough to expect a Christian writer who writes of spirit's ambivalence towards flesh to give the nod to spirit and valorize a flesh-restraining will. Augustine can be read, superficially at least, to fit that mold. He reports regaining his composure and coming to feel secure on the spiritual side of his will when a child's voice singing, "pick up and read" (*tolle, lege*), alerts his attention to a book of Paul's letters and to this, freely selected, verse (Rom 13:13–14; *conf.* 8.12.29): "No more wild parties and drunken fits, bedroom antics and indecencies, rivalries and wrangling; just try on Jesus Christ, your master, and don't look to lusts to care for your flesh." Augustine speaks of the heart-securing clarity that came with his encounter of this verse: his dark misgivings about his own resolve were scattered in the dawn of new confidence—"as if an untroubled light were to have flooded my heart" (*quasi luce securitatis infusa cordi meo*). He knew then that no partial will of his would ever lend him the strength to become whole again, but also that no doomed and desperate heroism was being asked of him as a condition of his redemption. Christ had already given Augustine the strength he needed to live forward, in spirit—the remnants of his old carnal life, still begging at spirit's door, would continue to annoy, but they no longer threatened subversion.

Readers from the monkish Pelagius to the scholarly moralists of our own day have been both fascinated and appalled by Augustine's *pas de deux* between human and divine will. From a place in his psyche mythically human and thus somehow Adamic, Augustine imagines himself to have willed his own fall from grace and descent into a psychology of conflict and blind ambition. Once into this postlapsarian life (the life that ironically begins for him at birth), Augustine has no prospect of willing his own way to safety. He is convinced that a purely human will to break with God can be converted and stabilized only by a grace that is free to invent virtues where it finds none. The part of this Augustinian spectacle that fascinates is its dramatization of an original choice: faced with the stark contrast between an unqualified good (life with God) and unqualified evil (life without God), a human being still apparently has a choice to make: either will the goodness of the good or be parted from all good. Is this kind of choice, assuming for now that it is a choice, of the essence of human responsibility, or is it already the expression of a perverse human desire to usurp creative control of anything of value? The ambiguity is rich enough to fuel a lifetime of uneasy moralism. The part of the Augustinian spectacle that tends to appall has to do with God's part in redemption. It is one thing for a human being to veer from God for no good reason (such veering can suggest culpability of will); it is quite another for God to find nothing of merit in those whom he raises (that just seems like bad parenting). The idea that a divine father would love his sons and daughters well in excess of their particular virtues is of course more reassuring than troubling, and even a Pelagian can take some honest comfort from it, but Augustine comes to insist on the far more radical notion that God loves in his children only the virtues that he implants there himself—even the very desire for a virtue is a divine gift.

Augustine arrives at his doctrine of gratuitous election in 396, the first year of his long tenure as bishop of Hippo. His friend and venerable mentor, Simplician, who would succeed Ambrose in the See of Milan, had asked him to comment on some passages from Kings and, more importantly, on two perplexing selections from Paul's Letter to the Romans: Paul's avowal in Romans 7 of his inability, as a carnal person, to adhere to a spiritual law, and his meditation in Romans 9 on God's seemingly arbitrary preference for one mother's son over another, for a Jacob over an Esau. In his responses to Simplician, Augustine stays with the reading of Romans 7 he had developed just a few years prior, in a cursory exposition of the letter. Paul, he claimed then, was not speaking in his own person when he spoke of being compelled by sin to act lawlessly; he was impersonating someone "under the law" (*sub lege*)—a person who sees the good of a divinely regulated life while being held, by a chain of habit, to lawless desire (*ex. prop. Rm.* 44). On the face of it, Augustine's agonized self-portraiture in *Confessions* 8 is his personal rendition of this condition: having acknowledged the preeminent goodness of an eternal life, unfixed from mortal flesh, Augustine finds himself still habituated to old loves—sex and reputation, but sex especially. The vanities whisper to him of his own fear of finality and freeze his resolve (*conf.* 8.11.26): "You are sending us away? We will not be with you ever again from now to eternity; from now on and for all time, you will not be permitted this and that." Augustine lets on that the "this" and the "that" are sexual fantasies, too graphic to spell out. What is he, or anyone caught between law and desire, to do?

On the basis of his reading of Romans 7, rehearsed for Simplician's benefit, Augustine comes up with the appropriate counsel (*Simpl.* 1.1.14): "This is what is left to human initiative [*libero arbitrio*] in this mortal life, not living up to justice whenever we want but turning in humble petition to the one whose gift makes such living possible." In short, it is human to pray for help, divine to deliver it. In his next response to Simplician, keyed to Paul's reading of the Jacob and Esau story, Augustine effectively abandons any suggestion that a true prayer originates in human extremity and not in God, the giver of all good things. He had at one time surmised, while wrestling with Romans 9, that God must have foreseen and rewarded not the weaker twin's virtue but his disposition, so unlike that of his rugged brother, to seek his strength outside himself (*ex. prop. Rm.* 60). Augustine does not rehearse that reading to Simplician; he offers it up for sacrifice. The virtue of faith, he finally admits, is no less a virtue than its cardinal offspring (courage and the rest); it too must be part of the package that God makes of a human life. At the end of his exegesis, Augustine recalls Paul's own conversion: he was knocked from his horse, not answered in his prayers, and out of the savage will of a persecutor God fashioned a preacher of the gospel. Augustine concludes from this that "wills are elected" (*Simpl.* 1.2.22). In other words, the divine hand is at work in the entire history of a redeemed life, the dark past as well as the dimly anticipated future; God does not enter into a life by invitation only.

Augustine looked back on his responses to Simplician and noted that a big change in his own thinking had taken place there. He had come to see that the beginning of faith (*initium fidei*) is a divine gift, not a human initiative (*persev.* 20.52); this led him to concede, with a not wholly feigned reluctance, that God's grace trumps human free will (*retr.* 2.1.1). There is no consensus in the scholarship over how big Augustine's big change really was. Had he come to a sudden rejection of the classical ideal of a self-sculpted life, or had he always been cool to perfectionist ethics? Granting that he consistently advertised the God-sculpted life in his writings, did he nevertheless lose perspective when responding to Simplician and come to believe that a human being, to the divine artist, is just a passive lump of living clay?

Having engaged with questions of this sort for the better part of two decades now, I am impressed with how little bare-knuckled appeals to the will tell us about Augustine's theological vision. Consider that faith-bestowing God of his, who gives the entire virtue. Augustine marks a distinction between two kinds of calling in his revised reading of Romans 9. Sinners like Esau, who are called but not chosen, can be expected to dissociate themselves from whatever gift of faith they may receive; their sin ultimately says more to them than does their rootless faith. For a Jacob, on the other hand, who is both called and chosen, there is no possibility of a permanent dissociation. God calls the elect "suitably" (*congruenter*; *Simpl.* 1.2.13), and their faith, despite the occasional waning, invariably waxes overall. It is difficult to determine in the abstract whether a providentially educated Jacob is his own person of faith or merely a vehicle for his creator's self-enjoyment.

No doubt it is tempting to conclude that God is self-relating through Jacob and that nothing distinctively human could ever emerge redeemed from this kind of divine soliloquy—not in Jacob's case, not in any case. But then there is this to consider. The faith that God creates in a person is not a virtue that Augustine imagines God to have or need; Christ has this virtue, to be sure, and has it perfectly, but he has it on his human side. Faith for Augustine is preeminently a creaturely virtue, as is any virtue that takes into its self-definition difference from God. A creature, but not God, has to endure not being God. There are virtues that facilitate this endurance, and however profoundly God may induce some human beings, the elect, to have them, these virtues necessarily have a distinctively human expression. Augustine surmises that God gives us two things in the gift of a virtue (*Simpl.* 1.2.10): *that* we will (*ut velimus*) and *what* we have willed (*quod voluerimus*). We share the "that" part, he explains, with God (God calls, we follow), while the "what" part, the good that is willed, is all God's doing. If no real division of labor were being described here, then not even Christ would know what the difference is between God and a human being.

The failing of a bare-knuckled appeal to the will, when applied to Augustine, is its utter impatience with the idea, admittedly difficult, that a creator who relies on nothing to create can have heirs who are creative, but less than absolute, in their self-expression. Put another way, this is the idea that a difference in being does not resolve, upon analysis, into God and nothingness. The absolutized human will, defined by its capacity to refuse the entirety of its inheritance and embrace the void, suggests both the fear and the impossibility of being essentially related to something; the God who addresses this fear by asserting his one absolute will against all pretenders to the throne merely validates the impossibility. Under the regime of an absolutized will, it is impossible to begin with God and nothing and not end there as well. Augustine seems at times to tire of the more subtle line of thinking. He advises his interlocutor in the dialogue *On Free Will*, the work of his most often used to construct his philosophy of will, to stop asking why a person graced with wisdom and virtue would willingly choose a path of ignorance and difficulty (*lib. arb.* 3.17.49). Don't ask not because the situation has been misdescribed, but because the only possible answer is maddeningly uninformative: that a person willingly does what a person wills to do. End of story. This will not be the last time that Augustine frames an act of will in such absolute terms (cf. *civ. Dei* 12.6–8). His tendency to subvert his own absolutism is nevertheless equally striking. One finds this subversion less in his abstracted remarks about the will than in the thick of the drama that he weaves into his most intimate choices.

II. Conversion Reframed

When Augustine sets the scene in *Confessions* 8 of his interior face-off, will of flesh against will of spirit, he recalls that his hope at the time was more for stability than clarity. "All the things inside my life's time were teetering," he writes (*conf.* 8.1.1.); "my heart needed to be rid of the old yeast." The instability of his badly leavened heart had everything to do with the desperate history of his erotic attachments and its legacy for him of incurable inner privation and hopeless craving for relief in partnered flesh—or as he puts it all, more succinctly: "I was to this point still knotted tightly to women" (*adhuc tenaciter conligabar ex femina*; *conf.* 8.1.2).

The flavor of Augustine's phrase "*ex femina*" (literally, "out of or from woman") suggests the originating context of his interior knottiness more than it does its cause. The origin of a thing is usually its cause, but, as in the paradigm case of God's creation of all things *ex nihilo*, this is not necessarily so: the nothingness from which all things come is not the *cause* of their coming to be. Augustine has learned from a few Platonic texts and from an ecstatic experience that more or less confirmed for him the truth of Platonism (*conf.* 7.10.16 f.) that immaterial spirit is the active and eternal cause of true creation. Nothing is in place "before" that cause gets to work, not even time itself. Fathered by immaterial spirit and mothered by nothing at all, it is little wonder that Augustine has come to think of his closeness to creation *ex femina* as a snare of some sort.

Agony in the Garden

He will hope to disentangle himself from this snare by living a celibate life. That much is clear from the way that *Confessions* 8 ends (*conf.* 8.12.30). Augustine tells his friend Alypius, who kept vigil while Augustine anguished, what has transpired—the agony, the voice, the verse, the resolve. Alypius selects his own verse from the Apostle's book, an injunction to care for a person weak in faith (Rom 14:1), and attaches himself, as the weaker vessel, to Augustine. Together they go to find Monica, Augustine's mother, to tell her the good news. Not only is Augustine intent on baptism; he is determined never again to have sex with a woman. Spiritually fecund *continentia*, or chastity personified (*conf.* 8.11.27), now has more allure for him than any future wife or mistress. Monica is delighted, her sorrow converted to a joy "more bountiful (*uberius*) than she had desired" (*conf.* 8.12.30) when her best hope for her son was for a good marriage.

It was likely Monica who had convinced Augustine to break from his concubine, the woman he considered his wife, in fact if not in law (cf. *b. conjug.* 5.5), and to whom he had shown sexual fidelity (*conf.* 4.2.2). A year into their long liaison together (371–385), begun when he was seventeen, she bore him a son, Adeodatus. When Augustine broke with her years later, ostensibly to secure a more socially advantageous match, Adeodatus remained in Italy with his father while she returned to Africa, vowing chastity.

In the short but densely significant description that he gives of his parting from her, Augustine never refers to his sexual partner and mother of his only child by name. That omission has been a source of disappointment to many of his readers, especially the modern ones, who would like to know this woman better. But instead of disclosing the individual to us, Augustine speaks of the effect of her loss on him (*conf.* 6.15.25): "My sins were multiplying all the while, and the woman with whom I used to share my bed, who was now an impediment to my marriage, was torn from my side; the heart in me, where once she was joined, was cut and wounded, trailing blood." Having experienced more a wounding than a parting, he concedes that he lacked the resolve to imitate his woman and live chastely. He broke faith with her soon after her departure and took up with another woman, a "stopgap mistress," to borrow a phrase from Peter Brown.[1] Augustine was to find the solace of mere sex rather hollow, however—an analgesic of sorts, but no cure. His wounded heart continued to cause him pain, "colder" than before, but "more desperate" (*frigidius sed desperatius dolebat*).

---

1. Brown (1988), p. 393.

Parting Knowledge

If the disappointment of getting a woman's love filtered through a man's grief can temporarily be put to one side, we can begin to address the allegorical ambitions of Augustine's description. The parting of a woman from a man's side recalls the Genesis paradigm of parting (Gen 2:21–25): so that Adam may have a partner and not be alone, God sends Adam into a deep sleep, opens his side, and crafts a living being out of one of his ribs—man and woman emerge from the process, unashamedly naked in one another's presence. Augustine is of course not simply illustrating that first parting in his account of his own experience; he is, as Danuta Shanzer has so ably shown, recalling it in a painfully distorted and corrupted form.[2] The original Adam was not wounded by having a woman parted from his side; he was initiated into a fullness that he could enjoy only in relation to his partner. And he did not lose her through parting, but through an act of disobedience that will for Augustine become an object of ceaseless, if horrified, fascination. Bearing in mind that the writer of the *Confessions* is always acutely aware that he writes after disobedience and the loss of original innocence, it is striking what he makes of his woman and her departure from his life. In her unnamed persona and her (apparently) easy embrace of a chaste life, she becomes for him a palpable reminder of the innocence that he has lost. When she leaves him, he is left with only his lusts to wed, all those cold and desperate desires that he is enjoined through a verse from Romans to put aside—if he really wants to have a life in the flesh.

The idea is not that Augustine thought of his flesh-and-blood partner, with a history no doubt as complex as his, as free from the distortions of love that get passed on from one generation to the next. That he chose not to emphasize her culpability for their imperfect partnership hardly means that he considered her wholly innocent. The more reasonable notion to entertain is that she reminded him of the difference between a chaste life and a sexless one. Given the way that he describes her entry into chastity, there was no world of difference between her sexual fidelity to him and her resolve, after their breakup, never to give herself to another man. For him, there was obviously a great deal of difference between his sexual fidelity to her and his grip on the virtue of continence. It does not require a deeply psychoanalytic reading of his text to imagine that his sexual fidelity to her had always been skin-deep. That, in any case, is what he would have us believe (*conf.* 6.15.25): "Because I was a slave of lust and not a lover of marriage, I got myself another woman, not a wife to be sure, but a means, as it

---

2. Shanzer (2002).

were, of sustaining and drawing out my soul's disease, at normal strength or worse, and of bringing my retinue of long habit into a wife's domain."

Augustine's sense of the perversely prophylactic work of lust, a vice that protects against intimacy, brings home the point of his otherwise bizarre speculation about sex in Eden. His Adam and Eve sin and fall before they ever get around to having sex, but he assumes that they would have had innocent, unproblematic sex had they maintained their sinless marriage. His assumption is significant in itself, as it suggests his belief in the original goodness of human sexuality—a belief that many of his critics, both then and now, have been quick to doubt. In principle at least, Augustine did not think of a chaste sexual life as a contradiction in terms; he thought of it as the life that was once meant to be. When he describes the "mechanics" of that life, most elaborately in *City of God* (*civ. Dei* 14.17–19, 21–24), he suggests the image of an extraordinarily controlled kind of sexual intercourse: the man calmly wills his readiness to initiate sex (all the relevant parts of his anatomy obey his wishes), and the woman in turn, with equivalent calm and self-control, wills her receptivity. There would have been, insists Augustine (*civ. Dei* 14.23), no strife or opposition of any kind between lust (*libido*) and will (*voluntas*) in paradise, no awareness even of the contrast between a capable will and an insatiable desire.

It is tempting to take Augustine's image of untroubled sexuality and read into it an anti-sexual desire for sexless sex—no passion, no abandon, no real nakedness, just a business meeting between two self-sufficient individuals. The failing of this temptation, as John Cavadini has well noticed, is its assumption, wholly contrary to Augustine's own, that we have an image of mutual self-presence that is not, by default, an image of two self-controlled individuals.[3] Augustine's hypothetical Adam and Eve have no need for self-control; they have, while still without sin, an effortless desire to intertwine themselves in one another's selfhood. The aim of the intertwining is not to meet two private agendas of need but to move from self-sufficient to self-exceeding and therefore procreative life. Such abundant knowing is hard to imagine on the other side of the fall, where procreation so easily devolves into the labor of dispirited bodies.

Augustine's image of untroubled sexuality turns out, upon closer inspection, not to be an image at all, but a warning against a corrupted imagination, mortgaged to lust and other privations. Lust, being a form of sin, is always a pathologized privation for Augustine—not a temporarily felt lack of something desirable, but an obsession with lack, reinforced

---

3. Cavadini (2005).

with each passing satisfaction. A soul in lust overtly craves the vitality of a bodily life; in reality it has confused this vitality with the desire for it. Admittedly the desire for more life is a common enough expression of vitality. Still the expression is not the fount. Life is not wholly the desire for more life, and desire cannot hope to fill its own void by feeding on itself. In this regard, lust can seem rooted in a surprisingly basic confusion between desire and life, and yet no one, thinks Augustine, simply mistakes the force of privation in a life; something willful happens, and suddenly we find ourselves wanting only the life we have yet to have—or have yet to envision. For what image can we have of a consummate life while our desires for life are so self-consuming and, by way of a ruthless solipsism, consuming of others? Perhaps what we need is not another image for the discarding but a disquieting thought: that sex without desire is not only possible, but is possibly not pornographic. This in any case is the thought that Augustine tries to offer his readers by way of his speculation about original sex.

In the portrait he gives of himself in *Confessions* 6, Augustine lacks sexual self-control in even the shabby form that would have allowed him some resemblance to his partner, whose vow of continence was, contrary to his long-standing imagination for the virtue, not solely (or even principally) a defense against lust. It is hard to pin down the continence he imagines seeking in *Confessions* 8: is it the usual will to resist temptation, or is it perhaps an old innocence, newly illuminated? Before he begins speaking about his crisis of self-division, he recalls the half-hearted prayer of his early adolescence (*conf.* 8.7.17): "Give me the continence of a chaste life, but not yet." If we read what he goes on to describe as his struggle at age thirty-two to *will* his more adult and less hedged resolve, then we are likely also to discount the partnership between Augustine and his woman, now just another prompt for his lust, and to view his conversion, mediated through the flesh of Christ, as a gift of willpower and not of vision. I have been laboring through some of the complexity of Augustine's thinking about sexual desire, especially his own, largely to make this reading less tempting.

But let's give the temptation its due and give into it, if only for a moment. The story of his conversion, reduced to its essentials, would be as follows. Augustine receives the cardinal illumination of his life, not when he reads Paul and tries on divine flesh (*conf.* 8.12.29), but when he reads Plotinus and comes to see that God, being immaterial, has no conceivable tie to a woman (*conf.* 7.10.16). Finding himself still beholden to that tie,

Agony in the Garden

Augustine appeals to the power of divine spirit to restrain his desire and seal his adoption in the spirit (thus his hope for stability in God). Habit alone keeps him tied to a good that his mind no longer credits, but he is forced to admit, in the pitch of his distress, that habit has a power, darkly material and maternal, to bind his resolve. That power is decisively broken for him, however, the instant he finds himself enabled to try on the flesh of Christ. With resolve greater than his own, he leaves his garden retreat and tells his mother not to expect more grandchildren. His conversion from flesh to spirit, despite an echo or two of an old habit, is essentially done.

The chief inconvenience of this reading is that it has Augustine perfecting the very kind of Gnosticism he has been so keen to disavow. During much of the time he would have considered the years of his regnant lust (roughly his twenties), Augustine was also an auditor of the Manichean religion, for him a form of Gnostic Christianity. The Jesus of the Manichees rescues children of the light from the enveloping darkness of a material world; he lets them know that they are not, despite what they may think, of this world. With better self-knowledge (*gnosis*), they can live more in accordance with the unseen world of spirit. The elite among them—not the auditors but the elect—vow to refrain altogether from sex and the eating of flesh, the two most tempting venues of spirit's tragic materialization. Although Augustine was initially attracted to the idea of a radical duality of good and evil, he soon came to doubt and eventually to detest the idea of a vulnerable source of goodness. Such vulnerability, to his way of thinking, spoke to a terrible confusion of creator with creation and so to an inability to conceive of God as spirit.

Augustine's Manichees do not seem to realize that only a material deity is subject to material bondage and that Jesus, minus his paternal inheritance, becomes just another casualty of a chaotic materiality. But if we let Augustine's Platonism supply him with a rigorous dualism of spirit and matter and then read his conversion as the emergence of his soul's desire for spirit alone, we make him into a more consistent Manichee than the Manichees he knew. Perhaps he was aware of this kind of reading when he inserted a long caveat against Manicheism into his analysis of his two wills (*conf*. 8.10.22–24). Whereas Manichees read internal conflict as the sign of mutually exclusive sources of selfhood, Augustine cleaves to the possibility of wanting what he does not want and still being essentially the person that he is.

Ultimately the mystery that frames Augustine's conversion is not the irrational power of habit over informed resolve but the coexistence of opposed desires within the same love. Augustine wonders (*conf.* 8.3.7), "What then is acting in the soul when its delight in finding and recovering the things it loves is more than if it were always to have had them?" God too, he recognizes, prefers a prodigal to a stay-at-home son. In the face of prodigal love, Augustine's sense of his beginning *ex femina* is no longer as obvious a contrast to his origins in God as it may have seemed at first—not if God too has a birth and inherits that knottiest of ties to woman. At the outset of *Confessions* 8 Augustine invokes his desire to be more stable in God, the fleshless father of his spirit; by that book's end, he confesses to feeling most secured by the God who has come into the world *ex femina*. If that God is truly his mother's son, then Augustine, like the Adam of the myth, may not be able to undo a tie simply by denying it.

III. Dramatic Choices

Augustine sets forth an odd but telling critique of Platonism in *City of God* 14, a book much preoccupied with psychological matters. In the chapter I have in mind (*civ. Dei* 14.5), he is ostensibly criticizing Platonists for holding a bad theory of the emotions. Although they are not quite Gnostic vilifiers of the flesh, like the sex-hating Manichees, they do, Augustine thinks, unwisely blame the body for subjecting the soul to a number of emotional disturbances (*perturbationes*), any one of which can dull moral vision and distort happiness. In Stoic theory the disturbances take four forms—craving, anxiety, abandon, and despair; Augustine knew that theory from Cicero's *Tusculan Disputations*.[4] He also knew from Cicero that the Stoics proposed to address the morbidity of emotions through right thinking and better judgment. The Platonist remedy, which presupposed the soul's immateriality, was more radical: seek, short of suicide, a clean separation of soul from body. If the Platonists were right about disembodied soul-life and the catharsis of death, then no soul free of its body and able to recall the depredations of bodily life was ever going to desire a return trip to the womb. Augustine does not dispute the idea of reincarnation (although he does reject it by this time); he argues that the Platonists do not really believe that death is so redemptive. They tell a story that belies their dogma.

Here Augustine refers to the part of Virgil's *Aeneid* where Aeneas talks with his dead father in the underworld and learns from the old man that even the purest of pure souls in Elysium eventually drink from Lethe,

---

4. The theory is laid out in book 4; for translation and commentary, see Graver (2002).

the river of forgetting, and desire, in their oblivion, to be reborn in a human body.[5] Aeneas has already expressed some trepidation about the soul's "dread lust" (*dira cupido*) for a body, but he accepts his father's unnerving suggestion—that even a pure soul chooses to resubject itself to that lust—without comment.[6] Augustine is prepared to comment. He thinks that the story, paradigmatically Platonist, of birth, death, purification, willful forgetting (drinking from Lethe), and return to the womb, has one clear moral (*civ. Dei* 14.5): "That the soul is stirred to desire and fear, to exult and anguish, not just from flesh, but, as the Platonists have conceded, it can also be moved to have these motions from a source within itself."

It is odd to think of Virgil, whose eclectic personal philosophy tended towards the Epicurean, not only as a Platonist, but as a "famous representative" (*locutor nobilis*) of that movement. I suspect that Augustine brings to this judgment a twofold assumption: that Virgil believes the story about reincarnation that he has Anchises tell and that the story, which Virgil poeticizes but does not invent, says more about pagan Platonism than does any theory about the soul's immateriality. Be that as it may, Augustine accepts the truth of what he thinks the Platonists, by virtue of their myth of soul, are implicitly committed to believing: that the soul, whether sick or sound, is the motivator of emotion, of movement outwards. Unlike simple physical motion (e.g., a body in freefall), the movement of emotion is always towards some good or away from some evil. It is not then the body that causes a soul to seek a good outside its own perfection; it is the soul's desire for such a good that causes it to seek a body.

The really telling part of Augustine's critique of the Platonists in *civ. Dei* 14.5 is that he allows the part of their story to stand where a purified soul, having no further wisdom to seek, seeks forgetfulness (cf. *civ. Dei* 10.30). We may be tempted to conclude, with some encouragement from Augustine, that sin begins there, with that unaccountable turn from plenitude, but this would be to give up on the question of motive and settle for outright paradox: wisdom will be seen to desire lapse, making it wise to be unwise. The other possibility is that the Platonists have been bending their myth of soul around a false assumption. Perhaps the separation of soul from body is not some great catharsis but is, as Augustine thinks, a tragic necessity; it may be love of the body that is native to soul. If this is true, then the point of narrative incoherence in the story, the soul's choice to

---

5. *Aeneid* 6:724–51; see lines 852–90, pp. 154–55 of Lombardo's translation (2005).

6. Lombardo renders "*dira cupido*" as "yearning," but that strikes me as far too tame a translation. This is desire that is akin to madness and rage; the *Dirae* are the Furies.

forgo closure and begin again, may not be the effect of a deficient motive (*causa deficiens*) but is perhaps the place where two different story lines have converged and a choice of story needs to be made.

Augustine does not subscribe to the story that he associates with pagan Platonism, even if he is prepared to draw an acceptable moral from it. His preferred drama of carnal desire is the story of Adam and Eve in the garden and not some metaphysical tale of a soul that alternatively flees and embraces life in the flesh. In his earliest commentary on Genesis (c. 388), where his aim is to allegorize where possible and counter Manichean contempt of too human a creator, Augustine does flirt with the possibility that the first man and woman begin as incorporeal souls, united in spirit, and only later, on account of sin, become creatures of flesh and blood (*Gn. adv. Man.* 1.19.30). It proves not to be a serious flirtation for him, however (cf. *retr.* 1.10.2), and he soon settles into his preference for carnal progenitors. In the second book of his early commentary, he counsels his Manichean readers not to discount God's power to make flesh out of mud—lovely, fully functional flesh, free of the worm of death (*Gn. adv. Man.* 2.7.8).

He will offer a similar kind of counsel to his *City of God* readers, when they are moved to deny sexuality to original flesh. No one of Adam's heirs may be in a position to remember what uncorrupted sexuality was like, but this does not prevent Augustine from insisting that flesh, in its untroubled beginnings, was more substantial than the flesh we now know. Only the resurrected flesh of Christ, free of the *possibility* of corruption, has even greater substance for him. Where a modern reader may see Augustine etherealizing flesh and robbing it of its true substance, Augustine imagines a contrary movement. No longer feeling any need to discount the originality of the body to human life, he is able to write his greatest commentary on Genesis (begun c. 401) as a commentary *ad litteram* ("according to the letter")—as a reading that hews as closely as possible to irreducible things: God, angels, human beings.

While it is important when reading Augustine to take in the difference between a blissfully bodiless spirit (an angel) and a happily incarnate human original, knowing no pain (an Adam), it is also worth noticing the similarity between the Adam of Genesis, as Augustine construes him, and that purified soul of the Platonist myth, poised to forget its way back into bodily existence. In both cases, Augustine envisions a poorly motivated choice for a less self-contained, naturally imperfect kind of life—a life that begins when the birth-tie to woman is cut and a less tangible but no less powerful tie to other flesh takes over, the libidinal tie. The Adam that he consistently describes in all of his Genesis commentary, early and late, has no external motivation to sow libidinal agony into Eden. His life with his partner, the woman, is, as Augustine's emphasizes in *City of God* (*civ. Dei* 14.10), a life of serene love (*amor imperturbatus*). The two of them have a great marriage, perfect health, idyllic surroundings, easy access to God, and basically no cause to want anything they have not been given. Admittedly they are forbidden access to the tree of knowledge, but as Augustine explains in his literal commentary on Genesis (*Gn. litt.* 8.6.12), this is not a tree whose fruit is naturally good or bad; the fruit *becomes* good or bad only in relation to what the man and woman decide to do. If they decide to remain obedient, the good of that is that they get to enjoy forever the fruits they have been enjoying already; if they disobey, the evil of that is that they lose those very same fruits and usher in mortal times. Augustine further assumes that they need no taste of knowledge to know the better course. Just as it is possible, he notes (*Gn. litt.* 8.16.34), to know what "nothing" means without having to undergo annihilation, so it should be possible to know, without first having to experience it, what a loss of happiness means.

The short of it is that the Edenic couple would have to forget what they know before thinking to risk their happiness for something greater. When Augustine considers the separate roles of the man and woman in bringing about the first sin, he treats the woman as if her fall were unthinking. She is for him the sensualist of the couple (*Gn. adv. Man.* 2.14.20–21), and so she has no inclination to question what the serpent tells her, that she has been forbidden a boon to life and can expect, if she disobeys, to see like a god and not to die. All that matters to her is that the fruit of disobedience, thus described, starts to look good—"lovely to the eyes, a delectable sight" (Gen 3:6); naturally she goes with her appetite and takes a bite. Meanwhile, her more sensible, less sense-driven husband realizes that the serpent's advertisement is lie, but not fast enough to be able to restrain his wife, and by implication, his own more sensual side. Augustine has him face a terrible choice: either he abandons his beloved partner to her fate, or he joins her in her transgression and risks alienating his divine father. He chooses to disobey because he cannot imagine her getting along without him—"she would wither away without his care" (*Gn. litt.* 11.42.59)—and because he assumes that God will forgive him for having made, in some respect, a faithful choice (*civ. Dei* 14.13). Augustine does not stop to assess Adam's assumption about his wife's weakness (though one can imagine); he finds Adam's assumption about the relative lightness of his offense appallingly shortsighted. Apparently even a mind unclouded by an unthinking lust for life has a hard time imaging how bad the beginning of an alienation from God can be.

Augustine's sense of the first sin as a two-part invention, his and hers, is in no small part a rehearsal of some of the dreariest tropes in the history of sexism: man as reason and sublime judgment, woman as sensuality and animal appetite, ideal human life as the rule of the male over the female principle. But more remarkable than his predictable fit within the history of sexism is his understated subversion, through the figure of Adam, of its flesh-denying imperative. To amplify what is understated in his Adam, we need to allow ourselves access to Augustine's readerly imagination, to his sense of a narrative's undisclosed possibilities. We can be grateful that as a reader of Genesis, Augustine does not restrain himself from counterfactual speculation. Suppose that the man and woman had successfully resisted temptation. What then? We know Augustine's answer: they would have had happy, lust-free sex and done their part to produce the preordained number of saints. The only problem with his answer is that it credits the wrong question. In Augustine's account of what actually transpired in Eden, the woman has no motive to resist a fruit she unambivalently desires; it is the man who has his desire tested—for her. So the better dramatic possibility to entertain, given Augustine's setup, is this: what would have happened to the Adam who parts himself from his partner and remains an obedient son?

We do not know Augustine's answer to this, not expressly, but he does give us a basis for making a reasonable inference. If Eden is, as he insists, a place of plenitude, where the obedient never go wanting, then a steadfast Adam would have a new woman, a replacement partner. And we should not expect him, as a member of paradise in good standing, to mourn the loss of his first wife: she is no longer, being lost, of any value to him. It is indeed difficult to imagine him remembering her at all. The irony of this counterfactual speculation is that it forces the love of a steadfast Adam into the framework of lust, where appetite crowds out mourning. Even the prodigal Augustine had the good sense once, while confessing lust, to acknowledge loss. His tie to his partner, though severed, persisted (*conf.* 6.15.25).

Augustine's non-hypothetical Adam, the one who fell, also felt a unique bond to his partner, and because he was "unschooled in divine severity" (*civ. Dei* 14.11), he assumed that God would sympathize. Although Augustine is clear in his exegesis that God did not, should not, could not sympathize, the absoluteness of divine will being what it is (i.e., absolute), it is nevertheless striking that he gives us an Adam who would have thought otherwise. Adam's tie to woman, the being taken from his side and later recognized by him to be "the mother of all the living" (Gen 3:20), speaks to the truth that any mother's son or daughter must eventually face: that attachment takes in separation. "What then is acting in the soul," Augustine wonders (*conf.* 8.3.7), "when its delight in finding and recovering the things it loves is more than if it were always to have had them?" Perhaps Augustine has hit upon the soul's desire to recollect the birth that will bring its entire self-conception into its manner of loving—a consummation, finally. Until then how could a purified soul not wish for another birth? How could an Adam bear a life forever apart from the mother of all the living? If God can sympathize with such questions, then, as Augustine's Adam suspects (but too naively), God is no stranger to life in the flesh. When this Adam, in a moment of truth, disavows the flesh of his flesh and implies that God is to blame for giving him woman-trouble, he turns his suspicion into a torment, for himself and his heirs.

"The woman whom you gave to be with me gave to me from the tree, and I ate" (Gen 3:12). Augustine does not think to root Adam's sin in his hasty denial of his marriage bond, whose subversion begins a long history of conflict between flesh and spirit. Although he clearly disapproves of Adam's apparent ingratitude for the woman and his hint at entrapment (*civ. Dei* 14.14), Augustine is disposed to move quickly from the ambiguities of Adam's carnal love to its deficiency as a motive for disobedience. An Adam who desires deficiency more than he desires the woman is going to be more of an antagonist to God than a misguided son. God, Augustine is convinced, both creates and perfects *all* that is good; to will deficiency in God's house, the created order, is to desire a way out of the house, even if into a wasteland. The woman is no more the direct object of such a manically narcissistic desire than is any other wasted good. We seem to have here an Adam disturbingly different from the one concerned (however paternalistically) with his partner's happiness.

It is possible to read Augustine's emphasis on the deficiency of a sinful motive as his attempt to secure human responsibility for sin. On the one hand, the desire to lack goodness is so bizarre that it hardly seems plausible as anyone's motive; on the other, it is certainly not God's motive and so whose motive, if not an Adam's, can it be? I prefer to think of Augustine's slip from carnal love to love of privation as his nod to an angelic drama of sin and fall. An angel, in Augustine's conception, is an immaterial being who is beyond the first death, but not the second. The first death, normally called just death, refers to the separation of soul from body; the second death, Augustine explains (*civ. Dei* 13.1), refers to the separation of God from soul or spirit. An angel, unlike a human being, finds its natural perfection in a bodiless existence. It is constitutionally incapable of loving flesh so much that its spiritual chemistry changes and it starts to experience the disincarnate life as a privation, like the soul in the Platonist myth. When an angel falls, it falls into its own self-created void and not towards another body (*civ. Dei* 12.6). Having never known the love that binds spirit to flesh, it skips the first death and proceeds directly to the second.

When Augustine gets to the part of Genesis where Adam faces his woman across a spiritual divide, he has to decide whether the story has essentially been about an angel or a human being. If a human being, then Augustine has some cause to expect God to show up, at some future stage of the story, on the woman's side of the divide. If an angel, then no offer of beauty, not even the beauty of divine flesh, is ever going to seduce a soul out of its self-induced privation. In a telling illustration of angelic sin, Augustine offers a case of two men and one beautiful woman (*civ. Dei* 12.6): although both men see "the same beauty" (*eadem pulchritudo*) and see it "equally" (*pariter*), one lusts and the other does not. Beauty has no bearing here on whether a man sins.

Augustine knew that no fallen angel could be saved. Why does he suppose that a human being who sins like an angel can fare any better?

IV. Conclusion: Desire Encore

In one of his rare attempts at biblical exegesis, the great philosopher of the Enlightenment, Immanuel Kant, saw in the Genesis story an inspired attempt to represent the unrepresentable.[7] He was referring not to the story's depiction of God but of original sin, the turn from good to evil. Kant's assumptions about that turn and its proper exegesis, in and outside of Genesis, are closely akin and perhaps beholden to Augustine's own, but with one crucial difference. Where Kant emphasizes the extraneous presence of the serpent, its interruption of the Genesis narrative, Augustine is more inclined to see in the serpent an anticipation of Adam's sin. Both men read into the serpent an absolute evil, a will disposed, when faced with all the

---

7. I'll have much more to say about Kant's reading of Genesis in chapter 10 of this volume. The exegetical move I refer to here can be found at the end of part 1, section 4 of *Religion within the Boundaries of Mere Reason*; see pp. 61–65 of the di Giovanni translation (1998).

advantages of the good, to want corruption. But only Kant seems to realize that an Adam who wills sin directly, without the mitigating factor of desire for the flesh, is beyond redemption.

I have been arguing throughout this essay that Augustine was an exquisite dramatist of the will, but not a great theorist. As a theorist, he assimilates human to angelic existence, robs spirit of its affinity for flesh, and turns the will to sin into a paradoxically self-assertive drive for self-privation. He does all this mostly for the cause of moral responsibility, but it is debatable whether a will that footloose in its disaffection can be responsible for anything. As a dramatist, Augustine exchanges will *ex nihilo* for desire *ex femina* and entertains the ambiguities of a carnal desire that does not always covet flesh. Lust in his dramas, both exegetical and confessional, proves to be the most gnosticizing of desires; it devalues the tie that binds a soul so particularly to a body by veiling the origin of that tie and making one woman seem much the same as another.

The proper contrast to lust of this description is not repressed sexual desire but an original experience of the flesh, known best to the God who remembers being born. The rest of us, Augustine suggests, are compelled to become better readers of our particular griefs—the losses that frustrate lust, cut the will to sin down to human size, and keep us open to beauty. A less-than-satanic Adam, worried about the heartbreak of his partner, is part of the myth of this reader. The Augustine who suggests the myth is part of the history that the myth portends. So is the other Augustine, who prefers a story about angels and tries to read the conjunction of male and female, fraught and full of promise, out of the divine image (*Gn. litt.* 7.24.35). Augustine's readerly struggle within himself to resolve on a beginning has given us, his readers, our most enduring myth of will.

2

Crisis Mentalities
Augustine after Descartes

IN AUGUSTINE'S PSYCHOLOGY, THE heart is a transgressive organ. It seeks the source of its animation beyond the limits of the particular body it has been given, as a physical organ, to sustain. Superficially the heart's desire resembles a bodily appetite, but only in the way that a mirror image both resembles and inverts its exemplar. It is in the nature of a bodily appetite to seek to incorporate an other, to direct hunger and thirst to food and drink; bodily appetite is satisfied (temporarily at least) when the object of desire is no longer other but a part of self. The heart does not seek to consume its desired other, but to find communion in difference. In its characteristic desire, the heart seems to defy what is so obvious and so often painful to a self defined by its appetites: the confinement of a single life to a single body. The odd business of living outside of one's body—familiar to anyone with a heart—finally makes sense in relation to God, the inexhaustible being whose otherness is the heart's food. Augustine says famously at the beginning of his *Confessions* that no heart finds rest until it rests in God (*conf.* 1.1.1: *inquietum est cor nostrum donec requiescat in te*). His words look forward to a resurrection, not a burial.

I round off my preliminary comments on Augustine's psychology with a musing on mind. If the notion of mind invokes not only the capacity but also the desire to know, as it surely did for Augustine, then mind and heart must have some connection. In his great work on the Trinity—which is the best source for his philosophy of mind—Augustine bids his readers to remember that "... no one is able to love at all what is altogether unknown" (*Trin.* 10.1.1). There is a certain obvious wisdom in this. When love is completely blind, nothing defines the beloved more than the emptiness in the lover's desire. Heart's desire moves perilously close to bodily appetite. On the other hand, Augustine should not be taken to imply that the heart always has to follow the mind's lead. Imagine this extreme, that nothing can be loved until fully known. If this were true, then the mind's desire to know would be distinct and wholly apart from the heart's desire for a beloved other, and the wisest lovers would all be Cartesians; they would not affect to love until they were first sure that they really knew what they thought they knew.

In at least one kind of knowing, that of mind becoming aware of itself, Augustine contends that seeking to know is not what knowing resolves, but what it becomes (*Trin.* 10.10.16): "the mind knows itself even as it seeks itself out." Self-love, by implication, is not the love of a special kind of object, one very close to home, but a transformation in how the self loves what is in its world. Experienced unreflectively, the world is other to the self only to the extent that an object can become an object of desire or aversion, a focus of want or a source of pain. On the face of it this is an unlovable kind of otherness; being rid of it brings relief to the self and some measure of pleasure. It is through love, not appetite, that the otherness of the world, or of some individuals within it, starts to become desirable in itself. What is it, though, that would occasion such a profound transformation of desire? Augustine's ultimate but least accessible answer is that the transformation is already at the heart of what we are now. We were made by God to love something, to exercise the heart's peculiarly transgressive capabilities, and even our meanest desires can be bent to serve that end. But admittedly this is the sort of answer, if it makes sense at all, that makes sense only in retrospect, when the question is (presumably) no longer urgent.

In the meantime Augustine offers us in his *Confessions* a vivid history of his own imperceptive but not quite blind heart's desire. In book 4 he recollects the rending grief he felt at the loss of a childhood friend, and he follows this grief into an awareness of dementia (*conf.* 4.7.12): "What madness [*dementiam*] it is not to know how to love human beings humanly!" The desired know-how has something to do with being able to take in the fact of a beloved's mortality. "What other reason was there for it," Augustine wonders (*conf.* 4.8.13), "that grief had penetrated me so easily and deeply, than that I had poured my soul into the sand by loving someone bound to die as if he never would?" He is wise enough to let that question haunt him. Too presumptuous an awareness of the mortal condition can have a chilling effect on love. If Augustine is right about his reason for slipping into a demented grief, would his rightly minded love lead him to love only what never dies? Or should he perhaps, through the adoption of some Stoic calculus, contrive to love a mortal being proportionally less than he would were that being really immortal?

The human need for some awareness of the mortal condition, and the difficulty of humanly having it, takes us to the crossroads of mind and heart in Augustine's quest for wisdom, and it is there that I wish to remain for the remainder of this chapter. As I have established matters in Augustine thus far, the heart but not necessarily the mind is a transgressive organ. As a mind, I naturally want to know all there is to know, but I am indifferent to the possibility that coming to know all this may never take me outside of myself. The heart, by contrast, dies from solipsism. As a heart, I need to be connected to someone whose well-being I come to regard as essential to my own. Being a person, I am not just a mind or heart but some conjunction of the two, plus what seems to limit each—the appetite for my own bodily preservation and pleasure.[1] As long as I have my beloved other before me, there is no antagonism between mind and heart; in fact, my mind helps me articulate and enjoy the otherness that is essential to my heart's desire. The loss of a beloved, however, through either death or disaffection, can precipitate a crisis—a parting of the ways between mind and heart, occasioning the need for a fundamental choice of direction.

The mind, unlike the heart, is not directly affected by loss. With the passing of one being or another out of existence, the world of the mind's acquaintance grows smaller, but the mind remains essentially undisturbed in its capacity to know. The mortal threat to the mind comes only, if at all, from the body to which it is substantially attached. If the mind should die along with this body, it does not know itself to be dead; it simply ceases to exist. Mind and heart suggest different ways of being limited by a body; they also suggest different ideals of immortality. As a mind I cannot experience my own death. As a heart I can; I experience it through the death of others, the ones I have loved.[2] From the mind's point of view, the immortal

---

1. I might have well have added "will" (*voluntas*) to the psychological mix, but I prefer to let that notion emerge out of the conflict between mind and heart. In any case, my use of psychological language is more heuristic than analytic. I use it to highlight unnoticed aspects of Augustine's philosophical portrait of the soul, not to submit human personality to a regime of faculty psychology.

2. See *conf.* 4.9.14: ". . . out of life lost to those who die comes death to those who live." Augustine's Latin is terse: *ex amissa vita morientium mors viventium*.

is what always remains what it is; it is the unchanging form that abides through change and corruption, untouched. The heart follows a different wisdom: it looks for life eternal in death and resurrection. If I were to love a friend in the way Augustine claimed once to love a friend, as someone not bound to die, I would not be loving with an awareness of the mortal condition. But would my failure here be one of heart or one of mind? And what would it cost me to have to choose?

As far as I can tell, Augustine never chooses between heart and mind, not even when they meet in crisis and seem to demand a choice of one ideal of immortality over another. Living reflectively between mind and heart requires a crisis mentality, but without the pessimism that such a mentality sometimes connotes—expectations of a terrible future, blows of bad fate. Augustine finds hope in a crisis mentality. I take this to be a strength of his philosophy, not a weakness, though it is not a strength that is easy to convey. Partly this is because philosophical sensibilities since Augustine have been so profoundly shaped by his alter ego in philosophy, René Descartes. Descartes invents the crisis that motivates his *Meditations on First Philosophy*, and his invention is so imaginatively compelling that it becomes nearly impossible for his heirs to imagine a crisis more relevant to the possibility of knowing. In response to this invented crisis, Descartes encourages a subtle, almost ineluctable displacement of the desire to know by the need for certainty. The very etymology of the word *certain* is suggestive of his achievement. The Latin *certus* (certain) is the past participle of *cerno* (to sort out), cognate to the Greek *krino* (also, to sort out), the verb at the root of the word *crisis* (a sorting out). Etymologically speaking, certainty just is the resolution of a crisis. It took Descartes to translate an etymological truth into first philosophy.

The affinities between Descartes and Augustine have long been the subject of scholarly study.[3] No one that I have read has ever made the suggestion that the crisis of radical doubt in the *Meditations* is just like the crisis of sin and self-doubt in the *Confessions*. I too am mostly struck by the differences between the two crisis mentalities. What I resist, however, is the disposition to think of the Cartesian crisis as the inauguration of a new philosophy and the Augustinian one as the impetus to transcend philosophy altogether. I am more inclined to think, with no disrespect

---

3. Here is not the place for an extensive bibliography, but I would like to mention three of the works that have most informed my own thinking on the subject: Gouhier (1978), Matthews (1992), and Menn (1998).

to Descartes intended, that Augustine's sense of a crisis is a good impetus to transcend Cartesian philosophy and its prescription for what ails knowledge.

Augustine after Descartes? I admit to the anachronism and to the risk of pinning too much of the future of philosophy to a dramatic choice (a mark of my own crisis mentality, no doubt). But I am not obtuse to the complexity involved in following the lead of any historical figure in philosophy. Philosophers who look to the past for inspiration are in the business of anachronism. Some kinds of anachronism are better than others. Here I work to free Augustine's inspiration from a retrospective Cartesianism. When Augustine is allowed his own sense of a crisis in philosophy, he is better able to shape the sense of crisis in a post-Cartesian age, or perhaps to challenge the presumption of the age to have moved beyond crisis-driven philosophy altogether.

I. Radical Doubt and the Place Like No Other (*Regio Dissimilitudinis*)

Descartes begins his meditations proper with the resolve to eradicate all of his former opinions, to pull them up by the root by means of a singular exercise of doubt. An opinion, as Descartes entertains the notion, cannot be held doubtfully, for an opinion, unlike a simple belief, always incorporates a presumption to know—a bad one.[4] Since opinions are always the expressions of intellectual vice (of unnecessarily subjecting the mind to error), it is not surprising that Descartes wishes to be as little opinionated as possible. It is rather more surprising that he contrives to do away with all of his opinions at once. He discloses his motive for his cathartic attempt at infallibility in the first sentence of the *Meditations*, the opening of the only autobiographical paragraph in his whole first-person narrative: "It came to my attention some years before now how many falsehoods I took for truths in my time of youth and how doubtful were all the things I have built upon them since."[5] I take it that Descartes is not of the *opinion* that

---

4. In the fourth set of objections to the *Meditations*, Antoine Arnauld encourages Descartes to underscore the distinction between belief and opinion, so as to dispel any impression that Descartes has no place in his philosophy for prudent or faithful belief. Descartes replies that the context of his *Meditations* as a whole renders this distinction clear enough. See volume 7, pp. 214–17, 247–48 of Adam and Tannery (1996), hereafter abbreviated as AT. For a provocative reading of the exchange between Arnauld and Descartes on the legitimacy of belief, see Menn (1998), pp. 331–36.

5. AT (1996), vol. 7, p. 17.

he has erred in the past; at no point over the course of the *Meditations* does he ever consider the possibility that his knowledge of his own error is no better off than the knowledge he would presume to have of anything else. There is one presumption to know, then, that evades both of the devices that he uses to radicalize his own doubt: his assimilation of waking consciousness to a dream-state, his supposition of a dream-world controlled by a deceiving demon.

Admittedly the knowledge of error is not much to stand on. In fact, it is the very knowledge that precipitates the crisis in knowing that Descartes is at pains to resolve. If he knows that he has erred, but does not know how he knows, then he has no practical control over his knowing. He may err in all kinds of ways that escape his awareness or his ability to correct. The knowledge he holds onto, that of his errant disposition, has a gift-like status at the beginning of the *Meditations*, but Descartes is in no mood to receive. Instead he imagines a world in which it would be disastrous and self-deluding to look for truth in an offering, whether it be from the senses or from some tradition of received wisdom. He expects his knowing self to emerge out of this world in defiance of it. The world will have been imaginary, but the self it has defined presumably not.

If knowledge of error stands behind the Cartesian crisis in knowing, as is my claim, then there has to be a fork of options in play for conceiving of knowledge and its possibility at the opening of the *Meditations*. Descartes makes it seem as if he had no choice but to follow the road into the self-sufficient certainty of the doubting self—the self that wears its doubt as armor. But he did have a choice. He could have looked at the other side of knowledge of error and noticed that its curse came conjoined with a blessing. But had he done that, he would have written a confession instead of a meditation. I will resist the temptation to speculate on how that might have given modern philosophy a different genesis and content myself with an attempt to unearth further some of the hidden features of the Cartesian crisis.

As fine a fiction as the dream-world is, Descartes does not need it to define the self that emerges out of doubt as a knower. He needs only the supposition that the world he experiences as a doubting self is governed by a malignant genius, intent on deceiving its other half. I say "other half" because his supposition of a deceiver follows from his having split and set at odds two expressions of his human ability to imagine a world. The doubting self expresses his ability to imagine that nothing given in the world is as it seems; the malignant genius expresses his (alienated) ability to imagine the world that never seems to be what it is. The malignant genius, under a different inspiration, might have suggested a redemptive possibility to Descartes, but Descartes chose instead to seek all his possibilities in doubt. He moves from his ability to deny the existence of what he can doubt to the stunning claim that he is essentially what he cannot doubt—the power to think the doubt, a thinking thing (*res cogitans*).[6]

The materialists of Descartes' day were most unimpressed with the inference, and even Arnauld—who was disposed to be sympathetic—had to admit that Descartes' logic had escaped him. Descartes' reply to Arnauld is remarkably sanguine. If as a doubting self I have arrived at the point of doubting the existence of my own body, I must have a concept of myself, he suggests, that is distinct from the concept of body. There is no contradiction, then, in supposing that I am essentially a thinking thing. Descartes makes this last point in a way that binds the reasoning of the second meditation (on the finite thinking self) to the reasoning of the third (on the infinite thinking self): ". . . since what I have in mind is sufficient for me to subsist with it alone, I am certain that I could have been created by God apart from the things I do not have in mind."[7] In other words, when I no longer have it in mind that I am my body (I have come to doubt it), I see that—God willing—I am really what I cannot discharge from my thinking: my thinking self.

There is both an element of prescience and of forgetfulness in this reply. On the prescient side, Descartes sees just how profoundly the self who cannot but doubt looks forward to a self who is altogether beyond doubt's possibility. The Cartesian God is in essence an ideal *res cogitans*, a being who knows all there is to know simply by knowing its own act of thought. Since nothing real is ever absent from this being's thinking, there is literally nothing for it to doubt. Descartes never bothers to explain to Arnauld why the God who could separate a thinking self from its ties to extended or bodily substance would most assuredly do so. I think that this is because, in Descartes' mind, there is no philosophically interesting difference between the separation from body that the mind requires for knowing and the separation from body that the mind would seem to require for its immortality. The relevant distinction between mind and body, the one that makes knowing possible, has already been revealed in the self-reflexive doubt of the thinking self. Knowing is being set up here as redemption.

6. AT (1996), vol. 7, p. 28.
7. AT (1996), vol. 7, p. 219.

On the forgetful side, Descartes seems to have overlooked something about what makes an act of doubt human. If I am moved to doubt the truth of what is given to me in my experience, it does not follow that nothing is given to me, but only that I am not in a confident position to say what it is. Descartes resolves to take a further step and assume the nonexistence of all that he is able to doubt. This kind of doubt is not just radical; it is supernatural. I could be assured of the nonexistence of doubtful things on one of two suppositions. Either there is a malignant intelligence at the source of things and so the world I doubt really is never as it seems (nothing is given), or I somehow have a divine power to think things in and out of existence. Descartes, of course, does make the first supposition, but as he moves into his discovery of his thinking self, he fails to keep the suppositional status of his earlier invention in mind. It is not that he ever forgets that his malignant genius is his own fiction; it is that he overlooks the dependence of his doubting self on his deceiving one. The hypothesis of the deceiver is what defines the doubter; without it Descartes would have no means for arriving at his notion of a self whose essence is to think. My claim, then, is that the distinctiveness of his concept of a thinking self depends on his having an intelligible motive for excluding his body from all his acts of knowing, and that no less than a contest with an ultimate deceiver will do. (Once again the flesh is handed over to the devil.) But if there is this dependence between doubter and deceiver, why is the doubting self any less imaginary than the fiction used to define it?

I think that Descartes is in trouble here. His concepts of self and God are far more indebted to his imagination than he is willing to admit, and when the imagination starts to have authority for more than fictions, it becomes a very lonely place for a self to inhabit. By the time he gets around to meditation 4, the solipsism of a mind left to its own devices has become a real problem, but Descartes has no way from within the meditation to recognize the problem for what it is.

Ostensibly his aim in meditation 4 is to account for the possibility of error. Descartes has already established from his project of radical doubt that he is essentially a thing that thinks; his only company in this meditation is an idealized version of his own thinking self—the infinite being whose will is reality. As a finite being, Descartes cannot always make his will reality, but in what really counts he thinks of the infinite and finite will as virtually equivalent: "For although the will is greater in God than in me by comparison, . . . it seems nevertheless not to be greater when viewed strictly as a power in its own right."[8] The essential power of a will is either to assent to or dissent from the truth, to embrace or to shun the good. For an infinite will this turns out also to be a power to create or destroy a world, but even for a finite will, which would have to be a part of whatever world the infinite will has chosen to create, the power of will is inviolate. A finite thinking self, as long as it is still thinking, retains its capacity to doubt and shun, to reject offerings of truth and goodness. If the offerings are from a malign genius, bent on deceit, then there is freedom in this dissent. If, on the other hand, the offerings come from God, then Descartes is willing to say that he would err to reject them and correspondingly diminish his freedom as a thinking being. As of meditation 3, Descartes has officially replaced the great deceiver with the infinite will of God. So where does he, as an expression of this will, derive his will to err?

The problem of error is a very tricky one in Descartes. It looks like a version of the standard conundrum of theodicy. A good God, with unlimited power of will, is supposed to have created all there is; if there is evidence of corruption in this creation—lapses or losses in goodness—how is God not ultimately the source of the problem? The resemblance is even more compelling if we take into account that Descartes' interest lies not in the bare possibility of the erring self, but in the fact of an errant disposition. The finite self is able to err simply by virtue of there being something beyond the veil of its doubt to get right or wrong; a disposition to doubt prevents error, but does not eliminate its possibility. What strikes Descartes in meditation 4 is the degree of error not attributable to the fact of finitude. Apparently he senses within himself something like a desire to err (he refers to it as a "privation" in his knowing), and it seems as if that should not be, not if he could have been created without it.

If Descartes is dealing with theodicy, then the terms that have set up the issue are themselves the problem. Look at his alternatives. If he conforms his will perfectly to the infinite will of God, he disappears. There will be only one will in evidence, the original one. If he wishes to retain a sense of his distinction from God (an infinite will), he has given himself no choice but to treat all offerings of truth and goodness as if they were the deliverances of a malignant intelligence. The disposition to err is not relevantly different in his *Meditations* from a disposition to doubt, and therein lies the real incoherence of the whole Cartesian project. As a thinking self, Descartes cannot be different from his God and still inhabit a world. His crisis in knowing has resolved itself into solipsism.

8. AT (1996), vol. 7, p. 57.

Crisis Mentalities

Augustine's Gordian knot in the *Confessions* is the problem of evil, a fuller bodied problem of error that shakes Augustine's confidence in the adequacy of his concepts of God and self, and shakes it to the core. For a not insignificant period of time he reports of having been enamored of Manicheism, a Gnostic dualism whose revision of the Delphic imperative, "Know yourself," more or less came out to be: "Know that you are not the evil of your flesh." But he is too impressed with his own love of the flesh to be comfortable finding the source of evil there, and even if it were there, why, he wonders, would he love something evil as if it were good?

Augustine's growing disenchantment with Gnostic denigration of flesh leaves him at a loss on the question of evil's origin. He takes it as a given that he has been disposed to will perversely, to love the absence of the good as if absence were itself good. This peculiar kind of corruptibility suggests to him his origin in an incorruptible being, whose will must be the measure of his own (*conf.* 7.4.6): "There is no way at all for corruption to violate our God, not by will, not by necessity, not by accident unforeseen: for God is God, and what God wills for himself is good, and that same good is God." It would be good for Augustine to have a will that loves the same good that God does; that would make him, by the logic of his concept of God, a part of God, of something incorruptible. But it is precisely the possibility of his connection to a will of inviolate goodness that perplexes him. If he is willed to be by this will, he should always be good beyond corruption, and if not, how is it that he is any good at all? He entertains the idea for a moment that the devil is the originator of all corruption, but he quickly recognizes that the devil should have the same perplexity that he does. How did the devil come to love the good that was not? "By these meditations," he writes (*conf.* 7.3.5), "I was once again weighed down and choked."

Descartes meets up with his problem of error after he has settled upon fixed concepts of God and self. Augustine brings to his problem of evil—or more to the point, his problem of sin—a questionable concept of self and a notion of God that is up for revision. Although Augustine is not disposed to think of God as limited in will (for him a Manichean temptation), he is not locked into thinking of God as will alone. He edges up against his profoundest revision of God's nature when he heeds the directive he finds in certain books of Platonist philosophy and turns within, into the inmost depths of himself. The directive of a return to self must have been especially striking to him, in that his problem of evil, which he pitches so relentlessly in the first person, has often made him seem a stranger to himself. Once within himself, he understands the reality of God better, but he is still apparently far from having a grip on his own (*conf.* 7.10.16): "When I knew you first, you took me up so that I might see that what I was seeing existed and that it was not yet me who was seeing."

It is tempting in translating the Latin to resist the vertigo of this statement and have Augustine communicate something like this: I saw that I was not yet seeing what I was supposed to see. But I think that Augustine intended the vertigo.[9] His words gesture at the incongruity of two perspectives: the one that he is being taken up into and the one that he is temporarily leaving behind. The incongruity speaks to the difference between time and eternity. Augustine abides in his vision as the person God sees him eternally to be, but for the man still trying to put together the narrative of his life, that is a person who is yet to be. Even within himself, Augustine sees that he remains outside of himself, but here in a way far more promising than offered him by sin. He will want to become that person outside of himself, a person, he is ecstatic to report, who is able to love God without missing the mark (*conf.* 7.17.23): "It was a wonder to me that I was loving you already and not some illusion in your stead."

There is more to say about this perspective of the self who is not yet. It is a window into redemption but also a reminder of what resists it. Augustine describes his incongruous point of view as a *regio dissimilitudinis*[10]—a place of unlikeness, a place like no other. Since I think that this is the place where the Augustinian crisis is best defined against its Cartesian shadow, I will begin by noting what makes it different from a space of radical doubt. First of all, Augustine is in an unlikely place, one he thinks of as far from God, because of sin and not because of doubt. He is still bound to a will that confuses good and evil. He is still inclined, that is, either to serve an illusion of goodness or to find fault and privation where there is none. However strange his inward exile may seem to him, it is continuous with the confused alienation of his outwardly directed life of sin, where he is also within God but without himself. The difference is that he has been made aware of his position; the *regio dissimilitudinis* is a spatial representation of

---

9. The Latin reads as follows: *et cum te primum cognovi, tu adsumpsisti me ut viderem esse quod viderem, et nondum me esse qui viderem*. O'Connell (1989), pp. 1–3, discusses the difficulty of translating this line; I follow him in his sense of the Latin syntax, but divert from his Plotinian reading of the meaning.

10. The term has antecedents in Plato and Plotinus. Augustine would have inherited the Plotinian antecedent (ἀνομοιότητος τόπος) from *Ennead* 1.8.13, the tractate on evil; see Armstrong (1989), p. 308f. For some of the peculiarities of Augustine's use of the term, see Solignac (1998).

Crisis Mentalities

his knowledge of sin. Literally this place is nowhere, occupied by no one; it is outside of the logical space of being. The last thing we should expect, then, to emerge out of such a paradox would be a *res cogitans*, or for that matter, any concept of an intelligible self.

But Augustine does say that there were things for him to see, realities for him to embrace, even from so odd a point of view. It is as if solipsism has been inverted for him. He is not yet in his life, but the source of his life is present to him, as are all the many other beings that have come from this source. God and world, but no self. His vision of God is difficult and indeterminate. The light of original being blinds him, drives him back into his place of unlikeness. Into that space, and from on high, come startling words, promising but with an edge of menace (*conf.* 7.10.16): "I am the food of the fully grown: grow and you will feed on me. You will not change me into you as you do the food of your flesh; you will have been changed into me." Soon there are other words, the signature statement of the redeemer of exiles: "I am who I am" (Exod 3:14); Augustine hears this in his heart (*in corde*), and his vision comes back into play. He notices the creation, the visible trace of God, and it strikes him that there is no evil in it, nothing wanting (*conf.* 7.13.19).

The choice before Augustine is the most fundamental of choices, a version of Hamlet's question: to be or not to be? Suppose he is moved to enter into the self who is not yet. If his crisis had a Cartesian inspiration, he would be deciding between God and world, but Augustine's God does not give him this choice. Communion with God apart from embracing the world of God's creation is self-abdication; by the time Augustine would have had his fill of God, the one who offers him food from afar, there would be no Augustine left, but only God. The direct route to God seems paradoxically to be a choice for nonbeing. What better defines Augustine's crisis is the difference between two ways of being other to God. There is first the fascination with willing other than as God wills, the disposition to sin and err; this is the impetus to otherness that lands Augustine and (unwittingly) Descartes in a place of exile from themselves. The alternative is not to put more faith in the ability of the human will to become godlike—an option that breeds resentment of mortality—but to look for forgiveness where it is least expected. The will to be other to God is not always worthy of punishment. When it is a will to be other than God is, it can be the expression of love rather than fear and resentment. Augustine refers to this possibility as the mystery of the Word made flesh (*conf.* 7.19.25). He admits that the lesson of this mystery is still before him.

I have said that as a thinking self, Descartes cannot be other to his God and still inhabit a world. He has no better way to be other to God than to will other than as God wills (to doubt, to err). In Augustine's attempt to return to his essential self, he discovers that he cannot inhabit a world without being other to his God. The shift between these perspectives happens in the blink of a soul's eye. Augustine will be periodically tempted to regard the body as too impoverished a thing to mark other than a punitive difference between divine and human. Those are the times when he is most apt to look for the essence of himself in his freedom from his flesh. In book 10 of *The Trinity*, for instance, he seems nearly to have embraced the Cartesian *res cogitans* as his own true self. There he employs indubitability as the key to self-knowledge. If as a mind I can doubt that I am essentially material, does it follow that I am essentially what I cannot doubt, something immaterial? It would, Augustine reasons, if it were true that "nothing is able to be more present to the mind than itself" (*Trin.* 10.3.5).

But is this true? In that particular book of *The Trinity*, the most apparently Cartesian of all his writings, Augustine seems to think so, but the immediate context is misleading. Augustine is on the way in the work as a whole to a reaffirmation of one of the signal insights of his *Confessions*—that his God has been more present to him than he has been to himself (*conf.* 3.6.11): "You were nearer than my depths, and ahead of my heights." In a tone less confessional, Descartes adverts to a similar wisdom, but one he never takes to heart: "I understand clearly that there is more reality in an infinite substance than a finite one, and that accordingly the perception of the infinite substance, God, is somehow in me before the perception of the finite substance, myself."[11] Somehow.

II. The Distance between Sin and Error

It was on Arnauld's advice that Descartes added this caveat to his synopsis of meditation 4 (AT, p. 15): "Note should be taken that sin is in no way dealt with there, or error that is committed in the pursuit of good and evil, but only error that is met with in the adjudication of true and false."[12] Arnauld must have noticed, as would any good reader with a modicum of theological training, that the form of Descartes' reasoning in that meditation invites a substitution of evil for error. But if so, and here Arnauld's theological instincts are again in evidence, it also invites a confusion, for

---

11. AT (1996), vol. 7, p. 45.
12. AT (1996), vol. 7, p. 15.

there is a world of difference between sin and error. It is possible to err by mistake. The best of minds can resolve not to err, remain resolved, and still err. Such is the liability of being finite. Sin, by contrast, is never simply a mistake; it has its source in a perversion of will. Arnauld does not think that Descartes himself is confused about this. His aim is only to spare Descartes the bother of having to defend his meditation against injudicious readers.

In meditation 4, Descartes is indeed aware of the distinction between error that is attributable to finitude and error that is not, but as I noted in the previous section, it is the latter kind of error and not the former that takes up his attention. Not only is it possible for a reader to draw an analogy between sin and error in this context, it is downright obfuscating to work to avoid it. Descartes concedes early in the meditation that God might have created him with an infallible, albeit finite, capacity to know. He would not know everything it was possible to know (no omniscience), but what he thought he knew he would know. He would never be inclined, that is, to presume upon knowledge he did not in fact have. Practically speaking he might have to act on beliefs, but beliefs are not opinions; his mind would remain secure in its own realm. In the face of this enticing ideal, Descartes wonders what reason God has for having created him with such an evident imperfection, that of a disposition to err and act on opinions. He gives up asking pretty quickly. It is not the business of a meditation to speculate on God's motives, which can never be known with certainty. It is enough to know that there is no contradiction in the notion of a human being who is disposed to err. Descartes takes further and considerable consolation from the fact that in a disposition to err there is no necessity implied (AT 7, p. 62): "For I shall certainly attain the truth, if only I attend enough to all the things that I understand perfectly, and then separate them off from the things left over, which I see in a more obscure and confused state."[13]

If the analogy between sin and error is overlooked, Descartes will seem entitled to his prudent disdain for theological speculation. But his disdain is not really prudent at all; it leaves an impasse in the structure of his meditation untested. Descartes does not have to know why he is disposed to err, any more than Augustine has to know why he is disposed to sin, but he does have to consider what it means to his meditation to

13. AT (1996), vol. 7, p. 62. At the end of meditation 4, Descartes outlines a discipline for eliminating error and remarks that this is where he finds his "greatest and foremost human perfection." More grist for a theological mill. Descartes sounds very Pelagian here, a possibility Arnauld would have wanted to discount.

be stuck with this as an irresolvable question. He would like it to mean nothing at all, or at most something for theologians to worry about. His efforts in meditation 4 are largely dismissive. There remains to haunt him, however, what his question of why has presupposed: that he has the disposition at issue. How does he know that? Descartes cannot put his knowledge of his errant disposition to the doubt without undermining the very motive he has for conducting a meditation, but he cannot include it within the meditation without having it raise questions about his foundational concepts of God and self.

Consider what is supposed to set apart God and self in the progression of a Cartesian meditation. It cannot be the body; before its differentiation into its finite and infinite modes, the thinking self doubted the body out of existence. It must be the case, then, that doubt itself is some kind of imperfection, for as of meditation 3, doubt is only what the finite self does. How is it though that this doubt has suddenly become a sign of imperfection? Since its radical inception, doubt has expressed the will of the thinking self to be free of error, to experience autonomy in its capacity to know. As the expression of an abstracted will to know, the finite thinking self is no less perfect than its limitless paradigm. Granted, the self that perfects its knowing in doubt has nothing but its own thoughts to know. In comparison, the infinite self is still no different; its knowing is just as willfully solipsistic. If there is some hint of imperfection in the neighborhood, it takes its cue not from a desire to know perfectly, but from a desire to know another: the heart's desire. Before the thinking self can notice imperfection in its doubt, it will have to want its body back—not as an appendage of its thinking, but as a means of becoming other to something else. It is the question of otherness in knowing, the question of the need for it, that puts a person at the juncture of mind and heart. Descartes has arrived there in meditation 4, but he has covered his tracks and described the place differently.

In the way that I use the terms, the heart mediates the relationship of mind to body, or to be more precise, it suggests the need for a transformation of bodily appetite, so that knowing can become a matter of knowing another. Since the heart has no express role to play in the Cartesian crisis of knowing, Descartes is inclined to think of the union of mind and body as little more than a barometer of pain and pleasure. In its substantial union with the body, the Cartesian mind will avoid some kinds of pain and pleasure, acquiesce to others, but as for determining what these sensations signify (self or other), the collaboration ends: "For it seems to pertain to the mind alone to know the truth about these things, but not to the composite."[14] If Descartes is right, I know my own body no differently than I know the body of another; both are equally alien to a thinking self. I may as a composite of mind and body feel intimately the privations and pleasures of just one body in particular, but this kind of intimacy is, for the purposes of knowledge, a source of constant confusion.

Compared to Descartes, Augustine wears his heart on his sleeve. He is much more apt than Descartes to be impressed with the fact that he sometimes seems to feel the pains and pleasures of others as if they were his own. Does he too take this to be a source of confusion when it comes to knowing where he stops and another life begins? Yes, but the worrisome confusion to Augustine is that he will think too much in terms of himself and miss what he is being offered. He calls the source of his confusion his "carnal habit" (*consuetudo carnalis*; *conf.* 7.17.23);[15] it is what keeps him from leaving his place of unlikeness and entering into the self that is yet to be—it robs him of his future, in other words. Many of Augustine's readers have read him to be condemning his habit of sexual desire, and that would not be wrong, were it also understood that his indictment is not of sex per se. For Augustine, sexual desire is not the bane of bodily appetite; it is its crossroads. In one direction there is the pleasure that comes of filling a void in desire, and in the other the delight of having a world of more than one. Standing at this particular crossroads he is reminded both of his body's poverty and of his God's assumption of the flesh. Being able to move ahead in both directions would be, by his reckoning, to know and receive grace.

III. Confession as a Genre in Philosophy

One way to mark the difference between a philosophical genre of writing and a devotional one is to notice what kind of authority the author gives to reason. Writers of philosophy may be expected to notice limits to reason, even to insist upon them, but reason will retain its exclusive rights to knowing. If there are things unknown to reason, unknown they remain. Writers of a more devotional bent may be expected to notice not only the limits of reason, but its imperfection as well, and to insist especially upon

---

14. AT (1996), vol. 7, pp. 82–83.
15. For a fuller interpretation of Augustine's notion of carnal habit, see Wetzel (2000).

this. "The heart has reasons," writes Pascal, "of which reason is unaware."[16] I mention this way of marking a difference in genre because I think that it is both common and misleading. Applied to Descartes and Augustine respectively, it makes Descartes out to be the philosopher, Augustine the philosophically engaging writer of devotion. If Augustine had been more philosophically inclined, perhaps he would have written a meditation instead of a confession. Would it ever occur to anyone to think that had Descartes been more philosophically inclined, he would have written a confession instead of a meditation?

My concluding thought will not be that Descartes should have written his first philosophy in the form of a confession, but only that he might have. If we take the mark of a philosophical genre to be not its commitment to the autonomy of reason but its fidelity to the desire to know, then Augustine may have the better claim. He confesses his knowledge of his own sin in order to claim a larger share of God's love (*conf.* 2.1.1): "For the love of your love I do this, this recalling of my worst ways in the bitterness of my recognition." His words sound devotional, and they are. They also express no less profoundly the integrity of his hope for knowledge. To love the love of God is to embrace an original desire—the desire that there be something rather than nothing. In a created being, this desire takes the form of an acknowledgment. Augustine wants God's love, and so he must acknowledge that he once loved an illusion in God's place. The end of this illusion is not to put God in illusion's place, but to remember what is wanted from the desire to know (the labor of a lifetime). It is the knowing of sin that is the real gift. For without it I live by mind alone.

The Cartesian meditation, rewritten as a confession, finds a different hope in the knowledge of error. Not that I may be as perfect as my will never to make mistakes, but that my knowing may be as generous as the love that goes before me.

---

16. From fragment 397 of the *Pensées*; see Le Guern (2004), p. 251.

3

The Alleged Importance of Free Choice

Augustine on Liberum Arbitrium

IN HIS TREATISE ON the free choice of the will, Augustine speaks of the value of having a free will in these terms (*lib. arb.* 2.1.3): "If being human is a good thing, and a human being cannot, unless he wills it, act rightly, then a human being ought to have a free will, without which he cannot act rightly." In the abstract, Augustine's sentiment is unexceptional. If we humans are good by virtue of what we do with our humanity, then free will is an essential part of who we are. But now add this to the mix. Suppose that it is possible for an intelligent being to will the good for all eternity and never be tempted in the slightest to act perversely. What then would be the value of having of a will that is free to act perversely? Surely God could have made us from the start to be more angelic in our humanity or human as Christ is human—as having no inclination to lapse. When Evodius, Augustine's interlocutor in *On Free Choice*, presses Augustine to clarify the value of free will, he has in mind the dubious freedom of being free to embrace a lack of goodness, a life apart from God.

Towards the end of book 2, Augustine will refer to the irresolute will, capable of deviating from what it first and fundamentally loves, as an intermediate or middling good (*lib. arb.* 2.19.53): "The will, then, that adheres to the unchanging good that is everyone's attains the first and foremost goods of human life, even though this will is itself some middling good." It is far from clear what Augustine means in this context by "some middling good" (*medium quoddam bonum*). He goes on to suggest a contrast between the steadfast will, loyal to the good, and the will that turns away to pursue more remote and less worthy loves. Are we to assume that the will, when abstracted from an orientation, is still intelligible as will and therefore identifiable as a kind of good, albeit "middling"? If so, then the life of the will takes three basic forms: a life that clings to the good, a life that cuts free, and a life that is poised between clinging and cutting. That last possibility, if it is to be credited, is the life that Augustine's Adam forever loses for the rest of us when he follows a woman into sin and (in effect) leaves his father's house.

I am going to argue, for what I hope are good Augustinian reasons, that it makes no sense to cast the will as a middling good. Of course I concede that Augustine wants it to make sense, that he has a vested interest in the difference between the original Adam, who has freedom not to sin, and Adam's doleful heirs, who have freedom only to sin. He speaks specifically about two regimes of grace, Adamic and Christic, in a late work, far into the Pelagian controversy. Scholars of Augustine visit the relevant passages in *On Admonition and Grace* often (see *corrept.* 11.29–12.35), like a favorite pilgrimage site. Adam is described there as having been given the prophylactic grace that would have enabled him, had he made use of it, to live safely in paradise (no need to fear serpents or women). Adam's heirs, who are born to a wilderness of human longing, are given the preemptive grace that undoes bondage to sin and enables a person to enjoy, though never fully in this life of travail, the freedom that Christ enjoys: the freedom of incorruptible love. Although it takes a Pelagian threat to get Augustine to associate Adam's life with a regime of grace, he has always held to the view that Adam's unique freedom was to be able, apart from Christ's grace (but not the Father's), to avoid sin.[1] It looks as if Adam's freedom is less desirable than the freedom of the saints, who are being led into a perfect grace, but more desirable than the freedom of reprobates, who are left to suffer a second death. It needs to be noted, however, that the grace that turns a reprobate into a saint is not a grace that passes through the way station of Adamic freedom. It is not Adam who stands between love and its pathology but Christ.

---

1. In *corrept.* 11.29, Augustine draws a distinction between the grace of God (*gratia Dei*) and the grace of Christ (*gratia Christi*). The latter is still God's grace, but specifically grace that comes through the life, death, and resurrection of Jesus of Nazareth (*gratia Dei per Iesum Christum*). Adam was not born into a flesh that wars against spirit, and so he had no need for the grace that wins that war. His only need, says Augustine, was for the grace that leaves him with the choice of continuing his paradisiacal existence.

The Alleged Importance of Free Choice

When Augustine decisively abandons the idea, sometime around the beginning of his episcopacy, that the freedom to refuse grace is a freedom worth valuing, he undermines his motive for making a special case of Adam's freedom. The constant of Augustine's reading of Adam is that Adam freely exchanges his life in paradise for something considerably darker and more difficult. Forget for a moment the difficulty of motivating that kind of choice. Is Augustine in a position to claim that Adam, among his many losses, lost a valuable kind of freedom? I don't think so. Adam, by falling, merely shows himself to have been in the same need of grace as any reprobate. His original need was to be fully sealed to God without force or manipulation; it is, for Augustine, the grace of Christ that does that kind of work. There is, by a certain Augustinian light, no other grace.

Since I will be arguing Augustine against himself, I plan to frame much of my argument in developmental terms. I begin with some general observations about Augustine's volitional psychology, but I soon move into the theological twists and turns that give his psychology life but not necessarily consistency. With some misgiving, I find myself pursuing a reading of Augustine that stands much at odds with the one urged by Goulven Madec. In a seminal essay of his on the rapport in Augustine between responsible and graced freedom, Madec discounts interpretations of Augustine that find radical discontinuity in his theology of grace and then fixate on that finding.[2] The temptation to do this must be formidable, as it takes in the likes of Peter Brown and Kurt Flasch. Madec takes Brown to task for sundering Augustine into an early classical persona, "more Pelagian than Pelagius," and a tragic theologian of grace, given to uncertain delights. Flasch, for Madec, amplifies Brown's mistake and turns the turn of *Ad Simplicianum* (*To Simplician*), Augustine's midlife meditation on Paul, into a crisis from which Augustine never fully recovers—his theology remains from then on "a nest of contradictions."[3] The besetting sin of such interpretations is that they fail, from Madec's point of view, to make proper use of Augustine's distinction between an unforced acquiescence to a relative good (*liberum arbitrium*) and an unreserved embrace of an absolute good (*libertas*).

---

2. "Du libre arbitre à la liberté par la grâce de Dieu," in Madec (2001), pp. 241–55; the essay originally appeared in Bedouelle and Fatio (1994), pp. 31–45.

3. Madec (2001), pp. 242–44; cf. Brown (2000), especially chapter 15, "The Lost Future," and Flasch (1980), especially chapter 11, "Gnade (ab 396)." While I tend to agree with Madec that Brown is too apt to contrast Augustine the classicist with Augustine the (tragic) Romantic, I still side with Brown and Flasch in seeing *Ad Simplicianum* as a radical turn in Augustine's theology, a point of crisis.

Parting Knowledge

I doubt whether any careful reader of Augustine's texts can fail to notice that he does make this distinction and that he considers it of cardinal importance. It is debatable, however, whether the distinction can bear the weight that Augustine and some of his most faithful interpreters, like Madec, intend it to bear. I will try to show that once *liberum arbitrium* is sorted out from the antipodes that take it in, graced freedom and bondage to sin, it loses most of its significance.

I. Terms and Distinctions

In Augustine's use of the term, *liberum arbitrium* is invariably short for *liberum arbitrium uoluntatis*—free choice of the will. Occasionally he will use other terms to mean *liberum arbitrium uoluntatis*, such as *uoluntas libera, libertas arbitrii,* and *libertas uoluntatis,* but he overwhelmingly favors the term *liberum arbitrium* for referring to a freedom to act on desire. If I act on desire in Augustine's sense of *liberum arbitrium*, I will think of my motivating desire as good in some way, if only in the attenuated sense of being less evil than my alternatives. By no means do I have to identify with my desire fully in order for my decision to act, my *arbitrium*, to count as free. Augustine observes in *Spirit and Letter* (spir. et litt. 31.53) that actions done unwillingly (*inuitus*) are nevertheless done with a will (*uoluntate*): "Even when someone is compelled to act, if he acts, he acts out of will; but because he prefers to act otherwise he is for that reason called compelled, that is, unwilling." If I act under duress, I may act contrary to my normal inclination to act, but what matters to Augustine here is that I will to suffer one kind of evil rather than another. That is enough will for *liberum arbitrium*. It is also enough will for *liberum arbitrium* if I act against my own best judgment and give in to a guilty pleasure. In book 8 of the *Confessions,* Augustine memorably describes his struggle to be free of his carnal follies with women. Whether he succeeds or fails, he acts with a will.

For all its supposed importance to his moral theology, *liberum arbitrium* is for Augustine a minimalist notion of freedom. By itself it fails to account for what makes sinners culpable for sin, being equally present in compulsive, addictive, and coerced behaviors, and it fails to account—though this is less obvious—for what makes saints recipients of grace.[4]

---

4. For a classic expression of the contrary view, see Léon-Dufour (1946). Basically Léon-Dufour contends that no calling is ever received apart from the consent of the recipient, even when the circumstances of that calling virtually guarantee consent.

The concept does not express fully either what Augustine means by will (*uoluntas*) or what he means by freedom (*libertas*). His basic notion of will is of a register of aversions and attractions, whose coherent articulation—if there is one—defines the characteristic love of the soul and a person's personality. "The will itself," he writes (*Simpl.* 1.2.22), "is not able to be moved unless something happens that stirs and delights the soul; that this should happen is not, however, in a person's power."[5]

Augustine expects love in this life to be opaque and conflicted. On the surface, human beings love many different things in tangled ways, but at the fundamental level of will, love is either of God's absence or of God's presence. If a conflicted love resolves itself towards sin, the soul ends by loving nothing as if it were something and love is undone. If love resolves itself towards God, then the soul ends by loving God as the Son loves the Father, and the antipathy between God and humanity—so apparent in human sin—forever falls away, since there is no further prospect of sin to motivate it. In relation to the deeper dynamics of love and will, *liberum arbitrium* is a snapshot in time, an image either of an emergent personality, heading towards greater coherence, or of an increasingly fractured psyche, hobbled by the violence and stupidity of its desires.

Ideal freedom, as Augustine comes to think of it, is a blessing of wisdom—a divinely bestowed wisdom to be sure, but for all that a wisdom having distinctly human benefits. If I am wise, then I am able both to delight in true value and to recognize and disdain its counterfeit. I do not have to worry that my desires might be leading me down a blind and hopeless alley; I am free to want what I want. Regrettably, it is unlikely that I am really that free. In Augustine's estimation, the only unambiguously free human being was Christ, when he walked the earth as Jesus of Nazareth. His was the freedom not to be able to sin (*non posse peccare*),

---

In response to Léon-Dufour, Burns (1980) elaborates and defends the truth of Lebourlier's hypothesis in Lebourlier (1955): that after 418 Augustine came to think of grace as renovating the sinful will from the inside out, thus making it difficult if not impossible for him to identify responsible human freedom with a person's freely given consent (*liberum arbitrium*) to either sin or grace. I have learned much from Burns.

5. Cf. Brown (2000), p. 149: "Augustine came to view 'delight' as the mainspring of human action; but this 'delight' escaped his self-control. Delight is discontinuous, startlingly erratic: Augustine now moves in a world of 'love at first sight,' of chance encounters, and, just as important, of sudden, inexplicable patches of deadness." Augustine's assimilation of *uoluntas* to *amor* is considered by most scholars to be both novel and important. See Arendt (1978), pp. 84–110, Burnaby (1938), pp. 226–34, Horn (1995), pp. 132–38, and Rist (1994), pp. 186–88.

not because he was forced into obedience to God, but because he grasped in mind and heart the wisdom of obeying.

To the extent that the contrast to ideal, Christlike freedom is ignorance of the good and not a failure of will, Augustine's conception of freedom is apt to seem Stoic.[6] The Stoics linked freedom to right judgment and were confident that a corrected way of seeing would issue in the appropriate affect, leaving the Stoic sage free of internal conflict. Although there is some affinity between Augustine's ideal of freedom and Stoic resolution, the affinities are greatly complicated by two features of his mature theology: his firm conviction that a graced love is still a conflicted love, even in as weighty a saint as Paul himself, and his dark insistence that the loss of Adam's original freedom—a freedom to choose obedience over death—profoundly colors the ignorance of his descendents. Inherited ignorance of the good of obedience is for Augustine a *culpable* ignorance. Unbaptized infants are damned on account of it.

Augustine had to work his way into his settled doctrine of grace and original sin. Some of his discarded views illumine the ground beneath *liberum arbitrium*, where two ideals of liberty are in tension, if not outright conflict.

II. Contextual Development

Much of Augustine's thinking about the nature and operation of grace emerges out of the context of his anti-Pelagian works, the writing of which preoccupied him from mid to late career and right up to his death. For Augustine, Pelagianism was basically a denial of the guilt and depravity that is the legacy of original sin and a corresponding inclination to underplay the depth and desperation of the human need for redemption through Christ, the better Adam. Although Augustine's thinking about both grace and original sin developed significantly over time, he claimed that he had come to his anti-Pelagian theology well before ever hearing of Pelagius. In his late work of self-review, the *Retractationes*, he looks back at the first work he wrote as a bishop, a set of exegetical reflections, and concludes that in his exegesis of Romans 9:10–29, he had been laboring to connect God's offer of grace to a prior act of faith, but that grace finally "won out" (*uincit*; *retr.* 2.1) and upstaged human initiative.

---

6. On Stoicism in Augustine, see Colish (1985), pp. 142–238, Verbeke (1958), and Sorabji (2000), pp. 372–84.

The Alleged Importance of Free Choice

The motivating question behind Augustine's exegesis of Romans 9, where Paul is pondering the relative favor in God's eyes of Jews and Gentiles, is whether God has any basis in human merit for his prenatal election of Jacob over his twin, Esau. In an exposition of Romans, written just a couple of years before his set of responses to Simplician, Augustine had already excluded the possibility of virtue-based election, but he was still disposed to believe that a person's *desire* to become virtuous, expressed in a faithful petition to God for help, could supply a reasonable basis for election. In electing Jacob over Esau, God must have foreknown that Jacob, but not Esau, would grow up to become a man of faith (*ex. prop. Rm.* 60). Augustine decisively repudiated this interpretation of his in his subsequent foray into Romans 9; having concluded that even an act of faith is a work that might feed the human appetite for vainglory, he embraced the idea that divine election is wholly gratuitous and never let go of it. Jacob's election over Esau, as with the election of any one sinner over another, is going to be a complete mystery from a human point of view. It is based, says Augustine (*Simpl.* 1.2.16), "on the most hidden kind of equity, far removed from human experience."

There is some question in the scholarship over whether Augustine's revised doctrine of election was quite as decisive as he made it out to be for shaping his anti-Pelagian theology.[7] Regardless of how this question is finally resolved, it is beyond doubt that his anti-Pelagian theology underwent at least one transformation that Augustine did not anticipate in his first year as a bishop. In writings directed against the argumentative Pelagianism of Julian of Eclanum, Augustine decided that he would have to revise his reading of Romans 7, where Paul speaks in anguished tones about doing what he hates and not what he wants to do, being still captive to the flesh. Whereas Augustine had long been assuming that Paul speaks in Romans 7 under an adopted persona and not as a graced apostle, he now finds himself compelled to admit—under the pressure of a Pelagian idealization of sainthood—that it is possible, indeed the case, that Paul is speaking autobiographically there.[8] The significance of Augustine's

---

7. I have already indicated Madec's view of the matter. For a broader view of the debate, see the précis in Burns (1980), pp. 7–12.

8. The new Paul, groaning under grace, makes his first appearance in *On Marriage and Lust* (*nupt. et conc.* 1.27.30). When Augustine is accused by Julian of having sullied Paul's name, he defends himself and his revised reading of Paul in *Against Two Letters of the Pelagians* (*c. ep. Pel.* 1.8.13f.), where he affirms Paul's struggle against concupiscence as a saint's paradigmatic struggle. Augustine came to his new view of Paul reluctantly. For some insight into that reluctance, see Dodaro (2004), pp. 84–86.

revision of Romans 7 resides in what it implies about grace and concupiscence. If the aim of grace is not simply to rectify action but also to renovate desire—to the point of eliminating temptation altogether—then the barest delight in the good, even if it should prove *ineffectual* as a motive, is wholly a gift of grace. In the last decade or so of his polemics against Pelagianism, Augustine never tired of hammering home the point that, left to its own devices, the fallen will is free only to sin.

The Pelagians themselves had little affection for anything Augustine wrote after his ascension to the See of Hippo. Pelagius was known to have had a strong dislike for the *Confessions*, particularly the part where Augustine petitions God for a preemptory obedience: "Give what you command," he asks (*conf.* 10.29.40), "and command what you will."[9] Julian recalled one of Augustine's early definitions of sin, in the anti-Manichean work, *On the Two Souls*, and characterized it as a rare find of gold amid a corpus of dung (*aurum in stercore*; *c. Jul. imp.* 1.45). In *Two Souls*, a work dating from the time of his priesthood, Augustine had defined sin as "the will to cling and grasp at what justice forbids, when there is freedom to hold off" (*duab. an.*) The old bishop was well aware of what a Pelagian like Julian would read into such a definition: an admission that everyone retained the freedom that Adam had originally, the freedom not to sin. Augustine was especially concerned that *On Free Choice (lib. arb.)*, the most philosophical of his anti-Manichean works, would read to Pelagians like a manifesto for their heresy. There he had insisted on making sin fully a matter a human responsibility, a free choice of the will (*liberum arbitrium uoluntatis*). Augustine never retracted that thesis, but he did offer this caveat to his readers (*retr.* 1.9.2): "It is one thing to inquire into the origin of evil, quite another to seek the source of a return to innocence or of a reaching towards a greater good."

Given Augustine's claim that his doctrine of grace changed decisively with his revised view of election, his insinuation that his early anti-Manichean emphasis on human culpability was compatible with his late, anti-Pelagian theology of grace is at best improbable. Incompatibility does not mean, however, that the Augustine of *On Free Choice* was a Pelagian in temperament and spirit.[10] It is important to consider where Augustine most diverged from the Manicheism of his youth. The Manichees, as Augustine saw them, preferred to split God in two rather than admit that an

---

9. In *The Gift of Perseverance* (*persev.* 20.53), Augustine notes how irksome Pelagius found the petition.

10. But for a provocative argument to the contrary, see O'Donnell (2005), pp. 271–78.

originally good soul could will evil. The Manichean view seemed simple enough—good comes from good, evil from evil—but Augustine had come to realize that it missed a cardinal fact of human existence: that basically good people do stupid and evil things. Once Augustine was prepared to admit that he in some perhaps incomprehensible way desired the evil that most threatened his self-worth, he ceased to define himself in terms of the evil he was not and started to look for his redemption from a God who could take in his evil and make something good of it.

What the Pelagian reading of the early Augustine misses is his sense that human freedom has more to do with fulfilling desire than with resisting it. Augustine's God allows him to experience his sin in a transformed way—no longer as a self-defeating love of nothing, but as a love of God that has yet to recognize itself as such. His late, anti-Pelagian emphasis on concupiscence as the cardinal problem of human freedom is thus in keeping with his early anti-Manichean turn: the persistence of disruptive desire in the soul's pursuit of the good is indicative of a still subverted longing for God. The soul is not yet free to want what it wants.

If Augustine were to have embraced only a doctrine of sin and grace and not also a doctrine of sin without grace, the Pelagians would have had nothing to complain about. It makes no sense to insist on an earned redemption, as if some further good—a reward for effort—could be added to the redemption given. Once God perfects the soul's desire for God, the soul becomes one with its desire, and its desire ceases to be a source of want. To desire God and to enjoy God's presence are now synonymous. Augustine insists, however, that God is not intent on perfecting everyone's desires.[11] Some are given a glimmer of redeemed desire only to have the glimmer flicker and fade away; others are left perpetually in the dark. The reality of damnation does fairly raise a question of desert, and Augustine never thinks it enough to say that the damned are responsible for their bad end merely because of *liberum arbitrium*, their freedom to follow their self-destructive impulses. Somewhere in the history of their psyches, they must have had access to an alternative path of desire. But it is hard for Augustine to credit this possibility once he associates the work of grace with a complete transformation of desire. For what would move a grace-bereft

---

11. Only God's elect are called in a manner that elicits their consent; they are called *congruenter* (*Simpl.* 1.2.13). There is no possibility that the elect will fail to fulfill their calling, even if at times they seem to falter (*corrept.* 12.38). Those who are not predestined to be redeemed will, on the other hand, inevitably fail to persevere in the good that they do (*corrept.* 13.42).

soul to seek God other than the grace that this wretched soul is by definition denied?

In order to account for the culpable freedom of the damned, Augustine is driven to link *liberum arbitrium* to a freely willed rejection of an original, but not ultimate, life of *libertas*. It is the murkiest move in his philosophy of freedom.

III. The Perplexing Case of Adam

It is in the wake of his revised view of election that Augustine finds himself compelled to speak of the original guilt (*reatus originalis*; *Simpl.* 1.2.20) that is passed along from Adam to his descendents. Before that, he would speak of heritable impediments to living the good life (*ignorantia et difficultas*; *lib. arb.* 3.18.52), but these never kept anyone from asking for a better wisdom.[12] Those who ask receive, and those who don't ask have only themselves to blame for their negligence. Once original guilt is in play, no one who is not expressly moved by God to do so will think to ask.

Augustine's Adam wrecks it for the lot of us by choosing his partner, the flesh of his flesh, over his creator. In his more elaborate exegeses of the Genesis story of a short-lived garden paradise, Augustine assigns the man and the woman distinct parts to play in bringing about the first sin.[13] The woman is a sensualist who unthinkingly believes the serpent when the serpent suggests to her that knowledge is life; the man is a rationalist who disbelieves the serpent but concludes that the woman would surely perish without him. The man's motive for disobedience, though other-regarding in appearance, is self-aggrandizing; he assumes that he has it within him to redeem the woman and secure the life of the flesh. Although the woman's disobedience is first in time, it is the man's that reflects for Augustine what is paradigmatic about all sin. Like the rebellious angels who fell before him, the man turns away from God to seek within himself independent resources of strength, beauty, and goodness. If, as Augustine believes, the man has no reason to think that his life with God is lacking, then he must

---

12. The impairment of post-Adamic agency has always been for Augustine part of the penalty of original sin, but this is a sin that, until *Ad Simplicianum*, he has attributed solely to Adam and Eve. As penalty for *their* sin, they are not allowed to produce heirs who are wiser and more morally able than they are. After the turn of *Ad Simplicianum*, Augustine associates post-Adamic difficulties with heritable guilt. We are penalized for what we have (somehow) done in and through Adam and Eve.

13. *Gn. adv. Man.* 2.14.20–21; *Gn. litt.* 11.42.58–59; *civ. Dei* 14.11.

also know that God is his fulfillment. For no specifiable reason, he fails to remain steadfast in that knowledge.

It is not clear from Augustine's analysis of the deficient motive (*causa deficiens*) behind sin whether he thinks that sin is finally a pure love of evil or always some deluded way of pursuing the good.[14] What is clear from his analysis is that the motive behind sin is ultimately irreducible to either flesh or spirit. There is no bodily good, no good of mind or spirit that can render sin intelligible.[15] Augustine is sometimes credited with having invented the idea of will, where "will" is understood as a motive power neither sensuous nor rational in origin, but some *tertium quid*.[16] If Augustine has such a notion of will, it corresponds to what he characterizes as a will to sin and privation. The Adam who can will in disregard of the delights of his God-given flesh and spirit is an Adam who has been made susceptible to solipsistic illusions. Augustine calls the cause of such susceptibility "deficient" (*deficiens*), but that designation—which gives a name to a mystery—applies as much to any sin as it does to the first. There is no conceptual difference between what Augustine describes as Adamic freedom and what he comes to see as the imperfect freedom of a Paul under grace: in both cases a divinely bestowed love of God fails to rule out unaccountable desires to test the darkness.

While it is quite clear that Augustine would have resisted a historicized Adam and a reduction to one regime of grace, it is equally clear that he was not looking in this life or the next for a restoration of the original Adamic freedom. Had it been restored, it would have necessarily left open the prospect of another fall. Augustine held out instead for the freedom of the second Adam, whose heart is secure.

The most perplexing aspect of the first Adam's freedom is its duality. Adam's freedom not to sin—which is, for Augustine, the basis of his culpability and that of his descendants—is equally an expression of his freedom from God. He can either sin or not because, unlike Christ, he is not of one

---

14. My suspicion is that Augustine needs it (impossibly) to be both. A desire for pure evil (i.e., a deliberate rejection of God) is what makes the first sin solely a matter of human culpability; a grossly misshapen, but still salvageable, desire for the good (i.e., an ignorant love of God) is what makes the first sin redeemable. For more on this, see chapter 1 of this volume.

15. Augustine analyzes the motive behind sin in *civ. Dei* 12.6–8 and concludes that it is inexplicably deficient. For contrasting views on whether a deficient motive can be a basis for culpability, see Babcock (1988) and MacDonald (1999).

16. The paradigmatic argument for this view is that of Dihle (1982), pp. 123–44. For a more recent attempt to define the Augustinian will as *sui generis*, see Harrison (2006).

being with the Father. It can hardly be said that Adam was in much of a position to *choose* this condition of his. His freedom from sin but not from the desire to sin makes his original liberty less than free.

IV. Freedom in Christ

It is hard to justify vicarious punishment. Adam sins and his descendents are punished as if his sin were theirs as well; that just does not seem fair. When Augustine gives voice to the many people who would make this their complaint, he adds this response in his own voice (*lib. arb.* 3.19.53): "Perhaps they would have a right to complain if there were no one of our kind to conquer confusion and lust." Of course he does not mean just anyone, but the one human being who is also fully divine and who brought to human awareness a new kind of freedom (*libertas*)—in retrospect the only kind of freedom. Augustine points out in *On Free Choice* that the sting of an unfair punishment is not worth complaining about if it becomes the occasion for a reward far in excess of what anyone deserves. A vicarious reward is easier to accept than a vicarious punishment. The former, but not the latter, can evoke love and generosity, though perhaps *reward* is the wrong word to use when describing an offer of love.

Imagine a world where there are two kinds of people: the many who endure a vicarious punishment to its bitter end and the comparatively few who are released from this punishment through no virtue of their own. It is possible, up to a point, to fit Augustine's doctrine of predestination into this imagining. He does divide the world into the saved and the damned when he writes his late works on predestination, and there is no basis in human merit for the way he draws that division. The saints do not deserve their salvation, and the damned deserve their damnation only in the problematic way that everyone, the saints included, deserve damnation.

The part of his doctrine that fits less well into this imagining is his take on Christ's humanity, the "clearest light" (*praeclarissimum lumen*) on predestination and grace. To get a sense of what that light is, it helps to live awhile with what is, for me, the most stunning question Augustine ever thought to ask (*praed. sanct.* 15.30): "To be taken up by the Word into a co-eternal unity of person with the Father, to be the one begotten Son of God—where does the man get the merit for that?" Where indeed? I take it that Jesus owes his merit to a divine source, for no human being, not even one free of original sin, can self-generate sufficient merit to win a life with God. The gulf between divine abundance and human privation is simply too great ever to expect that; only the initiative of a self-giving God changes the terms of an otherwise inevitable alienation.

When Augustine speaks in general terms of the unfathomable mystery of election and neglects to avail himself of its Christic framing, he tends to emphasize the fact that human beings are born tainted by original guilt and so are *unworthy* of divine favor; the fortunate few who get it anyway can boast of no special merit. This dark teaching of his obscures the cardinal insight of his theology: that divine love is generative, not reactive. An antecedent worthiness (or lack thereof) has nothing to do with the dispensation of divine favor. Being free of original sin, Jesus was not unworthy of the grace bestowed upon him, but neither was he worthy. The clear implication of Augustine's doctrine of grace is that Jesus never earned his incarnation. He was born into it. There is in fact no other way to be a son or daughter of God.

Augustine occasionally entertains the fiction of an Adam who refuses forbidden fruit and thereby earns the grace to persevere with God for all eternity: "If Adam had freely willed to remain upright and without vice, then," Augustine speculates (*corrept*. 10.28), "he would have received the full happiness that perseverance merits, the very happiness—doubtless free of death and difficulty—with which the holy angels are beatified; in other words, he would be beyond the possibility of a fall and he would know that most certainly." Why is this fiction not a Pelagian fantasy? Its suggestion is that God might have dealt out love differently, on the basis of a quid pro quo, had human beings been better behaved from the start. The Adamic regime of grace, which puts Adam in a position to preempt a divine gift (by persevering before perseverance is given), is not the lost alternative to the Christic regime: it is its antithesis. If one regime is possible, then the other is not. Either I can will good and evil before my will is ever very intimate with God, or I can will good and confess to evil only when God is within me (*interior intimo meo*) and I am within God (*superior summo meo*).[17] The first, dissociative kind of will is forever unresolved between a fiction of good and evil and a fully divine life (though human too). I don't think that this kind of will is real, much less a middling good. The other kind of will, really the only kind of will, is as real as divine love is. I trust I don't have to say where Augustine found his freedom.

---

17. In the *Confessions* Augustine uses these words to convey the compass of his soul's intimacy with God (*conf.* 3.6.11): "You were more within me than me [*interior intimo meo*] and higher than my highest reach [*superior summo meo*]."

4

Trappings of Woe
Augustine's Confession of Grief

AUGUSTINE ANNOUNCES AT THE beginning of book 4 of the *Confessions* that he spent a good nine of years of his life, from age nineteen to twenty-eight, publicly teaching the liberal arts and privately binding himself to a false religion. As if to underscore that he was not bound alone, he uses the first-person plural to set the mood for the confession to follow (*conf.* 4.1.1): "During these same nine years, ... we were used to being seduced and to seducing, to being deceived and to deceiving, in a variety of excitements." When he lapses back into the first-person singular and—grammatically speaking—extricates himself from his friends in seduction and deception, he more or less catalogues his life as a Manichee in Carthage.[1]

It is a catalogue of restrained vices. He versed students in the unprincipled art of rhetoric, greedy to enhance his own reputation for speaking, but he preferred the sort of student who was principled enough not to use rhetorical tricks to get an innocent person condemned. He took on a woman to be his sexual partner out of wedlock, hoping to have no more than the one unplanned child he had already conceived with her, but he remained faithful to her during their fourteen years together. He looked

---

1. Manicheism is a religion that takes its name and inspiration from Mani, a religious visionary who was born in Persian-controlled Babylonia in April of 216 and executed under the reign of Bahram I in February of 277. For a concise account of Mani and the religion he inspired, see Coyle (1999). In essence, Manicheism is a religion that emphasizes the dual and irreconcilable origins of good and evil and offers knowledge as a path to redemption. Augustine tended to view Manicheism as a distorted form of Christianity, one overly pretentious in its claims to divine knowledge. For the purposes of my essay, I will be looking at Manicheism through Augustine's eyes.

to astrology to relieve him of the responsibilities of his tangled human freedom, but he refused the ministrations of soothsayers, who sacrificed animals to win the favor of spirits that cared about things like poetry contests and who won them. All things considered, the life he describes was not an especially bad one, but neither was it especially good.

"Badly consoling" is a phrase that more aptly captures the flavor of Augustine's years as a committed Manichee. Consolation is bad or false in cases where the need for consolation has been misperceived, and the need is either not there at all or of the sort that demands consolation of a different order. At the heart of *Confessions* 4—its moral center of gravity—Augustine recounts and anatomizes an experience of howling grief. He is back in Thagaste, his hometown, having returned there from Carthage. A young man of about twenty at the time, he is full of enthusiasms. Carthage was the city where he fell in love with love, developed his taste for theatre, dedicated his passion to philosophy, and converted to Manicheism—a religion from which he expected answers to his most burning questions. Shortly after his return home in the fall of 375, he reconnects with a childhood friend, whom he soon convinces to become a Manichee. Although Augustine refrains from retrospectively describing his relation to this man of like age, background, and interests as a "genuine friendship" (*conf.* 4.4.7), the bonds of affection between the two young men were obviously heartfelt. When the "friend" (for lack of a better word) dies of a fever, Augustine is inconsolable. He drags his "broken and bleeding soul" around town, visiting familiar haunts—where "all things were a horror, even light itself" (*conf.* 4.7.12)—until he decides to leave home again and return to Carthage. There he will seek repair in "causes of other sorrows" (*conf.* 4.8.13): friendships seeded in the soil of a false religion.

In his commentary on book 4, James J. O'Donnell tells us that "this book is made up of reminiscences of Carthage (376/83) framing the Thagaste episode (375/6) in the mid-section of the book."[2] From a strictly chronological point of view (a view not always easy to apply to the *Confessions*), O'Donnell is surely right about the framing. When the imperatives of book 4's confession are weighed in, however, I am inclined to invert the picture. It is the Thagaste episode that frames Augustine's memory of

---

2. O'Donnell (1992), vol. 2, p. 203. O'Donnell's three-volume edition of Augustine's *Confessions*—the Latin text and two volumes of commentary—is a fabulous resource for scholars and advanced students of Augustine, but it is tough going for the Latin-less. For a more accessible, but still quite sophisticated, commentary I recommend Starnes (1990). O'Donnell and Starnes work through Augustine's text book by book, section by section (minus the last four books in Starnes).

Carthage and not the reverse. After Thagaste, Carthage became to Augustine what fleshpots were to dispirited Israelites wandering in the desert: a falsely consoling memory. The Carthage that Augustine escapes to in 376, fleeing from the familiarity of his grief-hued life, is not very different from the Carthage of 371, the "cauldron of dissolute loves" (*conf.* 3.1.1) that beckoned a seventeen-year-old boy to leave the house of his father. Admittedly he didn't know himself in 371 to be seeking solace for a wounded heart. His heart seemed restless, but not grief-stricken. But it would be premature to conclude that in 376 he came to Carthage knowing the grief that dogged his steps. His friend's death had turned his life into a "great question" (*conf.* 4.4.9), and it was the sort of question that his Manichean pieties had ill equipped him to entertain. Augustine had touched upon a grief in himself that defied limits and so defied chronology. It spoke to a loss in his heart that preceded all the losses of a finite reckoning, and to hear of this loss terrified him. He confesses that he ran from his heart rather than enter into the question of its grief (*conf.* 4.7.12): "My straying was my god."

When I speak of the imperatives of book 4's confession, I don't mean to set these imperatives apart from the confession that is the common concern of all the books. The basic imperative of confession holds constant throughout Augustine's thirteen tries at self-recollection and knowledge of God, and that is for him to face the great question of himself. Part of what it means for him to face this question is to suffer the death of his straying self; the other part is to surrender to the life that works through this death. These parts are as inseparable from one another as sin is from grace; hence all of Augustine's confessions have a twofold aspect: they speak of not hearing God, and they speak of God's having made use of the "not hearing" to be heard.

I am not going to try to make better sense of confession in general beyond trying to fathom the particularities of book 4's confession, which I have referred to in this chapter's title as "Augustine's confession of grief." The suggestion in my title is not that grief is always some kind of sin—perhaps a lack of faith in God's keeping—but that grief is sometimes God-bereft and to confess it as such is to be called home. For Augustine the return of soul to God is the heart's return to itself. His own suggestion, then, is that the human heart is always in God's keeping and so cannot express a God-bereft love that is not divinely claimable in the end. His view of love, it seems to me, limits the power of sin considerably (even to the point of making sin powerless), but not sin's misery. We are too rooted in God, in other words, really to have broken from God, but not so rooted that we can't feel like we have.

My main interest in this chapter is Augustine's theology of grief, since it is this theology that underwrites book 4's retrospective confession of a God-bereft grief. His theology of grief is also a psychology of grief. I would like to be as faithful as I can to Augustine's inspiration, and keep God and soul together, but this kind of fidelity is hard to come by. I am aware of two major difficulties that stand against me. These are in fact difficulties that stand against many readers of the *Confessions*, but the scholarly ones most of all.

One I will call a difficulty of address. How is Augustine best addressed by his interpreter? He is writing in a confessional mode. I do not take myself to be writing about him in a confessional mode. Is it possible then for me to hear Augustine's posing of his "great question" about himself—the question that he is—and not be moved to enter into a great question of my own? I would like to say that it is possible, or if it is not, that at least I have the option of posing my question privately and not have it burden my exposition of his. Reading *Confessions* 4 has troubled my hope about this, however. That book is largely about failed friendships, or the ways in which friends tacitly conspire with one another to keep great questions from being asked. When Augustine loses his one friend so painfully—the one who at a crucial moment had refused the conspiracy (as I will soon explain)—he abandons himself to all the virtual, not-quite-real friendships that were left to him. It is as if a whole world of affection had collapsed for him into a single death.

I have the uncomfortable feeling that if I try too hard to be the impartial observer, or to maintain too studied a detachment from his confessional mode of address, I risk perpetuating the very kind of conspiring that compelled Augustine at the beginning of book 4 to pluralize his confessional voice. Must he confess for me? My worry here is not that I will end up being a bad friend to Augustine, whatever that could mean, but that I will end up being a bad reader or bad guide to other readers—and perhaps that is all being a bad friend to him could mean in this context. To be a good reader of Augustine, I need to allow him the chance of addressing me and not restrict myself to erudite eavesdropping on his conversation with God. I give him this chance less by sharing his beliefs and empathizing with his experiences than by keeping an eye on the motive I have for reading him at all. What do I expect from Augustine?

That brings me to my other difficulty. I will call it a difficulty of expectation. Take the case of *Confessions* 4. I expect to be able to move from Augustine's episodic account of his dark bout with grief to a more general consideration of what makes his grief fit matter for a confession. The move to the more general issue raises the question of sin and grief: namely, where is the sin in grief? Here, it seems to me, comes the really hard part. How am I supposed to isolate, identify, and analyze the sin in Augustine's confession of grief? Let's assume for the moment I plan to do all this objectively—without concern, that is, for whether I share in the sin that Augustine confesses. I may not even believe that there is such a thing as sin. Let's assume I don't. I will want, given these assumptions, to treat sin as one of Augustine's constructs, as an artifact, that is, of his clime and culture, albeit a culture he has helped shape. I will leave it to him to be one of the architects of his own distant world, but not of my world, the one near to hand. Were I to try to bring him into my world, presumably I would be compelled to take his influence on my own terms—according to the constructs, that is, that govern my own world of experience.

Now let's apply the logic of this line of reasoning to the identification and analysis of sin in book 4's confession of grief. Sin there is what Augustine would have identified as a bad conceptualization of his experience of grief. Since he has been busy trying to discredit the Manichean beliefs of his young adulthood, it must be those beliefs—about God and soul—that frame and misshape his grief. And yet there is no way to test this hypothesis directly. The line of reasoning I have been sketching works on the assumption that experiences *just are* conceptualizations of experience, and so there is nothing to compare to a conceptualization except a further conceptualization. The interpreter of Augustine is thus left with the task of determining whether his description of his troublesome grief is of a piece with his once Manichean conceptions of his own psyche. Simply put, are the conceptualizations consistent?

I don't think that the question of consistency is a useless one to pose. In his commentary on *Confessions* 4, Colin Starnes has done a brilliant job of helping readers see the consistency between Augustine's adherence to Manicheism and his descriptions of his life's miseries during that time.[3] One moral of this consistency is that Augustine, like most any one of us at one time or another, has been the prisoner of his own mindset. When he conceptualizes important matters badly, he is not likely to live much better than he conceives. But what else is consistency supposed to tell us

---

3. Starnes (1990), pp. 89–112.

here? That Augustine's Manichean beliefs were the *cause* of his sorrow?[4] We expect too little of him if we are apt to conclude this. He would want us to honor better his struggling love of the truth and ask what it is about *him* that has led him to seek his truth in a false religion. Of course it is a much safer, much neater proposition not to seek the truth when reading him and focus on words and their life-shaping possibilities. The results may be diverting, even alluring, but so restricted a focus will never reveal to us Augustine's basis for making his words and their life-shaping possibilities his own.

Not to care about Augustine's basis for selection is not to care about reading him. He is too alive as a writer to the difficulties of putting himself in his words to be read as if his words and their historical currencies automatically defined his much-desired sense of self. His words are hopeful gestures to selfhood or halting attempts to break his soul out of its infancy. We won't read these gestures well unless we can imagine like gestures in ourselves, and that requires not just a concern for the possibilities of words but for using words to speak the truth. I don't mean that we ought to bring some crude defensiveness about truth to reading Augustine and then join him in rejecting what he rejects. I mean that we ought to care enough about truth to notice *how* Augustine goes about seeking his. For all his talk about Manicheism as a false religion, he says precious little about why it is false. If we read him with that question in mind, we are left with a short list of things not to believe: that God is material, that evil is a substance, that God is passive in the face of active evil, that souls are either purely good or purely evil.[5] This listing, however accurate as a list of untruths, skirts the issue of what would move anyone to believe things of this sort in the first place. That is just the issue that Augustine refuses to skirt in his confession. It may be the case that Manichean doctrines are false, but the falsity that counts most for him—because it does the most damage—is falsity of heart. If the words are true, but the heart is false, the words are of no avail.[6]

---

4. Starnes (1990), p. 106, seems to think so: "He has not proven that the Manichees' doctrines were wrong or that in following them he was actually going away from the truth, but he has shown how the actual misery and futility of all his actions in these years were a direct consequence of his adherence to their position."

5. My sense of Manicheism as it is represented in the *Confessions* is greatly indebted to chapter 5 of Brown (2000). Brown's book remains, in my estimation, the single greatest work on Augustine in English.

6. I am not claiming that Augustine never had any interest in representing and refuting Manicheism as an abstract set of beliefs. He has a host of polemical writings that are usually grouped under the heading of "anti-Manichean treatises." My claim is that his confessional approach to the Manichees is as I have described.

Parting Knowledge

Augustine's concern for truth, when set in the register of the heart, comes across as a problem of articulation. To be truthful it is not enough for him to declare and believe true things; he must also be present in and through the truth he declares; otherwise there is a real sense in which *he* hasn't declared anything. The grief that Augustine confesses to in book 4 is false not so much because the beliefs that frame it are false, but because he uses those beliefs to keep his distance from himself. His grief was noisy, but inarticulate. His confessional mode of remembering his grief is his attempt to give his grief a better voice—a voice that says better what was lost and what there is left to hope for.

When I think of Augustine's confession of grief in this way—a way that has some hope of meeting my difficulties of address and expectation—my mind tends to wander to *Hamlet*, Shakespeare's great drama of a man's belated self-conception. I think especially of the problem Prince Hamlet had in making his grief believable. Hamlet lost a father and clung to black mourning; his mother lost a husband and wed herself to her husband's brother. She wants to know from her son why his grief persists. He is not the first son to lose a father; he will not be the last. Death is the common lot of mortals. Why should one death seem so particular to him? He answers her as follows:

> "Seems," madam? Nay, it is. I know not "seems."
> 'Tis not alone my inky cloak, good mother,
> Nor customary suits of solemn black,
> Nor windy suspiration of forced breath,
> No, nor the fruitful river in the eye,
> Nor the dejected 'havior of the visage,
> Together with all forms, moods, shapes of grief,
> That can denote me truly. These indeed "seem";
> For they are actions that a man might play.
> But I have that within which passes show—
> These but the trappings and the suits of woe.[7]

Hamlet tells Gertrude, in effect, that she has not seen the particularity of his grief for his father, but only its inadequate forms—"the trappings and the suits of woe." He knows in himself that he feels his father's loss uniquely, but also that he is powerless to convey that uniqueness to her or anyone else; he can only seem to. What he has within, he says, "passes show."

---

7. *Hamlet* I.ii.76–86; Farnham, ed. (1970), p. 37.

I take his point to be not that his grief is too much for sighs, tears, and a dejected visage, but that he is not play-acting. His grief isn't *for* show. Hamlet's curse, as he sees it, is that he was born into a world where men and women commonly play-act feelings for personal gain and so debase the common language of feeling. Have enough people show grief and not mean it and it becomes hard, if not impossible, for a person to mean grief by showing it. "Denmark's a prison," Hamlet tells two of his uncle's spies.[8] It is the sort of prison that keeps his heart confined to silence—a prescription for madness.

Augustine lost his father years before he lost his unnamed friend. He records the death of his father with all the affect of a necrology: "... when I was eighteen and my father had already been dead for two years" (*conf.* 3.4.7). The thought of his father's death is tacked on to another thought, about receiving money from his mother for books; it doesn't even rate its own sentence. By contrast Augustine is eloquence itself when it comes to the death of his friend (*conf.* 4.4.9):

> My heart was wholly in grief's shade, and death was whatever I looked at. My native land was a punishment to me; my father's house a strange and luckless place. The things I had shared with him turned and tortured me cruelly in his absence. My eyes kept seeking him out everywhere, and he was gone. I hated everything because nothing had him; nor could anything still say to me, "look, he is on his way," as when he was alive and just away. I had become a great question to myself.

If I could put to Augustine a form of the question that Gertrude put to Hamlet, I would want to know why the death of his friend should have seemed so particular to him. The difference between Augustine and Hamlet, aside from the difference in their respective occasions for grief, is that Augustine has anticipated my question and posed it of himself. Hamlet casts doubt on even the propriety of his mother's question. The barest suggestion from her that he may be unnaturally affected offends him. How could she, whom he takes to be false herself, possibly be in a position to tell?

The burden of Hamlet's knowledge is indeed heavy. Casting himself as the only true soul in a world of pretense and theater, he has no way to act in his world except as a pretender of pretense. The irony finally undoes him, and in the end he is left with no other resolution to his life's drama but death. Augustine is also aware that he has been born into a world of

---

8. *Hamlet* II.ii.241; Farnham, ed. (1970), p. 75.

pretense and falsity. But unlike Hamlet, Augustine acknowledges his human lot. The curse of his birth, as he sees it, is not the singular exception of his life, but his commonality with all the world's pretenders—the curse of original sin. So where Hamlet sets himself the impossible task of inventing a wholly original language of action and emotion (who would understand it?), Augustine works to redeem his use of familiar words and gestures.

I turn now to the particulars of Augustine's efforts in *Confessions* 4 to recollect himself in grief and thereby redeem his language of grieving. The need for such redemption will show up in his peculiar failure to be in his grief. Augustine's description of this failure—which is anything but a *simple* failure of memory—takes in a psychology of self-escape. Augustine's return to himself and to his reluctantly human expressions of grief is a possibility he vouchsafes to theology. Because I will proceed as he does and begin with the psychological complexities of his remembered grief, I need to issue this caveat at the outset: Augustine's transits from psychology to theology are misleading if we read him under the assumption that his theology takes up where he psychology leaves off.

The sense I get from the *Confessions* as a whole is that all of us have to begin a quest for knowledge with psychology, in that the human desire to know is everywhere twisted and hobbled by bad presumptions of self-knowledge. But it is not Augustine's view that we work at a question of self whose answer is then revealed to us from above—as if we were simply in need of further information. His perspective is more radical than that. It is the *question* of self that is the revelation. We take this question to God, the maker of selves, but God's answer is already implied in the continual opening of the question. Augustine's respect for the piety of faithful questioning—a respect he shares with Plato's Socrates—runs throughout the *Confessions*. Book 4 is a paradigm case.

I. The Word for Grief

First I need to say a few more words about that friend of his. Augustine doesn't furnish us with many details about his friendship at Thagaste, beyond his saying that it was an "exceedingly sweet" affection, "cooked in the fervor of like enthusiasms," and snatched from him all too soon—scarcely past a year into it and well before he had had his fill (*conf.* 4.4.7). The most telling part of Augustine's recollection picks up the friendship at its end. Sometime over the course of a long fever, when the friend seemed to his family very likely to die, they had him baptized. The sick young man was quite out of his senses at the time, and for his part Augustine simply assumed that his friend would laugh off the baptism once he came back to consciousness and was told of it. Their friendship, after all, had been built on Augustine's success at turning his friend from the Catholic faith to the religion of the Manichees. (For the Augustine barely into his twenties, this would have been a choice between a superstitious and authoritarian faith and a philosophical, if somewhat esoteric, quest for truth.) When he finds his friend temporarily revived and lucid, Augustine is surprised, stunned really, at his friend's response to his jests about baptism (*conf.* 4.4.8): "He was horrified at me, as if I were his enemy, and with an astonishing and sudden sense of independence, he warned me that if I wanted to be his friend, I would have to stop saying such things to him." Augustine's immediate reaction to his friend's change of heart is one of disbelief and reserve. Because he can't quite believe that the change in his friend is other than illness-driven, he decides to wait for a better time to work on his friend and restore him to his more compliant disposition. That time never comes. The fever returns a few days later, while Augustine is away, and the friend dies.

Thinking back on his last encounter with his friend, now with the benefit of distance, Augustine is prepared to find some consolation in a death that had opened a black hole in his heart (*conf.* 4.4.8): "That one was taken abruptly from my madness, so that he might be safe with you and a consolation for me." There are really two distinct offers of consolation acknowledged here in Augustine's confession: one is of being able to know that a beloved is safe with God, and the other is of being able to know that a beloved is safe from oneself. These consolations are intimately related in Augustine's confession, and ultimately they must be read to reflect a single consolation and a single source of redemption. The desired convergence of the consolations—the convergence that makes consolation consoling—is best approached, however, by way of distinction.

Consider first the consolation that Augustine would take from knowing that his friend is with God. This will be the hardest consolation for him (and his reader) to take in directly. The difficulty is that it is all too tempting here to confuse being with God with being dead—as if his friend or any friend were *better off* dead. The flip side of that confusion is to suppose that the living are not yet with God. Neither sentiment makes a bit of theological sense, but Augustine's alternative sentiment isn't easy to understand either: that we are always with God but not always or even usually with ourselves. A paradoxical psychology of self-escape needs to be confronted, it seems, before anyone can ever hope to take much consolation from God.

Augustine comes up against just such a psychology in himself when he tries to take the other kind of consolation from his friend's death. He thanks God for putting his friend out of reach of his madness and therefore for sparing Augustine the guilt of having corrupted his friend for a second time. And it would have been a far worse corruption than the first. The first time that Augustine had convinced his friend to reject the Catholic faith and share in his Manichean fixations, his friend was young and impressionable and "not deeply rooted" in "the true faith" (*conf.* 4.4.7). The second convincing, were there to have been one, would have worked against the forthright independence that Augustine was so startled and disturbed to see emerge from his friend. No longer would Augustine have been misleading an impressionable youth, whose principal failing up to then had been his uncritical desire to please his charismatic peer; he would have been turning a man against his own best conviction, robbing his love of his love of truth. But thankfully, recalls Augustine, the worst was not to be. His friend's death left Augustine alone with his madness, and under the guise of a bereft lover, he tried desperately to escape himself.

I am suggesting that there was a significant element of pretense in Augustine's grief over his friend's death, that his grief was not a reliable measure of how much he loved this person in life. In suggesting this, I am entering into an aspect of Augustine's own puzzlement over his motives and behavior. He would like to know, looking back at his days of weeping, what made him hold on so long and so tightly to his grief, as if something bitter could itself be a relief from bitterness. He wonders whether his grief might have harbored some hope of having his friend restored to him, so that in holding onto the grief he was holding onto the hope. He rejects the idea. Hope would have made his grief into a kind of prayer, and he had no God to pray to then, but only the phantom of his Manichean imagination—a divinity as helpless as he was. The closest he comes to answering his question is this further question, left poignantly unanswered (*conf.* 4.5.10): "Or is weeping really a bitter thing and pleasing only in place of the distaste we have for the things we formerly enjoyed but now shrink from in horror?" If Augustine means to ask this question of himself, then he has to face the terrible prospect of getting this answer: that his grief had less to do with mourning his friend than with avoiding his own guilt. The prospect is terrible because his guilt may suggest to him that he never loved his friend at all.

In his confession, Augustine is sufficiently aware of the ambiguities in his grief back then not to want to return to it too precipitously. For confessional purposes, it would be good of course for him to face his guilt about the friendship and unearth his sin from there. But if grief was once his way not to face guilt, then recollecting grief may simply harden and renew his defenses. Augustine pauses to survey his motives for continuing (*conf.* 4.6.11): "Why do I talk about these things? Now isn't the time to be asking a lot of questions, but to be confessing to you." He continues nevertheless to entertain the question of his grief. He has no choice but to continue with it, for his confession turns on the answer. So what does he think his grief was finally all about?

His first attempt at a definitive answer ends on a false note. He applies a poetic trope for the bond between two committed friends—two halves of one soul—to his own case, and then he uses this trope to suggest a reason for why he preferred a miserable life to joining his friend in death (*conf.* 4.6.11): "Perhaps I was afraid to die, because then the whole of him, whom I loved so much, would be dead." In his *Reconsiderations*, a review of his life's writings written three years before his death, Augustine will look back on that sentence in book 4 and admit that it seemed to him more like a "trifling disclosure" than a "serious confession" (*retr.* 2.6.2). Actually, I find it hard to believe that Augustine's intent was ever other than serious while he was writing book 4, the offending line included, but I think I get the old bishop's point. There is something theatrical or showy about Augustine's image of himself as half his dead friend's soul, and theatricality in his *confessional* self-image is wholly out of place. A "serious confession" would expose, not perpetuate, the theatricality of his friendship. It would expose, that is, what was false or affected in Augustine's love of his friend.

Augustine has already in fact supplied us with a means to take a more sober view of his friendship and begin to see through its pretense. He has said that death was God's way of removing his friend from Augustine's "madness" (*dementia*). Let's consider what manner of madness that might be. I don't think it can simply be the madness of wanting to reinduct his friend into a false religion. At the time Augustine doesn't believe that Manicheism is false, and it isn't especially mad behavior for him to want company in his convictions. It would be mad behavior on his part only if Manicheism were so wildly implausible a religion that it would have been crazy for him ever to have put any trust in it and crazier still for him to think he could have elicited a like trust from others. But it wasn't a wildly implausible religion. The aspects of Manicheism that came most to disturb

69

Parting Knowledge

Augustine—its materialism, its limited view of God, its us-and-them dualism, and its obsession with a God-given purity—have appeared in many different forms in the history of human consciousness and are likely to have a long future. And with his gift for persuasion and his rare intelligence, Augustine was more than capable of making just those very aspects seem seductive. He had good reason to believe that he would have won his friend back over to his side, had he been given the chance. He won others to his side in Carthage, and he was consoled by their attentions to him.

Seen from another angle, however, it is Augustine's very confidence about what would have happened with his friend that betrays his kind of madness. The thought never even occurs to Augustine that his friend, had he lived, might have been the one doing the convincing. I don't mean to suggest that his friend would have had a whole new arsenal of arguments to marshal against Augustine and a newly discovered ability to use them effectively. *He* had not been, after all, the man to master Aristotle's *Categories* at the tender age of twenty, and without benefit of instruction (*conf.* 4.16.28). That was Augustine. Nor had he been the man known to possess the "quickness of mind" and "sharpness of insight" that made him a natural for the study of the liberal arts (*conf.* 4.16.30). That was Augustine too. No, it was only out of "some unknown higher instinct" that Augustine's friend took his deathbed baptism to heart and refused Augustine's mockery of the sacrament.[9] Augustine did not of course owe his friend *belief* in

---

9. The phrase I am invoking here to describe what moved Augustine's friend to accept baptism—"some unknown higher instinct" (*superiore aliquo instinctu nesciente*)—actually occurs in a different section of book 4. This is the section where Augustine describes how "a man of keen intelligence," whom he will later identify in book 4 as the renowned physician Helvius Vindicianus, had been trying to dissuade him from looking for knowledge from astrology (*conf.* 4.3.5). The sticking point for the young Augustine was that many of the forecasts of astrologers seemed to come out right. Vindicianus doesn't argue the point. He simply offers Augustine the observation that in many cases of divination, whether it be the use of lots, horoscopes, or a chance reading of some passage of a book, there is a congruence between the seeker and the sign or utterance, in accord with "some unknown higher instinct" of the soul. The moral of the observation is that astrology is false not because astrologers are always wrong, but because the language of astrology is of no use for exploring the truths that astrologers sometimes divine.

The moral is a telling one as well for the case of Augustine's friend and his divination of the correctness of his baptism. Whether his baptism were a true sign of his condition would depend not only on the correctness of his intuition but also on the aptness of the Catholic faith to articulate that intuition. Suppose, to be more specific, that Augustine's friend would have been right to connect his baptism to a profound feeling of personal liberation. If that is to be other than a chance divination on his part, it must be the case that Catholicism offers him the right terms for expressing and exploring the liberation.

the face of his friend's transfiguration, but he did owe it to the friendship not to dismiss out of hand what had elicited his friend's independence of heart and mind. It would have been enough had Augustine been willing to question his own self-certainties before his friend had to die. That is the sort of questioning we offer to someone, not out of respect for a superior argument, but out of love.

"Oh, what madness it is," Augustine exclaims (*conf.* 4.7.12), "not to know how to love human beings humanly!" He refers to the same madness that had distorted, if not falsified, his friendship. His mind could accept the basic truths about loving other human beings—that they were different from him, that they didn't live forever—but his heart could not. His heart preferred to have a friend who would be wholly the creature of his desires, specifically his desires not to have to face his own corruptibility. Those were the same desires that drove Augustine to embrace Manicheism. The madness in all this was that Augustine loved his friend on terms that made it impossible for him to have a friend. The consummation of his love would have been, spiritually considered, his friend's death.

But there is more to the story of Augustine's love than his fear of death, or he would have found a perfect consolation in the friends who were willing to reconfirm him in his Manichean fiction of himself—that the part of him that was right would never die. Instead he speaks of his love for these friends as having taken the place of his love for God, this being the continuation for him of "a tall tale and an old lie" (*conf.* 4.8.13). Once again Augustine was wedding himself to a bad pattern of loving and to the extravagant mythology he would need to justify it to himself, but he is not in retrospect entirely condemning of his heart. He doesn't think that he never loved his friends at all (that he was just pretending, in other words), but that he loved them only after he had rejected a profounder love.

The effect of this rejection on his or anyone else's love is to place an impossible burden on the human desire to know the unity of love. "This unity is so loved," he observes (*conf.* 4.9.14), "that we feel guilty when we don't love the one returning love to us, or if we don't return love to the one loving us, seeking nothing from his body but signs of a good will." Augustine's complex use here of the Ciceronian coinage *redamare*—"to return love for love"—suggests his belief that if we refuse God, whose love is always first in the order of loving, it becomes too late for us to return love to others, a belatedness that darkens and adds guilt to grief. Behind this belief lies the story that is his alternative to the Manichean mythology of human beginnings. In Augustine's version of Genesis, we were all somehow present in the choice of Adam and Eve to turn from the love of their heavenly father and seek an abundance of life by other means (the quest for divine knowledge). But as there is no way to secure immortality other than by responding to the love of God, they bound themselves to seek immortality where it could not be found. Their original sin, thinks Augustine, has altered the disposition of the human heart. All of us are now disposed to substitute some other love for the love of God, but this is less the direct substitution of one love for another (we lack the imagination for that) than it is the terrible impoverishment of the love we have always had.

Original human love, as Augustine conceives of it, is love that has what love most wants, at least until the day that love decides it wants something else. It is a paradoxical notion, to be sure, to be moved to want less than what you want most, but I won't enter here into Augustine's intricate and (as far as I can tell) not always coherent reflections on the psychology of original sin.[10] I invoke his notion of original love in this context to help frame what he thinks human love is like on the *other* side of the paradoxical choice to seek life's fruition "in the land of death" (*conf.* 4.12.18). It is like knowing that your best chances at love are always behind you. When Augustine tells us of how his dying friend set new terms for their friendship, he also tells us of how he felt threatened by this—as if he had been made out to be an enemy—and of how he resolved in himself to reject those terms. From his confessional perspective, Augustine casts himself then as having rejected God's offer of love, at that very moment when his friend, in the deepest sense of the words, had come to his senses. Augustine's friend had not rejected him, nor had God. It was Augustine who was doing all the rejecting. But he came to understand this long after his friend had died, when it was too late to respond to the love he most wanted.

Most reflective people will know something about the pathos of Augustine's kind of hindsight. His readers may be forgiven for wondering, however, what good it does to cast the follies of missed opportunities in love in the form of a rejection of God. There is no easy or quick answer to

---

10. For those interested in teasing out this psychology in detail, I recommend looking at these three places especially in Augustine: his account of the angelic fall in *City of God* 12.6–8 (where he introduces the notion of a deficient cause); his account of the original human fall in *City of God* 14.10–12 (where he makes a distinction between being seduced into sin and sinning out of pride); and lastly his confession of his theft of pears in *Confessions* 2.4.9 to 2.10.18 (where he uses his own sin to suggest the way in which all sin is original). And for some discussion of these texts, see chapter 5 of this volume.

Trappings of Woe

that question, I think, but we would do well to remember that Augustine's God is a God of both judgment and forgiveness. The judging side of God commends us to our responsibilities. We are not free to consign all our failures at love to the waste bin of bad luck; we will be found wanting for the love we have overlooked and trampled upon in the name of some other value. The forgiving side of God commends us to the judgment that is not our own and so releases us from the hell of self-torment. We are not free to absent ourselves from God, despite our best efforts, and so we are not the final arbiters of our love's imperfections. That is why confession of sin is for Augustine a hopeful act.

These two sides of God—punishing and forgiving—come together in Augustine's description of Christ. His description is worth citing at some length (*conf.* 4.12.19):

> He who is our life came down to us, took up our death, and killed it with his own life's abundance: and like thunder, he called us to return to him from here and into that hidden place from which he first came forth to us—the virgin womb. It was there that humanity was wedded to him, mortal flesh, not to be mortal forever. And like a bridegroom from the bridal bed he leapt with joy from there, a giant to run his course. For he did not delay, but ran calling out with his words, actions, death, life, descent, ascent—calling out for us to return to him. He left our sight, so that we might return to our heart and find him there. He went away, and look: here he is.

Augustine's imagery here, especially his use of Psalm 18:6 (RSV 19:5), conveys the idea that human life, from birth to death, is a love affair with God. It would be a depressingly unrequited love were we the ones to determine the terms of God's absence. Those terms would dictate a life lived in God's absence, free of the heart's responsibilities, but bound to the demands of the flesh and mortgaged to death. Augustine's God has preempted this humanly willed absence and willed an absence of his own. The place where either out of despair or pride we hope to be rid of God is the place where he awaits our return.

Consider once more the consolation that Augustine hopes to take from knowing that his friend is with God. His pride would tell him that his friend, as a creature bound to follow Augustine's madness, could never have been with God in life. His pride would be wrong. It is not the friend's death that informs Augustine's confession, but his living voice, speaking against irreverence. It has become Augustine's voice too. His despair would tell him that he has heard the voice of his friend too late, well past the time for responding. His despair would be wrong. The friend's death conveys to Augustine God's absence. This absence calls Augustine to return to himself and be in his love for others. Were he to think that loving others would not also be to love the one departed from view, he would still be looking with his eyes and not with his heart. Perhaps he would still be caring too much for his old madness—as if it were ever his madness alone.

Augustine finds something consoling in the thought that his friend, by dying, had moved beyond his love's madness. But this is a thought that is more about Augustine or his friend than about his friend's absence, and so it has nothing directly to do with what need there is for consolation. Augustine passes through this thought in his confession in order to get to what turns out to be the only kind of consolation possible for him: the hope that life is (still) in God's keeping. Getting to that hope is partly, if not wholly, a matter of taking the true measure of a beloved's loss.

II. The Aesthetics of Sin

"Back then I didn't know about these things; I loved lesser beauties, and I was sinking into an abyss" (*conf.* 4.13.20). Augustine describes here, near the end of book 4, the quality of love that would animate his friendships in Carthage. "I used to say to my friends," he continues, "'For what else do we love if not beauty? What is a beautiful thing? What is beauty? What is it that attracts and unites us to the things we love? If it weren't for the grace and beauty in them, they would move us not at all.'" The fascination that he had for beauty in the years immediately following his friend's death had a telling blind spot. His thoughts did not give him a way to comprehend his love of the dead.

Around the age of twenty-six, Augustine began to pull together some of those thoughts, and the result was his first book, a study of the difference between absolute and relative beauty. Something relatively beautiful needs the right context to set it off: as part of a body, for instance, a foot can be pleasing, but when met detached, it tends to horrify. Absolute beauty isn't like that. It is "as though whole" of itself (*conf.* 4.13.20). Augustine called his study *On Beauty and Aptness*, a title that signaled his inclination to think of relative beauty not as a kind of beauty but as something of a different category: not as "beautiful" (*pulchrum*), but "apt, fitting" (*aptum*). We don't know all the details of how he worked out this distinction. His work was lost some years later, and thinking back on it from the vantage

Trappings of Woe

of the *Confessions*, he can't remember when it got lost or even whether it was originally divided into two books or three. What he does remember of his first work, however, is sufficient for his confessional aims in book 4. In particular he is able to use his piecemeal recollection to frame better what he was forgetting back then, when he didn't know the things he needed to know to be a good friend and to mourn a good friend well.

In one respect it is not hard to identify what Augustine didn't know at the time. The things to be known make up a list of big truths: that God is spirit not matter, that God's spirit has become incarnate in Jesus of Nazareth, that Jesus is the Christ, that souls are redeemed through Christ's death, resurrection, and ascension into heaven. The list could be emended or its items elaborated, but the list would still be a list—and there's the rub. Augustine is very aware of his education in the concluding sections of book 4, or the years he spent reading every book he could on the liberal arts and feeling that he had grasped them all. He wonders what he really learned from all that. Let's stipulate, for present purposes, that the items on my list of big truths are all true, and that these truths are often encountered in traditions of liberal study. But to bring the example closer to home, let's just say that some tradition of liberal study includes the works of Augustine, and that this tradition takes Augustine to be an authority—a reliable teacher, that is, of the truth. Would a reader in this tradition, reading book 4 of the *Confessions*, have the benefit of the truths that Augustine names there but sees as having been absent from his understanding during his student years?

Even were the reader a "believer" (as we now tend to use the term), Augustine's answer to my question would still have to be this: that it's not for him to say. Sure, he may have presented some big truth persuasively enough to convince his reader to consent to it; still, he suggests, the benefit to the reader may yet be lacking. I take that suggestion from his summary assessment of his own years of greedy reading and study (*conf.* 4.16.31): "I had my back to the light and my face to the matters illuminated, and as a result my face, my means for looking at these matters, was not itself illuminated." The big truths either take in the truth of the person trying to grasp them, or they are diminished truths and therefore dangerous (in that they may continue, though diminished, to be believed big).

This brings me back to the "great question" that Augustine's grief had made of him. It was clearly not a question he was ready to have posed. Perhaps no one is ever ready for this kind of question at the time of its posing, but few have been as eloquent or as insightful as Augustine about their lack of readiness. In one of the more lyrical passages of the *Confessions*, he speaks of the belatedness of his love for God. His words recapitulate the psychology that has turned his grief into a wasteland (*conf.* 10.27.38): "Late have I loved you, beauty so ancient and so new, late have I loved you! And look you were within me and I outside; there I looked for you, and into the beauties you made I rushed, misshapen myself." The beauties of his misshapen affection and the "lesser beauties" of his Carthage years are one and the same. His trouble then and later would lie not with beauties that pale in comparison to God's beauty (there is no scale here), but with his inclination to use beauty as a venue for self-exit. He hoped, in effect, not to have to be included in his knowledge of the whole.

This is not to say that he was directly seeking the "abyss" of nonbeing. Quite to the contrary, he was seeking a self that seemed to him better, more beautiful, than the one he was fleeing. His youthful reflection, *On Beauty and Aptness*, suggests his terms for success. He offers two key disclosures about that text in book 4. One concerns his motive for writing it. Augustine had been moved to dedicate his work to the orator at Rome, a man named Hierius. Although he had no personal knowledge of Hierius, he loved and admired the image of the man in cultured circles: an unusually gifted speaker of both Greek and Latin, well versed in the subtleties of philosophy. Augustine had been used to getting recognition from those who craved his (his friends); now he was the one craving to be recognized. He was after his ideal self, whose beauty would be confirmed or denied for him in a word from an important man.

Although that word never came to him in either form, Augustine tells us that he continued to think well of what he had written. His other important disclosure about *On Beauty and Aptness* speaks directly to its content. Augustine's conception there of a supremely good soul, one good enough to be called divine, was that of a "monad," a mind free and clear of erotic disturbances and conflicting desires ("a sexless mind"); its contrary he called a "dyad," a soul at odds with itself and so constantly prey to lust and anger (*conf.* 4.15.24). The basic idea seems to be that it is good to be single-minded, bad to be diversely driven—not the easiest of ideals for a spirited personality, such as Augustine's, to attain. But he wasn't envisioning himself as having to move from dyadic to monadic life. His exotic Pythagorean categories spoke to wholly distinct genealogies. Either he was carnal or spiritual in essence; if spiritual (the only sane possibility), then the carnal "part" of him was there to be excised, not redeemed. His judgment in book 4 upon this way of thinking was succinct (*conf.* 4.15.24): "I didn't know what I was talking about."

I take Augustine at this word, but why then does he spend time in his confession rehearsing thoughts from a lost book of nonsense? The answer has to do, I think, with the seductiveness of the nonsense at issue. Suppose you are a reader who brings to your reading of the *Confessions* an aesthetic sensibility akin to Augustine's in *On Beauty and Aptness.* You are not likely to find the grief that Augustine describes in book 4 any prettier than he did. There is too much evidence in that description of a soul torn between conflicting impulses—to live or to die. But what then would be your ideal expression of grief? I don't think that you can have one. Even the expression "ideal of grief" is inept. Grief is at best appropriate, but never ideal. It is not properly part of the beautiful.

There are two broadly metaphysical intuitions that can underwrite such an aesthetic sensibility, and I wonder whether Augustine would have been all that careful to distinguish between them in his earliest work. In one the wholeness that is absolute beauty has no involvement with vulnerable beauties, and in the other that wholeness takes in vulnerable beauties and gives them their ultimate significance. The first intuition suggests that we ought to be indifferent to goods that we can lose; they are to be held as of no account. The second intuition allows us to value these goods as good, but it calls us to value them from the perspective of the whole, where loss drops from view.

Augustine's sense of God discounts both intuitions. His God is neither the whole that is indifferent to the divisible wholes, nor is he the whole that is the sum of all the parts. That leaves human beings searching for a wholeness that they can never fairly hope to comprehend. Although this lack of comprehension is meant to be a liberation for the spirit and not a depressing feature of finitude, human resentment of finitude is usually potent enough to suggest otherwise. As he gets older, Augustine gets less tempted to heap contempt directly upon the vulnerable beauties of this life, but he never quite gets over his desire for a world-disdaining faith. In book 9, where he describes his intense grief over the loss of Monica, the vulnerable beauty who was his mother in life, Augustine is unapologetic but defensive. He sends God this note to pass along to a judgmental reader (*conf.* 9.12.33): "Let him read and interpret as he wants; if he should see sin in my having wept for my mother a small portion of an hour, the mother who died before my eyes and wept for me many a year that I might live before yours, let him not deride me, but rather—if he is someone of great charity—let him weep to you for my sins." Part of what stands against Augustine's grief is his faith that his mother died in God's grace and so lives without want. Does he think, then, that were his faith perfect, there would be nothing for him to grieve? Does the reader "of great charity" weep for his lack of faith?

A perfect faith—or the closest that human beings ever get to *knowing* that all life is in God's keeping—does not, in fact, rule out grief. On the contrary it is what allows grief its truest expression: sorrow, pure and simple, over the loss of a beloved. We will miss the person who continues to be with God but who is no longer with us. In a less than perfect faith, we get distracted by other claims on grief, most of them coming from guilt and its two allies, resentment and fear. Those claims are ignored at one's peril, though they are the hijackers of grief and not its natural ally. Augustine is probably wise to confess that his most faithful grieving may yet have an element of falsity to it, some mere trapping of woe. Perfect confession is like perfect faith: it invites love.

III. Summary Reflections

Book 4's theology of grief is a confession of loss and of the heart's confusion over the magnitude of loss. This confusion, for Augustine, has to do with sin and so with the prospect of ultimate and irredeemable loss. Not long into his *Confessions*, he comes up with this concise characterization of his sinful disposition (*conf.* 1.20.31): "My sin was this, that I was seeking pleasures, sublimities, truths not in God but in his creatures—me and the rest—and in this way I was heading into pains, disorders, errors." It is easy to notice Augustine's apparent antithesis here between God and creatures without paying too much attention to the work that the preposition "in" does to define a branching of human desire: for good things *in* God, or for good things *in* creatures. (This is an "in" of origination and could be happily translated as "from.") It is generally easy, when reading Augustine, to turn God and the created world into competing objects of desire. The ease and temptation of this reading, which is in fact a disastrous misreading of Augustine, is due not to his concision or carelessness as a writer, but to a disposition he would have identified as sinful.

Book 4 is the greatest check in the *Confessions* against one potent form of a sinful disposition: the craving for an absolute antithesis between God and humanity. As sin in this form obviously entails a denial of a divine incarnation—either its possibility or its importance—it is no accident that book 4 is one of the most explicitly christological of the *Confessions'* thirteen books. The God who calls Augustine home walked the earth as a human being, tried to teach other human beings how to love humanly, and suffered a human death. The christological emphasis in book 4 on the absence of Christ from human eyes—on the passing, that is, of Jesus of Nazareth into history—figures into Augustine's attempt to reassess his own human losses. He was not alive to see Christ die; he did live to see others die: both of his parents, his son Adeodatus, the unnamed friend of book 4, still others. Somehow Augustine hopes to find in Christ's death the measure of all his palpable human losses. That is the hope of his confession in book 4. How is a reader to conceive of it?

In making his way to a connection between Christ's death and the deaths of his own experience, Augustine is having his heart freed from having to choose between loving God and loving a human being. In book 4, he describes having done his level best to love a mortal human being as if he were immortal and presumably divine. The result was not that Augustine loved something of lesser value in place of something greater, but that he lost touch with the man he was loving and so had no way to take in the magnitude of his loss. Augustine's grief was painful, disorderly, erroneous. If the sin in his grief had been a matter of his loving his friend in place of God, then he would have been guilty of loving his friend too much. The idea of loving someone too much strikes me as confused, but even if it makes some kind of sense, it's not the idea that Augustine's confession conveys to us. He failed to love his friend *in* God, and this left his friend to be the creature of Augustine's fears and desires—or it did, at least, from the point of view of the prodigal Augustine, who had abandoned his father's house.

The terrifying prospect of Augustine's confessional logic is that love is an all-or-nothing affair. Either we love someone well and therefore in God, or we love a fiction of our interior poverty, a desperate projection of sin. Apart from God, in other words, we never get outside the fiction we take to be the self. It is only the vision of God as a redeemer who passes through death that diverts Augustine's logic from its all-or-nothing disjunction. If it is possible to love Christ after the death of Jesus, not abstractly but in the palpable form of love of neighbor, then it is possible to redeem a lost love by loving the ones who come after. This speaks to the solidarity in love that goes along with and even presupposes solidarity in sin. The redemption of love from sin allows us the consolation of love that admits of degrees.

Parting Knowledge

More profoundly but infinitely harder to grasp, it releases us into a greater-than-human perfection.

5

Prodigal Heart

Augustine's Theology of the Emotions

A MAN WHO CASTS his affections as his soul's feet and who envisions his life's journey as his heart's quest for repose is not likely to neglect the emotions in his philosophy. The dazzling display of emotional intelligence that gives the *Confessions*, Augustine's most famous work, its resonance for students of the inner life is evident, albeit in more muted hues, in nearly everything that he wrote: sermons, letters, scriptural commentaries, polemical and apologetic works, theological meditations. Augustine made it his practice to use his heart as an organ of illumination.

There is of course an important difference between speaking from the emotions and speaking about them. Theorists of the emotional life will find much that is of interest in Augustine, but it would be misleading to attribute the theorist's ambitions directly to Augustine himself. In one of his earliest works, the *Soliloquies*, he claims to want to know only two things: God and soul. The conjunction is important to him. There is no disclosure of soul that is not God's disclosure of soul. Whatever Augustine has to say about the emotions (a matter of soul) will have to be read, then, in the context of his theology. Apart from that context, his invocation and use of some classical theories of emotion—most if not all of which he would have taken from Cicero's attempt, late in his political career, to Latinize Greek philosophy—will seem disappointingly derivative. Set within their proper context, Augustine's insights into the emotions form part of his strikingly original attempt to confess to the ambivalence of his soul's love of God.

Take, for instance, Augustine's general characterization of emotion in book 14 of *City of God*. He opens that book with his influential distinction between two cities, one ruled by flesh (*secundum carnem*), the other by spirit (*secundum spiritum*). The first kind of rule is really an abdication of rule, a surrender to a chaos of mind and body that is sometimes driven, but not always, by bodily appetite. It is possible to be under the flesh and abstemious if carnal restraint is serving the vices of a malign intelligence. Because Augustine does not equate living by the flesh with sensual indulgence, he is quick to distance his sense of rule by the spirit from a Manichean hatred of sex and from even the milder contempt of the body that Platonists exhibit when they blame the body for subjecting the soul to emotional disturbances. "It is the quality of a person's will that matters to emotion," he writes (*civ. Dei* 14.6). "If the will is perverse, then so are the person's emotions; if upright, then those emotions are not only innocent but praiseworthy as well. Will is in all the emotions; emotions are indeed nothing other than expressions of will."

If we want to know how something as seemingly involuntary as an emotion can express willfulness, Augustine will explain to us that emotions have two aspects to them. There is first the involuntary impression that something about to happen or happening is an object of aversion or attraction; then comes a judgment. We either agree or disagree with the value—good or bad—that has impressed us involuntarily. It is the mind and its judgment, not bodily reflex, that finally determines the quality of an emotion. On the face of it, Augustine is adopting a Stoic account of emotion, where there is a clean distinction between an impression (φαντασία) of some good or evil and consent (συνκατάθεσις) to that impression. The original inspiration of this view is likely to have been Chrysippus, Zeno's successor among the early Stoics, but Augustine gets his Chrysippus by way of Cicero. Witness Cicero in book 4 of *Tusculan Disputations*, encapsulating the Stoics on emotions: "It seems to me that the whole argument about the mind's susceptibility to emotion comes down to this, that emotions are all in our power, all of them express judgment, all are voluntary."[1]

So far the Augustine I have described is blandly Stoic in his understanding of emotion. To leave the matter there, however, is to miss altogether the theological involvement of Augustine's notion of will. In

---

1. *Tusc.* 4.5. I follow Margaret Graver in translating *perturbatio animi* as "emotion" rather than "disturbance of the mind" or "affective disorder." Although the term *perturbatio* can carry a negative connation, in this context it clearly does not: the proffered account of a *perturbatio* applies to desirable as well as undesirable movements of the mind. Later Latin authors, Augustine included, will tend to use *affectus* or *affectio* to designate emotion in the neutral sense, leaving *perturbatio* to its negative connotations. See Graver (2002), p. 80.

some of his earliest writings, notably the first book of *On Free Choice* (*De liberum arbitrium*), Augustine invokes an unanalyzed and relatively unencumbered kind of consent to account for human responsibility. The view of that particular book is that we are free, and most free, when consenting to wise desires; when we consent to foolish ones, full of false promise, we are less free, having wed ourselves to delusory happiness, but still accountable. Consent, whether to wisdom or foolishness, is our own. This early Augustine *is* blandly Stoic, at least when it comes to his ethics, but Augustine soon comes to outgrow his Stoicism.

Certainly by the time he ascends in middle age to the episcopate of Hippo, he has ceased to presume upon the innocence of consent. It becomes his habit to look intently at the motives behind consent, the sources of delight and aversion that land human beings in one of the two cities. Undoubtedly, the turn in Augustine's thought has come with his set of responses to Simplician, an aged priest, soon to be Ambrose's successor in the See of Milan, and a man who, a decade back, had helped Augustine find the will to convert. Augustine is asked by his old friend to tackle some exegetical problems, the toughest coming from Paul and the ninth chapter of Romans: what is it about Jacob, and not Esau, that finds favor with God? Augustine ponders the mystery of election in his response, and he comes to the conclusion—a surprising one for him at the time—that election has to remain a mystery. There is no basis of merit that distinguishes a Jacob from an Esau, a saint from a lost soul. God elicits and elects the whole of the good will, leaving nothing of independent worth for a human being to contribute. Consent to a wise desire is not, then, what a human being adds to divine gift (Augustine's earlier view); it is part of what is given with grace. To suppose otherwise would be, by the reckoning of the new bishop, to leave the soul a veto of its election—a denial of God's capacity to delight.[2]

Despite the thorny problems of accountability that his revised view of consent left unresolved, particularly in regard to unelected souls, Augustine never reverts to a quasi-Stoic concept of consent. When he identifies emotions with expressions of will in *City of God*, a work that extends well into his episcopate, he is presupposing that redemptive consent, the kind that commends us to our better selves, is divinely mediated and no longer simply up to us. Consequently he will make the substitution of love

---

2. For a moving description of Augustine's turn of mind and some further sense of its context, see "The Lost Future" in Brown (2000), pp. 139–50. Martha Nussbaum develops an important qualification to Brown's interpretation in Nussbaum (2001), pp. 535–43.

for will in his definition of emotion, as if love and will were somehow the same thing (*civ. Dei* 14.7): "And so a straightened will is love that is good, and a twisted one is bad love." Good love, an expression of delight in the good, and good will, a resolve to work goodness, are naturally one only in God. For human beings, it takes a labor of love to bring together the two, whose usual separation feels like a split in will: wanting the good and not wanting it. The labor, thinks Augustine, is both God's and ours, but the initiative, he insists, is solely God's.

Again, no study of Augustine on the emotions can do him justice and not engage directly with his theological animus. His God is infinitely distant from his flesh-and-blood feel for his own humanity, and yet, at the same time, his God is his humanity. The mystery of the incarnation—of the intimacy between a divine and a human way of being—is tied in his mind to the mysterious perversity that both necessitates and denies him his confession: he loses himself in self-love, and, worse, he is blind to many of the forms that his self-love can take (some look patently self-denying). If Augustine has to generate self-love on his own, it will be hard for him to envision external sources of delight and dismay—the loadstones of emotion—other than as threats to his personal integrity. Augustine evades this trap only because he encounters God as a mediating presence in his self-love.

In the relatively brief compass of this chapter, I hope to open a window on Augustine's theology of the emotions. Basically, this will be a two-part undertaking. In the first part I take a closer look at Stoicism in *City of God* and Augustine's eventual rejection of its theory and practice of emotion. Augustine's rejection of Stoicism is importantly symptomatic of a shift in his notion of will, from a facility for consent to a focus of internal conflict and incoherence. In the next part, I attend to the connection between sin and self-undoing by entering into Augustine's fascination with a first or original will to sin. My primary resources here are his psychological analysis in *City of God* of the Adam and Eve of Genesis and his parallel analysis of himself in *Confessions*, where he describes a fall of his own. I conclude this chapter with a reflection that bridges its two parts.

I. A Stoic Stalking Horse

The eminent classicist Richard Sorabji delivered his 1997 Gifford Lectures on the theme of emotion in ancient philosophy. The book that came of his lectures is mostly devoted to the Stoics, whom Sorabji calls "the driving force of the whole ancient discussion," but the final part ventures into early Christian transformations of Stoicism, where Augustine plays the dominant role in the narrative. Sorabji presents us with an Augustine who thinks of what the Stoics called "first movements" or "pre-passions" as *emotional* responses, laden with implicit value judgments. This is a misreading of the Stoics, Sorabji argues, but one that will allow Augustine to construct a sinful experience of temptation out of what counts, for Stoics, as simple bodily agitation.³

Sorabji's provocative reading of Augustine focuses primarily on Augustine's use of anecdotal evidence in *City of God* (*civ. Dei* 9.4) to discredit Stoicism. The anecdote comes from *Attic Nights*, the journal compiled by the second-century amateur philosopher Aulus Gellius during his visit to Athens. Gellius tells of being on board a storm-tossed ship in the company of a Stoic who turned pale, apparently with fright. When the storm passed, Gellius asked the Stoic to explain the meaning of his pallor, since actual fright would have been inconsistent with the equanimity of a true sage, able to discount adversity. In response, the Stoic fetched from his bags a compendium of Stoicism, composed by the first-century Stoic luminary Epictetus. The relevant part covered how everyone, wise or foolish, experiences involuntary impressions (*phantasiae*) of what seems desirable or not. Only the fool, however, acquiesces to the impression; the wise person consents only to what is reasonable. The Stoic wanted Gellius to know that his pallor, fleeting and involuntary, gave no reliable indication of what he was really thinking or valuing at the time.

Augustine invokes the anecdote to decide a question about the emotions that had left the various schools of philosophy divided. Namely, does a wise person feel passion? Read "passion" in this context (Greek *pathê*, Latin *perturbatio*) to refer to feeling that tends to subvert a person's better judgment. Aristotelians and Platonists (Augustine lumps them together on this issue) concede that a wise person sometimes experiences passion but, being wise, never gives into it. The Stoics, by contrast, deny that the sage ever has passions. The crucial difference between the two sides is that the passion-touched sages of Aristotelian wisdom are willing to call "good" (*bonum*) goods that are beyond a person's ability to control fully, whereas the passionless sages of Stoic wisdom call those same goods "advantages" (*commoda*) and refuse to lament their loss. Take the case of our Stoic at sea. He does not have full control over either his physical well-being or his material possessions, both of which can be taken from him by storm.

---

3. See Part 4 of Sorabji (2000), especially pp. 375-84.

He presumably does have control over his own virtue (his courage, for instance), which he cannot lose except by consenting to its loss. All things being equal, our Stoic finds it preferable to have both his virtue and his health, but if he cannot have both, he continues to define his virtue as his *whole* happiness. His Aristotelian counterpart would define *most* of his happiness that way, but if he loses some vulnerable good, natural for a person to want (his health, for instance), he will feel the pinch. More relevant than the feel of the pinch, though, is that the pinch is powerless to induce our Aristotelian to compromise his virtue, the better part of his happiness.

Along with Cicero, who argues the point at length in On Good Ends and Bad (*De finibus bonum et malorum*), Augustine takes the distinction between "goods" and "advantages" to be a distinction without a difference. Rather than rehearse Cicero's argument, Augustine is content to draw a simple moral from an anecdote (*civ. Dei* 9.4): "Surely if the philosopher in the story were giving no weight to what he felt he was about to lose by shipwreck—life and limb—he would not have so shuddered at the danger as to give witness to fear with pallor." The pallor Augustine has in mind is not like a pang or an ache or the pastiness that comes of having the flu: it is pallor bound to fear, fear bound to an impression of impending harm. This impression, Augustine insists, discloses the philosopher's sense of value, albeit without his consent. Consent is not necessary because (if Augustine is right) a person's sense of value is not always, and perhaps not even usually, a deliberate judgment. It lodges in involuntary feelings. In subjecting one representative Stoic to such feelings, Augustine seeks to deny the philosophical schools their last best hope of finding happiness in personal integrity and perfectly controlled judgment. Even assuming—as Augustine would not—that virtue is the part of happiness that a person controls, the virtuous life is never all the life that a virtuous person values.

Sorabji's point against Augustine and on Stoicism's behalf is that Augustine begs the question against Stoicism when he builds fear into his description of the shipboard Stoic's involuntary state of mind. Pallor does not, in and of itself, indicate fear. Sorabji notes that Aulus Gellius is not so careful to distinguish between two verbs—*pallescere* (to become pale) and *pavescere* (to begin to quiver)—in his paraphrase and gloss of Epictetus. Augustine has a vested interest in not making that distinction clear. When "becoming pale" is allowed to slip into the more emotionally invested notion of "quivering," the Stoic becomes subject to involuntary emotion. Sorabji reminds us that Augustine needs to do more than presuppose the emotive content of involuntary impressions. He needs to argue the point.

It is not clear to me, and perhaps it was not so clear to Augustine either, how an impression can be an object of assent or dissent without also having some propositional content (at least implicitly). I do not dissent from an itch, although I may choose not to scratch it; I can dissent from a fear. My fear tells me that some danger or unpleasantness is impending. If I discredit that perception, I go some way, if not all the way, towards dissolving the fear. If the Stoic sage really did not consider his physical safety a good, but only an optional advantage, would he have grown pale during the storm (assuming, of course, that he was not just seasick)? Sorabji's reminder is nevertheless perceptive. If Augustine is arguing against the possibility of Stoic *apatheia*[4]—freedom from passion—in book 9 of *City of God*, he is not going to convince many Stoics with his anecdotal argument. They can always conclude either that the situation has been misdescribed or that the Stoic, thus described, is not a very good Stoic. The argument of book 9, construed as a case against *apatheia*, is a poor one.

But what if Augustine hoped to discredit less the possibility of *apatheia* than its desirability? Chapter 4 of book 9 is still not that argument. Augustine's ambition there is to use the issue of the passions to house the various schools of philosophy under one roof. There they will all be heard to preach the gospel of virtue against the chaos of passion. They will all seek to reshape and refine a person's value commitments, to the point where that person may hope for a reasonably consistent happiness, secure in its core values. Augustine's composite portrait of the genius of philosophy as it flourished in the polytheistic culture of Greece and Rome is designed to be attractive. Stoicism's loss of its claim to perfect *apatheia* is everyone's gain of a reasonable hope. It is still reasonable, as of chapter 4, book 9, for philosophers—Stoics included—to marshal their virtues to restrain and diminish their passions. The passions may never be eliminated entirely, but real progress is possible.

In book 14 of *City of God* Augustine includes within his account of the origins of human sinfulness an attack upon the ideal of *apatheia*. He aims his ire squarely at the desirability of a passionless life. Stoics continue for him to be the chief promoters of *apatheia*, being the self-described purists of reason, but we already know from book 9 that Augustine has denied them their purist credentials. So why then does he bother to critique

---

4. The Greek word *apatheia* is the root of the English word *apathy*. I am nevertheless going to refrain from making the translation. Apathy connotes lethargy and inner deadness and is generally accounted a vice; *apatheia* does not carry any of this baggage.

a way of life that he believes no one lives in practice? A balloon, once deflated, is hardly worth bursting.

Stoicism in *City of God* plays the role of stalking horse for any philosophy that adopts an ethics of autonomy and so turns the pursuit of virtue into an essentially self-referential affair. It falls to the Stoics to display the deadly logic of this pursuit. Because Stoics refuse to call good what has yet to elicit their consent, they affect not to be affected by unacknowledged sources of value. Informed and voluntary consent to an impression of something desirable or repellant is taken by them to determine the entire range of their emotional possibilities. Although in theory it is possible to consent to the goodness of a good that can be lost involuntarily, in practice the Stoics would restrict their consent to the one good that seems unassailable to them: the reasonableness of the world's order. The terrible irony of Stoic practice, as Augustine describes it in book 19, chapter 4, of *City of God*, is their sanctioning of a reasonable suicide—for the loss of goods whose goodness they would (in theory) disown.

The obvious alternative to Stoicism is for a person to acknowledge goods whose goodness exceeds or has nothing to do with an exercise of self-possession. Augustine's Platonists and Aristotelians do this explicitly; his Stoics repress the acknowledgment and are constantly compelled to disown their own involuntary impressions of value. Any acknowledgment of such goods, sometimes called "external goods" (*bona externa*), is bound to move a self out of self-containment. Cicero calls this movement a *perturbatio*; the word means passion or emotion and connotes a shake-up. Augustine uses the word in book 14 to enumerate the passions that *apatheia* is meant to eliminate. His presentation there of the four cardinal movements of soul, the *perturbationes*, parallels Cicero's in book 4 of *Tusculan Disputations*. In both accounts, the soul is moved in one of two basic ways: by attraction or by repulsion. When the soul anticipates what attracts it, it experiences desire; when its desire is satisfied, it feels joy. When the soul shrinks from what repels it, it feels fear; when its fear is realized, it knows grief. The four cardinal movements of soul are desire and joy, the two modes of attraction, and fear and grief, the corresponding modes of repulsion.

It may seem odd for a Stoic or anyone else to want to live a life free of desire and joy. Even fear has its uses, as a tonic for mental clarity and a call to avoid avoidable grief. If any of the cardinal passions is worth missing, it would be grief itself, the passion that weds the soul to loss. Cicero spends all of book 3 of *Tusculan Disputations* making the case that Stoic sages are strangers to grief. When he takes up the question of the remaining passions in book 4, he imagines ideal Stoics not to be free of joy, desire, and fear, but to be free of the *disorder* of those affects. Grief is not redeemable, but apparently the three other *perturbationes* are. When a *perturbatio* no longer perturbs, the Stoics call it a *eupatheia*, a well-tempered passion. Cicero's Latin designation for the good kind of passion is *constantia*, a condition of constancy. The idea behind his choice of term is that a soul can be both constant and emotional if its emotions admit of measure: fear, when measured, becomes prudent caution, joy becomes just satisfaction, desire enlightened resolve. Augustine notes that when Cicero speaks of grief, he uses the word *aegritudo*, a term that can signal physical as well as emotional distress. Augustine prefers *tristitia*, in order to narrow distress to pain of soul. "Regarding grief [*tristitia*]," he writes (*civ. Dei* 14.7), "the tough question is whether there is a good sense of it."

His eventual answer to that tough question, based in part on scriptural evidence (Paul and Jesus both seem to have grieved for others), is that grief can be a good thing. He does not mean by this that grief is ideal. As he reads the story of the human start in Genesis, humanity's parents could have inaugurated a tradition of obedience to God and passed it on to their descendents, who would have led happy, immortal lives untouched by loss. Instead, Adam and Eve looked for a greater life in a break from God, and their willfulness injected loss into human happiness. It is now too late for those born to history to live beyond loss and, Augustine would add, too ungenerous for them to try. The three *constantiae*, when made to serve a private, impregnable integrity, define smallness of soul.

Augustine's rehabilitation of grief marks his profoundest break not only from the cognitive therapy of Stoicism, but from all the various forms of philosophical self-help that he associated with classical culture.[5] Even his beloved Platonists, who seemed to him to love the one God, desired too blithely the soul's separation from the body, as if this were a liberation of life and not the disintegration of personality that comes of sin and death.[6] They failed to comprehend, as would any school of philosophy untutored in scriptural wisdom, the first form of grief: the soul's loss of God.

---

5. Augustine's break from Stoicism on the issue of grief is well described in Colish (1985), pp. 221–25. For the broader matter of Augustine's break with classicism, I recommend Cochrane (1944) and Harrison (2000).

6. Augustine valued soul over body, but unlike other Christian Platonists, he put no value on the soul's separation from the body, or what Plato defined as death. For an illuminating discussion of Augustine's attitude towards death, see Cavadini (1999) and Brown (1988).

Parting Knowledge

My next section on Augustine explores the willful element of that loss and its effect on human affect.

II. Three Degrees of Disaffection

The story of the man, the woman, Yahweh, and the serpent, as recounted in Genesis (2:4b—3:24), was a source of constant meditation for Augustine. The story begins with Yahweh, a heavenly deity, fashioning a human being, Adam, out of the clay of the earth. Yahweh breathes life into Adam's clay and places him in a garden where two trees are singled out—one of knowledge, the other of life. In his first words to Adam, Yahweh tells his creature not to eat from knowledge, as even a taste would bind Adam's life to death. Adam's humanity is differentiated into male and female when Yahweh sends Adam into a deep sleep and sculpts a woman out of one of his ribs. A shrewd serpent soon appears on the scene and convinces the woman that eating from knowledge is life, not death, and that she will come to know as a god knows. She eats and then offers the fruit of her knowing to the man, who also eats. When Yahweh discovers that the man and woman have both tasted of knowledge, at the serpent's instigation, he curses the three of them and expels the human couple from the garden. The man and woman are not to have access to the tree of life. Yahweh consigns humanity's parents to labor in the soil of human origins, where they and their descendents will know life conjoined to death.

In *Genesis according to the Letter* (*De Genesi ad litteram*), his most extensive commentary on the creation narrative, Augustine insists that it was disobedience, not knowledge, that rendered mortal a potentially immortal human nature and caused other troubles (*Gn. litt.* 8.6.12): "The more I consider the matter, I can hardly express how strongly I agree with the view that food from the tree of knowing was not harmful to humans— for the one who had made all things very good would not have planted an evil in paradise—but disobeying the command not to eat was." Augustine's decision to put the entire burden of mortality on an original, transhistorical act of human defiance was to have fateful consequences for his theology and the history of its reception, including the part that pertained to emotions.

In book 14 of *City of God*, right after his critique of *apatheia*, Augustine begins to speculate about the emotions of the first man and woman in the time prior to their disobedience. He believes that neither of the two would have been subject to emotional disturbances, the *perturbationes* that so concerned the Stoics (*civ. Dei* 14.10): "Their love for God and for one another, as they lived in a true and trusting partnership, knew no disturbance, and this love brought them great satisfaction, since what they loved was never denied them. Their avoidance of sin was peaceful, and while it remained so, no evil of any kind broke in to cause them sadness." If his speculation is to be credited, then Augustine is describing characters with no motive to break faith with their creator and risk losing their already complete and secure happiness.

He does pause, if only briefly, to consider an alternative possibility. Given his somewhat convoluted assumption that the original man and woman were not created immortal, but only provisionally not mortal (their ultimate status to be determined), Augustine wonders whether fear of death and desire for an immediate immortality may have been motives for the original disobedience. The motives he is considering would be reasonable motives were it reasonable for a human being not to believe Yahweh, who is for Augustine the one God. Augustine cannot bring himself to conceive of a situation in which this would be reasonable. Were he then to attribute desire and fear of the above sort to the newly created couple, he would be reading *perturbationes* into sinless human psyches. He adamantly refuses this option and insists instead on the perfect contentment of Eden's Adam and Eve.

As Augustine's analysis of original felicity progresses, his portrait of emotional life in Eden begins to resemble an exaggerated Stoicism. In the beginning Adam and Eve have all of their desires completely under rational control, their sexual desires included. In chapters 23 and 24 of book 14, Augustine ventures his audacious theory that Adam must have been able to command his erections with the facility that most men have now for raising or lowering a finger. He has less to say specifically about Eve on this topic, perhaps out of modesty, but clearly he believes that she too commands her arousal at will. The moral he wishes his readers to draw from his excursion into the sex lives of Adam and Eve is that conflict between will and desire entered human life only after sin.

Now that we have one side of Augustine's sketch of emotional life in Eden, it is time to consider the other: two reasonably contented people, with no emotional baggage to unload, are moved to disobey a divine command and invite death and chaos into their lives. Taking his cue from Paul in 1 Timothy 2:14 ("It was not Adam, but Eve, who was seduced"), Augustine reads different motives into their joint act. The woman, he says, was driven by sensuality. She saw a kind of carnal beauty in the fruit of knowing and wanted to add the fruit's life to her own; the serpent's lies encouraged her in her desire. The man acted out of pity and condescension. He knew that the serpent was lying (and so was not seduced), but he had no wish to be parted from his partner, whom he believed too weak to manage on her own. Consequently he favored his flesh-hewn bond to her over his spirit-infused bond to God. Augustine uses the difference in motive to suggest the alliance of a weakened will to unthinking appetite, but differences aside, he places pride (*superbia*) at the root of all sin and preeminently the first sin. The man and woman, he concludes, sinned because of pride.

It is not easy to grasp what Augustine means by pride. It is harder still to motivate the turn from reason to folly that he attributes to supposedly reasonable beings. Of the latter difficulty, at least, Augustine was keenly aware. In several of the chapters of book 12 of *City of God* (6–8), he carefully develops the idea that the cause of an evil will, or a disposition to desire a lack of goodness, is always deficient (*deficiens*), never effective (*efficiens*). Although the specific case he has in mind is that of the fallen angels, who turned from God's light to pursue satanic illusions of power, he intends his analysis of deficient motivation to apply equally well to the human case. The pride that deficiently caused Adam and Eve to sin may not tell us why they sinned, as it would were it a sufficient motive, but it does tell us what genuine good they obscured in their twisted attempt to acquire it. "Pride," observes Augustine (*civ. Dei* 12.8), "is not a vice that belongs to the administering of power or to power itself, but to the soul's perverse love of its own power, in contempt of power that is higher and more just." Deficient pride is not effective because, in distorting the good of power, it finally loses the good it seeks. The vices that are heir to pride—lust, greed, anger, vanity, to name a few—are bound to do likewise.

Augustine's best explication of deficient motivation takes the form of a gloss on a sin of his own, confessed in book 2 of his *Confessions*. In itself the sin seems remarkably unremarkable. Augustine is sixteen years old at the time and in Thagaste, his hometown in his native North Africa. One particular evening, he and his gang, all adolescent males, conspire to steal pears from a nearby orchard. They carry off armfuls, food to be thrown to pigs. Although there is no reason to doubt the historicity of the episode that Augustine describes, he clearly intends his theft and waste of pears to carry allegorical significance. The pears, as forbidden fruit, recall the fruit of first knowledge and humanity's original sin; as wasted food, thrown to pigs, they have their association with the prodigal son of Luke's Gospel

(15:11–32). Anxious to live by his own devices, the younger of two sons in this parable leaves his father's house, squanders his resources, suffers impoverishment, and resolves to return home when he finds himself coveting the food of pigs. As Augustine looks back at his youthful transgression and its prodigal outcome, he tries to bring his original motive into focus and discovers, in ways scarcely imaginable to his adolescent self, a shifting affection.

More specifically, he recollects three degrees of disaffection in his theft and waste of pears, each degree a rejection, in ascending order of ambition, of a value-sanctioning authority. Disaffection of the first degree is criminal in nature. "When the motive for a crime is being sought, the motive is not credible," Augustine writes (*conf.* 2.5.11), "unless it takes the form of an appetite for having or an aversion for losing some one or another of the goods we have been calling the lowest." The goods he refers to as "lowest" (*infima*) include material wealth, social prestige and position, physical beauty and power, and pleasures of the flesh; in short, they are just those goods that Stoics think of as advantages, but not goods in and of themselves. Seeking one's own advantage is not a crime, but doing so at the expense of the public good is. Augustine considers his petty theft a crime in the sense that any crime is a crime: it violates communal standards of value. He also remembers all too well what made his petty theft peculiar. Most thieves want what they steal. Augustine cared not a whit for the pears (*conf.* 2.6.12): "I threw away the ones I picked, with only the delightful taste of injustice to enjoy; if any one of those pears did make it into my mouth, it was my crime that was the flavoring."

The love of crime for crime's sake puts a person at the extremity of a criminal disaffection. Even there, however, the disaffection is still serving an apparent good, in this case the good of being subject to no authority alien to one's own—a negatively defined autonomy. The hard part about getting one's autonomy that way is having to determine who or what is alien to oneself. Augustine recognizes that he never would have behaved so meanly that evening in Thagaste had he been alone and facing no prospect of feeling shame, but he also recognizes that he was in no position back then to consider his fellow instigators his soul's kin. They were just so many threats to his criminally defined autonomy. Tyrannize or be tyrannized: there is no other logic to a criminal disaffection.

From the perspective of his confession, Augustine sees this logic well enough, which is why he takes so little consolation from the pettiness of his theft. But he is also able to see past the logic, to the next degree of disaffection. The instability of criminal disaffection lies in its excessive dependence on competition for self-definition; it opposes the self that is one's own against all other selves, without ever defining an alternative principle of selfhood. Eventually the disposition must fold before this paradox: if I am to recognize some self as a self to be opposed, I must first know what self I am; but I cannot come to know what self I am except as a self to be opposed. The next degree of disaffection, emerging out of this paradox, belongs to the perverse or evil will. It is disaffection felt towards the authority of any self, whether corporate or individual. Augustine recalls that he was insufficiently motivated to steal the pears—meaning not that he refrained from stealing them (he did not refrain), but that his motives somehow failed to convey *him* in his act of theft. He had become to himself "a place of emptiness" (*regio egestatis*).

Being a deficient cause, the evil will has to present itself in the guise of what it is not. Mostly it looks like criminal disaffection. It looks that way to Augustine, too, until he tries to confess to criminality. His motives for theft lose for him their expected, albeit criminal, intelligibility, and where he would expect to find a confident selfishness in himself, he discovers instead a strangely evacuated desire for selfhood. That place of emptiness, somewhere between a womb and an open grave, remains undetermined. He senses that he has insufficient motive to love himself—regardless of which self he takes himself to be, the one he was or the one he could be. His love's deficiency, when made into the object of his confession, puts him in mind of his third and final degree of disaffection, felt towards God.

As the self behind any pretended self, God is present in both criminal (selfish) and evil (self-undoing) disaffection as the unconfessed object of attraction. When it becomes apparent to Augustine that the first two degrees of disaffection are forms of the same disaffected love, he is able to begin his confession. What is it, he wonders, that his soul feels it lacks from God? He contemplates a variety of his human vices, all illustrative of the disparity between his pathetically independent efforts at happiness and God's perfect goodness. It is power, apparently, that his soul wants from God, specifically the power to live beyond loss (*conf.* 2.6.13): "Grief pines over the loss of goods that were desire's diversion. My soul does not want it so, but would have it be true, as it is for you, that nothing can be taken away."

Augustine goes on to lament his soul's fornication, its stepping out on God to seek pleasure in a world of God's absence. In confessing to this degree of disaffection, he admits to the element of theft and distortion that is present in all breakaway human desire. The theft lies in affecting to take from God what only God can bestow: a fruitful way of desiring. The distortion shows up in what is actually taken: a love of nothing, sin. A soul that loves nothing is beyond loss, but also beyond love. Augustine's God has nothing to lose by loving, but also, and unlike the human case, nothing to gain. It is a sign of generosity that his God loves anyway. It is a sign of pride that his soul forgets this generosity and seeks to be secure in its own desires.

Pride in Augustine's analysis ultimately comes down to faulty self-regard and the desire not to be beholden to the love of others. The cause of this pride, being deficient, has to remain a mystery for him, but he is confident of the love that is pride's undoing. To love himself humanly and well, Augustine knows that he must learn to love more than himself—a lesson that is generosity's gift. There is grief in the lesson as well as delight. To will away the grief, as his Stoics try to do, is to learn the hard way that there are things in this mortal life worse than grief.

III. The Will's Apocalypse

Over the course of this chapter, I have used Augustine's construct of Stoicism as a measure of his willingness to admit emotions, especially the unsettling ones, into the saintly life. When I speak of his "construct" of Stoicism, I do not mean to imply that his Stoicism has been solely his mind's invention and so carries no force against the schools of philosophy—Stoic and the rest—that he took to task. I happen to think that Augustine is an astute but not scholarly critic of the core ambitions of historical Stoicism. Be that as it may, the student of Augustine on the emotions still needs to see his Stoicism essentially for what it is: a temptation that Augustine resists. He is especially tempted, as he looks to Genesis for some hint of a lost human integrity, to turn *apatheia*, a vice in desperate and corrupted times, into an original virtue: if only Adam had felt no grief at the prospect of losing Eve, the flesh of his flesh, he might have resisted his impression that something unique would be lost to him and stayed his course. What is remarkable, however, about Augustine's ultimate reading of Adam's motives is that it is *precisely* as a man of upright will, able not to sin, that the first man stumbles and wills deficiently to follow his heart.

Augustine is sometimes credited with having invented or significantly clarified the notion of will.[7] I am more inclined to think that he

---

7. Albrecht Dihle elaborates an argument for this in his Sather Classical Lectures,

helpfully obscures a notion of will, the one that puts a person in a secure position to survey his or her desires and choose one to follow. Many a philosopher has pondered the means for determining the rightness of that choice. Augustine takes a step back and wonders about the security that he or anyone else has in choosing. Maybe *apatheia* would seem to be the ideal kind of internal security were it possible to see outside of time and free of the claims of conflicting desires. But Augustine thinks that no one can. Our best Adam falls.

It is surely no coincidence that Augustine receives his "light of security" (*lux securitatis*) when he stumbles upon these words of Paul's, while agonizing over the conversion he kept postponing (*conf.* 8.12.29; Rom 31:13–14): "No more wild parties and drunken fits, bedroom antics and indecencies, rivalries and wrangling; just put on Jesus Christ, your master, and don't look to lusts to care for your flesh." The citation is just as it appears in the *Confessions*; it is not Paul's complete thought, but an imperative, broken off in mid-sentence—a fitting metaphor for Augustine's sense of his own will. Paul's words suggest to Augustine a contrast of desires: there is what the flesh desires, and there is what the flesh desires when Christ is doing the desiring. To put on Christ is to will one kind of flesh rather than another, but what is the difference? One kind dies, the other dies and lives again—a difference between death and death conjoined to life.

Based on the evidence of the remaining books of the *Confessions*, it is doubtful whether Augustine thought his light of security gave him any special insight into the difference between abandoning his life to death and offering his life to others. His security seems to have come from his confidence that he would be taken into a greater wisdom by not presuming upon his own. That included his wisdom about himself. Lack of presumption, at its best, is neither a willed humility nor an affected ignorance, but an openness to the good that is yet to be known. This is the openness that makes emotion genuinely a motion towards something. Augustine called that movement grace.

Dihle (1982). For my response to Dihle, see Wetzel (2002).

6

Life in Unlikeness

The Materiality of Augustine's Conversion

"What ultimately stills the fear of death is not hope or desire,
but remembrance and gratitude."

—HANNAH ARENDT

PHILOSOPHICAL REFLECTION, IN MY practice of it, has been a long meditation on obscure goods. I hasten to add that the source of the obscurity is not always or even usually the good under consideration; more often, I suspect, the obscurity lurks in my manner of seeking. But in the case I wish to consider here—the good of materiality—I lack a good intuition about what to suspect. Materiality may well be the paradigm case of a goodness that is inherently obscure; it may alternatively be true that this is a complete misapprehension and that some very powerful prejudices about goodness are busy doing their obscuring work. If the former proves to be the case, then I have Augustine to thank for his guidance. He knows all too well that materiality, once set within the context of a created order, is necessarily a shadowy good. But if the latter holds true, then Augustine does not know what he thinks he knows and there is substance in a shadow. In that case I will have him to thank for the ingenuity of his obfuscation. Presuming I can see through it, I will be much less likely to fall for a similar ingenuity of my own.

97

Parting Knowledge

For purposes of focus, I am going to bring the putative goodness of materiality to the scene of a conversion and ask what good it is doing there. Specifically I am going to bring it to the scene of Augustine's conversion, the episode he famously describes in book 8 of the *Confessions*. The setting is a garden courtyard in Milan, at the house where Augustine is staying. He has retreated to the garden in order to play out in private an interior struggle that has become intolerable for him. His friend, Alypius, discretely follows behind him and stands by in silent witness as Augustine weeps and gesticulates and gives himself over to self-reproach. Augustine cannot seem to bring himself to will wholeheartedly what he professes is his heart's desire: to leave his sex life definitively behind him and take up, with a new innocence, a life of celibate Christian devotion. While he is wondering why God is delaying to intervene and supply him with the requisite will, he hears a child's voice coming from some nearby house and chanting the words "*tolle, lege*"—"take up and read"—over and over again. He decides that this is no coincidence, that the words must be meant for him, that his God wants him to pick up his book of Paul's letters, open it without premeditation, and read the passage that first comes to view. Augustine does just this and lands upon a verse from Romans 13 (cf. *conf.* 8.12.29): "No more wild parties and drunken fits, bedroom antics and indecencies, rivalries and wrangling; just put on Jesus Christ, your master, and don't look to lusts to care for your flesh." The words have an immediate effect. Augustine reports having a securing light (*lux securitatis*) flood his heart and drive out his doubts, down to the last shadow. He has, from then on, the resolve he had asked to receive.

All this is familiar stuff to even the most casual reader of the *Confessions*. But in spite of the publicity of the "*tolle, lege*" episode, relatively few readers, I would wager, have fully taken notice of the fact that what Augustine is describing in book 8 is less his conversion to Christianity than to celibacy.[1] The protagonist that we meet at the outset of book 8 is in most ways already a convinced Christian: he subscribes to a transcendent God of spirit, he admits that the way to this God is through the Son, and he concedes that his old lifestyle of secular ambition and money has become burdensome to him and grossly unappealing. All that holds him back from his baptism is his tie, still tenacious, to women.

---

1. For some insight into why celibacy should have been for Augustine the *sine qua non* of his conversion, see "Lusting for Celibacy," in O'Donnell (2005), pp. 74–78. O'Donnell's biography of Augustine is wonderfully ingenious and highly controversial. For my review of it, see Wetzel (2005).

Life in Unlikeness

Augustine uses the phrase "*ex femina*" to characterize the nature of that tie (*conf.* 8.1.2).[2] Normally the preposition "*ex*" in Latin suggests a point of departure or source of origination. Think of the phrase "*ex nihilo*" in "creation *ex nihilo*." God pulls being out of a void and creates something that is no longer nothing but still not God: it is being that is constituted *ex nihilo*. To claim an origin "*ex femina*" is to admit to being born of a woman—in most contexts an unremarkable claim. But if women as well as men are taken to be, at bottom, beings *ex nihilo*, then the claim to have come into being *ex femina* can certainly muddy the waters. Imagine an Augustine keen to reclaim his birthright as a child of immortal, eternal spirit and (the) nothing else. He might not be so keen to be tightly tied in his habitual self-awareness to mothered and mortal flesh. And yet it is clear from the context of where the phrase "*ex femina*" appears that Augustine intends to make an issue of his sexual ties to women and not his natal tie to his mother. In the very next sentence he remarks that there is no Pauline injunction against Christian marriage; Paul in fact recommends marriage to erotically challenged new converts who lack the willpower to keep their focus squarely on the Second Coming. It is his own *personal* imperative that is preventing Augustine from permitting himself what the apostle permits him and others. This makes a certain amount of superficially psychological sense: Augustine has given up his worldly ambitions but not his ambitions; he refuses to settle for a mediocre spiritual life.

But that sense is only superficial. If we discount the natal implications of the phrase "*ex femina*" and leave Augustine hell-bent in *Confessions* 8 on recollecting and mastering the history of his lusts, then his divine rescue, mediated through a child's voice and an apostle's imperative, makes for an extraordinarily anticlimactic conversion. Apparently, Augustine cannot command himself very effectively to obsess less about sex, but when he reads a higher authority into his self-imperative, he finds himself suddenly able. And so his conversion, his putting on of Christ Jesus, his master, basically becomes a matter of his surrender to a power of self-control greater than his own. The Augustine who once prayed (*conf.* 8.7.17), "Give me chastity and self-control, but not yet" no longer has to redeem the desires that have been bleeding his psyche into alien flesh: he can consign them to a remote corner of his capacity to love and wait confidently for his otherworldly transfiguration into a sexually autonomous and angelic being,

---

2. *sed adhuc tenaciter conligabar ex femina.* [*trans.*: But I was to this point still tightly knotted to women.] I have yet to find a good way to translate "*ex femina*" in that sentence: "*femina*" is singular, and "*ex*" means "from," not "to" or "by."

utterly untroubled by unsettling desires. On this reading of what a conversion is supposed to be, the God from on high descends, gestates in Mary, walks the earth, and dies on a cross in order to introduce a greater power of self-control into the muddled world of human desire.

Here I cannot resist quoting at some length from Mark Jordan's contribution to the tri-authored book *Seducing Augustine*. It is a beautifully written book and deeply insightful, but arguably mistitled relative to his part, for Jordan shows no apparent interest either in seducing Augustine or being seduced by him. He writes in the persona of someone quite done with the relationship. Witness this wonderful paragraph from his postmortem on Augustine's put-on body:

> Put on Jesus, but do not fall back into the habits of bodily imagination. Put on Jesus, but do not perform a spectacle or treat him as an actor's mask. Put on Jesus, but not as a second and more sensitive skin. What remains of Jesus' body in the Pauline verse works to mortify what remains earthly in your body. It quells the demands of any flesh beneath. This new body comes to Augustine's flesh not as a miraculous touch or even a gospel episode heard at liturgy. It arrives in hortatory words read at random from a didactic passage in scripture. Augustine succumbs at last to divinely seductive words. He puts on the body of Jesus, but that body consists only of examples and counsels. It is a "body" of ethical words delivered without any risk of making a spectacle of divine incarnation. *Confessions* refuses to figure Christ in this decisive act of reading. It refuses even to savor the pleasure of the figure, since savoring it would mean touching the skin of a god with your own.[3]

Clearly Jordan is none too impressed with Augustine's feel for an incarnation. His Augustine has exchanged the Word-made-flesh for a fleshless imperative to drive the body into hiding and foreground words. Jordan is hardly the first to level this kind of critique at Augustine and the tradition of Pauline piety that draws from his authority. Nietzsche can be heard from time to time railing at Christians who find perverse and self-deceptive ways to turn an incarnation into an excuse for a crucifixion.[4] But Jordan's critique is more devastating than the Nietzschean one. Partly this is because his critique is less hyperbolic, but more to the point he manages

---

3. Burrus, Jordan, and MacKendrick (2010), p. 58. Jordan is the author of chapter 2, "The Word, His Body."

4. I have in mind the second essay of *On the Genealogy of Morality*, especially §21. See the translation of Clark and Swensen (1998).

Life in Unlikeness

to convey a palpable sense of *disappointment*. Jordan may not be open to further seductions with Augustine, but I get the feeling that he was open once, that at one time he might have loved Augustine.

What can I say, as someone still working through his relationship with Augustine, other than that I find Augustine more complex than Jordan does? Well, suppose that my Augustine *is* more complex than his. I do not find complexity inherently seductive, and so I do not take myself to be offering Jordan and the many other sensitive readers who find in Augustine a dispirited lover a motive to take up or renew a relationship with his ancient animus. Read me as confessing something about my own readerly sensibilities. I sense a desire to slip free of the flesh in Augustine's willingness to read a gift of sexual continence as the fulfillment of an incarnational imperative. But I also sense that this desire is for him as much a temptation as it is a virtue. In the Pauline struggle between the spirit and the flesh, Augustine has always lacked a clear ally, or, more tellingly, an unambiguous enemy. When he confesses in book 8 to having an internally divided and therefore self-defeating will, I take him to be confessing as well to a divided wisdom. "While I was deliberating about whether to serve the Lord, my God, which," he writes (*conf.* 8.10.22), "I had long been disposed to do, I was the one who was willing, I was the one who was not: it was all me." If Augustine were wholly identifying with spirit, he would be finding himself unaccountably hampered by some other being's flesh—a Manichean nightmare he is anxious to discredit. The truth of the matter is that his willing spirit and unwilling flesh somehow complete another, and yet they persist in fracture.

At the end of *Confessions* 8 (*conf.* 8.12.30), Augustine discloses the result of his conversion: he no longer sought to have a wife, and his careerism had come to a full stop. He is less explicit about the resolution behind the result, or what it really meant to him to be turned from himself to God. I say this on the assumption that there is more to his conversion, much more, than the fortification of his celibate resolve. But apart from having some insight into the illumination that Augustine speaks of as heart-securing—the *lux securitatis*—I lack a good sense of how that resolve, clearly of great importance to him, befits his conversion. I plan then to enter into that light, treating it not as a private reserve of spirit but as the offering of a less divided wisdom. This may seem, at first, a crazy undertaking. Augustine is ancient dust, a corpse long dead and buried, and even were I to have before me more than his disembodied words, I would continue to lack a perspective from within his flesh. How would I know what he experienced, even were he to tell me, as, admittedly, he often does? And yet it is not the distance between my materiality and his that prevents me from sharing the light of his spirit; it is my fear, which I have scarcely outgrown, that materiality is in some very basic and unavoidable way spirit-entombing. I am going to want to revisit the converting imperative of *Confessions* 8—the injunction to put on Jesus—and look, with Augustine's assistance, for some deliverance from my fear.

But before I can return there, furnished with new illumination, I have to travel with Augustine through a thicket of materiality. The route is apt to seem meandering and full of confusing forks in absence of a map. So here I offer a map, broadly sketched.

In the section I call "Strange Matter," I work through Augustine's attempt to abstract matter from all the forms that matter materializes. Matter, insists Augustine, is the product and not simply the palette of divine creativity; such insistence credits God, the absolute maker, with the creation of formlessness. When Augustine tries to conceptualize an absolutely formless object, or matter per se, he finds that he has nearly nothing in mind, a thing that resists thinghood. The matter that God speaks into being curiously resists being objectified in thought. So is matter unthinkable? Yes and no. If matter is being made out to be absolutely formless, then thinking supplies form to formlessness and necessarily changes the subject. The alternative, and here I borrow a line of reflection from Wittgenstein, is to remember that I can often speak to the reality of something, say, my own pain, without having to objectify it.

This brings me to the section I call "Thoughtless Love." I mean by the phrase not a love that is stupid or negligent but one that preempts preconception and exceeds expectation—a love, in short, that has the power to relieve thought of its rigidity of thinking. In the dialogue *The Teacher* (*mag.*), Augustine dramatizes a conversation he is having with his son, Adeodatus, and early into that drama he tries to convince his son that they each use words only to convince the other of a preconceived meaning. This view of speaking makes the mind of another, even a beloved other, into a formless receptacle for form, into unthinkable matter. But roughly halfway into the conversation, Augustine reverses himself and contends that no human being has the power to import a meaning into the mind of someone else. The minds of others must already be well informed, or our words would convey nothing to them. Is the implication then that God, whose intimacy with form and formlessness far exceeds our own, imposes the form that we cannot?

In the final section of my essay, "Livable Unlikeness," I argue that Augustine has resources for resisting the idea that God, as creator and Word-giver, is basically all informer or a will to be understood that is rendered absolute. The "unlikeness" in the section title refers to materiality; God, as the one who truly is, is unlike material beings but unlike them in two fundamentally different ways. Augustine reminds me that I have the desire, as a sinful being, to resist having my life informed by God. That resistance, an expression of my desire to absent myself from God, amounts to a will to formlessness, to a faux materiality. God is absolutely unlike faux materiality. In the other sort of materiality, the real stuff, I am materially important to those who love me. They have some investment in informing my personality (especially if they happen to be my parents) but not without also having some indication of the limits of all such informing. In book 7 of the *Confessions*, Augustine describes being taken up by God into a "place of unlikeness" (*regio dissimilitudinis*); there, I contend, he is offered a window into the difference between the materiality that alienates and the materiality that binds without constraining. It is precisely the offering that Augustine needs before he can put on Jesus and still feel at home in his different flesh. At play here is not a mystery of metaphysics but the logic of love.

I. Strange Matter

Let me begin with what is likely to be misleading about the phrase "the materiality of a conversion." We who live on the post side of modernity are familiar enough with investigations into the material conditions of conscious experience. In the first lecture of his great-souled study, *The Varieties of Religious Experience*, William James marks an important methodological distinction between an existential judgment and a spiritual one.[5] I evaluate existentially, in James's sense of existential, when I look to specify the originating conditions of an experience—its natural but not necessarily normal setting. An existential judgment about Augustine's conversion might well take in his psychologically stressed relationship with his overbearing mother, his narcissistic tendency to dramatize his psychological crises in religious terms, and the cultural and historical specificity of the religious terms that he has available to him. When I move to a spiritual judgment, in James's sense of spirit, I am now concerned about the value

---

5. James (2004), p. 17. The edition I am using, with notes and introduction by Wayne Proudfoot, is based on James's revised edition, published in August 1902.

of the experience that comes out of this brew of natural conditions. What good does it bring about either for Augustine or for the world that the converted Augustine has helped shape? James is insistent that I not base my spiritual judgment on my assessment of existential conditions. For all I know, an abnormal psyche makes for a better conduit of spirit than the workaday psyches that most people are assumed (perhaps unfairly) to have. If I insist anyway on the reduction of spirit to nature, aiming to discount the independence if not the very existence of spirit, then I am, from James's point of view, acting prejudicially.[6] The prejudice, to boil down a great deal of his subsequent foray into saintliness, comes to this: of all the ways we have to know the body, the way of loving it counts the least.

Augustine is well familiar with the prejudice—he calls it "sin"—but he lacks the conception of materiality that would allow him to frame an existential judgment and enter into the great modern debate over various forms of reductionism. It never would have occurred to him that the material conditions of his conversion experience might be preempting its spiritual significance. In no small part this is because he has a far more determinative conception of spirit than he has of matter. To hear him talk of it, he barely has a notion of matter (*materia*) at all. In *Confessions* 12, or one book into his extended endgame meditation on Genesis, Augustine tries to wrap his head around the "unmanifest and discomposed" stuff that God's hovering spirit converts into an organized world of intelligible forms (*conf.* 12.3.3; cf. Gen 1:2). He recalls how he used to think of prime matter when he kept company with the Manichees: not really as formless stuff but stuff so overburdened with form as to be deformed and therefore deprived of beauty. But this will not do, he concludes. The materiality out of which God creates perfect order is no anti-creation, laden with such a resistance to divine orchestration that the likes of a Plotinus might be tempted to think of it as eternal cacophony.[7] It is, on the contrary, so intimate to the created order as to be conceptually inseparable from it.

---

6. Note James (2004), p. 25: "To plead the organic causation of a religious state of mind ... in refutation of its claim to possess superior spiritual value is quite illogical and arbitrary, unless one has already worked out in advance some psycho-physical theory connecting spiritual values in general with determinate sorts of physiological change."

7. Plotinus, arguably the greatest inspiration, next to the gospels, of Augustine's conception of God, does think of matter as evil (κακόν), but without having to demonize bodies. See especially *Ennead* 1.8 in Armstrong (1989). For an insightful take on Augustine's break with the Platonists, and Plotinus especially, over materiality, see Marion (2008), pp. 333–34.

Life in Unlikeness

Augustine does in fact try to conceive of the materiality of creation apart from form, but his attempt ends in failure. He writes (*conf.* 12.6.6): "I was quicker to suppose the nonexistence of what altogether lacks form than to think of something between form and nothing, neither formed nor nixed, but unformed, nearly nothing." His next move is to forgo all further attempts at a totalizing abstraction and direct his focus on the mutability of the bodies that he either senses directly or entertains in his imagination. He surmises that in all the change from form to form there must be something formless that is the ultimate recipient of the change: he thinks of it as mutability itself (*mutabilitas*). But what is that really? This is what Augustine would like to know. He is tempted to say that mutability is a nil-thing (*nihil aliquid*) or a not-being (*est non est*), but he readily concedes that it must have some kind of prior existence if it is able to sustain a visible order of forms.

Matter in Augustine's mind has become a mutability that is both essentially unformed and infinitely receptive to formation. This gives his conception of matter a forced philosophical grammar, to borrow a trope from Wittgenstein. In the sections of the *Philosophical Investigations* where Wittgenstein is looking at some of the ways we talk about and express pain, he calls into question whether we ever have to postulate an inner object, invisible to others, to account for the pain that we know.[8] Suppose I am tempted to say this: whereas I always know for certain when I am in pain, I have at best a belief about the pain of someone else. Wittgenstein's counter to this kind of temptation is simply to point out to me that there are many cases where I am in no doubt whatsoever about another's pain, that I would no sooner think to doubt it than think to doubt some excruciation of my own.

But now the deeply metaphysical puzzlement settles in. Suppose I suggest to Wittgenstein that he risks effacing the crucial difference between pain and pain-behavior. In my own case I do not have to infer my pain from pain behavior; I simply have my pain. In the case of someone else, whose pain I never have, I use behavioral cues to make an inference. Assuming that I really do believe that this is what I do, Wittgenstein's apparent failure to recognize the role of pain in pain behavior is going to puzzle me to no end. "You again and again reach the conclusion," I tell him, "that the sensation itself is a Nothing." He offers this wonderful response to the persona I have been wearing: "Not at all. It is not a Something, but not a Nothing either! The conclusion was only that a Nothing would serve

---

8. Wittgenstein (2009), roughly §§286–315.

just as well as a Something about which nothing can be said. We've only rejected the grammar which tends to force itself on us here."[9]

So now let's take a closer look at the grammar that is forcing itself on Augustine.

He wants to think of matter as some kind of Ur-object, as the thing that lends substance to form and transformation, but matter such as this is as easily thought out of existence as thought into it. The "almost nothing" (*prope nihil*) object of Augustine's unresolved thinking is not quite a nothing but not a something, either. It might as well be either, for all that Augustine can say about it. From one perspective, the one that Jean-Luc Marion sets out with extraordinary care and insight in *Au lieu de soi*, Augustine's failure to grasp an object of thought here is good news. For it is, when all is said and done, not matter that subtends the created order but divine love, and divine love is known only in the acknowledgment of it: a matter of praise and confession. The alternative would be something metaphysical. Construct a world in thought by affecting to combine formless stuff with stuffless form, and then submit the ensemble to some kind of transcendent judgment. Marion is absolutely right, I think, to underscore the fundamentally non-metaphysical bent of Augustine's thought or, better, his philosophy.[10] But then there is Augustine against Augustine. There is something forced in his admission that the basis of created change is not especially thinkable. It is this forcing that I wish to bring to the fore.

II. Thoughtless Love

Return for a moment to Wittgenstein. If I were to admit, with Wittgenstein's blessing, that a logically privatized and epistemically privileged construal of pain leaves me with a nothing-something, so to speak, I would not be swapping out one expression of philosophical grammar for another. I would be admitting to the temptation to shoehorn pain into an object of thought. A "nothing-something" is not a fancy bit of grammar; it is a paradox. "The paradox disappears," writes Wittgenstein, "only if we make a radical break with the idea that language always functions

---

9. Ibid., §304, both quotations.

10. Marion (2008), p. 23: "Bref, la philosophie ne s'accomplit que dans l'amour de Dieu, ou bien elle s'y oppose et ne constitue qu'une imposture. En ce sens, le philosophie telle que l'entend saint Augustin s'oppose à la philosophie au sens de la *metaphysica*." [trans.: In short, philosophy either completes itself in the love of God or opposes itself there and becomes a fake. In this regard, philosophy as Augustine understands it pits itself against philosophy in the guise of metaphysics.]

in one way, always serves the same purpose: to convey thoughts—which may be about houses, pains, good and evil, or whatever."[11] I can, of course, entertain the thought of a pain; Wittgenstein is not denying that possibility, nor is he legislating against it. But when I face the cries and petitions for consolation of my young son, who has once again dropped something relatively heavy on one of his toddler feet, does it really serve for me to doubt whether he is in pain, take a step back in thought, and come to some sort of probabilistic assessment of his inner state?

"Just try—in a real case—," Wittgenstein dares us, "to doubt someone else's fear or pain."[12] I can honestly say that I would not try to doubt my son's pain. But I have a good idea of what would happen were I to do so: I would become disconnected from his pain and disconnected from my natural response to it; I would be alienating myself from him and, strange as this may sound, alienating me from myself. We philosophical types tend to think of thinking as an unmixed virtue and only grudgingly concede that there are times when practical urgencies compel us to think less and act more. But Wittgenstein is reminding us of the times when our *knowing* is better served by our receptivity than by our gift for abstraction. His call for a radical break with the idea that language functions only to convey thoughts is his reminder to us of a less alienated, more naturally knowing form of life.

The receptivity that binds a father to a son and a son to a father, and binds them without constraint, is a form of materiality; it is, in fact, materiality's original form, to take a hint from the Trinitarian wisdom that Augustine honors. It is when Augustine seeks to know the nature of this matter, to render it an object of thought, that he sets himself up to overlook or forget what there is for him to know. Let me offer one very telling illustration of the sort of forgetting I mean. The forgetting is insinuated in the *Confessions* passage that Wittgenstein uses to launch the *Philosophical Investigations*. Augustine is affecting to remember how, as an infant, he first came to use words and thus to move out of infancy. The section of the *Confessions* that describes this is somewhat longer than what Wittgenstein chooses to excerpt, but for now I will confine my attention to what Wittgenstein takes to be the relevant part.[13] It translates as follows (*conf.* 1.8.13):

11. Wittgenstein (2009), §304.
12. Ibid., §303.
13. Wittgenstein's motives for bringing his favorite saint into the *Investigations* are, to say the least, complex. I explore them in my essay "Wittgenstein's Augustine," chapter 13 of this volume.

> When adults were calling something by name and doing so by moving their bodies in accord with an utterance, I would notice this and commit to mind the sound they were making when they wanted to point this thing out. That they wanted to do this was further apparent from their body language, the language that is, as it were, the natural speech of humankind: a change of countenance, a look, a gesticulation of limbs, a tone of voice that indicates an intent to seek and possess something or reject and avoid it. Over time I made the right associations between words in sentences and sounds frequently used to point out objects, and once I had wrung the requisite sounds from my mouth, I used them from then on to announce my desires.

Augustine's recollection suggests that he has a direct memory of his infant days, but he has earlier described this time of his life as sunk within his mind's darkness (*oblivionis meae tenebras*) and forgotten, like his time in his mother's womb (*conf.* 1.7.12). What we have above, then, is an inference dressed up as a recollection, an inference based on how Augustine and some of the adults of his acquaintance have come to experience infants. But undressing the inference hardly makes the passage less strange. For whether Augustine is remembering or inferring the infant he describes, he is describing a peculiarly self-directed child, much less of a dependant than many of us would have expected. It is as if the child were born into the world with fully formed desires and needed only someone else's labels to be about the business of getting those desires met.

Wittgenstein likens the child in Augustine to a tourist in a foreign land, lacking the language spoken there: "that is, as if he already had a language, only not this one."[14] What I find most striking about this child is his studied detachment. He overhears the adults speaking around him and pays close attention, but he does not interact with them—except perhaps at the end, when he has already learned what he wants to learn, and he is ready to announce his desires. To me he is less of a tourist than a spy or an eavesdropper. So is this really the way Augustine experiences an infant—as a touristy, eavesdropping, preternaturally self-directed desire-monger?

I have already disclosed that I have a small boy, a toddler who is just beginning to add words to his repertoire of grunts, coos, gurgles, and excited pointings. Over the past several months, I have learned not to underestimate his capacity to grasp the meaning of words I have not been teaching him to say and to clue me in, usually when he wants something, to the increasing range of his untutored comprehension. He really

14. Ibid., §32.

is a cunning little eavesdropper—and a desire-monger. But there are also those many times that he and I interact and read one another's body language with a kind of playful devotion. I venture a word, and he returns what I optimistically interpret as a prototype of my word. As our interactions thicken, it becomes clear to me not just that I am teaching him my language, but also that he is teaching me his. I begin to adopt some of his prototypical discourse in my own, trading sophistication for melody, and I find myself a more engaged reader of tone—his and my own. It is also true that my son and I are getting to know one another better, and as the desire for mutual recognition takes hold of our language-play, we each lose some of the separateness of our respective desires.

It is hard for me to imagine that Augustine, who had a son of his own, had such a radically different experience of fathering that he could, without missing a beat, leave all the body language reading to the child. And yet there is no father evident in Augustine's passage out of infancy—no Patricius for Augustine, no Augustine for Adeodatus. The father figure has faded without a trace into that group of anonymous adults who are talking and gesticulating but paying no particular attention to the infant observer in their midst. But I do not have to imagine Augustine either as a father or as fathered to know that *Confessions* 1.8.13 is a forgetful passage. Wittgenstein leaves the oblivious part out of what he excerpts. Here is that part:

> Emerging from out of infancy I came into boyhood, did I not? Or rather did boyhood come into me and replace infancy? Infancy didn't depart: for where did it go? And yet it was no longer there. For I was not a speechless infant but already a talking boy. I remember speaking, and later I discovered how it was that I learned to speak. Adults did not teach me when they furnished me with words in some order of instruction, and, a little later, a grammar; but using the very mind you gave me, my God, I resorted to a grasping memory when I was wanting to convey my heart's intentions and get my way with cries and assorted noises and flailing limbs and I was not getting all that I wanted from all the people I wanted it from.

The syntax of this passage in the Latin is difficult to work out, and some commentators take Augustine to be claiming more directly than my translation suggests that he taught himself how to speak.[15] Still that claim can be

---

15. See, for instance, Burnyeat (1987), p. 2, n. 3. O'Donnell masterfully sets out the syntax issue and the implications for punctuation in O'Donnell (1992), vol. 2, pp. 57–58. I follow O'Donnell's resolution, but none of the available resolutions is entirely convincing.

fairly inferred, I think, from both his dismissal of any adult contribution to his education and his appeal to his prodigious powers of observation and retention as an infant. But what matters more than the explicitness of his claim to be a linguistic autodidact is his apparent failure to name God as the true and only teacher of what words mean.

Augustine advances the thesis in *The Teacher*, though "thesis" is perhaps the wrong word here, that God or, more precisely, the Christ within, is the soul's exclusive educator.[16] The dialogue, which, Augustine assures us, replays a real dialogue between Augustine and his son, starts off on the decidedly other foot.[17] Augustine tries to convince his son, who has linked word use to two fundamental activities—teaching and learning—that language is really only about teaching. Take teaching and learning in a very broad sense here. To teach (*docere*) is to inform, to convey an intended meaning, and to learn (*discere*) is to be informed. I find the world that Augustine is commending to his son's attention bizarre, if not hellish: everyone is trying to inform everyone else of something, but no one is willing or able to be informed. I imagine a large room of orphaned infants and unrelated adults: the infants, all with the kind of inner life that Augustine has imagined them to have, are frantically looking for signs in the adults of infant desire, and the adults, if they are paying attention at all, are trying to get the infants to think and speak like adults.

Adeodatus is not unduly anxious to buy into his father's fiction and accept it for real. He notes that praying is a common enough form of talking and that praying can hardly be construed as a means of informing God. And of course he takes it for granted that God has neither the need nor the desire to be informed. Augustine's response to his son's challenge is uninformative, but perhaps that is appropriate given the world that is being imagined between them. He tells Adeodatus that true prayer comes from within and does not need to be voiced (*mag.* 1.2; cf. Rom 7:22). If someone, say, a priest, were to utter a prayer out loud, then he would be signing others, but not God, into his inner life. God always lives there and so never has to be signed in. Let's just grant that Augustine is right

---

16. *The Teacher* is a promising text for those looking for a theory of illumination in Augustine. But I am wary of the notion that Augustine's perceptual analogy for knowledge—that soul-sight is to God as eyesight is to sunlight—is best parlayed into epistemology. God's light is love. If that makes sense to an epistemologist, then fine: Augustine has a theory of illumination. For a judicious comment on the status of the interior light of truth in *The Teacher*, see Madec (1999), pp. 543–45.

17. In *conf.* 9.6.14, Augustine credits Adeodatus, then sixteen years old, with the ideas attributed to him in the dialogue. The write-up dates from about 389, right around the time of the boy's death.

about the nature of prayer. How is a wordless inner petition any less of an attempt to inform God than the chatty variety? Once Adeodatus has accepted the idea of an uninformed but always informing God, he has implicitly accepted the notion of a purely formative language, one whose function is to inform without being formed in turn, to create meaning *ex nihilo*. His proviso about prayer is not, then, a challenge to Augustine's fictional world; it is its foundational principle. Let prayer not be an informing of God; let all such informing be impossible. It remains for God to compel himself to be heard. And what can this hearing be for a would-be human speaker but a form of suffering?

But no matter. Augustine dismantles his fiction in short order. He gets Adeodatus to admit that communication, so far a matter only of informing, depends in large part on the effective use of signs, like words (*mag.* 2.3f.). Now I can use a word like *dog* to signal to my young son the smelly, shedding creatures that seem to fascinate him so, but I have no means to keep him from applying that word to what I mean by "squirrel" or "eats directly out of a dish" or to some possibility I would not even think to guess. Teaching for Augustine is not a mind-to-mind transfer of meaning; if it were, I could in principle exteriorize my sense of what a dog is and convey it perfectly to my son. No, for Augustine teaching is the use of a sign to invoke a meaning that a person already has available. My son already knows what a dog is. If he didn't, then my use of the word *dog* would have no shot of bringing the requisite intention to his toddler mind. I will have taught him nothing. But even supposing that he does know what a dog is, what is it about my use of a word that gets him to attend, in that moment, to what he knows? Nothing that I can manipulate or perfect. Augustine might have continued to think that we talkers and writers are still teachers, albeit imperfect ones. Instead, he introduces towards the end of the dialogue the idea of the interior teacher, no less than an eternal wisdom within us, and with the interior teacher on board, we lose altogether our status as teachers.

Because Augustine says so little about how the interior teacher teaches, he makes it tempting to suppose that Christ, God's eternal Word, does by supernatural means what paltry human words always fall short of doing: that is, fixing a mind perfectly within an intention of meaning.[18]

---

18. After having argued that both Wittgenstein and Augustine share a similar sense of both the privilege and the isolation of the first-person point of view, Burnyeat (1987) ends matters by noting that Augustine, but not Wittgenstein, resorts to a supernatural guarantee of communicability. Supernaturalism of this sort will tend to disincarnate Augustine's Christ, as Phil Cary makes clear in Cary (2008), p. 99:

But this is a temptation, I think, that is well worth resisting. Augustine is not setting up a skeptical problem of meaning in the dialogue. He does not move from the ever-present possibility of miscommunication to the worry that no communication ever happens.[19] And when it does happen, why should he exclude from its domain the playful exchange of unfixed meaning that elicits more delight than it does doubt? It is no accident that *The Teacher* is a dialogue between a father and a son who clearly love one another. Perhaps the function of the interior teacher is less to build an inner citadel than to cast out fear.

But I understand the temptation to conclude otherwise when reading Augustine. When he divides the original act of creation into the creation of matter, on the one hand, and the imposition of form, on the other, he tends to think of formation as the really divine part. This gets him into trouble, and that trouble is nowhere more evident than in *Confessions* 7, the book commonly read to describe his discovery, with some Platonist prompting, of the immaterial God. I will now sketch an alternative reading of that crucial book, the cipher of Augustinian interiority, and by way of this reading I aim to wed the interior Christ to the imperative to put on Jesus.

III. Livable Unlikeness

At the beginning of *Confessions* 7, Augustine introduces us to an Augustine who is well over the bad old days of his adolescence. He is no longer living with the woman, his partner in the flesh, with whom he once made a pact of lust and in the heat of a moment conceived a son (cf. *conf.* 4.2.2). It is likely, though not clear, that he has also given up the interim lover he procured when his brokenhearted partner returned to Africa and he still had two years to wait before he could enter into an arranged marriage (*conf.* 6.15.25). What is clear is that he has become a good deal more sober about his libido and its increasingly dim satisfactions. His problems with

---

"Augustine understands the inner teacher as the very condition of the possibility of rational knowledge and understanding, and thus of the kind of learning that any good student of the liberal disciplines can accomplish. This is an accomplishment for which one need never have heard of the man Jesus Christ, much less believed in him as God incarnate."

19. On this point, see especially his discussion in *mag.* 10.32 of how the art of bird-catching may be conveyed without the use of signs. If it is possible to get what it is by seeing it done, then it is possible to get it again later by being told about it. Augustine is willing to stipulate that successful communication happens all the time.

the physical are now more abstract but, as it turns out, no less tormenting. He finds that he cannot shake the habit of thinking of God in material terms, not crudely in the form of a big human body but nevertheless as a "corporeal something" that is poured out over the places of infinite space (*conf.* 7.1.1). When he tries to subtract the stuff and, more mind-bendingly, the space from his conception of God, he is left with nothing.

Since we know of Augustine's parallel thought experiment in *Confessions* 12, where he tries to subtract all the form from matter and is left with nearly nothing, we can fairly say that his persona in *Confessions* 7 has even less of a notion of God than he imagines. He is certainly no better versed in God's investment in materiality than he is in God's complement of spirit. All that he has in mind is an orphaned notion of a body that is cast scattershot into great unknowns. But it is not the paucity of his conception of God that torments this Augustine most. It is his conviction that he has willfully absented himself from this God's presence, however shadowy and diffuse that may be. Augustine firmly believes that he is the one, not God, who has the freedom to wreck perfect orders and will the undoing of something good. The only thing obscure to him is how God, his absolute creator, could have allowed him this one terrible venue of independent initiative. The implication is either that evil impossibly comes out of goodness or that Augustine, as a good child turned bad, owns no further part of God. It is a thought of absolute corruption, on the one hand, abject abandonment, on the other. "I was once again weighed down with these thoughts," Augustine writes (*conf.* 7.3.5), "and they were suffocating me—but I wasn't yet to the point of being sucked down into that hell of error where no one confesses to you because evils are thought to be what you suffer rather than what a human being creates."

When Augustine first gets access to certain books of the Platonists in a Latin translation, probably an assortment of the *Enneads* and a bit of Porphyry, he is ripe to have his world rocked. It isn't simply his conception of God that is lacking in life; his self-conception is equally sterile. He seems determined to tie his human distinctiveness to his capacity to alienate himself from the source of his life—presuming, of course, that something in him still has some workable sense of what that source is. Somewhere in the Platonist books, he encounters an admonition to return to himself; with invisible guidance, he enters into his inmost places. There his soul begins to see in the context of love's light, the original and eternal power of creation, and finding the light familiar, he has his first knowing of God. But given what he describes next, it becomes questionable whether he really has anything. His language conveys disorientation and dispossession (*conf.* 7.10.16):

> When I first knew you, you raised me up so that I might see that what I was seeing existed and that I, who was seeing it, did not exist yet. You gave a jolt to the infirmity of my sight, radiating violently into me, and I shook with love and an awestruck dread. I found myself far from you, in a place of unlikeness, and I was hearing your voice, as if from above: "I am the food of the fully grown: grow and you will feed on me. But you will not change me into you as you do the food of your flesh; you will have been changed into me."

The resonant phrase "place of unlikeness" shows up in Plotinus, in the *Ennead* on the nature and origin of evil. Matter is the place of unlikeness for Plotinus; it is the place into which beings enter and become unlike themselves—just as, to use the illustration that Plotinus uses, the food that enters into a dog becomes part of the dog.[20] While it is quite likely that Augustine lifts the phrase from his Latin translation, he does not seem to be applying a Plotinian meaning to it. True, he is, in the experience he describes, unlike himself. He is seeing in a whole new way, and he sees, to his understandable discomfort, that he has not made the scene of existence. But note: he sees not that he doesn't exist but that he has *yet* to exist (*nondum me esse*). The further transformation that is offered from on high will be taking place in God, not a dog, and it is safe to say that it differs rather profoundly from digestion.

The Platonist reading of Augustine's experience is true as far as it goes, but it gives out pretty quickly. From his place of unlikeness, Augustine mutters to himself that truth is surely not nothing when it is not poured out into space, and he immediately gets his reassurance from the God of exiles, who cries out to him, "I am who I am" (Exod 3:14; *conf.* 7.10.16). Hearing this with his heart, Augustine would have sooner doubted his own life than the truth behind the created order (cf. Rom 1:20). Somewhere in all this, Augustine has had his imagination cleansed and his mind freed to touch upon immaterial spirit. That much of a catharsis seals his bond with Platonism. But spirit for him, while independent of creation, never leaves its finite places. He sees its truth established there. The deeply cathartic revelation of his experience of spirit, the one that allows him to see his manner of seeing, has everything to do with his own sense of place.

---

20. *Ennead* 1.8.8, Armstrong (1989), p. 301.

Life in Unlikeness

Augustine has been experiencing his life from a place of unlikeness. His God recreates that unlikeness for him and invites him to see through it. Of course Augustine is, from his place in creation, unlike God. He is a creature, and God is God, the truth behind those two little words: *ego sum* (I am). The unnecessary unlikeness between Augustine and his God, the alienating kind, originates from Augustine's resolution to cast himself as the perverse lover, the lover who rejects his beloved and embraces undoing. Speaking as to a soul in self-exile, Augustine's God shouts across a wasteland of unlikeness and assures Augustine that spirit is not bound by Augustine's sense of place. And as a child of spirit neither is Augustine. He is not the being he imagines himself to be; he is not where he thinks he is. He has no history to undo, and creation is not the plaything of his imagination. He is already forgiven, has been from the start.[21] Now he lives in God. "Grow and you will feed on me. But you will not change me into you as you do the food of your flesh; you will have been changed into me." The words speak to gestation, not digestion. When Augustine is ready to leave the womb and take his place in creation as a divine being, he will truly have put on his flesh and walked with God.

But before he is ready to do that, he does leave the place of unlikeness that his God has specially created for him. This is the hardest part of his experience to interpret. He speaks of an astonishing revelation—that from within that specially created place he is already the lover of God that he wishes to be: "I was loving you," he recalls (*conf.* 7.17.23), "not some figment I had imagined in your place." But he also recalls, as if he were just extending the same thought, how quickly it all ended. Again more astonishment (*conf.* 7.18.23): ". . . and I was not standing firm in my enjoyment of my God; I was snatched away to you by your beauty and just as quickly snatched back by my weight. I crashed with a groan into lesser things. That weight was my flesh's habit." The passage is hard to interpret because Augustine does nothing to soften the apparent antithesis between enjoyment of God and what is going to pass for his flesh's habit: a sexual desire so dispirited in its expression that it leaves Augustine feeling abandoned and corrupted in the midst of his very desire to connect. The habit-forming nature of this desire reflects Augustine's disposition to be unlike himself but not the gift of unlikeness that he has been given. He is still wed to his self-portrait as a bad lover. The missed disclosure of his inner Christ is that

---

21. I think here of Simone Weil's sentiment in Weil (1988), p. 17: "Moi aussi, je suis autre que ce que je m'imagine être. Le savior, c'est le pardon." [*trans.*: I too am other than I imagine myself to be. To know this is forgiveness.] For further elaboration of this notion of forgiveness, see chapter 8 of this volume.

a spirited being already has the habit of loving the flesh well. Augustine is not being sent back to prison; he is being returned to the place where he can experience love for all the beings, himself and others, who are being changed into God's flesh.

What he takes to be a necessity—his habit of faithless love—is actually his choice. If it were otherwise, Augustine would have found no illumination, no security, in an imperative to put on Jesus and stop with all the lusting. The problem with lust is not that it is too flesh-obsessed but that it makes for a very bad parent. That may seem an odd claim or worse, given the importance the difference between sexual and parental love, but the two forms of love do share this profound kinship: they both seek to elicit and celebrate non-alienating knowledge of separate flesh.[22] In short, they are both forms of love. Lust is love that has lost its trust that the flesh of others can be loved and still remain inalienably their own. For that very reason, lust lacks a sense of its own flesh. When Augustine imagines an essentially parentless transition out of infancy, he reads the logic of lust into the learning of language and robs the word of its consort with flesh. When he imagines that celibacy is the ultimate solution to alienating sex, he forgets his faith in the good of marriage and leaves his partner in the flesh with an increased burden of memory. My point is not that he should have been a better lover. Who am I to judge? The one who is his judge, Jesus the Christ, his *dominus*, speaks to him first through the voice of a child: "Take up and read." Go to the Word, yes, and submit humbly to its authority, but when you are enjoined to put on the flesh of Jesus, remember that God too was a child once and that his flesh elicited a parent's playful attention. The command of love is less a condemnation of sin than an extraordinary vote of confidence in the original possibilities of spirit. God's incarnation in Christ reminds us that materiality is indeed part of what God has created. And this materiality is not simply an excuse for form; it is a relief from it as well.

At the beginning of my essay, I said that I didn't know what to suspect about the good of materiality. Is it an inherently obscure good, or is its simplicity simply too much for anyone to bear? When I look to Augustine for my answer, I am tempted to think that somehow the answer to both questions must be yes. But I also know that at the end of this particular road, my only honest answer is this: the good is as obscure as I choose to make it.

---

22. I have learned much about the complexity of affective ties—natal, sexual, parental—from Kathleen Skerrett. She of course is not responsible when I turn complexity into confusion. See her beautiful essay, Skerrett (2009).

7

A Short History of Philosophy

Augustine's Platonism

THIS CHAPTER IS ANIMATED by two fundamental convictions. One is that Augustine's conception of philosophy is still largely an undiscovered country. The other is that his conception is intimately bound up with his sense of the history and significance of Platonism. I explore Augustine's sense of Platonism in order to get at his conception of philosophy.

My way of proceeding will be to compose the philosophical equivalent of a two-part invention. The first part, focused on the opening sections of book 8 of *City of God*, sets the theme: that Augustine's reception of Platonism—particularly its doctrine of two worlds, one sensible, one not—is thoroughly determined by his theology of creation. From the evidence of book 8, where Augustine starts things off with a short history of philosophy, pre-Socratics to Plato, he seems not to make *any* distinction between the immaterial perfection of a unifying idea and the God who lovingly creates a world teeming with material forms. Since we who live on the other side of modernity have grown used to thinking of Platonism as a form of idealism, it will not be easy for us to read Augustine's Platonized God other than as an idealizer of matter, a creator who, in effect, creates an illusion of material substance. But, in fact, it is Platonic idealism and not biblical materialism that gets evacuated of content in Augustine's rendition of a divinely ordered world. His God confirms the substance of the world by entering into creation and walking the earth as Jesus of Nazareth.

In the second part of my invention, I continue with the theme of Augustine's theological transfiguration of Platonism but this time with attention to the surprise of incarnation. It is surprising that God, the sublime creator, would have chosen to become so particularly human; it is also surprising that Augustine, created by God to be a particular human being, would have chosen to become something else. The surprises are related. In book 7 of the *Confessions*, the textual focus of part two, Augustine speaks of Platonism in more personal terms, less the grand turn in philosophy's history and more the catalyst for a new self-awareness. Augustine wants desperately to see through to the immaterial God of pure spirit, and just when he seems to have what he wants, the inconvenient fact of his neglected incarnation begins to reassert itself—a blessing that comes across to him (at first) as a curse. Augustine soon comes to see that he has always been relating to God in an irredeemably flesh-bound way, but irredeemable because no redemption is finally necessary. Flesh is not foreign to God.

The upshot of my two-part invention will be a Platonism that is christological at its core. There is no knowledge of the ideal that is not a knowledge of creation, and there is no knowledge of creation that is not a love of the particular beings whose particularity has been reaffirmed and sanctified by the creator's incarnation. This species of Platonism is not Augustine's ideological point of departure in philosophy; it is the aspiration towards which his thoughts and desires, sometimes haltingly, tend.

I. Up to Plato

In book 8 of *City of God*, and notably in chapters 5 and 6, Augustine is full of praise for Platonists. They are the philosophers who come closest to Christians, and they more or less know who God is: the bodiless, self-subsistent being on whom all beings depend for their existence, well-being, and value. This description could apply equally well to Plato's Form of the Good or *Noûs* (divine intellect) in Plotinus. From a modern vantage, Augustine can seem to be imposing a theological agenda upon ideas whose drift is more towards the secular; in this regard, he can be said to be "baptizing" classical thought.[1] But if he is adding God to a God-free mix, basically by making eternal ideas out to be divine thoughts, then Platonism must be for him a form of idealism. I do not think that it is. It is fundamentally for him a doctrine of creation.

For purposes of explication, I will be keying my notions of the classical and the modern in philosophy to Christine Korsgaard's view of their

---

1. The metaphor is common enough; it is used to describe what Augustine and a whole host of medieval thinkers do to Plato, Aristotle, and the Stoics. For a magisterial working out of its implications relative to Augustine, see Rist (1994).

contrast in her short history of Western metaphysics, the prologue to her historically informed analysis of the nature of value.[2] In her short history, Plato is the great exemplar of a classical value theorist, one who ties value to perception: the better we see the world, the more it presents itself to us as a realm of commanding presence, full to the maximal extent possible of goodness, beauty, and truth. But since this way of seeing the world is at odds with most people's experience, the great problem of classical value theory will be the problem of ignorance. How have we come not to know what is truly real, and what can be done about this? The modern way to think about values, Korsgaard goes on to say, begins with an inversion of the classical perspective. The real is no longer ideal, but material, and matter is knowable to the degree we refrain from confusing what is of value with what is. Modern values have their source in norms, not in things, and norms are possible because we are the sort of animal that binds itself, in reflection, to its own law. But since it is not altogether obvious what authority a law has when legislation is self-imposed, the great problem of modern value theory will be the problem of justification. What gives us not only the right but the obligation to impose forms of value upon material beings?

The pivotal figure between a classicism epitomized by Plato and a modernity epitomized by Kant is, for Korsgaard, Augustine—the overtly religious thinker in her narrative. She has only a few words to spare for him, but the ones she offers are weighty. "In Augustine's hands," she writes, "the Form of the Good is transformed into a person, a lawgiver, God, whose business is to impose excellence on a reluctant, recalcitrant, resistant humanity. Why we were this way of course remained a mystery, the mystery of the Fall. But the upshot was that we became obligated."[3] On this way of reading Augustine, he shifts the focus of value theory from idealized perception to rectified will.

The role that Korsgaard assigns to Augustine in her narrative of metaphysics is neither novel nor especially controversial—which is why she can afford to be so brief in her remarks. I cite her largely because of that lack of novelty. Her reading of Augustine is a modern retrospective on his place in the history of philosophy, and it is limited by what is most often limiting about this kind of retrospection. Augustine enters the narrative not as an active reader of his own modernity, that of an ascendant Platonism, but

---

2. Korsgaard (1996a), pp. 1–5. She titles her prologue, "Excellence and Obligation: A *Very* Concise History of Western Metaphysics, 387 BC to 1887 AD."

3. Ibid., p. 4.

as a proto-modern, impossibly waiting for Descartes or Kant to finish his sentences. This reading of Augustine may seem to elevate Augustine for his foresight; in truth it works to remove him, discreetly but decisively, from the history of philosophy proper. Plato may have been wrong to base the real on the ideal, but his mistake still falls within modernity's domain of the philosophically possible. I can be a justified knower—which is the only kind of knower that modernity recognizes—of an idealized world. Think of Descartes' attempt in the fifth meditation to demonstrate that bodies are part of the subject matter of pure mathematics. The point is that Platonism can be made to fit the modern fascination for autonomy in knowing: I see the ideal form of things when I attain through self-rule the ideal form of the knower and become, in effect, justified in my claims to know. The catharsis required may not be easy—no Platonist, modern or ancient, ever said that it would be—but it is sufficient for knowing in an idealized world.

Augustine's God, by contrast, is not so accessible to would-be knowers. He gives himself over to be known by a selective illumination and with little or no regard for the virtues, intellectual or otherwise, of those whom he illumines. In the context of a modern retrospective, Augustine is not the first philosopher of the will;[4] he is the first philosopher of the alien will, of God's will. The uniqueness of God's will lies in its otherness—it is always the will that is too late for fallen, God-resisting human beings to have. Augustine appears to want to base both his knowledge and his human capacity for goodness on heteronomy. Now it should be clear: Augustine's proto-modern place in Korsgaard's story implies that he is neither a Platonist nor a philosopher.

I am not excluding the possibility out of hand that he is neither, nor am I claiming, despite how it may be sounding, that Korsgaard is just a bad reader of Augustine. I think that she is, like most gifted philosophers with a modern sensibility, an indifferent reader. Augustine lives in the margins of her philosophical consciousness; when he has the brief opportunity to take center stage, he enters the scene as the return of a repressed religious moment in a philosophical genealogy, the father that is hard to acknowledge but also not so easy to forget. I am sufficiently restless in my own modernity to want to prolong Augustine's moment and resist its reduction to a religious interruption. Two things are necessary for this to happen:

---

4. In the second volume of her Gifford Lectures, Hannah Arendt gives us an Augustine who is "the first philosopher of the will." See Arendt (1978), pp. 84–110. She is not the only philosopher to have credited Augustine with such inventiveness.

Augustine needs to be accorded his own sense of modernity, and we need to become more self-conscious about the modernity that is otherwise used to define his place in the history of philosophy. Korsgaard talks about a modernity that is Platonism's inversion and so is, by implication, the inversion of Augustine's modernity. It is unlikely, however, that Augustine would have viewed the inversion of Platonism as the postulation of a value-neutral material world. If we adopt *his* reading of Plato's two worlds and reverse the relation between them, putting sensibility before intelligibility, or matter before form, we get something considerably darker than a world of a raw material. We get a Gnostic's nightmare, a world that blocks our self-awareness at every turn and binds us to illusions of happiness and virtue. This is the world that Christ must overcome.

Augustine was perfectly capable of conceiving of a value-neutral material world. In his short history of philosophy, he recounts, without a great deal of enthusiasm, the succession of figures in the Ionian school of philosophy, whose founder was Thales of Miletus—a philosophical naturalist who was good at predicting eclipses and who saw in water the unifying element of the world's material diversity. The Ionian luminaries to follow all had an abiding interest in the analysis of material diversity. Some, like Thales, were inclined to use a single-element analysis; others, like Anaximander, were more inclined to postulate a plurality of material first principles. Augustine refers to a number of Ionian naturalists who added the workings of a divine mind or intelligence to their sense of material order, but he seems singularly unimpressed by the addition. One is reminded of the criticism that Socrates makes of Anaxagoras in the *Phaedo*: that he invokes mind (*Noûs*) as an explanatory principle without having any sense of what kind of principle mind is.[5]

Socrates enters Augustine's account of the history of philosophy as a disaffected student of Ionian naturalism, and Augustine offers two rival theories about the nature of his disaffection (*civ. Dei* 8.3). Either Socrates was bored by an endless parade of obscure theories about the causes of things and wanted something better to do with his time, or he came to the conclusion that it was corrupting for anyone to seek knowledge of the cause of everything—the highest good (*summum bonum*)—without

---

5. Socrates casts himself in the *Phaedo* as having once been an avid student of the causes of things. His vocation as a philosopher comes out of his disillusionment with too flat-footed a conception of that kind of investigation. He still seeks the causes of things, but he also worries about being blinded by a good that his eyes cannot see. To avoid blindness, he resorts to truth-seeking by means of argument, a retreat into words. See *Phaedo* 96a–100b.

also seeking release from the tyranny of territorializing desires (*terrenis cupiditatibus*).

The Socrates who separates off the question of the highest good from the study of natural causes has given up on the naturalness of value. If it is possible to study the good apart from its naturalness, then the world is not in any philosophically interesting sense a created order. I will not need to know anything about my own nature to get along well in such a world; I will just need to convince others that my conception of the good is superior to theirs. Augustine notes that Socrates was skilled at exposing the stupidity of those who claimed ethical expertise and that he exercised this skill without ever revealing the basis of his own ethics. Imagine that this skilled and secretive Socrates is also the Socrates whose lack of interest in natural knowledge has left him keen to defend his self-willed conception of the good. He does this both by keeping his conception to himself and by attacking what others are willing to say about theirs. If we take this defensive strategy as our clue to the nature of what is being defended, our conclusion would have to be that Socrates is wed to the idea of the good being his conception alone.

Augustine claims, somewhat cryptically, that no one can know either the causes of things or the good of life who is polluted by *terrenis cupiditatibus*. The Latin phrase is not in itself esoteric or unusual; it readily translates as "earthly desires" or, perhaps, "earthly lusts." The ready translation does not help us much, however, if we think to ask what makes an earthly desire polluting. The implication of the Latin phrase in its context is that an earthly desire is not a desire to know the earth and the oneness that is the source of earthly order, but is instead a desire to preserve and defend an unreflective, deceptively natural kind of oneness: the oneness of one's own body. I am inclined here to extend the meaning of *terrenus* into the idea of territorializing. A *terrena cupiditas* is a desire that confines soul to a narrowly defined, if ferociously defended, territory, that of a body that is deprived of love and knowing—a colonized world of one and perhaps not even that. Augustine does not, in fact, think so ill of Socrates. He believes that the great teacher of Plato disdained the ramshackle oneness of the territorialized soul and sought in its place the oneness that only a purified intelligence is given to experience. This experience, says Augustine, is of a constant light without bodily source (*incorporei et incommutabilis luminis*), the light in which the things of this world are seen to live securely (*stabiliter*).

A Short History of Philosophy

When Plato enters into Augustine's narrative, he enters not as a philosopher who is prepared to return to a purely contemplative path, but as a student of Socrates, better able than his beloved teacher to avoid an overly adversarial philosophical method. Here is Augustine on Socratic contentiousness and its effect (*civ. Dei* 8.3): "In Socratic disputation, where Socrates asserts, advances, and destroys all views, it is never evident what the highest good is; because of this, people have assumed what they please, counting as the good in its finality whatever their impression is of it." Plato takes his leave of this tenuously philosophical culture after Socrates is put to death, and he travels to Egypt and Italy to study with new teachers. Plato's Italian teachers, the Pythagoreans, have already received a bit mention in the story; they are the contrast to the Ionian school, and their founder, Pythagoras of Samos, is the first person, says Augustine, to have called himself a philosopher or seeker of wisdom—this being his attempt to disavow having wisdom but not his desire to be wise. It is worth noting that Augustine makes Pythagoras out to be a humble man. Pride is the great enemy of philosophy, as far as Augustine is concerned, perhaps its greatest enemy—it encourages a person to claim wisdom and turn a blind eye to further revelations of the good. Augustine's Plato learns from Socrates how to care deeply about the question of the good; the Pythagoreans teach him that the contemplative enjoyment of the good need not wait for an interminable argument about goodness to end. Plato returns to Athens with the same insight that the Apostle Paul speaks from in Romans 1:20, the verse Augustine uses most often to bridge philosophy and biblical wisdom: "From the creation of the world," Paul writes, "the eternal things of God, though invisible, are seen and understood through the things made."

Augustine does not blink at the idea that Plato is, as a philosopher, an avowed theist; in fact, Augustine seems only too happy, based on his appreciation for Platonic theology, to identify philosophy with the love of God. We can nevertheless safely assume that the Platonists who figure so eminently in the *City of God* could have not guessed that their sublime and transcendent deity is also fully human; Jesus of Nazareth will be the visible disclosure of that peculiar divine truth. But perhaps these Platonists of old, being such prescient theists, were in a position to reason to the reasonableness of some such incarnation, if not to the specific case of a first-century male Nazarean Jew named Jesus.

Augustine is not tempted to think so. I quote from one of his earliest writings, where his confidence in Platonic reasoning is never greater (*c. Acad.* 3.19.42): "The most refined kind of reasoning would never return souls to the intelligible world once they had grown blind from the many shadowy forms that error takes and forgetful in the face of the meanest things of the body—not unless God on high, out of a liberal forbearance, were to bend and lower the source of divine intellect to the level of a human body." If I follow the logic of his sentiment, Augustine is suggesting that the humanness of God is not an irrational thought but a revelation of spirit's stake in even the meanest things of the body. What cannot be rationally anticipated is less the particularities of God's earthly life as Jesus (though that is true enough) than the depth of the love that is revealed through these particularities.

For Augustine, such love is the stuff of ongoing confession: we are always learning to speak with and through the love that keeps us from foreclosing on our life's narrative and succumbing to self-condemnation. The knowledge that this love affords—call it knowledge of God—is passed down from generation to generation and, through the grace of an illumined retrospection, passed back. Unanticipated love has an unnerving way of unfixing the past, making it, no less than the future, an open book: God's book. But it is still a nice question as to what Augustine's Platonists, the ones long dead before Christ's advent, can be said to know of God.

Augustine praises them above other philosophers for having known that God is not a material object (*nullum corpus esse Deum*; *civ. Dei* 8.6). As I have been urging, he is not praising Platonists for being idealists and knowing that God is one kind of object—an immaterial one—and not another. He credits them, on the contrary, for their insight into divine simplicity. All beings not God—whether they be material, like human beings partly are, or immaterial, like angels fully are—are complex: they have an essence that differs from their existence. It is, for example, of the essence of my humanity that I have the capacity for intelligence, and it is arguably of my individual essence that I am human. I cannot continue to be human apart from my capacity for intelligence, and I cannot continue to be me apart from my humanity. But were I to cease to exist, the terms that would allow others to speak *in memoriam* of my intelligence and my humanity do not thereby cease to exist. Were (impossibly) God to cease to exist, then so would the terms any of us have for speaking of God's existence and derivatively of our own. Thriving life, living intelligence, and abundant perfection are what God is and what we (for a grace period) have.

In his reading of Platonism, Augustine fatefully conjoins two ideas: that God is simple and beyond change, that God is the creator. "Because they understood that God is simple and beyond change, the Platonists also understood that God has made all things and is himself not able to be made from anything," concludes Augustine (*civ. Dei* 8.6). Many centuries later Thomas Aquinas would reverse the order of insight: it is on the basis of God's status as a first cause that anyone would know him to be simple and immutable. But Augustine has somehow managed to see in Plato's Form of the Good theism's most radical possibility: a source of being that is itself not a kind of being.

It is still not obvious, however, what Augustine's Platonists know of God. Indeed, the question has deepened. How does the being that is not a kind of being ever avail itself to anyone's manner of knowing? "It is one thing," Augustine famously writes, with Platonists in mind (*conf.* 7.21.27; cf. *civ. Dei* 10.29), "to see the homeland of peace from a wooded height and not have a way to get there." "It is quite another," he continues, "to keep to the way leading there, secure in the care of the heavenly sovereign." If some Platonists find themselves stuck on a wooded height—where presumably they see better than they are seen—the suggestion of book 8 of *City of God* is that they are still too wed to their own ideas about how things are. Augustine credits capable learners with knowing that God, whose mind eternally holds the "primary idea" (*prima species*) of things, always knows better. They know this not because they have taken in God's mind and compared it with their own cracked vessel but because they have not let their fixed ideas stand in the way of their education. For God is revealed to us not as a fixed idea but through the changing things that God has made.[6]

The addition of Christ to Platonism is no more going to change Platonism for Augustine than the addition of God. But this is only because God has never been an addition to his Platonism. Augustine takes there to be a manifest connection between simplicity of form in Platonism and the stability of a created order. In his short history, he does not say that Platonists were implicit theists who needed someone like him to bring out their theism; he says that they were theists who helped him understand something crucially important about his own God. With modern hindsight, we might want to say that he makes too little of the distinction between Plato and Plotinus, but we should also notice that Augustine's God is not in any case much like the Demiurge or the One. If he has found his God in Platonism, then regardless of what we are disposed to find there, we owe him as readers some attempt to look at his Platonism from

---

6. Augustine fittingly ends *civ. Dei* 8.6, the crucial chapter on Platonic natural theology, with an allusion to Rom 1:20.

the inside out—based, that is, on some understanding of Platonism in his own story.

To this end, I turn my attention to book 7 of the *Confessions*, where Augustine describes dipping into a number of Platonist texts (*libri Platonicorum*), being led within himself to a very strange place, and finding there his path to the immaterial God—or, better yet, to the homeland of peace.

II. Contrary Motion

In the second half of *Confessions* 7, Augustine reports the results of his having taken to heart a Platonist admonition to return to himself and look there, where no body is, for his truth. He discovers, much to his amazement, his profound love for God (*conf.* 7.17.23): "It was a wonder to me that I was loving you then, and not some figment in your stead." But just as much to his amazement, he discovers that his love of the bodiless God is no stable thing (still 7.17.23): "As quick as I was snatched to you by your beauty, I was snatched back from you by my weight, and with a groan I shipwrecked into familiar stuff." The weight he speaks of is both carnal and habitual (*consuetudo carnalis*); it has to do with his history of loving bodies and wanting some conjunction with them—women's bodies especially. Despite his newly unearthed love of God, he finds himself forcibly returned to the flesh he wishes, apparently prematurely, to leave behind.

It is tempting to conclude from *Confessions* 7 that Augustine walks away from Platonism with a concept of a bodiless beauty, immutably spiritual, and that this is his favored conception of God. Being in love with this God is, on this way of reading him, his favored conception of himself. So what then would this Augustine expect from the God who descends into flesh? "I was craving not to be more certain of you," he writes at the beginning of *Confessions* 8, "but to be more stable in you." That certainly sounds as if he is looking to Christ for a less flesh-craving spirit, and indeed, when he finds himself better able to love spiritual things, Augustine adopts this verse from Romans as his new imperative (Rom 13:14; *conf.* 8.12.29): "Put on Jesus Christ, your master, and don't look to lusts to care for your flesh." But still: how is Christ, who is not only perfectly but also distinctly human, supposed to be helping Augustine with his conceptualization problems? If he is having trouble restricting his attention to bodiless truths, then he needs a lesson in mathematics, not a story about a resurrected Nazarene. He needs to be meditating on first philosophy.

What we need to notice, as we part with our modern philosophical prejudices, is that Augustine's Platonically prompted return to himself actually works to destabilize his self-conception. He does not move from the darkened consciousness of an enfleshed soul to the impregnable clarity of a Cartesian *res cogitans*; he moves from his sense of himself as a flesh-craving God-forsaker to something considerably less defined. "When I first learned of you," he confesses to God (*conf.* 7.10.16), "you raised me up so that I might see the reality of what I was seeing and that I, who was seeing, was not yet real." There are three points of reference to this assumption from within: the God who beckons, the real world, and the self who is neither with the one nor part of the other. Not yet.

Augustine speaks of finding himself in a place far from God, a place unlike any other. From there he heard these words from on high: "I am the food of grown-ups; grow and you will feed on me. You will not change me into you, as you do the food of your flesh, but you I will change into me." The words evoke in Augustine the thought that God is not material at all. And in that thought he caught the cry of the God of exiles, still far-off; it said to his heart, "I am who I am." His doubts were driven out. "I would sooner have doubted I was alive," he writes, "than doubt the truth that is seen and understood through the things made."[7]

His invocation of Romans 1:20 is clearly proleptic. He has not been pondering the particular beauties of creation; he has been listening to voices from a place within himself that is both far from God and removed from the material order of things. We know that his "place of unlikeness" (*regio dissimilitudinis*) is not a part of creation because he describes surveying from that place all the beings that are not God but derived of God (*cetera infra te; conf.* 7.11.17); it is his next order of interior business. His survey leads him to two contradictory conclusions, whose contradiction, let alone resolution, he has yet to see. One is that the created order is a realm of privation. The things there exist insofar as they are from God; they lack existence, in the sense that they are deprived of it, by not being what God is: a fully real being. If this is what Augustine wants to believe, then it is his very difference from God that is the source of his human corruptibility.

He has, however, been given another way to look at creation. It is the beloved order, beautiful to God, and, as such, it is unmarked by ugly deprivation. Livings things still die, but in this alternative vision, mortality

---

7. All the quoted material is from *conf.* 7.10.16, including the allusions to Exod 3:14 and Rom 1:20.

is a form of life, not life's defeat. As for the unnatural causes of death and suffering, the devices of sin, Augustine is surprised to see that these have been left out of the picture. He comes to a startling conclusion: "There is simply no evil for you," he tells God (*conf.* 7.13.19), "and not only for you, but for the world of your creation; for nothing is able to break in from the outside and wreck the order you have set in place."

Augustine often has been credited—or burdened—with an aesthetic theodicy, where the beauty of the whole trumps the evil of the part.[8] While there is some evidence from his writings that he is drawn to theodicy of this sort, there is none from book 7 of the *Confessions*, where theodicy is simply not the issue. Consider where Augustine is when he sees the inviolable beauty of the created order. He is not part of the order he sees. He is not part of God. He is, as he says, in a place of unlikeness. There are two ways of construing the place, and they are closely connected.

It is first of all a place of illusion, literally a view from nowhere. Augustine is given a miraculous insight into the way he continues to subvert his own life. He has put his bad old days behind him, such as they were, but he has yet to escape the idea that his sin defines for him his distinctiveness. It is a strange kind of piety that allows God only sinning children; the rest are absorbed into their father in heaven, like shadows into the sun. Augustine's vision of the beloved order invites him to see, on the contrary, that sin—here a will to be deprived of one's beginnings—is never a source of creative difference. Sin just doesn't materialize, and as long as Augustine insists on seeing himself in terms of his will to sin, he will never be able to see himself as part of a material order.

The other way to read his place of unlikeness is as a place of gestation. Augustine is not yet real there in the sense that he is not yet born; he remains within the womb of spirit. Exiting the womb is going to require differentiation. What is it that would give Augustine his creative difference from God? It cannot be his will to become what God is not. That turns out not to be an ability. It is like trying to will one's own birth or will its undoing. The effort is always belated. Nor can it be God's power that makes all the difference. What I mean by this is that God cannot will *ex nihilo* the difference that is Augustine. That kind of power would undermine difference in the very act of creating it. Difference would be something as coming from God but nothing as coming from the *nihilum*—an unthinkable parentage. Whatever creation *ex nihilo* is finally taken to mean, the

---

8. John Hick famously makes a case for an Augustinian tradition of aesthetic theodicy in Hick (1978). For a counterproposal, see Williams (2000).

"w*ex*" cannot be the "*ex*" of material origination. Matter, like spirit, must have a divine source.

I am far from suggesting, then, that Augustine needs a Platonic demiurge to release him from his place of unlikeness. A demiurge imposes the perfection of form upon unruly matter. Augustine needs a deity not to restrain his material possibilities but to be in love with them. Some of those possibilities have to be Augustine's alone and not God's. As any mother knows, the moment of that first differentiation is the moment of birth. "The food which I craved in my weakness Christ mixed with flesh; the Word was made flesh," Augustine writes (*conf.* 7.18.24), "so that in our infancy we might nurse from the wisdom that you used, God, to create all things." These words are not just a pious addendum to the doctrine of creation *ex nihilo*. They transform the doctrine by reading pathos into will: Christ, the eternal logos, descends into flesh and becomes more human than any one of us. But at least we can grow and learn. Such is the wisdom of creation.

III. The Upshot (Reformulated)

I have already alluded to the Pauline imperative that releases Augustine from a life of unresolved inner conflict and binds him to a better-spirited love. It is a two-part imperative: put on Christ, and stop lusting. In the *Confessions* narrative, Augustine is able to apply this imperative to himself only after he has taken his lessons from the Platonists and noticed their limits. He recalls having become a pseudo-expert on the God-concept: the being who is infinite but not extended in space or subject to time, eternally perfected and utterly immutable, and yet willing to create a shareable reality. "I chattered openly about all this, as if I were an expert," Augustine writes (*conf.* 7.20.26), "but until I began to seek the way to you in Christ, our redeemer, I was not skilled but scuttled." Augustine faults himself, and by extension the Platonists with whom he has self-identified, for undervaluing or missing altogether the role that humility plays in the philosophical life. By humility he means not his self-contrived efforts to abase himself (that's a parody of humility), but God's descent from an eternally unreachable summit to the created order. We are unlike God anywhere else—but, of course, there is nowhere else to be.

Platonism, without Christ, is not for Augustine a difficult form of idealism, best appreciated from an out-of-body point of view. It is an attempt, not without insight, to get at simplicity without having to become

Parting Knowledge

simple. Of course one is never simple as God is. Augustine's Platonists knew that. Metaphysics forbids the equation. But then there is the temptation to style oneself a master at not being God. Platonism does not help Augustine with that one. There are still Platonists living after Christ, he notes (*conf.* 7.21.27), who never mention God's life and death as Jesus. They overlook the generosity of God's way of not being God.

So stop lusting. Stop living as if your bottomless needs and wants owned the rights to your flesh. And put on Jesus. Allow yourself to love others simply and without reserve. Those you love will defy your powers of description, but your words will always speak more than you can say. Such is the mystery of the Word made flesh.

Cultivation

8

Some Thoughts on the Anachronism of Forgiveness

MAYBE SAMUEL BECKETT WAS poking fun at T. S. Eliot when he made this line a move in *Endgame*, his play about the game of redemption: "The end is in the beginning and yet you go on."[1] Eliot does seem anxious in *Four Quartets*, his poetic ode to the limits of poetry and the possibility of forgiveness, to find his beginning in his end. He concludes that all of us who explore seek this: ". . . to arrive where we started / And know the place for the first time."[2] Beckett is not so sure. If you want to arrive at where you started, perhaps you would have been better off staying put. Why go on if the end is the beginning? There is no good answer to Beckett unless beginning and end somehow meet in forgiveness; if that can be imagined, then Eliot and the other explorers among us have only one answer to offer: why else?

I. Preliminaries

Some kinds of knowing call for a being known. You can know many things that are simply objects of your attention. They do not attend back, yet you still know what they are. It seems to me that you cannot know another person this way, though you can doubtless know many things about the person. When you are not known in what you know, you know an object—something you can define and perhaps manipulate, but nothing

---

1. Beckett (1957), p. 77.
2. Eliot (1943), pp. 241–42 ("Little Gidding").

that gives you a sense of where the boundaries are between your person and the next. The knowing of persons awaits a mutual trespass of preconceived boundaries; at the intersection, usually slender, of knowing and being known, a knowing comes to be that owes its metaphors more to touch than to sight. You are touched by the persons you know. Unlike the knowing that goes in one direction, this kind of knowing is particularly vulnerable to disaffection.

I am going to take two controversial claims for granted in this essay. The first is that there is this deep difference between personal and objective knowing, more or less as I have described it. The second is that disaffection always veils, never reveals, the person. Someone whose treatment of you is indifferent, deceptive, or overtly malicious shuts you out; you can see and shun what this person does, but you have no insight into who this person is. Of course I do not mean to imply by this that there are no bad people or that it never makes sense to call a person wicked. My second assumption, rephrased, is that becoming wicked is never a way of defining a personality, even if many persons seem to have a go at it.

In assuming what I assume, I am clearing the way for a reflection on forgiveness, or the resumption of mutual knowing in the wake of disaffection. What disaffection reveals is that persons have the capacity to veil themselves. Once in evidence, this capacity seems substantially to reduce, if not exclude, the possibility of future knowing. For if I have betrayed you or have inadvertently thrown you back upon yourself, how can you not become a skeptic when it comes to knowing me? Skepticism is fine for viewing suspects, but fatal for touch.

Within skepticism, forgiveness is the benefit of the doubt. You may doubt whether my good actions toward you are revelatory of my actual disposition, since I have acted badly in the past, but you reckon your doubt to be less than decisive. You are willing to take me to be, for now at least, largely the person that my good actions define. Outside of a skeptical context, there is something anachronistic about forgiving. There it seems closer to a recognition of rebirth than an offer of probation. I will be at the end of my essay before that thought makes much sense, but I can at least suggest at the outset what motivates it.[3]

---

3. A colleague once remarked to me that forgiveness is either offered ahead of time, before the offense, or it is offered too late. Her remark made no sense to me at first, but I could not shake it from my thinking. It has taken me years to begin to see for myself the "anachronism" of forgiveness. If there is any wisdom in what I have written, I probably owe it to Anne Freire Ashbaugh; she is certainly not responsible for the messes I have made of her insight.

Some Thoughts on the Anachronism of Forgiveness

A negotiation of forgiveness usually involves an explanation for disaffection. Suppose that I wrong you, repent of it, and then ask for your forgiveness. If my hope is not simply to end your resentment but to regain your trust, I am likely to offer you motives for what led me to lose it in the first place. In the context of forgiveness, this is a very particular and easily misconstrued offering. I offer you motives that make sense to you as motives—that is, they are motives that you can share—but I am not offering you excuses. If you hear me offering excuses, you hear me saying that I had good reason to violate your trust. You may then reasonably expect me to do it again if similar circumstances present themselves.

Alternatively, you recognize that I am trying to dissociate my intelligible motives from the disaffection that has set in between us. I ask you to accept me as precisely the sort of person who is not intelligibly moved to abuse your trust. We will then both share some incomprehension over my former disposition. The mutual incomprehension is important, and so is your acceptance of the motives I have offered you by way of explanation. If you allow me some claim to these motives short of their rationalizing my betrayal of your trust, you help me salvage *from* my disaffection a basis for relating to you in the future. In effect, I invite you to stand in the place where disaffection once held sway. The forgiveness that would incline you to do this is neither blind nor forgetful, but anachronistic. Past innocence is put ahead of transgression: having forgiven me, you expect to meet me in my motives, as if I were returning to the person who had never raised a question in your heart.

The anachronism may seem less radical than it is if forgiveness is confused with a kind of mitigated moralism: you decide to forgive me because you concede that no one is perfect and because my particular lapse is, in your estimation, less than morally debilitating; you still have some reason to hope that my failings will not write my life's story. As tempting as it may be to base forgiveness on faith in a person's capacity to improve morally, despite the occasional setback, it is nonetheless a confusion. Forgiveness involves a recognition of imperfection but is never a concession to it. Just because it is so tempting to think otherwise, I will devote a chunk of this chapter to forgiveness in a moral context, where anachronism disappears and forgiveness along with it.

The proper space to imagine forgiveness is religious rather than moral. There has been a good deal less of this space in which to think, however, ever since philosophers got into the habit of turning religious reflection into moral idealization: God as the omnipotent moralizer. I would say that this became habit-forming after Kant.[4] Be that as it may, I will borrow some of Anselm's premodern inspiration to reimagine greatness of being and how a being who embodied an excess of it could conceivably be forgiving.

The more I manage to disentangle my religious imagination from moral idealization, the more I find myself in a meditation on incarnation. The heart of this chapter emerges from there. I would not want to imply by my reliance on Christian imagery that the religious imagination for forgiveness is indelibly Christian or that my way of interpreting the imagery is especially traditional. If, for instance, it is traditional to see in Christ's death a compensation for sin, I am not traditional at all. Those who care about the tradition should know that it has not been my ambition to advance and defend a Christology, even as I admit my great debt to theologians—like Anselm—who do. I end in the space of an incarnate imagination because that is where my thoughts on the anachronism in forgiveness tend.

II. The Moral Measure of Forgiving

In this section I try to imagine forgiveness from a moralist's point of view. The term *moralist* can connote someone who takes unwholesome satisfaction from telling other people what to do. I use the term stripped of this connotation. Let a moralist be anyone who thinks of human value as a question of moral worth. Moralism can have a religious context, but it need not. Of the two moralists I discuss, Aurel Kolnai writes about forgiveness "in spite of the Christian tinge of the concept," while Jean Hampton plans to test the moral limits of her Christian duty to forgive.[5] In neither case is the moral framework of forgiveness altered much by religious commitment or its lack.

---

4. For more on Kantian moralization, see chapter 10 of this volume.

5. See Kolnai (1973–74), p. 91; Hampton (1988), pp. 10–13. Hampton's core writings on forgiveness appear in a book that she coauthored with Jeffrey Murphy. As she notes in the preface to *Forgiveness and Mercy*, her exchange with Murphy is less a dialogue than an exercise in mutual provocation. Each philosopher reflects on issues and questions that the other raises, but there is no attempt on either side to offer a point-by-point response. This makes it relatively easy for a reader to consider Hampton's views apart from Murphy's or vice versa. For my purposes, I have chosen to focus on Hampton, whose moralism—unlike Murphy's—is religiously inspired. I would also like to mention that I met and spent some time with Jean Hampton not long before her sudden and untimely death in April 1996. Philosophy has sadly lost one of its most sensitive practitioners. I write with her example very much in mind.

Some Thoughts on the Anachronism of Forgiveness

What is essential to any kind of forgiving moralism is a selective deployment of moral skepticism. As a moral skeptic, you may doubt whether there is such a thing as moral value, or you may accept the notion that some acts are knowably right or wrong but doubt whether these acts are revelatory of moral personality. I will argue that the moralist must make use of the second kind of skepticism in order to grant the possibility of forgiveness in a moral context, but also that there is no principled way for the moralist to move from skepticism to forgiveness.

Vagueness in the notion of moral worth already invites a certain dose of skepticism. Is moral worth read directly off the quality of a person's actions, or is it inexpressible to some extent? Does it admit of corruption, or does every person have the same claim to moral worth? Theories of moral worth are metaphysically tendentious and thus endlessly debatable.[6] I think that they are hard to fix upon because they have to negotiate knowledge of persons. Part of what defines a person is a person's own power of self-definition, but it is not simply that, or no one would have anything to learn about what a person is from anyone else. In the face of a negotiable boundary between self and other, it will always be easier to define respect of persons negatively. Treat other people as if they counted only in your self-definition and never in their own, and you deny them proper respect, as if they did not count as persons.

If it is hard to define what positively counts as proper respect of a person, it is harder still to determine when you have a case of *restored* respect. Is it enough that I regret my disrespect, apologize, and stop treating you badly, or must I do more to warrant your forgiveness? Kolnai finds an inkling of paradox in the difficulty this kind of question raises. He calls it the "Logical Paradox of Forgiveness," and it goes something like this: if I really have had a change of heart, I do not need your forgiveness, having already liberated myself from my offending part; if I have not made the change yet, you cannot forgive me without seeming to condone my offense.[7] Each branch of the paradox suggests that there is something morally unsavory about forgiveness. Sitting on the first branch, you assume a claim over my self-definition to which you have no right; I am no longer the wrongdoer your forgiveness would define. Sitting on the second, you abdicate too much of your own right to self-definition. You are passively guilty of not respecting your own person.

---

6. For a good discussion of what ambitions a theory of moral or human worth can be expected to have, see Hampton (1988), pp. 45–49.

7. Kolnai (1973–74), p. 91.

Kolnai admits that his paradox is artificial. In real life, there is the moral middle ground that stretches between irredeemable corruption and perfect changes of heart. As long as there is some reason to hope for movement in the right direction, the offender, Kolnai concludes, can legitimately be forgiven. What manner of forgiveness this will be, however, is not clear. It depends on the sort of reason that is taken to underwrite hope. At one extreme, hope is perfectly tailored to evidence of a person's will to change; the better the evidence, the greater the hope. Kolnai is suspicious of so calculated a hope, especially when forgiveness has been figured into the cause of the hoped-for moral reform; then much of the offender's self-definition will have been taken up into the forgiver's ability to assess and shape potential. The other extreme is to base hope wholly on faith in undisclosed moral potential: here there is little to distinguish forgiving from condoning. At every point in the moral middle ground, the decision to forgive is dogged by possibilities of manipulation and moral lassitude, of being too hard or too easy.

Kolnai does not define a way out; he settles for keeping moralism open to the distinction between condoning a wrong and having faith in a wrongdoer's essential goodness: "The sin and the sinner are not separable but they are distinguishable, and this suffices for the *possibility* of one kind of forgiveness. It is possible to 're-accept' somebody—the essence of forgiveness—without exculpating him and without hoping for anything like a thoroughgoing repentance on his part."[8]

In moralism the path from doubt to faith—cynicism to approval—involves progressive disinterest in evidence for irreversible moral rot. Reflecting on what she takes to be her Christian duty to forgive, Hampton writes, ". . . let me propose that the injunction to forgive is not merely the injunction to encourage in oneself the reapproval of others based on real evidence of decency, but also the injunction to reapprove of others through faith in their decency despite a lack of evidence for it."[9] Her proposal is made with Kolnai's concerns in mind. To keep from seeming to endorse an overly lax will to forgive, she has to appeal, as Kolnai did, to the Augustinian wisdom of hating the sin without hating the sinner.

This is not an easy wisdom for the moralist to apply. In order to avoid condoning a wrongdoer's wrong, the moralist has to insist that the wrongdoer will always be the person who acted wrongly. Forgiveness never changes that basic fact. The implication is that wickedness is at root

---

8. Ibid., p. 104.
9. Hampton (1988), p. 155.

personal; there can be no sin without a sinner. You cannot then separate the two without eliminating the sin and thus exculpating the sinner. That would be too much forgiveness for a moralist to credit. The alternative is to tie forgiveness to an exercise of charitable skepticism: grant that wrongdoing may sometimes hide the heart rather than express it; try then to give the wrongdoer the benefit of the doubt. Perhaps the wrong is not very telling.

Doubt of this sort finds its terminus in cases of extreme perversity, the stock and trade of the indignant imagination. Hampton is prepared to acknowledge a morally appropriate, albeit rare, hatred, directed against sinners too identified with their sin ever to be forgiven. She crosses this line into hatred, she says, "for moral reasons,"[10] but I cannot think of what those moral reasons would be. If the heart is at least partially hidden from the judgment of the eyes, as a forgiving moralist would have to assume, there is no moral basis for hating a person. This does not mean that it is always possible to forgive or even desirable to try. If to admit forgiveness you have to affect a trust you do not have, I do not see how you can manage more than pretense; a show of forgiveness is often worse than none at all. Psychological limits to forgiveness deserve respect, but not moral sanction. There is no moral injunction not to forgive.

The contrasting injunction, the duty to forgive, is often assumed to be what differentiates a religious from a strictly moral approach to the question of forgiveness.[11] What morality permits, faith commands. There is a neat division of labor here, as long as faith commands nothing morality would disallow: then an ethic of faith can be, morally speaking, a life of supererogation, inspiring to all, but required only for those specially called to it. The wreck of this economy comes when forgiving begins to look more like giving up than giving more—that is, when it begins to look like a craven capitulation to evil. Who can tell, though, when forgiveness has become too much of a good thing? Moralists who are stuck with this question, as I think all moralists are, are apt to find themselves in fairly useless reflections on whether Nazis, child abusers, and the notorious general in *The Brothers Karamazov* can ever be forgiven.

---

10. Ibid., p. 153.

11. If there is a duty to forgive in some religious traditions, as Paul Lauritzen and Louis Newman argue for Christianity and Judaism respectively, then from within those traditions the duty is not an addendum to morality but part of its proper extension. The notion of a "strictly" moral point of view presupposes that morality makes perfect sense apart from religion. See Lauritzen (1987); Newman (1987).

I say "useless" because however well intentioned such reflections are, they inevitably reveal more about the human imagination for sadism than they do about the limits of forgiveness. The charitable doubts of a forgiving moralism are all framed ahead of time: it is a presupposition of moral judgment that the inference from wicked deed to wicked person is unreliable. You can imagine as many cases as you care to where the inference is practically irresistible. From a moralist's point of view, you are imagining something about the psychological limits of moral skepticism, but nothing about its propriety. That is why I think Hampton would have to give up her moral reasons for hating.

I cannot refute the skepticism that gives moralism its only access to forgiveness, but I do reject it as unlivable. I would not be sorry, of course, to lose my right to hate, but I would be sorry to lose what else I would end up losing if I managed somehow to incarnate a moral skepticism. The doubt that blocks me from reading malice into a heart also blocks me from reading in love; a principled skepticism cannot forbid the one inference without forbidding the other. Even if my own heart were somehow to remain indubitable to me, no one else would ever know when I was trying to offer love and when I was trying to elicit it. The world of the moral skeptic strikes me as a ghostly world of surfaces, where every heart wears a mask and bodies touch and part without intelligence. At best, it is a world of frustrated longing; at worst, it is a graveyard of hearts.

The moral I draw from moralism is that forgiveness has no measure within a moral point of view. You can be an expert in differentiating the permissible from the obligatory from the supererogatory and still be quite at sea when it comes to forgiving. The breaker of the moral point of view is the notion that is often taken to soften it: that sinner and sin are separable. I don't mean "separable" just in the sense of "distinguishable." I mean that sin is removed from the sinner, as if time could be undone. The moral point of view can manage the distinction but not the separation. What the distinction grants is a space for unknowing, a gap between knowing the deed and knowing the doer, expressed in time as a delay of final judgment. What the separation grants is an actual anachronism, a paradoxical memory of future innocence.

I have no way to make sense of the anachronism that does not undo it and return forgiveness to the strictures of moralism. What follows, then, is less an occupation and defense of a position than a revision of its borders. I look from the outside in and try to imagine what it would be like to be on the inside looking out. This act of imagining moves me from moralism to religion.

III. Exercises of Religious Imagination

As a philosopher of religion, I find myself speaking on occasion about what things look like from God's point of view. This is an occupational hazard, I suppose, but it disconcerts me nonetheless. Of course, I cannot know whether I ever see what God sees or whether God ever sees what I see, but it is not my arrogance at presuming a convergence (however minimal) that most concerns me. I admit readily that I am imagining and not describing what is beyond my ken. My real worry, and this may point to a subtler kind of arrogance, is that my discourse of imaginings is all unintended soliloquy. I talk to myself obliquely about myself because in the one space where transgression is a virtue, I remain complacently situated in my habits of judging and feeling.

Anselm is the patron saint of those who have my kind of worry, and that is why I make use of his inspiration throughout this section. He had a sense in the *Proslogion*—the work of his most admired by philosophers—of what it takes to shake the imagination from the doldrums of soliloquy into a mode of thinking that is not so much about God as open to God's possibilities. It is a hard mode to describe, let alone sustain, but I will try to do both as I move on to the possibility of forgiveness and its anachronism.

The revision I have in mind of what defines forgiveness from the outside—from, that is, the imaginer's point of view—is at root a revision of the moralist's source of despair: the realization that no one ever deserves to be forgiven and yet everyone stands in need of it. I hold to the truth of this conjunction, but I do not think that it can be a truth defined within the moral point of view. I depend again on Anselm to direct my mind toward a different kind of definition, but this time direction is by indirection, as I will be working against Anselm's own residual moralism.

Anselm and His Fool

In the Psalms (14 and 53), the fools are the ones who say in their hearts that there is no God and then behave abominably. I pause at what it means to be moved "in your heart" to deny God. This must involve more than a simple failure to be convinced. Something in the heart is damaged in the avowal, or it would not be so easy for those affected to "eat . . . people as they eat bread," to borrow the psalmist's image. When the psalmist ends the psalm on the hope of a future reckoning, I recall that consolation has its limits and disconsolation its dangers. You can say in your heart, "There is no God," when you refuse to be consoled for the madness of fools. If your refusal should become your heart's desire, you risk becoming mad yourself.

There are other ways to deny God's existence in your heart, and most all, I think, will be beholden to a defiant grief. What is curious about Anselm's fool, whom he imports from the Psalms, is that this fool is incapable of the requisite denial. He can form the words, but he cannot frame the intention. His denial veils what is still conceivably in his heart—some sense of the divine. What sense that may be is what Anselm aims to discover in the *Proslogion*, whose title signals writing in the form of an address or allocution. Usually the *Proslogion* is read as if it were addressed to the fool, and a rather academically minded fool at that, but it strikes me that the fool is the one person whom the work cannot meaningfully address. It may be about the fool, or against the fool, but it cannot be *to* the fool. For the fool would never hear what Anselm or anyone else has to say about God, or more precisely, he would hear only the words. Circumlocutions for God—such as Anselm's famous tag, "the being greater than which none can be conceived" (*cogitari*)—would be of no avail. The fool is insensible to how things refer to God.

The pressing concern of the *Proslogion* is not, then, how to convince a fool, but how not to become one. Anselm says in his preface that he writes in the person (*sub persona*) of someone who wants to understand what he already believes: that he and others have need of a being who has no need of them, but who nevertheless is at the origin of all need. This labyrinth of need is the setting for Anselm's contemplation of God. If he cannot find along the way some thread of an original connection between his own needy being and a being of sublime self-contentment, he moves closer to the persona of the fool, whose manner of speaking is self-absorbed and, by Anselm's reasoning, insignificant.

Anselm grants that there are two ways of speaking significantly. You can use your words to refer to something, or you can refer to your words and thereby attend to your manner of word use.[12] His fool manages to

---

12. *Proslogion*, chap. 4. I will refer to Anselm's texts in one or both of two ways. If I cite Anselm at length or make a claim that depends in part on how I am translating his Latin, I will indicate the relevant volume and page number in the standard critical edition of his works, edited by Schmitt (1946); otherwise, I will simply note the section of the work under discussion, which is enough information for consulting any of the current translations.

confuse these two kinds of signification, to disastrous effect. Whenever he denies God, the fool opens a question about his use of words, but he has neither the wit nor the heart to enter into it. The result is a hedge of language between God and fool: what the fool says stays with the fool, and what is said to the fool stays without.

Anselm's manner of avoiding a fool's confusion is to imagine the limits to his imagination for God. Say that God is the being whose greatness is never exceeded by a humanly imaginable greatness. It is supposed to follow that God is greater than anyone can imagine and as such fails to conform to even the greatest of conceivable fictions. Posterity has condensed the complexity of Anselm's reasoning into something called "the ontological argument," whose proof of God's existence rests on the inconceivability of God's nonexistence. I follow posterity in associating Anselm with this line of argument, but not in considering it the point or aim of the *Proslogion*. It is not the thought of God's inconceivable nonexistence that arrests the mind with divine presence. As of chapter 3—the usual terminus for the ontological argument—Anselm has yet to sort out the ambiguity in his affirmation of God's existence "in reality" (*in re*). At root, he takes his affirmation to mean that God is not his mind's fiction (he will try to inhabit that thought), but there are at least two ways for God not to be a product of his or anyone else's imagination: God exists prior to what anyone imagines, or God is by nature beyond imagining. The first must be true if God is real, and the second may or may not be true. Since Anselm aims to sense God, it does not do him much good to affirm the existence of an unknowable God in place of a fool's imagining.

After the first few chapters of the *Proslogion*, Anselm addresses the ambiguity of his ontological proof and begins the real work of imagining God. Further meditation upon the "being greater than which none can be conceived" yokes together two conceptions of God, neither adequate in itself: there is the being who is the greatest conceivable (*deus in intellectu*) and the being whose greatness is beyond that (*deus in re*). The God of his interest is conveyed in the conjunction of these two conceptions, if indeed they conjoin. Note that the first defines a God who can be sensed. What you can conceive of has some possibility of becoming a part of your experience. The second secures the originality of God. You cannot conceive of what is there before anyone's conception.

The last claim warrants further comment, as it seems to depend on an equivocal use of "conceive." In the bodily mode of conceiving, originality is everything. No one gives birth to someone already born. In the mental mode of conceiving, matters are less clear. You can call to mind a great many things you have sensed before, and with some extrapolation from your experience, you can imagine many things you have never directly sensed. So as long as you are not claiming to give birth to a being who is absolutely original, why should its originality prevent you from conceiving of it?

The answer must appeal to the priority of sense over imagination, but not priority in the simple way that an image depends on what is imaged. In the sphere of the senses, perception is always selective and continually calls into play shifting qualities of attention and desire. The sensible world takes shape in the crucible of attention, but it gets its gravity—that is, its capacity to sustain attention—from desire. As desire tends to be less dependent on attention than attention on desire, it is usually desire that extends sense into imagination, where objects of desire seem less like givens and more like creations of the mind imagining them. Before there was ever an imagined object of desire, there first had to be a sensed one. But what about after that? Need the priority of what is given hold?

If you think of imagining as free-form representing, the priority of the sensible is hard to contest. Your imagination has to borrow in order to create: the paradigms for imaged touch, taste, sight, sound, and smell all originate in the senses. In the realm of desire, however, you seem to have more autonomy. Many of your desires may have originated in the needs of your body, but you can, and probably often do, imagine entertaining desires that have nothing to do with such needs. Now try to imagine the greatest being you can conceive of as an object of your desire, but not as a bodily need. How good can your imagination be here? If good enough to conceive of God, then God would be—if bodiless—a complete fiction of your desires. If other than a fiction, God would have to have a body to be sensed, but even here your imagination would be contributing all the gravity. In order to escape from an imagination that is caught up in its own desires, Anselm refuses to separate the conceivability of God from an original and more fundamental inconceivability. All the goods that he can imagine wanting, he attributes to God. They are tributaries that lead back to their source. The source itself, the one ultimately desirable good, attracts with unimaginable gravity.

In conjoining greatness of being to an inexhaustible, original, and essentially mysterious source of attraction, Anselm opens his imagination to a beloved whose nature is to defeat expectations. It takes quite a dance of the mind to remain open to this beloved's beauty. Too much originality defeats recognition as well as expectation; Anselm often laments that God is hidden in light. Too little leaves the beloved veiled by imagination; Anselm finds himself grasping at his mind's shadows. The beauty that comes through in a transgressed expectation is invariably a test of heart. You have to know when to leave your expectations behind, and when not to. As the *Proslogion* draws to a close, Anselm mixes self-indictment into his disappointment. He has not sensed the beloved in whom he subsists, mostly because, he surmises, the senses of his soul have suffered from a "long-standing, sin-induced languor."[13]

The ultimate cause of Anselm's insensibility may well lie, as he says, in sin, especially if sin can be thought of as a fascination for the wrong kind of transgression—the kind that veils rather than discloses beauty. His mode of meditation in the *Proslogion* betrays the influence, however, of a more apparent, perhaps proximate, cause. When Anselm imagines greatness of being, he invariably imagines strength of will. The greatest will conceivable creates apart from a context of creation and knows only negative limits to its power. It is incapable of willing loss, division, corruption, or self-diminishment of any kind. Necessarily it is self-possessed and complete. Anselm assumes that this will is bodiless. If it had a body, it could be affected. To be affected is to be acted upon. Is this not a capacity for self-diminishment? In short, Anselm describes a being who is pure will. To others it always comes across as effect, never presence. It is not surprising, then, that he has no sense of this being. What is sensed is always one remove or more from an original act of will.

Sense and imagination are fundamentally at odds in the *Proslogion*, but their antithesis is obscured by the one inconsistency that it never would have occurred to Anselm to question: that pure will changes in response to human perversity. We were brought into being to love God, but we have loved something else. God responds by damning some, forgiving others. How is this not being affected by what humans do? Anselm has no answer to this question. The best he can do is to imagine that the divine will is uniformly just in its two radically different responses to the eruption of sin, or what is unhappily original in us; uniformity follows, he thinks, from taking justice as the effect, but not the motive, of whatever God wills.[14] His reasoning, if it holds together at all, underscores his deeper problem. A pure will has no motives because it is never moved. The question that nags him is not, then, "How just is it for God to have two different responses

---

13. Chap. 17, Schmitt (1946) 1, p. 113.
14. Chap. 9 especially.

to human perversity?" but "How can God be imagined to have a response at all?"

This last question puts me at the limit of Anselm's inspiration in the *Proslogion* and on the edge of a different kind of imagination for divine forgiveness. With the inconsistency of the *Proslogion* removed, there is no longer a question to be resolved concerning who gets forgiven by God and why. Either there was an original disposition in God to keep human company, or there was not. If there were no such disposition, we would not be in existence to wonder whether there was. The disposition to keep human and divine together must therefore be original in God. If as human beings we nevertheless feel abandoned, that must have something to do with the burden of our own peculiar originality.

Human willing is intertwined with affect. We can be affected by how we will. Somehow the flesh remembers. The most burdensome affect of all marks the betrayal of love. To be affected by your own betrayal is to sense that you always have it within you to will contrary to what you love. Unlike the original being, who wills unaffectedly, human beings have a capacity—apparently inalienable—for self-diminishment. If it is within God to punish us for our betrayals, the punishment is simple: just give us more time and leave us to our own devices; we will work out lives of diminishing returns. I have no heart, however, for imagining this. (Who would need to imagine it?) If it is within God to forgive us, then the originality of God must be reimagined. There must be a way to wed will to affect without having to imagine a diminishment in being.

A Balancing Act

The two works that Anselm is most remembered for—the *Proslogion* and *Cur deus homo*—are, metaphorically speaking, both studies in gravitational attraction. In the former, the movement of desire is from human to divine, and in the latter, from divine to human. By Anselm's reckoning the latter movement compensates for deficiency in the former. The human soul never makes it into the divine orbit of attraction on the strength of desire alone. Its original capacity for love has been too much diminished by diversion. The divine compensates by drawing near to the marrow of diversionary love, the flesh and its excesses. Incarnated divinity subjects the distracted human heart to the pull of incalculable forgiveness. I plan to follow Anselm into the incarnation, but without subscribing to his notion of compensation. It is not the need of having to compensate for imperfection that moves God to forgive.

In a sense, Anselm would agree. His professed aim in *Cur deus homo* (Why the God-man?) is to determine "by what reason or necessity" God was moved to take shape in a woman's womb, walk the earth, and die by human hands.[15] Since Anselm does not imagine that God is the sort of being who can have needs, he does not find in God a need to forgive, for any reason; the necessity lies on the human side of things, and it takes the form of an infinite need to be forgiven. By moving to the human side, God introduces an excess of love into flesh that knows mostly poverty. It is fitting, thinks Anselm, that at least some human beings begin to sense the restoration of balance that has taken place. They will be reclaimed by God, though never fully "in this life" (*in hac vita*).[16] In *Cur deus homo*, Anselm reflects on the gravity of human neediness and the means that God has to address it, but he says little about what would incline God to apply them. This is not so much a question of need as of attraction. What is so great about a human way of being that it should draw the divine into it?

I do not mean to imply, by my way of putting the question, that I imagine human beings to have a kind of greatness that is lacking in God. Attraction based on need is bound to be short-lived; either the need is met, or the spectacle of neediness becomes irksome. I imagine instead that there is some beauty in human beings that continues to call forth humanity from God. This humanity is not a new and perfect creation that is set over the original as an indictment, nor is it humanity that no human being can ever live up to. It has to be a way of being that is fully human as well as fully divine; otherwise, there is never a knowing of the divine that is not humanly self-diminishing. A humanly knowable divinity is other to you but not alien to your humanity; it could imaginably take the form of another human being. Analogously, a divinely knowable humanity is other to God but not alien to divinity. I would not say here, though, that God could imaginably meet up with another God. There is a distinction between humanity and divinity, even in a being who is fully human and fully divine. Beauty is always original to God, whose power to attract is without limit. The beauty of the human being is, in comparison, either some poor shadow of an originally nonhuman beauty, or it is divine beauty that has somehow become other (but not alien) to God. It is the otherness of beauty, and not its imperfection, that has the profounder effect on

---

15. Sec. 1.1, Schmitt (1946) 2, p. 48.
16. Sec. 1.10.

gravitational attraction. Beauty that is God's other—the beloved—actually inverts gravity, so as to draw a being of unimaginable attraction into the orbit of human sensibility.

Two ways of being other to God have been much remarked upon by theologians, and neither gets singled out for its beauty. There is the difference that the body makes and the one that the will makes. The body seems to render human life irredeemably incomplete: there is always some further desire to satisfy until one's death, when life either ceases altogether or is fixed in a perpetual condition of unhappiness. For its part in making the difference, the will subverts the natural order of things, reduces justice to the law of desire, and turns death into a bad end. It is usual to consider the body as naturally other to God, but not naturally perverse or loathsome. In itself, the body has its own kind of limited beauty. The will, by contrast, is native to the divine being. When it becomes other to God, it infects the body with unwholesome needs and wants; in particular, it directs the body to what is other to God: death and the void. It also seems to direct the body obsessively to itself, and that is perhaps the most insidious and common way to will otherness to God. A self-absorbed body loses the benefit of its natural otherness. Eventually it senses other living beings only as effects of its own will to feel; an unnatural insensibility sets in, like a kind of deadness.

In most traditional accounts, otherness of will is what opens the distance between divine and human. Insofar as these accounts tend as well to assimilate divinity to greatness of will, the distance becomes absolute. The body, as naturally other to God, has too limited a beauty to motivate a renewal of connection; the human will, as unnaturally other, is downright ugly in God's sight. Even if this will were miraculously to develop eyes for its own ugliness, it would lack the capacity to reform itself.

Anselm describes the impasse imaginatively in one of the most intriguing sections of *Cur deus homo*. In chapter 21 of the first part, he tries to convey to Boso, his sometime student and interlocutor in the dialogue, the weight of a single sin.[17] First he asks Boso to place himself in a scene of temptation. He is in God's field of sight (*in conspectu Dei*). Someone unidentified directs him to look in a particular direction; God says to him in turn, "Under no condition do I want you to look there." Anselm asks Boso to consider what would make that look worth taking.

The answer Anselm is fishing for is that nothing makes it worth taking, because nothing can compensate for the loss of the will's original

17. Schmitt (1946) 2, pp. 88–89.

integrity. Compensation means here a return with interest, or as Anselm puts it, "You haven't done enough until you have given back something greater than that for the sake of which you ought not to have sinned." In the case Anselm has envisioned, your disobedient look, however trivial in itself, ruins the good of a will in perfect submission to God. You owe in return something better than what you have ruined, and I suppose that would have to be, given the context, a will that was incapable of transgression. Clearly it is already too late for you to will this kind of will. Time stands against you, and your life from now on is a debtor's prison.

It is tempting to wonder whether the compensatory will, which is beyond anyone's paying, should have been in place from the beginning. If transgression opens up a black hole of imperfection, why not begin with beings who are impassive to transgressive motives? Origins are a divine prerogative; if God values submission above all else, you would expect this end to have been accounted for in the beginning. There is some question, though, as to whether a constitutionally perfect being could have been a human being. Perhaps the capacity to sin—to will to be alien to God—is simply part of what it means to be human. This possibility lends tragic pathos to the human condition and, for that reason, has a certain romantic appeal, but it also suggests what can be absurd about tragic pathos. If it is human to want to be different, how is it that wanting this creates a need to become more than human? Being human is no longer a way of being; it is a way of becoming something else. And if Anselm's logic of compensation holds, it is an impossible way of becoming.

What I am pointing to is not a contradiction in human nature, but an often unnoticed incoherence in how human distinctness is imagined to register with God. Take God's originality of will to mean that God creates the substance and value of things. The human will, as a derivative power, is left room either to affirm or deny the order of the good. A submissive will is essentially the divine will in moral image. It is the will to stay focused on what falls within God's line of sight: the original order. Yet when it comes to the will and its desires, satisfaction is always a matter of defeating an opponent or overcoming an obstacle. It is never submitting. Think in this context of the unidentified tempter of Anselm's invention, the one who weds transgression to a human way of seeing. This is the voice of the will itself, expressing its natural desire for distinction, for some measure of its own originality. The absurdity of its situation is that it is always too late to be distinct. Its best, but still empty, hope of originality lies ironically in a will to self-defeat: transgression simply for the sake of being contrary, or the spiritual equivalent of chasing your own tail.

Anselm adds to this context a mediator who carries a perfect will into desperate human times. As God incarnate, Jesus is incapable of feeling the pull of dark, ungodly desires. He has his father's will; only his human side is subject to death and dissolution. I see the makings for compensation here. Jesus has the compensatory will but no need to compensate; his fellow humans have the need but lack the will. The balance is supposedly tipped when Jesus suffers the one death that has not been mortgaged to sin. His sacrifice will have elicited an excess of divine favor, to be applied to those who need and ask for it.[18]

The sticking point of this reasoning is that the damage of transgression is wrecked upon human beings, not God. It is redundant to return perfection to God or revisit it in the divinity of Jesus; it is the runaway human will that stands in need of a radical perfecting, presuming, of course, that you are still fixing upon the moral gravity of sin. What I do not see in Anselm's work—or in any of the Christologies of compensation—is how the application of divine favor can be an application of forgiveness. If perfection is actually effected and the human will is relieved forever of its impetus to transgress, it will not be perfection in this life. No one for whom time still matters can be that perfect. Does it follow, then, that under the expectation of an afterlife, the time of this life—the body's time—is relieved of its burden of perfection? Such relief would not be forgiveness; it would be the forbearance of a divine victor. God would cease to vie with opponents who have already defeated themselves.

As a game of the will, redemption is unforgiving. I am not sure whether this is because the will is too narrow an imaginative space for conceiving of forgiveness or because the will itself has been too narrowly conceived. Consider for a moment the distinction between love and will. Normally you cannot just will to be loved; love comes to you naturally from those who are disposed to love you. Yet what makes you distinctive as a beloved presumably has something to do with the self you are willing to express. If will did not condition love, would love discriminate at all?

Unconditional love, or what passes for it, has a veneer of philosophical disrepute about it. Sigmund Freud, whose sobriety about love was always impeccable, captured the disrepute perfectly in two well-chosen indictments: "A love that does not discriminate seems to me to forfeit a part of its own value, by doing an injustice to its object; and secondly,

---

18. Sec. 2.20 especially.

not everyone is worthy of love."[19] It is possible to respond, as has much of Christian theology, that no one is worthy of love and so no one is slighted when all are loved unconditionally. The weakness of this kind of response is that it is often too indebted to the reasoning it seeks to displace. If the claim that no one is worthy of love is taken to mean that all of us are *unworthy* of love, nothing has been said to dispel the impression that some of us are more unworthy than others. The least worthy are perhaps those who know nothing of their unworthiness; thus does the competition begin for the most delicate conscience. (This is the competition that Nietzsche was so good at despising.)

So what is a forgiving God to do? Incarnation hints at a divine love of life in the flesh and of all who live it. Maybe it is not just a hint, but an outright declaration. The latter is hard to imagine. We know too much about what is unlovable about the mortal vale and its denizens, and so our imagination for incarnation is correspondingly halfhearted. Let the divine keep its sublime sense of discrimination intact while it walks among us. It will need it. Only a will greater than we can conceive of could negotiate the labyrinth of time and desire and manage to retain all of its original innocence. The hardest thing to imagine in God is a will whose center of gravity is body rather than spirit, a will subject to the touch of time. Anselm's Christ is incarnate in all but will. The flesh is to him still confusion at a remove. That is why he can show mercy, but not forgive. You cannot forgive what you have never loved.

An incarnate will is somewhere in the neighborhood of unconditional love, but I mean by "unconditional" a love that is unreserved, not indiscriminate. In the imagination of a moralist, it is impossible to pull these thoughts apart: if love is not reserved, then it must be indiscriminate. I am inclined to invert this wisdom. Unreserved love, if it can be imagined, must be the most discriminating of all. In imagining this, my mind bends towards the "moral scandal" of Christian fascination: Jesus nailed to a cross, rejected by those whose humanity he had hoped to touch. Luke is the one evangelist who turns the crucifixion into a moment of forgiveness: "Father, forgive them, for they do not know what they are doing" (Luke 23:34). John leaves Jesus with a terse "it is finished" (John 19:30). Matthew and Mark relate words of stunning pathos: "*Eli, Eli, lema sabachthani?*" ("My God, my God, why have you forsaken me?") (Matt 27:46; Mark 15:34).

---

19. Freud (1961), p. 49.

Parting Knowledge

The voices of the evangelists reinforce a symbolism that weds forgiveness to incarnation. Jesus can forgive his tormentors because he has entered into the human condition without reserve. He knows what sin feels like. He tells us in Matthew and Mark. It feels like being forsaken, untouchable, beyond love. Take this anachronistically. Abandonment is supposed to follow sin, as a punishment follows a crime. On the cross, Jesus puts the abandonment before the sin; he thereby opens a space within grief for forgiveness. The moral is not that you have to suffer grief in order to be forgiven, but rather that in moving from sin to grief, will to pathos, you do not have to suffer diminishment. At the crossroads of sin and destitution, a burden of separation has been taken up into God. It is finished—has been from the start. Human beings do not have to will to be other to God or to one another; they are already naturally other, being set apart. The natural otherness of another sentient being is an invitation to know and be known. To become incarnate. The alternative is to turn the cross into a scale for weighing sin against the perfection of self-sacrifice: the anachronism disappears, and forgiveness degenerates into making excuses for the flesh and its ignorance.

The anachronism of forgiveness is ironic. Usually anachronism is a violation of time. Here it is time's restitution. It is not God, after all, who is resentful of the limits that allow for touch. We are the ones who insist on a temporary incarnation, who cannot refrain from holding time before a mirror of eternity. In eternity, the end is in the beginning; in time, you go on. Can God accept one apart from the other? Can we? In the incarnation these come to the same question.

IV. Absolute Time

I have been writing about anachronism with the line from Beckett in mind. It is Hamm, one of the principals in *Endgame*, who announces in the midst of a story he has been telling that "the end is in the beginning."[20] When he adds, "and yet you go on," it is not clear whom he is addressing, though earlier he billed his story as a soliloquy. Let it be Hamm's story, or yours, or mine. In this story, one person is perpetually indebted to the service of another, and after a time, neither can stand to be with the other, or without. The story could be anyone's. What catches me in Hamm's statement is its ambivalence. Is going on when the end is in the beginning hopeful or pointless? That depends, I guess, on whether a beginning worth

20. Beckett (1957), p. 77.

Some Thoughts on the Anachronism of Forgiveness

recapturing has been lost or forgotten along the way. There is no way to tell in Beckett's drama. His characters begin in the endgame of a contest of wills: one person's jaded desires vie against another's inarticulate needs, to no resolution. In what Beckett imagines, winning or losing may turn out to be just another way of continuing the game.

Beckett never cared much for the imagination of his interpreters. As a dramatist his interest was in, as he put it, "fundamental sounds."[21] The other sounds heard, the "overtones" of the interpreter's art or indulgence, were not his responsibility. Both the pleasure and frustration of interpreting Beckett lie in trying to determine where your responsibility begins and his ends. I know of no dramatist who better taxes a person's imagination for what is fundamental. There are allusions throughout *Endgame* to a missed beginning, whose recollection promises to lend the game of ending some direction: to a future as likely to be damnation as redemption, but in either case to the next and possibly last move. The allusions fail in the end, however, to carry against the sentiment, expressed early on, that "all is absolute." There is nothing more fundamental in *Endgame*, it seems, than the recognition that you are here, and not there, that the time is now, and not then. Time, as absolute, has been untied from all absolute beginnings and endings. There is no game of redemption or damnation to play, and that in itself may seem like damnation—or redemption. Hamm, ever the ironist, puts it like this: "Use your head, can't you, use your head, you're on earth, there's no cure for that!"[22]

I invoke Beckett by way of concluding because I think he poses the right challenge to the religious imagination. In some absolute beginning or ending, there is life as it is meant to be: free from the pain of loss and untouchable in its perfection; in short, something finished. If you imagine this life as your own, your time is always either behind you or to come. You will have imagined, certainly, a life more than human, but can you be as sure you have not also imagined one less than divine? The hope for a life beyond life's imperfections sometimes comes to little more than the curse you put on time. To live between a curse and a hope is to enter an endgame without end, or life in the mean time.

When I try to imagine what can be absolute and original about an incarnate life, I think of a being who has fully accepted being human before any one of us has. If this being is God, then the time the rest of us have to become incarnate is still before us. Forgiveness is what we begin with. I do

---

21. As cited in Bair (1978), p. 470.
22. Beckett (1957), p. 61.

Parting Knowledge

not imagine that going on will be easy. There is no compensation for any of the time that human beings have used to postpone their humanity; perhaps this is because becoming human is not a compensation. In that last possibility, I begin to sense a resurrection, but in my own anachronistic way, I would take it as a birth.

9

A Meditation on Hell
Lessons from Dante

"Keep your mind in hell, and despair not."
—ST. SILOUAN THE RECLUSE

HELL, IT SEEMS TO me, is an idea that is as hard to live with as it is to do without. Those who claim fervently to disbelieve in the place are often inclined, if sufficiently provoked, to wish others there—or themselves, if sufficiently disheartened. Those who do believe in the place often wish they didn't have to, but it is sadly easier for them to disbelieve in heaven. Those who are either utterly content to believe in hell or who see nothing in the idea but a primitive anger they have gladly overcome are not my intended audience. But they are most welcome to follow along, if only out of curiosity.

I offer here a meditation on hell that takes seriously what is difficult to accept and even scandalous about hell, but concentrates on what is theologically compelling about the idea. There is also for many of us something psychologically compelling about the idea of hell, but that will not be my primary focus. My meditative guide, or source of inspiration, will be Dante. His *Inferno* is not only a stunning work of the imagination; it is also a very profound piece of theology. I hope that some of that profundity will come through in the use I make of him, but he is not to be blamed, of course, for shortcomings in my exposition. I am particularly taken by one line of the famous inscription he places over hell's gateway, at the opening of canto III: "No things were before me not eternal; eternal I remain" (3.19.5–6).[1] The suggestion here, as I read the line, is that hell is part of the original order of creation and not an *ad hoc* response to human sin.

It is possible to read the line otherwise. Suppose that Dante means to suggest that God has foreknown from all eternity that a human being, when given the chance to sin, will freely do so; hell has been divinely set up to be the eternal destination of those of us who never get over this disposition. I don't discount this reading, but I don't follow it either. And that is partly my excuse for taking up the theology of Dante after others—such as Singleton, Gilson, and especially Freccero—have already done such interesting things with it. I don't believe that too many commentators have done much with the idea that hell is original to creation and not part of a default plan. But I take that idea to be both central to Dante's vision of hell and essential to any vision of hell that wishes to be free of revenge fantasies and tragic pathos.

My meditation falls into three parts. The first is on the scandal of hell, or the difficulty of conforming hell to a model of retributive justice. The next two take up Dante more directly and his alternative theology of hell. The first of these sections, itself divided in two parts, is largely a reading of the *Inferno* and especially of the figure of Virgil, Dante's designated tour guide through hell. Understanding Virgil's authority and place in hell goes a long way towards understanding the theology that animates the text as a whole. My last section continues my reading of the *Inferno*, but gives more attention to the broader implications and interests of the theology that has been emerging.

I. The Scandal of Hell

In one of the testier sections of *The Genealogy of Morals*, Nietzsche accuses Dante of having committed "a crude blunder," albeit one of "terror-inspiring ingenuity," in making this a part of the inscription over hell's gateway: "I too was created by eternal love."[2] Can love be a motive for hell's creation? Dante would have been more justified, suggests Nietzsche, had

---

1. Whenever I quote Dante, I will be using Pinsky's translation (1994). My method of referencing quotations will be to give canto, page, and line number(s), in that order.

2. Section 15 of the first essay of the *Genealogy*, trans. Kaufmann (1967). Nietzsche is paraphrasing rather than quoting the *Inferno*, where the relevant part of the inscription reads (3.19.4–5): "Justice moved my high maker, in power divine, wisdom supreme, love primal."

A Meditation on Hell

he placed over the gates of paradise, "I too was created by eternal *hate*." For what other than hatred would move the blessed or those aspiring to be blessed to relish the spectacle of the never-ending torment of their enemies—the so-called enemies of God?

I take it that Dante's blunder is crude in that he has disguised a terrible truth with only a transparent veil and so would have, from an aesthetic point of view at least, done better without the veil. As matters stand, he has tactlessly disclosed what is for Nietzsche the open secret about hell: that the place is the favorite fiction of resentful moralists. The "terror-inspiring ingenuity" of Dante's blunder is, I assume, its unwitting insight into what Nietzsche is attempting painstakingly to reveal in a genealogical study. Nietzsche discounts the idea that Christian moral values have their source either in eternal reason or the immutable will of God and returns them to a human history—a history driven in no small part by dark forces of fear, anger, hatred, and deceit.

Although I don't happen to share Nietzsche's judgment, either about Dante or the significance of hell, I readily concede that he has uncovered a common and all-too-human motive for wanting hell to exist. It is a natural human desire—call it an appetite of will—to want to win rather than lose and even to crave the contest that makes winning or losing an issue. We tend over time to define our individual selves against challenges that come from those we deem like us in some way, a form of individuation that is often benign. The desire for hell can be read as a distortion or perversion of a basic human desire for competitive recognition. Healthy competition depends on there being some form of individuation at work for those competing that is *not* fundamentally competitive; otherwise, to lose to another is to lose part of oneself to another; it is to be hurt. If more than being defeated by my opponent, I am hurt, I may react by wanting to hurt my opponent in turn. If I am sufficiently aggrieved by the hurt and take it as an offense, I may want to see my opponent, who is now clearly my enemy, suffer endlessly. I consign my enemy, in thought if not in deed, to a hell that reflects my own feeling of having been wounded beyond hope of redemption.

Admittedly this reading of the doctrine of hell, as the resentful projection of a wounded psyche, is very cynical. It assumes that the traditional apology for hell—that it answers to a principled demand for just retribution or punishment for sin—is so bankrupt that no other explanation for hell's appeal other than a darkly psychoanalytic one will do. As will become clear over the course of this essay, I believe that the doctrine of hell has a theological integrity that resists reduction to the psychology of resentment or to any kind of psychology that tries to do without a theological perspective. Nevertheless, I share Nietzsche's suspicion of retributive justice and doubt whether a doctrine of hell based on such justice could be other than some sort of deceit. Granting that justice can sometimes be retributive in aim (and I wouldn't normally grant this), a retributively conceived hell would be a theological disaster area.

Consider that the basic logic of retribution is that of proportionate harm. I harm you culpably, and so I am justly made to suffer the same degree of harm (an eye for an eye, a tooth for a tooth, and so on). If I am made justly to endure an unending life of torment, the implication is that I have caused you to suffer irredeemably. So how can you be said to be other than in a kind of hell yourself? By the very logic of retribution, a retributively conceived hell implies a "heaven" of perpetual victims. In truth there would be no heaven to set against a hell of retribution; there would only be two kinds of hell, the one readily convertible to the other—the hell of having to hate others and the hell of having to hate oneself. I suppose one could say in response that all sins are ultimately against God, not other people, but then God by the logic of retribution would have to be vulnerable to irredeemable harm.

It is worth noting here that some of the recent defenders of the doctrine of hell have given up on retribution.[3] Their revised logic of hell, based on the absolute good of human freedom, goes something like this. Souls are in hell not because God has forced them to reside there, to serve out an eternal sentence, but because they have chosen to be there, and God, out of a moral or metaphysical imperative, respects that choice. God's imperative would be moral if it should turn out that a coerced redemption is of even less value than a freely chosen damnation; it would be metaphysical if the idea of a coerced redemption should turn out to be incoherent and therefore beyond the pale of possibility. On one view of freedom—usually referred to as "libertarian"—it is simply a contradiction to speak of the cause of freely willed act. So in a libertarian's hell, which is the one most likely these days to get a philosophical hearing, the damned have the final word on their damnation. God cannot save the damned against their will without in the process violating their humanity in some fatal way.

The libertarian conception of freedom is not uncontroversial (I do not myself subscribe to it), but even if it were, it is hard to fathom what

---

3. See, for example, Swinburne (1983), Stump (1986), Walls (1992), and Kvanvig (1993).

would move a person freely to will a permanent break from God. Of course, one can imagine a person wanting to break from God thinking that some kind of good is served by it (the good of autonomy, say), but if a person were to see that God is, as most theologians claim, the source of all good, the choice for a break would be unaccountable. Thomas Talbott has advanced this kind of incomprehension against the libertarian apology for hell. His basic rejoinder to the apologists is that no one would choose to be in hell except on the basis of a delusion that a loving God would have sufficient motive to correct.[4]

Although I have a good deal of sympathy for Talbott's point of view, I am not prepared, as he is, to reject the doctrine of hell altogether. There are certainly bad reasons for believing in hell, and most all of them, I would wager, frame God's justice retributively. The libertarian conception of freedom allows the apologist for hell to avoid the appeal to retributive justice—the move Nietzsche castigated as resentful and weak—and play up the value of integrity of will, or the inviolate capacity of a free being to act for itself, even unto damnation. The merit of this strategy is twofold: it keeps reflection on hell from having to postulate two contrary dispositions in God—one of gratuitous mercy, the other of strict justice—and it suggests that self-determination, when exercised independently of God's will, is what lands a human being in hell. I think that both of those points are theologically apt.

Still I feel bound to reject the libertarian apology for hell, though for reasons that take me to a different conception of hell—Dante's—and not to a moral condemnation of the doctrine. The libertarian apology makes it seem as if the independence of the human will from the divine will is simply a constitutional requirement of freedom. And if freedom is really like that, I don't see much point in talk about the will's redemption. The value of the will that is presupposed here—its absolute liberty of choice—can neither be lost nor redeemed as long as there is a will to speak of. I can't say that I am not myself tempted by the thought that not even God can take from me my power of self-definition, for in this thought I become, in

---

4. Talbott (1990). Talbott has an ancillary argument against hell's apologists, which he develops only in brief and which I will mention only in passing. If it were conceded that responsible people could conceivably will to damn themselves, then, claims Talbott, God would have compelling reason to prevent them from doing so, even if it meant interfering with their freedom. The issue for the libertarian, however, is not whether God *ought* to interfere with a person's freedom to refuse redemption but whether God *can* and still in some interesting way be redeeming the person. In that Talbott never offers an analysis of or an alternative to libertarian freedom, his ancillary argument is at best question begging.

effect, the author of my own being. And I don't mean by this that I think to create myself literally out of nothing. I mean that I am tempted to identify myself with an absolute power of will: never to have to accept the value of what is given, always to be able to refuse a claim to value.

Like most temptations, this one has its element of truth and its element of delusion. The delusion is to suppose that the human will, or perhaps only the will to sin, is an autonomous power, free of the authority of divine law. The truth that this delusion distorts is of the genuine and legitimate good of self-determination. As far as I can conceive, human beings cannot be persons of any kind unless they have some power to determine the persons they become. The question here, however, is of how best to conceive of this determination. If the tempting thought of an absolute but humanly available power of will is given credence, then self-determination will seem to require a human exodus from the created order and its laws, or at least the possibility of one. This is to tie human freedom essentially to the will to sin.

When Dante attributes hell's eternal motivation to a trinity of divine virtues—justice, wisdom, and love—he suggests that the entire divine will, and not only a portion of it, is invested in what he imagines hell to be. Nietzsche took Dante's suggestion to betray the imagination of someone who resented others for their natural superiority and so had to invent a place where superior strength of will and spirit would be punished by a God who (ironically) sided with weakness. I take Dante to be suggesting that strength or freedom of will, if defined in opposition to the divine will, is an illusion; it doesn't exist even in hell, the place traditionally imagined to be God-forsaken. Where Nietzsche reads Dante's hell to indulge a conceit, I read it to expose one. We may take comfort or solace from the thought of being eternally divided from other human beings, either because we deem them or ourselves unworthy of further association, but there is no way to move from that thought to a vision of real damnation or redemption. Dante's hell is designed to expose the conceit of assuming otherwise. If we think we can tell who belongs in hell, we blindly usurp a divine prerogative of judgment and deceive ourselves about the freedom we have to take leave of others. Dante offers nothing to assure us that the conceit of a humanly contrived hell can't last forever; he simply shows us its hopelessness.

I recognize that my basic reading of Dante is apt to seem opposed to what is arguably the canonical reading of the *Inferno*: that its carefully crafted hierarchy of sin and punishment—the art of the *contrapasso*—is poetic justice, a matter of the punishment fitting the crime. I am *not* denying that there is often, if not always, an uncanny fit between punishment and sin in the poem, to the effect that the punishments bring the sins into relief and allow them to be read. What I deny is that Dante is theologically committed in the *Inferno* both to the propriety and the interminability of divine retribution—a conjunction Nietzsche did well to render suspect. For the rest of my essay I will try to make good on an alternative reading.

II. Hopeless Desire and the Sin that Is None

Virgil in Hell

My reading of the *Inferno* centers on the figure of Virgil, who is cast by Dante to be his guide and mentor throughout the tour of hell and (though beyond my purview) for a good bit of the way up Mount Purgatory. I follow most scholars of Dante, but especially John Freccero,[5] in holding to the importance of the distinction between the narrator's perspective (the poet who is telling the story) and that of his protagonist (the poet who is living it). These are two points of view within a single life. In bringing them together, Dante is telling us, "This is who I was." Self-disclosure of this kind is inescapably ironic. A self is claimed in the very act of taking leave of it: "This is me, but me no longer." Virgil is there to help the protagonist of the *Inferno* with the leave-taking. We ought to wonder where Virgil gets his authority to do so—obviously from the poet of the *Divine Comedy*, but to stop there is to ignore altogether the theological interest of Dante's art.

Theological interest in Dante often takes the form of psychological perplexity. It is out of the soul's confusion, or more precisely, out of the soul's awareness of its own confusion, that space is cleared for a humanly unanticipated intelligibility to a life's journey. In the canto that introduces both the *Inferno* and the *Comedy* as a whole, Dante famously puts himself "midway on our life's journey,"[6] where he is lost in dark and tangled woods and unable to recall how he came to enter there. The simplicity of his metaphor for spiritual confusion, as well as his decision to speak of his life in the plural (as *our*, not just *my*, life's journey), suggest Dante's intent

---

5. His major essays on Dante, from 1959 to 1984, are gathered together in Freccero (1986).

6. Pinsky (1994), 1.1.1.

to describe a journey that is in some sense everyone's.[7] For now I want to focus just on the commonality of the point of departure. The moment of departure is midway on life's journey. If we are in a position to know when our life has come to be and when it will cease, then "midway" means "half of the way" and Dante has in mind something like a midlife crisis. If we cannot presume to have a working knowledge of our life's limits, then "midway" has to mean "life that is already underway and not yet done." We live in the middle of life because there is no other place for us to be—not that we can see.

The midway crisis, whatever we take that moment to be, is most basically the loss of the right road, leaving the choice of a detour (an erring) or no movement at all. Being faced with this choice is perplexing. How does anyone come first to abandon the true and the good if not by the illusion of some false good? And if some false good, then hasn't the step off truth's path already been taken? Dante acknowledges the difficulty here of trying to recollect the first misstep, the fateful deviation, the original sin: "how I came to enter I cannot well say, being so full of sleep whatever moment it was I began to blunder off the true path."[8] Being full of sleep is already to have entered into the world of the dream, where the true and the false good are hard, if not impossible, to distinguish, and the right road is lost. Once in this world, Dante cannot locate himself by recalling the moment and motive of his entry. And so he proceeds by indirection. He will not try to fathom what good it was that lured him into dark woods. He will focus instead on trying to recollect the good he found there: "I feel the old fear stirring: death is hardly more bitter. And yet, to treat the good I found there as well, I'll tell what I saw."[9]

The retrospective posture of Dante's words suggest his perspective is that of the poet—the one done with waywardness—and not that of the protagonist, who is the source of the old fear. Ideally the task of recollection should fall to the poet-narrator. He is the one who knows the journey's end, and so he presumably is subject no longer to the errant disposition of his protagonist, his old self. It is only the protagonist, however, who has a clear motive for wanting to find the good in dark woods. The good is his way out. From the poet's perspective of retrospection, this same good is

---

7. This oft-made observation is magisterially developed in Singleton (1957); see the chapter on allegory.

8. Pinsky (1994), 1.3.7–10.

9. Ibid., 1.3.4–7.

more apt to seem like a way back in—hence the old fear stirring, a fear of becoming lost again, of returning to one's old and wayward self.

The ambivalence that fuels Dante's hesitations between an old self and a new one has everything to do with the figure of Virgil. For in an obvious way, Virgil just is the good that Dante resolves in the face of fear to remember. Think of the protagonist's plight in the opening scene of the drama. After wandering some in the trackless forest, his spirits lift at the sight of a hill whose slopes are "mantled in rays of that bright planet that shows the road to everyone, whatever our journey."[10] But his hope is short-lived. Three animals appear on the scene suddenly and in succession, straight out of some nightmare bestiary of the unconscious. They block the protagonist's ascent. An encounter with a leopard, spotted and wicked quick, eats up his morning; a lion, proud and defiantly hungry, comes next, presumably at midday. By the time the last animal is met— a grim and persistent she-wolf, whose leanness compressed a world of hunger—the day is nearly done, and the protagonist finds himself driven back to "where the sun is lost."[11] He realizes then that he has run out of light. Dante recalls the history of his inner states to that point: first hope yielded to fear, then fear to despair. Virgil arrives in deus-ex-machina fashion to relieve the younger poet of his despair and offer him, if not a way up, at least a way open. So on one side of Dante's ambivalence there is the Virgil who restores his hope in a time of despair; on the other there is the Virgil who is stuck forever in a hopeless place. In short, Dante loves a man in hell.

Dante's commentators and, I suspect, most of his sensitive readers have been keenly aware and not a little discomfited by the apparent fixity of Virgil's place in hell. How can Virgil know the way out of hell and yet still be condemned to remain in the limbo of the unbaptized? Or to put the question differently, why is Dante so damning of the very poet he took to be his poetic father? In more traditional commentaries Virgil ends up as an allegorical figure, less the Mantuan poet of the *Aeneid* than a disembodied persona of Reason. This is a reading that dulls the blow of Virgil's damnation. It isn't so much that a man is condemned; it is more that Reason, in its pretension to be redemptive, has been duly humbled. The problem with this reading is that the complexity of Dante's characterization is out of keeping with allegorical abstraction. More recent commentators, many of them influenced by Charles Singleton's development

10. Ibid., 1.1.14–15.
11. Ibid., 1.5.45.

of the notion of theological allegory, have tended to take Virgil's historicity for granted.[12] And when Dante's Virgil is taken to be first and foremost the historical Virgil, we are returned to the spectacle of Dante's ambivalence. Virgil is loved for his virtues and damned for his time of birth. He had the simple misfortune of living before Christ and serving the Rome of Caesar, not Peter and Paul. The best a modern interpreter can do, when convinced of the unyielding conservatism of Dante's theology, is to read tragedy into Virgil's infernal fate.[13]

My own view is that Dante's Virgil is neither a tragic nor an allegorical figure. He is basically what every other character is in the *Inferno*, with the exception of the protagonist: he is the incarnation of a particular kind of sin. Virgil is unique, however, in two respects. He is a figure who is particularly loved by Dante, and his sin, when seen through, undoes the illusion in other sorts of sin. I intend really two claims when I say that Virgil is loved by Dante—both that the character of Dante loves the character of Virgil (love as an artifice of the drama) and that the poet of the *Comedy* loves the poet of the *Aeneid* (love as a source of dramatic inspiration). The allegorical reading of Virgil's fate distances the character of Virgil from the man, out of a kind of sublime disinterest, and the tragic reading conflates the two, condemning the man for the character's flaw.[14]

The allegorical reading is wrong, not because it distances character from man, but because it cultivates the wrong kind of distance. Allegory banks on abstraction from the particular; if the Virgil of the *Inferno* is only loosely or accidentally connected to his historical inspiration, he can be taken to represent all kinds of lives and not just one in particular—a gain of universal meaning. This kind of logic, which is hard to assail in the abstract, is utterly disastrous in the context of the *Inferno*. It blinds the reader

---

12. In theological, as opposed to poetic, allegory, the literal sense of the narrative is not fictive. Singleton derives this distinction from Dante's *Convivio* and then offers his reading of the *Comedy* as theological allegory. "With its first meaning as an historical meaning," he writes (1957), p. 93, "the allegory of the *Divine Comedy* is grounded in the mystery of the Incarnation."

13. Two examples of this: Ryan (1993), pp. 136–52, and Hollander (2001), pp. 114–21.

14. Hollander on Dante on Virgil (2001), p. 120: "For Dante, Virgil is the most welcome of sources, the most needed of poetic guides. It is simply impossible to imagine a *Comedy* without him. And no one before Dante, and perhaps very few after, ever loved Virgil as he did. At the same time there is a hard-edged sense of Virgil's crucial failure as poet of Rome, the city Dante celebrates for its two suns, Church and empire, but which Virgil saw only in the light of one (and perhaps even then not clearly). For Dante, that is his great failure."

A Meditation on Hell

to the monstrous irony of an incarnation of sin. There is no such thing, not literally, as sin incarnate; literally it would be nothing—an absence of body as well as soul. Here it is useful to remember one of the presuppositions of Dante's drama: all of the action in the *Inferno* takes place prior to the day of last judgment—prior, that is, to the time when the denizens of hell are reunited with their bodies. The physical torments described in hell are not, despite the appearances, the torments of suffering *bodies*. Only the protagonist in hell can be presumed to have a body, and here I am strongly inclined to think of the protagonist not simply as the character of Dante but as any reader of the *Inferno*. (Here is the one place, in other words, where an allegorical reading works.) Dante's challenge to the reader of hell—himself included—is to see through the various seductions of false incarnations (lies of the soul), so as to be prepared, after a struggle, to have a share in the one true one.

Virgil's incarnation in hell is no less illusory than all the others, and this is what the tragic reading of Dante's Virgil misses. The tragic reading weds Virgil to his body ahead of time (preempting the Last Judgment) and tragically cannot imagine his incarnation other than damningly. But is it ever humanly necessary or fitting to anticipate a final judgment? If Dante is read to think so, his vision of hell will come across as a preview of who will end up there, and we who follow along with him will be tempted to second-guess his prescience. It strikes me, however, that the *Inferno* is the least prophetic of texts. It isn't giving us a foretaste of the afterlife of the wicked; it is showing us the limits of a retributive imagination. Assume that the wicked inevitably suffer and that some of them suffer without end. (I don't think that Dante is denying either possibility.) It still wouldn't follow that any one of us has a particularly good imagination for what this suffering is or when it is a person's only possibility. To assume otherwise makes for bad prophecy and worse.

The last line of hell's inscription reads as follows: "Abandon all hope, you who enter here."[15] This can and mostly has been read as a counsel of despair. It lets the damned know what not to expect of life in hell: that it ever comes to any good. The hopelessness of life in hell should be reason enough, then, for anyone to leave. So why isn't it taken to be so by hell's denizens? If Dante were tailoring his vision of hell to fit a retributive paradigm, the question would clearly be out of place. In a hell of retribution no one is *allowed* to leave; wanting to leave would just be an additional torment. But Dante doesn't set up his hell that way. To the souls in the

---

15. Pinsky (1994), 3.19.7.

Inferno, hell is a place where God is not and therefore a place where there is nothing from God to fear. Those who enter do so willingly. Dante speaks of his having seen a throng of souls crowded on Acheron's shore, clamoring for passage into hell's dominion. Virgil glosses the image for him as follows: "My son, here are joined the souls of all who die in the wrath of God, from every country, all of them eager to find their way across the water—for the goad of divine justice spurs them so, their fear is transmuted into desire."[16] Souls who desire some good of hell, whether it be freedom from punishment or some antinomian pleasure, are either discounting hell's imperative of hopelessness or aren't noticing it at all.

Of the two souls who do notice the imperative, Virgil and Dante, only Virgil reads the imperative to suggest a motive for entering hell. It suggests to him a test of courage: "All fear must be left here," he tells Dante, "and cowardice die."[17] That is a heady and heroic-seeming way to face hopelessness, and at first Dante acquiesces to its desperate appeal. But in the poet's recollection of how his journey would unfold, it isn't courage that finally allows his errant self exit from hell, but a certain kind of practical wisdom. He eventually comes to realize that any image of virtue in hell—the courage of his guide included—is bound to be fatally misleading. It leads to no good, to absence. This ending is never easy to see, except perhaps in the abstract, where the seer stands outside of sin altogether and so sees in sin nothing at all. But who can lay claim to such a view? Not the poet of the *Inferno* and even less the self whose passage through hell he is attempting to recall. Dante's task of recollection here, like that of his journey forward, is to be a good reader of signs. If he reads them well, they will convey to him hell's utter barrenness and therefore his lack of any motive for being there. In short, hell's imperative to abandon hope, etched in eternal stone over its gateway, needs finally to be read for what it is: neither a counsel of despair nor a test of courage, but an invitation to leave.

In my concluding section, I will say more about Dante's exit from hell and how it may (and may not) be said to differ from Virgil's. Although Virgil and Dante emerge from hell together, Virgil leaves Dante for good in canto XXVII of the *Purgatorio*; the strong presumption of most readers is that Virgil ends where he began, in the circle of hell designated for him and his kind. I am more inclined to think that any presumption about Virgil's ultimate fate is itself presumptuous. I prefer instead to focus on the larger issue of whether Dante's vision of hell, when viewed without

16. Ibid., 3.25.100–105.
17. Ibid., 3.19.11–12.

resort to either the consolation of tragic pathos or the dark pleasure of retribution, leaves something for hell to be. I think that it does, and that is what makes Dante's achievement—both poetic and theological—so remarkable. For the remainder of this section, however, I want to keep the focus still on Virgil and now with an eye to his sin.

Virgil's Sin

The infernal Virgil—and by that I mean simply the Virgil whom one meets in the *Inferno*—does not believe that he *has* sinned. To hear him tell of it, his torment in hell is the one truly pitiable fate there and so is deserving of some sympathy. He is, he imagines, part of a unique and exclusive circle of hell's own, that of the great pagan figures of antiquity, poets and philosophers among them, who have been condemned for their bad luck and not for their vices. Souls in other circles of hell, who ride the tide of fear and antinomian hope, have only their vices to blame for their torment; indeed, their vices are a great part of their torment. Virgil will admit at most to having an accidental vice, born of circumstance. Because he did not live to know of Christ's advent in the world, he never learned the right way to worship. But it is far from clear what kind of fault Virgil takes this to be.

When characterizing the suffering of those in his circle, Virgil alludes to the dubious sin of being uninformed about the religion of Christ: "Through this, no other fault," he notes, "we are lost."[18] But when he adds the punishment to this fault, his words suggest something other than an indictment of sin: "we are lost, afflicted only this one way: that having no hope, we live in longing."[19] It is certainly plausible to take him to mean that good people, for no other cause than an ill-fated birth, have been denied hope of the ultimate good and that they suffer in hell only because they prefer a hopeless seeking of the good to no search at all. That is, I would venture, just about the noblest kind of punishment anyone has ever imagined. The sin of Virgil and his kind looks remarkably like courage.

It is hard to see what darker possibility of sin lurks behind the veneer of Virgil's courage, but that is as it should be. Dante's art respects the fact that sin is often hard to read. And even when some sin has the clear markings of vice, as we see in more violent acts of self-aggrandizement and hatred of others, it may yet seem that there is some profit in vice. The metaphysical truth that sin is no good, a ticket to nonbeing, is usually hard

18. Ibid., 4.28–29.30–31.
19. Ibid., 4.29.31–32.

to credit in the face of some particular sin. In Virgil's case, the veneer of his goodness in hell is so thick that commentators simply take him at his word when he describes his own sin, or really non-sin. When I advocate a reading that is more cynical than this, I am not hoping to psychoanalyze a Virgil who is, when all is said and done, a character in Dante's fiction, nor am I implying that Dante had some deep and unacknowledged Oedipal resentment against the man who inspired his fiction.[20] My intent is to follow the logic of Dante's characterization of Virgil as it is set and shaped within the theological logic of the *Inferno* as a whole. Based on the broader logic of the narrative, we should expect the infernal Virgil to be most misleading when speaking of his own sin, and we should further expect that what misleads there misleads elsewhere.

Both expectations, I believe, are borne out. When Virgil tells us that it is his fate, in effect, to be forever brave in the knowledge that he will always be denied sight of the ultimate and perfect good, he does not tell us what the other good is that his courage is so bent on protecting. Here reconsider, with some suspicion, Virgil's description of his sin and its torment. The hopelessness of his infernal life is not his fault; God has chosen to be alien to him. He, on the other hand, resolves never to capitulate to the evil of despair. The picture is of a virtuous man, unbroken by suffering, steadfastly defending his integrity against arbitrary power. One thinks of Job here, but where Job aims to defend himself *before* God, Virgil is defending himself, albeit discreetly, *against* God. For Virgil, unlike Job, has no desire to learn the ways of God from God. He already knows why he has been damned; it is because right worship and ritual is more important to God than desire for the truth—a view that makes God out to be superstitious. Not far beneath the surface of Virgil's apology, then, is a cultured pagan's indictment of Christianity. Virgil, the seeker of truth, affects to defend himself against a God whose favor of one person over another is taken to be without reason.

It is in Virgil's circle that we find the amply lit and multiply fortified castle of the liberal arts, the only place in hell having its own source of illumination. We can take it for granted, I think, that Dante is not

---

20. I am not in principle against psychoanalytic readings of authors and their characters. Authors have psyches after all, and their fictions—if they are good ones—are invested with psychological complexity. My worry here is that the Oedipal reading of Dante's Virgil makes too little of Dante's theology. Harold Bloom, who is happy to make little of Dante's theology, offers an ingeniously Oedipal reading of Dante in *Ruin the Sacred Truths* (1989). Bloom, I should add, is not uninterested in theology; it is just that his theology happens to be literature. He looks to writers of the sublime—Dante among them—for knowledge instead of faith, Self instead of God.

using the image to cast doubt on the value of education or to condemn reason. Far more likely his image suggests a walling-off of classical ideals of wisdom from new sources of inspiration. Reason isn't being defended in hell's circle of philosophers and poets (but no philosopher-poets); it is being entombed. Possibly this is Dante's way of defending Christianity and its scandalous insistence on a crucified God from cultured pagan disdain, but I am more persuaded that Dante has a less partisan moral in mind. It is after all part of Virgil's self-presentation, when speaking of his own sin, to offer the view that sin can be solely a matter of being in the wrong party. If this were Dante's view too, there would be nothing about the virtues of his Virgil that he should want to exclude from his own developing character, from the Dante that is destined to meet up with Dante. And if there is nothing worth excluding, then it is wholly arbitrary of Dante to give his own character but not Virgil's poetic access to a narrative of redemption. Dante would be saving himself for no better reason than God has for picking Dante over Virgil—according to the infernal Virgil, for no better reason than no reason at all. If this Virgil is to be believed, then Dante has reason to revisit hell endlessly. For he will always be drawn to the poet who is abandoned there, as the one true good that heaven lacks. (And the poet left in hell is either Virgil or Dante himself, the distinction between them having become moot.) The theology of the whole *Comedy* is at stake in Virgil's fate. Is there, upon closer reading, a way for Dante justly to take leave of his Virgil? I ask this without assuming—in fact I explicitly do not assume—that a case against the infernal Virgil is a case against Virgil the man.

Against the infernal Virgil at least this much can be ventured. Virgil sins not because he has come to the wrong view of God, but because his confidence in his own rectitude has left him without a God to seek. Those who, like Virgil, suppose that being mistaken is their only fault are bound to make their own integrity their highest good. They will tend to surround themselves with those who confirm their rectitude; the rest they exclude. The first circle of hell enshrines a partisan wisdom and rejects humility as weakness; it should come as no surprise then that Virgil, its representative at large, can think of God in no other than a partisan way.

A good indication that the infernal Virgil has more to do with sin than with classicism is that he ends up misrepresenting both the ethics of Aristotle and the plan of hell itself at a key juncture in the narrative. It is commonly assumed, largely based on what Virgil recounts in canto XI, that the hell of Dante's invention is set up to punish three kinds of sin, whose circles are arranged in groups of descending order and along a path of increasing gravity—the farther down a circle is, in other words, the more dire its sin. The extreme depth of hell is at the center of the earth, where Satan is fixed. It is further assumed that each of the three kinds of sin corresponds to one of the beasts that show up to torment and frustrate Dante's errant self.

Provisionally let's take the leopard, the first of the beasts encountered, to signal a love to deceive, either oneself or someone else. This is the love that hates truth. Let's then take the lion, the next beast to appear, to represent an intemperate love of triumph, or the desire to have one's will vindicated at any cost. Finally, the last and most wretched of the beasts, the she-wolf, can be taken to convey the desire to have it all, where "all" means whatever is conceivably an object of desire. In short order we will have reviewed the three determinants of human psychopathology: a deluded mind, a wounded will, and an insatiable appetite. I believe that my provisional reading of the three beasts and what they represent is in keeping with how the psychology of sin unfolds throughout the rest of the *Inferno*. Nevertheless, in canto XI, Virgil offers a perplexed Dante (and a perplexed reader) a different key to the psychology of hell's threefold partitioning, one supposedly cut from book VII of the *Nicomachean Ethics*. "Don't you recall a passage in your *Ethics*," Virgil asks Dante, "the words that treat three dispositions counter to Heaven's will: incontinence, malice, insane brutality? And how incontinence is less distasteful to God, and earns less blame?"[21]

Virgil implies that of the three dispositions he mentions, incontinence is the least grave and most lightly punished, whereas insane brutality is extremely bad and merits the harshest treatment. The picture is not especially Aristotelian. The condition in Aristotle that is supposed to correspond to "insane brutality" (*la matta bestialitade*)—or alternately translated, "mad bestiality"—is for Aristotle not even a condition of vice. The insanely bestial person is a barbarian, or someone whose horrific and unnatural acts indicate a complete lack of reason. (Bestial persons act more like beasts than human beings.) By contrast the vicious person in Aristotle is someone in whom reason is still present, but perverted. This person does wicked things, reasoning that wicked things are good. There is a logic and articulation to wickedness that is lacking in pure brutality.[22]

21. Pinsky (1994), 11.89.77–82.

22. Aristotle encapsulates the contrast between vice and bestiality in *Nicomachean Ethics* 1150a. See Irwin (1985), p. 189. In a vicious person the part of the soul that calculates and chooses is corrupted; in a bestial person this part is altogether absent.

A Meditation on Hell

So where Aristotle marks a category shift or difference in kind (vice to bestiality), Virgil stays within the boundaries of vice and observes a difference in degree (malice to insane brutality).

What's important to notice here, however, is not that Virgil misreads Aristotle, but that Virgil's quasi-Aristotelian reading of hell is very favorable to the likes of a Virgil.[23] Consider the sins that Virgil deems the least grave, the ones falling under the Aristotelian category of incontinence, or *akrasia*. Those who suffer from this condition know what the good is, but cannot bring themselves to choose what they know. Their appetites subvert their reason, and they become lustful, gluttonous, slovenly, and the like. If we go with this picture of sin-lite—a phenomenon of unruly appetite—then those in Virgil's circle of hell are better than even the mildest and most well intentioned of the sinners. There is no war between appetite and reason in Limbo. There is only an appetite for the good that goes hopelessly begging. And it goes begging not because the good souls of Limbo desire something other than the good, but because the good that they desire has been withheld from them. Not only, then, is their suffering noble; it is the very mark of a temperate or virtuous soul.

It turns out that Virgil is a particularly bad reader of the sins that are the closest to him. The sins associated with the she-wolf, the sins of appetite, simply do not correspond to Aristotelian *akrasia* or what the medievals referred to as *incontinentia*. There are at least two good indications of this, both conveyed by the figure of the she-wolf. First, it is late in the day when the she-wolf arrives to block Dante's path to illumination, and her effect is decisive. Dante loses his resolution to continue. If the she-wolf were simply a bearer of unruly appetite, she should come first, as a sign of a lack of discipline. Second, the condition of hopeless desire—the condition that describes both the hunger of the she-wolf and Virgil's punishment in Limbo—is already far removed from incontinent desire, where

---

That difference makes bestiality, in Aristotle's judgment, less evil than vice, but more alarming.

23. Not everyone agrees, in any case, that Dante's Virgil is misreading Aristotle. See Triolo (1998) on canto XI. Triolo observes that Dante inherited a tradition of interpretation that allowed Aristotelian bestiality to be thought of as an intensification of malice or vice. "Thus 'bestiality,'" writes Triolo, "to which Dante prefixed the adjective 'mad,' is simultaneously a disposition in its own right and an extreme form of the malice of intemperance" (p. 159). I am in no position to quarrel with Triolo's knowledge of the medieval tradition of Aristotle's reception, but what he has just described makes no sense. Bestiality can't be both a vice and not a vice. It is either a vice, or it is a disposition in its own right. Aristotle himself is quite clear that bestiality and vice (or intemperance) are different.

hope resides in knowing what is ultimately of value. The she-wolf, it would seem, values nothing other than appeasing her own hunger, but as Virgil himself notes, "her nature is so malign and vicious she cannot appease her voracity, for feeding makes her hungrier."[24]

Virgil is describing a strange kind of hunger, one that takes hunger as its own end. The hunger for hunger is, in one sense, the desire to have a body and be released from the isolation of a needless perfection. In another sense, hunger of this sort is an imprisonment of soul and a refusal of the body's death and resurrection. In the *Inferno* it is the damning side of the she-wolf's desire that matters. Virgil can describe the desire and call for its end, but he cannot see what is damning about it. Instead he clings to a life of hopeless longing and embraces the very hunger he decries. For what is the difference, finally, between a resolutely hopeless desire for the good and a hunger that is closed in upon itself? To take leave of the infernal Virgil and his deadly kind of integrity, it is necessary to face the she-wolf not just at the beginning of one's wandering but also at the end. It is to that ending in the *Inferno* that I now turn.

III. Hopeless Justice and the End of Desire

The last image of hell is of a tower of hunger. A three-headed Satan stands at hell's center, fixed up to his waist in ice, each mouth of each head raking the skin off the back of a betrayer. Satan derives no satisfaction from his endless meal. The more he eats, the more he is moved to grieve. "He wept with all six eyes," recalls Dante, "and the tears fell over his three chins mingled with bloody foam."[25] Does Satan weep because he has been defeated by a more powerful adversary, or does he lament having lost forever the love of God? Or is there yet another reason for his suffering? Dante doesn't speculate. This is the point at which his character is no longer tempted to enter into a hopeless, gnawing desire. He and Virgil remain literally and figuratively on the outside. Dante holds onto Virgil, and Virgil grasps the matted hair and ice of Satan's frozen flank. The two of them scale down the tower of hunger, pass though the center of creation, and then come to see that from an altered perspective a way down can be a way up. They reach the sight of stars together.

So at the end of a difficult journey into darkness, with imperfect guidance, there is finally some illumination. It is not the bright light of

---

24. Pinsky (1994), 1.7.74–76.
25. Ibid., 34.297.54–55.

A Meditation on Hell

the sun, but, then again, it is only the kindness of the night that allows a plurality of suns to be seen—a vision of an illuminated community. I want to raise two questions about the illumination won. What light does it shed retrospectively on the significance of hell, as Dante has conceived of the place? And what about Virgil? If he is as imperfect a guide as I have made him out to be, he ought to have been left behind to languish in hopelessness. Instead he carries Dante piggyback out of the depths of darkness. A tragic poet lifts up the poet of redemption. The irony is comic.[26]

Since both of my questions have something to do with getting beyond hopeless desire, it would be convenient if desire could speak for itself. Then we would know what it wanted and could invest or divest ourselves accordingly. Dante's Satan never speaks, and so there is no help directly there. But in the penultimate scene of the poet's progress, a talking hunger is encountered, and satanic hunger, rage, and grief come through in an all-too-human voice. It is at the end of canto XXXII that Virgil and Dante stumble upon the spectacle of two souls stuck neck-deep in ice, the exposed head of one gnawing fixedly on the exposed nape of the other, "the way," observes Dante, "the starving devour their bread."[27] Dante notices anger in the hunger—a "bestial hatred" he calls it. In this image of a perversely conjoined humanity, two of sin's beasts are immediately apparent: insatiable appetite (the she-wolf) and an angry will (the lion). If the third is there as well—a deluded mind (the leopard)—then Dante will have before him a consummate image of sin.

The ideal way to face any sin, I suppose, is to see through it and be drawn to the good it has absented from view. If this were easy to do, then all ascents to wisdom would be free of detours, and no Dante would ever need his Virgil. But even when sin loses its appeal, it almost always retains some claim to be a lesser good—a consolation, if not the prize. So before the wanderer in hell can take his leave of the place, he must face a final temptation: the temptation to affirm life in hell as a lesser good, a consolation for love's failure. The failure can take many forms, but one of the most potent—imagined of God himself—is the failure of a parent's love to protect a child from harm. God lost a son. Count Ugolino, whose shade gnaws bestially at the head of his enemy, Archbishop Ruggieri, lost two sons and two grandsons. He is undoubtedly not the first human being to feel he has more cause for grievance than God. He tells Dante's character his story.

---

26. For a wonderful discussion of the redemptive significance of Dante's kind of comedy, see the essay on comedy in Agamben (1999).

27. Pinsky (1994), 32.281.127.

Parting Knowledge

In life Ugolino and Ruggieri were sometime allies but eventual enemies. While pretending alliance, Ruggieri conspired with the Ghibelline leadership of Pisa to have Ugolino—whose Ghibelline loyalty was suspect already—imprisoned in a tower, along with his two sons and two grandsons. Ugolino refers to the tower as "Hunger's Tower." He tells Dante that it was named after him, for there he and his children all starved to death.

In recounting his story, Ugolino skips over the details of what had consumed him in life—the political scheming that was to bring down his house—and harps instead on the suffering of his children. Evidently Ugolino wishes to suggest a world of difference between his enemy and himself. Ruggieri never gave a thought to innocent suffering, whereas Ugolino now spends an eternity devoted to avenging its cause. If this is to be believed, then hell really does have its distinctions of rank and nobility and an in-house order of virtue. Ugolino may be a sinner in his own eyes, and rightly punished, but he also sees himself as an agent of justice, a bringer of righteous retribution.[28] Consoling for him, but is it true? Here truth rests on the durability of the difference between Ugolino and Ruggieri, and more particularly, on whether Ugolino's vengeance is truly a memorial to the suffering of innocents. There are hints in what Ugolino recounts, in his *manner* of recounting, that suggest the contrary.

He reports having had a strange dream while locked in the tower, a dream about a wolf and its whelps being hunted down and devoured by lean hounds. It is an image that recalls a prophecy of Virgil's from canto I, where Virgil speaks of the day when the Hound of God will arrive to give the ravenous she-wolf her painful death.[29] The image of a wolf's defeat is of no more use to Ugolino, however, than it is to Virgil, who, like Ugolino, thinks of divine victory in terms of superior force. Ugolino sees his defeat by an adversary who got the better of him, and nothing more. He awakens from his dream to the cries of his children for bread. And when it begins to dawn on his children that their father is wholly preoccupied with his own hunger and has no idea of how to respond to theirs, they offer to feed him instead. Ugolino recalls their words: "Father, our pain will lessen if you eat us—you are the one who clothed us in this wretched flesh: we plead for you to be the one who strips it away."[30] To Ugolino, whose hunger is hardly the sort that responds to sacrificial love, the words amount to no more than the

---

28. The parallel between Dante's Count Ugolino and Dostoevsky's Ivan Karamozov is inviting. Ivan also fashions himself a damned champion of the religion of retribution, whose first commandment is to avenge the suffering of innocent children.

29. Pinsky (1994), 1.7.77–87.

30. Ibid., 33.287.56–59.

offer of a gruesome meal. He keeps silent for six days, one shy of a creative cycle, or the time it takes for all of his children to die of hunger. One of them, Gaddo, cries of being forsaken before he dies at his father's feet: "Father, why don't you help me?"[31] And then for two days Ugolino calls out names over corpses. After that—was it on the third day?—he meets his end. "The hunger," he admits to Dante, "had more power than even sorrow had over me." Those words end his story; the infernal eating resumes.

Ugolino's parting words to Dante are ambiguous. Did he die of hunger or did he consume his children? In his case this is a difference without redemptive significance, for his kind of hunger is indifferent to the distinction between self and others. The other is seen to be just another part of the self—a part that exists, like the self it disjoins, to be consumed by desire. Ugolino has this telling recollection of a moment when a small ray of sunlight entered his cell and allowed him to see the faces of his children: "I made out in their four faces the image of my own; I bit my hands for grief."[32] He adds that his children mistook his grief for hunger. They were not so wrong.

When Dante first asks Ugolino to recount his reason for being so hungry for revenge, Ugolino hesitates: "You ask me to endure reliving a grief so desperate," he says, "the thought torments my heart even as I prepare to tell it."[33] But Ugolino tells his story with a vengeance once it occurs to him that his words may have as much bite as his teeth do. He speaks to defame his enemy and thus to continue his revenge by other means. Where grief comes into the picture is not at all clear. Revenge has been Ugolino's way not to acknowledge, and therefore not to have to mourn, the loss of his children, and he has given Dante no reason to hope that loveless justice can be anything other than the last metamorphosis of a blind hunger. Ugolino claims the moral authority of a bereft father, but it is impossible for him to have felt the loss of what he has never taken the time to love. His revenge, like his hunger, is oblivious.

Being loathe to imagine God as a more righteous and fatherly Ugolino, I am further disposed to think that it is not the cause of retribution that makes Dante conceive of hell as a place of divine wisdom, love, and justice. This should not be taken to imply, however, that the people in Dante's universe don't ultimately get what they deserve. I have no reason to deny Dante his faith in a providential order. But I do believe, based

31. Ibid., 33.289.65.
32. Ibid., 33.287.53–54.
33. Ibid., 33.285.4–7.

on my reading of the *Inferno*, that Dante thought people got their just deserts ultimately by getting what they *wanted*. The she-wolf's desire for a consumed good, the lion's for a defeated good, and the leopard's for a false good collectively frame the strange desire that animates the hell-bound soul: the desire for no good at all, or, put otherwise, the desire not to be. Is it really and truly possible for a soul to crave absolute nonbeing and not be chasing after some illusion of being? Like most human beings, I know something about illusions and their power to seduce, but also like most human beings, I don't know enough to be able to see past the illusions and into a despairing heart.

Let's suppose, though, that true despair is possible. It is for this possibility and perhaps for this possibility alone that hell exists—not to *punish* despair, but to allow it a place within the divine being. The only way to punish a soul for despair would be to force the despairing soul to continue to live. But if death in God can be life, despair in hell can be hope. That apparent paradox is at the heart of Dante's insight into the theology of hell; hell is not what we humans would make of it (an awful place, no doubt), but what God has made of it (a place to defeat the hope of the despairing).

In Dante's broader vision, the created order has been conceived to include all possibilities of being and nonbeing. These possibilities—heaven, hell, and the realms between them—are not a matter of human mastery, but divine governance. The human will has no special autonomy in matters of death and destruction, the beastly powers of sin notwithstanding. Practically speaking, the existence of hell means that we can neither ignore the possibility of despair in ourselves or others, nor presume to control it. But to acknowledge that possibility is emphatically not to wish hell on anyone. Only God knows how to invoke the hell that serves love, justice, and wisdom. And that hope of faith brings me back to Virgil and the fate of all imperfect guides.

It is part of Virgil's wisdom to know when he is no longer needed. In canto XXVII of the *Purgatorio*, he leads Dante to and through a purgatorial fire, reminds him of his destiny with Beatrice (the other love that inspires Dante's poetry), and exits in order to encourage Dante to follow his own will freely. Like any good teacher would, Virgil knows that taking leave of his student means admitting to his own limits as a teacher. Dante, after all, is not Virgil's creation, and it would be no homage to Virgil for Dante to think so. Neither one being the creator of the other, each has the chance to share in a common inspiration and therefore a common redemption. There is nothing in Dante's description of Virgil's leave-taking that suggests Virgil's confinement to hell, or the wholesale identification of Virgil with his infernal counterpart. Of course there is *some* connection between Virgil and the infernal Virgil, just as there is some connection between Dante and the infernal Virgil. The sin of arrogance is a live possibility for Virgil, Dante, and any human being who is tempted to think of wisdom and virtue as a personal possession. (Perhaps they are more like a personal responsibility, but even that way of putting it, I suspect, is misleading.) My point is that the connection between Virgil and his infernal counterpart is not essential. Dante is not consigning his beloved Virgil to hell, and certainly he is not consigning Virgil to hell because Virgil is a pagan, born before the time of Christ. The logic behind that kind of condemnation is exposed and subverted in canto IV of the *Inferno*. To accept the logic without irony is in effect to take Virgil's part and place in hell.

I much prefer the redemptive logic behind Virgil and Dante's mutual departure from a hopeless place. The logic follows the idea that nothing living is ever justly left behind by a sojourner in hell. Dante takes the living with him on the way out. Or he leaves alone and lives in the illusion that he won't have someday to return. The lesson to be learned here is not that hell is an illusion, to be dispelled by the power of human love, but that it is illusory to think that we can live by a distinction between who is redeemable and who is not and not fall into the very despair that makes a soul hell-bound. To illusion such as that, a God of love offers hopelessness. It is up to us to realize that, under the circumstances, there is nothing more to be wanted.

10

Myth and Moral Philosophy

THE BIGGEST MYTH IN moral philosophy is arguably the biblical myth of the Fall. I mean biggest in the sense of most influential. The idea that the moral life is to be measured against a lost beginning, a time when human beings were better than anyone is now in a position to remember, is one that has haunted the moral imagination of the West for millennia, mostly in its biblical form. There are other ways to read the biblical myth, of course, and other ways to mythologize a lost beginning. I will want to take a good look at one of these other ways—Plato's—before I offer my considered thoughts on why the biblical myth has been such a source of vexation and insight for moral philosophy. My way into the thick of the issue between myth and moral philosophy is through Kant and, more particularly, through Kant's moral interpretation of Genesis in one of his last and most controversial works, *Religion within the Boundaries of Mere Reason* (hereafter referred to simply as *Religion*).[1] As a moral philosopher of influence, Kant is big enough for my purposes.

I begin with a simple notion of myth, and it won't get much fancier as matters progress; the complexity of my argument resides almost entirely in the relation of myth to moral philosophy. I think of a myth as a story that is at least partly about divine or supernatural beings. I also have in mind the connotation of a myth as a false or childish story, but I don't subscribe to that view of the biblical myth or of many of the myths we may presume ourselves to have outgrown. Myth owes its connotation of falsehood in no small part to the cultural influence of science. It becomes harder to believe that stories about gods can be true in any straightforward

---

1. My references to Kant's text will be keyed to di Giovanni's translation (1998).

way once we are sure that we don't need divine help to be able to know things. If we are thus convinced, it doesn't necessarily follow that the old stories will be of no value to us. There are indirect ways of getting at the truth, ways that circumvent a story's apparent indifference to the facts as we have come to know them. I will call the effort of translating talk of gods into talk of values an attempt at demythologizing a myth.

It is important not to confuse demythologizing with debunking. We debunk the stories we hope to outgrow (like the one about the tooth fairy); we demythologize the ones we hope to carry with us, in some transformed way, into adulthood. Kant demythologizes the Genesis story in order to lay bare some of the difficulties in moving from a childish belief in a supernatural father figure of inscrutable will to a prudent and mature recognition of the divine or sublime nature of the moral law. If this is not to be a debunking, the story cannot be read to presuppose the truth of the childish belief. It must instead be credited with having a narrative structure subtle enough to suggest both the temptation of the childish belief and the means of transcending it. For Kant, it is only from the point of view of moral philosophy that it is possible to tell the difference between a morally subtle myth and a morally corrupt one.

There is a certain modest necessity for demythologizing in any reading of a myth. We have to stop and think about what the gods love and how they love it before we can have a good sense of what or who the gods are. But this is not a claim that makes the gods out to be different from human beings. We too are beings defined by what and how we love, but not always—if ever—transparently so. Kant's program of demythologizing makes essential use of the difference between divine and human disclosures of value. His gods (he calls them angels or bearers of a holy will) are beings of pure reason; they can no more will the contrary of what they value than they can not be gods. In this they are like ideals; they represent an absolute standard of conduct for beings, like us, who must struggle to be good. It is not the case for Kant, however, that a divine being is simply a human projection and personification of a moral ideal. The opposite is closer to his position. It is the moral ideal that gives shape and form to human personality; we are personified by it. Kant's God, the root power of the ideal to determine nature, is not very personal at all.

I confess that I fail to see what there is to be learned from most of the more ambitious attempts at demythologizing. If I go to the Bible looking for confirmation of the values I already hold dear on moral grounds, I come away feeling disappointed if I don't find them and vindicated if I do;

in neither case do my values change. Kant's attempt at demythologizing, though plenty ambitious, is not like most. The more he tries to demythologize the biblical text, the less transparent it becomes to moral reason, and yet he does not conclude from this that there is a better story, morally considered, to be told. Kant looks to myth for a representation of the *limits* to moral reason. It is hard to say whether success here should count as demythologizing a myth or remythologizing a philosophy. As it is the ambiguity that I find instructive, I turn to Kant's efforts without prejudice.

I. Kant and the Mystery of the Serpent

Not everyone who reads Genesis finds a fall described there. Those who do find a fall find it in the section of narrative that begins at Genesis 2:4b, the start of an apparently new creation story, and ends at Genesis 3:24, the expulsion of the first human couple from the garden of Eden. Biblical scholars attribute this section of Genesis to the Yahwist source, named for its characteristic use of the name Yahweh to name God. I am not going to speak directly to whether I think the Yahwist is telling the story of the Fall (for my answer would turn out to be, unhelpfully, yes and no); instead I will confine my attention to the Fall that Kant notices and then sets out to demythologize. But before I do that, I need to set the stage with some narrative details.

There are four principal characters in the Yahwist's tale of creation, in this order of appearance: Yahweh, the man, the woman, and the serpent. The man's name has been commonly assumed to be Adam, though in the Hebrew text "Adam" is not a proper name but the word for human being.[2] Yahweh creates the human being by forming him out of the clay of the earth and breathing life into his nostrils. There is a pun in Hebrew between *adam* and *adamah*, the word for "earth"; to be called human is to be recalled to one's earthly origins (as an earthling). Yahweh next places the human being in a cultivated garden, Eden, where two trees are singled out for special mention: the tree of life and the tree of knowledge, good and evil. The human being is to have the run of the garden, to watch over and till it, and may eat from any of the trees but one. Among Yahweh's first words to the human being is this prohibition (Gen 2:17): "From the tree of knowledge, good and evil, you shall not eat, for on the day you eat from it, you are doomed to die." The thought then occurs to Yahweh that it is

---

2. Robert Alter points this out in his translation and commentary on Genesis. See p. 5, n. 26. My citations of Genesis are all from Alter (1996).

bad for the human being to be alone and that he ought to have someone to sustain him. Yahweh's remedy is to fashion the woman out of a part of the human being (his rib). Once the woman is on the scene, we have humanity that is male and female. Indeed, it is not implausible to think of the creation of the woman more basically as the creation of sexual difference.

The serpent enters the narrative abruptly and tries to draw the woman into an apparent misreading of Yahweh's original prohibition (Gen 3:1): "Though God said, you shall not eat from any tree of the garden..." Before the serpent can finish the thought, the woman interjects that it is only the taste and touch of the fruit of the tree in the midst of the garden that is forbidden and brings death. It is worth noting that she names the tree by location, not type, and that both trees—life and knowledge—happen to be in the place she specifies. The serpent certainly encourages her to identify (or confuse) the two trees, first by cunningly implying that not eating of knowledge is like not eating at all, and second by telling her directly that it is not death but a divine point of view that comes of knowing. The result is that seeing becomes both the object and the expression of the woman's vivid desire: "And the woman saw that the tree was good for eating and that it was lust to the eyes and the tree was lovely to look at" (Gen 3:6). She eats with no apparent hesitation, and her male partner follows her lead. Eventually, Yahweh will expel the man and woman from Eden in order to prevent them from eating also of the tree of life (the two trees are apparently very different for Yahweh). Before that happens, the man will call the woman by the name of Eve. Her name in Hebrew sounds like the Hebrew verb meaning "to live"; there is also, for the etymologically promiscuous to ponder, a similarity between her name and the Aramaic word for serpent.[3]

I have passed over or touched lightly upon some of the details in the narrative that don't figure into Kant's reading of the Fall and included some that will become important only when I begin the work of revising Kant's reading. There are two key elements to his reading. One is his assumption that divine and moral law are essentially the same. Not only does this assumption govern his reading of the original prohibition in Genesis, it more generally establishes his authority as a moral philosopher to read and evaluate sacred texts. Kant's other assumption is that morally significant opposition to the divine law has to come from a divine and not merely a natural source, as if divinity were to carry within itself the principle of its own negation. The serpent will come to represent for him the demonic side of divinity (the anti-moral law), but the representation of

---

3. Alter (1996), p. 15, n. 20.

this can never be other than veiled. Kant's best efforts at demythologizing leave him laboring to fathom what has to be, by virtue of his two assumptions, the impossibly perverse wisdom of the serpent.

The two assumptions I have just mentioned are not unrelated. They are in fact the twin birth of a peculiarly Kantian psychological insight: that there is no possibility of freedom apart from a law of freedom. Kant proceeds from this insight to argue for only one law of freedom, the moral law. When Kant scholars seek to explicate his reasoning, they often focus on his two paradigmatic formulations of a purely practical imperative in *Groundwork of the Metaphysics of Morals*: (1) act so that your rule of acting can be willed as a universal law, and (2) act so that the humanity you and others share is always respected as an end and so never is reduced to a mere means. An imperative is purely practical if its reasonableness as a rule of acting is independent of the particular personalities involved; all that matters is that a capacity to reason be operative. I am going to forgo the usual preoccupation of the Kant scholar here—the question of whether either formulation of a purely practical imperative captures something essential about moral obligation—and fill out Kant's notion of the moral law in reference to the law that resists it.[4] Although Kant's official position is that there can be one and only one law of freedom, in *Religion* he comes very close to affirming the impossible possibility: an immoral law of freedom, or an imperative always to make immorality the end of one's actions. Impossibility in this context is neither physical nor logical, but practical. Unless I can assume that I was deliberating badly, I cannot make sense of myself as having acted against my interests as a free and rational being. An immoral law would actually bind my deliberation to acts of self-undermining. Hence this paradox: the more responsibility I take for the evil that I do, the less sense I will have of myself.

The paradox of the evil will is alive and well in Kant's representation of the serpent, but it is misleading, I think, to move immediately to a consideration of the paradox and whether it is real or contrived. For then the question of the evil will is apt to become, is it possible for someone to will evil for evil's sake? And that sounds like a question about how bad people can be. However illuminating a debate over this question may be—and I doubt whether it is ever *very* illuminating[5]—Kant is pursuing a different line of inquiry. His interest in the possibility of an anti-moral law proceeds

---

4. For those interested in the more traditional approach to Kant, I recommend Korsgaard (1996b). See especially her two essays "Kant's Formula of Universal Law" and "Kant's Formula of Humanity."

5. See chapter 8 of this volume, the section on the moral measure of forgiving.

quite naturally and without paradox from his disposition to think of freedom in terms of the will. We don't become conscious of having a will until we become conscious of having our will opposed. Wanting to overcome what opposes the will is what having a will is mostly about. The opposition, moreover, must be of a very particular sort.

Suppose that I am one of Kant's beings with a holy will, a good angel. It is in my nature as a holy being to be morally upright. But I am no more obligated to be moral by a moral law than an object in free fall is obligated to respect the law of gravity. It just does. If I can be said as a holy being to have any kind of will to be moral (and Kant would say that I do), it is will in an attenuated sense. Granted that nothing in me directly opposes my will to be moral, I may nevertheless experience opposition as coming from without. I am presuming here that I would have some interest as a holy being in promoting the moral development of less than holy beings, or beings who were morally inclined but imperfectly so. The opposition of these imperfect beings to my efforts on their behalf could conceivably give me some sense of my own will to be moral. That would depend on how much I have identified myself with those I am trying to serve.

But enough of angelic psychology. I am not in fact a holy being but a human being, and as a human being, I have a side of my nature that identifies with holiness and a side that does not. The side that does not supplies me with amoral desires and ambitions. If I were to reflect on what kind of being those amoral desires and ambitions define, I would come to a conception of a human being who has to compete with other human beings for its share of pleasure and recognition. The humanity of others would be merely a means to my own. The other side of my nature, my moral side, is what furnishes me with my will not to identify with humanity of that conception. Ideally I would like to have in view the alternative conception, the humanity that shows me how it is possible to perfect myself without having to diminish others, for then I would know what the good is that my will serves. Short of that ideal, I have to have in view the conception of humanity that I disown as debased. Notice that I cannot disown what I have not first identified with.

It is tempting when reading Kant to think of the body as the source of human imperfection. For if I didn't have a body to identify with, I wouldn't have a troublesome source of desire to disown; all my motives would be naturally rational, my will would be good by default, and I'd take my place among the angels as a matter of course. Kant's own view, however, is achingly more subtle than this. Although he certainly thinks of the body as a troublesome source of desire, he does not think of it as the agent of human corruption. The agent is a person's willingness to let bodily desire define personality. In other words, I give authority to the desires of mine that lock me into a humanity of one and ultimately of no one. When I come to oppose these desires, I oppose my own will.

The subtlety of Kant's view, as well as its perplexity, is aptly illustrated in his demythologized reading of the serpent's seduction. On a naïve reading, it looks to Kant (and, he presumes, to most readers) like the serpent tempts the human being to put other interests before his interest in obeying a divine command. It is the man's temptation and not the woman's that is of interest to Kant, even though the Yahwist source is remarkably terse about what moved the man to eat. Basically the woman ate, handed over the fruit to the man, and he ate; his motives for eating have to be inferred. Kant can admit of two kinds of motive here and still stay within the naïve reading. The woman hands the man a lusty piece fruit; he is being tempted to value bodily pleasure over law. It is the woman, his natural partner, who hands him the fruit; he is being tempted to value human company over law. If he gives into either of these temptations, he mixes good with evil and defines himself essentially as a body—something doomed to die. The naïve reading ends for Kant when he presses the further question of what makes the man susceptible to temptation at all.

Perhaps this is to ask one question too many. If I tell you that I sometimes act badly for the sake of material gain or social recognition, and you want to know why I sometimes do this, I am at a loss. Am I to wear my humanity on my sleeve? If you press me further for explanation, I may be tempted to tell you that the devil makes me do it. Though aware of the force of this kind of rejoinder, Kant is prepared to press his question about the origin of evil. In the place of a satanic figure who *causes* a human being to be evil, he finds a serpent-tempter who represents the mystery of evil's origin:

> Evil can have originated only from moral evil (not just from the limitations of our nature); yet the original predisposition (which none other than the human being could have corrupted, if this corruption is to be imputed to him) is a predisposition to be good; there is no conceivable ground for us, therefore, from which moral evil could first have come in us. The Scriptures express this incomprehensibility in a historical narrative, which adds a closer determination of the depravity of our species, by projecting evil at the beginning of the world, not, however, within the human being, but in a *spirit* of an originally more

sublime destiny. The absolutely *first* beginning of all evil is thereby represented as incomprehensible to us (for whence the evil in that spirit?).[6]

Part of Kant's message in this complex passage pertains to the logic of freedom. If evil is an expression of free will, I have nothing more fundamental than freedom to appeal to when I want to know why evil comes to be. Suppose, for example, that I want to know why the serpent—Kant's "spirit of an originally more sublime destiny"—lost its good will and ended up being a spoiler of perfection. Whatever story I end up telling here will basically be of a good spirit who gives into a bad temptation. I will then have a further story to tell about a new tempter. So either I look for a story with an infinite number of serpents in the drama, or I get clued into the idea that there is no good reason for something good to become evil. The Yahwist had the sense to stop with one serpent, and that is why Kant credits the Yahwist with having told a good story about the origins of evil.

Kant's is a demythologized reading of the serpent in as much as he is prepared to trade in the mythical figure for a moral truth. He is, to a large extent, prepared to do just that. The story tells us that the serpent and the human being—tempter and tempted—are two separate beings, but from the standpoint of moral philosophy, they are identical. I am not responsible, morally speaking, for succumbing to temptation unless I have already freely willed my subjection to corrupting influences (my original sin). The serpent in my life is always my own evil will. Kant is not insensible to the psychological cost of this kind of demythologizing. The internalized serpent appears in the human psyche as the demonic will, a hopelessly paradoxical disposition to will evil as the good. It is less a will than the will's question mark. I will never have an answer to the question, why do I will evil? None, that is, that I can rest with. Kant would have me live with a question when living with an answer to it would be worse. It is admittedly tempting to let temptations, or all those amoral desires that segregate my humanity from that of others, stand as the explanation for the evil that I do. But then I would in effect be splitting my nature in two. There would be the moral side and the amoral side—two independent sources of value—and never the twain shall meet. My attempt to explain evil will not have explained evil at all; it will have indicated only my surrender of part of myself to its dubious authority.

There is nothing about this demythologized reading of the serpent that Kant takes to be a correction of the biblical text. The serpent's sudden

6. di Giovanni (1998), pp. 64–65.

appearance in the drama, its past history and present motives a mystery, is for Kant the sign of a pregnant omission. We aren't told what good the serpent thinks it is serving, and that should make us think about the limits of our own knowledge of good and evil. This is where moral philosophy comes in, not to fill in between the limits, but to fix them. We are never to suppose that we have knowledge of pure evil, of the nature of the tempter; instead we must presume that the tempter stands unknowingly behind our human knowledge of good and evil, our often ineffectual awareness of being tempted by what is no good for us. To take responsibility for this knowledge is to take something unknowable into ourselves.

The ironic effect of demythologizing the serpent is to lend greater mystery to the moral life. Kant relieves us of a false clarity about good and evil and returns us, as it were, to a time before the divine knowledge of good and evil has been taken. But neither literally nor figuratively speaking can this be quite what has happened. To be relieved of a false knowledge of good and evil is not to be returned to a state of innocence, where desire for the knowledge of the gods is not yet in evidence. The temptation to want to know more than is the human place to know hasn't gone away. When Kant confines his attention to what makes us morally responsible for giving into temptation, he makes us out to be the agents of our own liabilities, and the serpent disappears. When he shifts his attention to the question of moral redemption, or whether it is still possible for us to be other than perennially subject to temptation, he reverts to the myth's separate depiction of a serpent-tempter and finds his hope for human redemption there. The story is telling us—in a way that apparently can't be demythologized—that the human spirit has not been "corrupted fundamentally"; in this respect, says Kant, the human spirit is unlike a spirit whose basic impulse is to be a tempter, "one, that is, whom the temptation of the flesh cannot be accounted as a mitigation of guilt."[7]

I think that Kant is wise not to want to make too total an assimilation of the serpent's significance to an anti-moral freedom, and yet it is very hard to see what he can do with the remainder. From a demythologized point of view, the temptation of the flesh—the serpent's stock and trade—has no redemptive value, not even in the very minimal sense of mitigation of guilt. How could it be otherwise? Nearly the whole point of demythologizing the serpent has been to dispel the impression that amoral desires are the biggest threat, or really any kind of threat, to the integrity of the good will. Kant favors this view of amoral desires, not because he has contempt

---

7. Ibid., p. 65.

for the body, but because he places such an extraordinarily high value on autonomy. If autonomy is the key to my identity and value as a person, I won't need Yahweh's command to know what the law of my freedom is, and I won't need the serpent's seduction to be tempted to free myself from even my own law. I will need Yahweh's command and the serpent's seduction to imagine myself as a being who can *become* autonomous. Yahweh and the serpent are two powers, in other words, that work to alienate me from myself and then return me there. Are they finally antithetical projections of my own will? I cannot know them to be such without making redemption—my will's perfection—an impossibility. But nor can I know them to be otherwise.

The economy that gives Kant's moral philosophy its working relation to myth depends crucially on his being able to separate off the will to live responsibly from the desire to see into the heart of good and evil. To put it figuratively, he has to forgo the knowledge of the gods in order to keep his human possibilities of redemption open. The economic division of labor here, between seeking to know and seeking to be right, can be taken to suggest either the demythologizing of myth or the remythologizing of moral philosophy. I have explored the former in this section. In demythologizing the serpent, Kant has transformed the serpent into an internal feature of the human will to self-rule, but at the cost, of course, of having to give up what the serpent in the myth had to offer: divine knowledge of good and evil. In the sections that follow, I take a closer look at desires for perfection that rest on refusals of knowledge; these quests for perfection, which can be both good and evil, are best cast in a remythologized moral philosophy. I begin by taking up a myth that invites a critical and yet forgiving look at the quest for perfection of the body—the quest that Kant has had to demonize in order to underscore the preeminent value of the good will and the imperative of its redemption.

II. Plato and the Comedy of Human Desire

Plato tells a story in the *Symposium* that bears certain affinities, as at least one of his translators has noted, to the biblical story of the Fall.[8] He puts the story in the mouth of Aristophanes, the same Aristophanes who once comically skewered Socrates in *The Clouds*. But Plato shows no evidence

---

8. With one small exception, I will be following Benardete's translation. See Benardete (2001), pp. 186–87, for his thoughts on Plato's Aristophanes and the biblical account of the Fall.

of having any ill will towards the mocker of his teacher and friend. On the contrary, he has the character of Aristophanes deliver a speech of great comic genius that manages at the same time to carry deeply tragic undertones. The perfect comedy in Plato's impersonation of a comic art becomes perfectly tragic. That in itself is comic—a tribute to Aristophanes—but also an invitation to move beyond comedy. For Plato's art, like his teacher's, is neither comic nor tragic, but philosophical.

I think of comedy and tragedy as both having to do with the disparity between nature and aspiration, between what we are given to be as human beings and what we may think or wish ourselves to be. If a dramatic representation of the disparity has been crafted to draw the sympathy of the audience to the side of nature, then the art is comic; if it has been crafted to ally the audience with aspiration, then the art is tragic. A third possibility, that the disparity is overcome and nature and aspiration made to align, is not a possibility of either comic or tragic art, where the disparity is taken for granted. In a comic or tragic universe, the parts that are human fit badly with the whole.

Plato's Aristophanes tells a story about parts and the whole. In keeping with the convention of the rest of the *Symposium*, he offers his story as a eulogy to Eros—the rarely praised Greek god of desire—or, more mundanely, as an account of why desire, especially sexual desire, is a beautiful thing. The eros that Aristophanes has in mind, however, is only accidentally sexual. Essentially it is desire of the whole, or perhaps better, desire to be whole. The choice of formulation turns on how the beginning of his story is to be read. Aristophanes takes us back to a strange time, a mythical time, when human beings have a nature apparently very different from the one they have now. There are originally three kinds of human being, or rather three kinds of doubled being: male-male, female-male, female-female—all the imagination that most of us have for sexual pairings. Only these are not pairings to be made; they are given at birth, as offspring of the sun (male), earth (female), and moon (androgynous) emerge from the ground in the form of a circular person-pairing, genitals on the outside. Procreation is more vegetative than animal for these circle people, who sow their seed not in flesh but soil. There is not much eros to speak of here, not if we are bent on giving eros a sexual origin, but we soon learn that these original human beings—whose circular shape suggests the perfection of physical form—are far from contained in their native desires.

In their original condition they have, as Aristophanes puts it, "big thoughts."[9] These thoughts are big and bold enough to move the circle people to attempt an assault on the Olympian gods, who have grown accustomed to receiving devotions from below. Since this is a story where the question of what is original is ever important, it is important to keep in mind that the Olympian gods—Zeus, Apollo, and company—are not the first generation of gods. The originals are planetary in shape and motion. Were the circle people to ascend to a sufficient height and get a good look at an original heavenly body, they would see the form that is parent to their own. Instead they lose out to a usurping generation of gods, who have the look that human beings have now. It is Zeus, the Olympian patriarch, who contrives the transformation in human nature and appearance. Wishing to end the hubris of big thinking, but not by killing off the thinkers and thereby forfeiting their devotions, he orders his son Apollo to cut all human pairings in two. The intended result is that of a weakened human being, whose original desire has been diverted into seeking its other half.

Initially the plan seems to have backfired. The diverted desire is so powerful that split human beings want only to cling to one another. They neglect to feed themselves, to make sacrifices to the gods, to do anything but cling; eventually they die of want. Zeus lessens the desperation of this altered human condition by making one alteration further: he moves the genitals of human beings from back to front. From now on, sexual release can offer human beings partial relief from their otherwise tyrannical desire for wholeness.

Reflecting on the tale he has told, Aristophanes wonders about the nature of the wholeness that the descendents of the circle people, their human heirs, still seek so desperately from one another. It cannot, he thinks, be sexual union, since that is, as unions go, only temporary. He asks his fellow symposiasts to imagine Hephaestus, the god skilled in the art of binding, making this offer to two human lovers: "Is it this you desire, to be with one another in the very same place, as much as is possible, and not to leave one another night and day? For if you desire that, I am willing to fuse you and make you grow together into the same thing, so that—though two—you would be one."[10] Aristophanes encourages everyone to suppose that the answer is obvious here. Of course this is what we all want, to be forever one with a beloved and restored to what was lost. It is of the essence of eros to desire and pursue original wholeness.

---

9. *Symposium* 190C, φρονήματα μεγάλα; my translation.
10. *Symposium* 192E; Benardete (2001), p. 21.

Parting Knowledge

I have now set out enough of the story to begin to suggest what makes it analogous to the biblical account of the Fall. Both stories seem to be about the loss of wholeness in human life, a loss prompted by a human desire for a divine point of view and exacted by the god whose point of view has been challenged. The man and woman, the perfect couple, will see as Yahweh does if they eat of the fruit that weds life to death; the circle people, all perfect couplings, will have a god's eye view of the heavens if they take the hill from Zeus. In each case the cost of wanting to know is spoilt perfection.

I don't deny that the two stories invite this kind of reading, and to the extent that they do, they lend support and encouragement to the perfectionist impulse in the moral life. As a perfectionist, I hold myself to an absolute standard of conduct. Whatever the imperative is that I choose to give myself, I must abide by it wholeheartedly or lose my sense of self-worth. The problem with perfectionism, as every perfectionist is destined to learn, is that people change, or to put it less prosaically, if there is an imperative that can define the value of a human life absolutely, it would have to be one that admitted of an indefinite, perhaps an infinite, number of interpretations. The serpent in Genesis encourages the woman to think about the meaning of the first divine command. Did Yahweh want her not to eat of the fruit of any of the trees? That would be to deny her a future, to condemn her to sterility. (For remember that a fruit is a seed; taken within a soil or a womb, it becomes a conception of new life—a conception not only of a beginning to life but also of a release of life and therefore of life's end.) If Yahweh is a god of life and not death, then how can he resolve to kill his children for wanting to know as he does, for wanting to grow up and know life as a parent does?

Questions like these—which emerge only when one is willing to depart from the letter of the text and start interpreting—can all be attributed to the serpent's inspiration and condemned as corrupting. A perfectionist like Kant has to take them that way. As far as his perfectionism is concerned, the serpent in Genesis is there to represent the universally human disposition to lessen the severity of the law's demands. The appeal of a less severe law is obvious. The morally perfect life is, to understate matters comically, hard to live. But even granting the difficulties of a perfectionism whose law is always absolute, I don't see any necessity to the thought that interpretation is transgressive. Not all those who interpret the law are seeking to defy it.

Return for a moment to the big thoughts of the circle people. Benardete translates the Greek phrase for big thoughts more elaborately than I have, rendering it as "great and proud thoughts." His translation underscores the element of hubris in the assault of the circle people upon the gods. There is no question that this element is there and there prominently. Plato's Aristophanes begins his tale of human origins by placing the first human beings under the rule of gods whose nature is alien to their own; to be subject to alien rule is just what it means to be tyrannized. Part of what moves the circle people to assault Olympus is therefore their desire to shake off their tyrants and rule themselves—a desire for autonomy.[11] The obvious hubris in this is that human beings think to do violence to divine beings without thinking too much (if at all) about the power of these beings to do violence to them in return. Aristophanes, after all, never describes a battle royal with gods, but only the ease with which Zeus and Apollo put their human subjects to shame.

The hubris that is really damning to the circle people is, however, less obvious. For it is hubris that has less to do with recklessly defying tyrants who conquer by dividing than with recklessly denying thoughts that seek wholeness beyond division. To begin to detect this level of hubris in the story, it is important not to read the "great" in "great and proud thoughts" to signify only an intensification of hubris. There are great thoughts that aren't proud. I think of them in the context of the story as big because they make bodily images of wholeness seem small. The circle people begin an ascent—a path of mind and heart, as well as body—in order to have the vision of the wholeness that is their birthright. This is not a matter of their having a perfected vision of what they take the body already to be, or they wouldn't have to defeat gods whose primary claim to fame is their power over bodies. To defeat these gods is not to beat them at their own game, but to release divinity from a tyrannized view of the body and its desires. (This is no different from the philosophical task of separating soul from body.)

One way to tyrannize the body (in thought) is to restrict all of its desires to expressions of poverty and lack of being; the desire for wisdom, or more basically, the desire to know good and evil, is thereby conceived to be alien to bodily desire. In this way of thinking, it will be of the essence

---

11. This reading gets further textual confirmation from the single other appearance of the phrase, φρονήματα μεγάλα, in the dialogue (*Symposium* 182C). Pausanias, who comes before Aristophanes in the order of speakers, uses the phrase to describe the mindset of Greek lovers whose eros for one another moves them to fight against tyrannical rulers (the Persians, for instance).

of bodily desire to want to preserve and perfect bodily form, the essence of wisdom to expand desire beyond the interests of bodily form and serve the good. If the desire to know the good (and so too evil) is itself a kind of need, it will be a need more contemplative than consumptive in nature—more, that is, like the need to respond to beauty than to satisfy a hunger.

In both the biblical story of human origins and the fanciful tale in Plato of the circle people, an original desire to know is veiled as something else, and this veiling is to my mind the deepest point of analogy between the two stories. In Genesis, the human desire to know good and evil and share in a divine way of seeing is veiled as a desire to break from Yahweh's protective but perhaps also stifling influence; in the speech of Aristophanes, the desire to know the highest things and to see one's own nature reflected there is veiled as a desire to be free of having to serve gods who are jealous of their honor and in need of constant praise and acknowledgment. In short, a desire to know is being veiled or subsumed in each case by a desire for self-rule. If this subsumption is not noticed and challenged, then the two stories have to be about loss of wholeness in human life and the futile but inalienable drive to recover it.

Aristophanes tries to gloss over the irrecoverable part by tempting his listeners to hope for some divinely contrived restoration of their original wholeness: honor the gods in their Olympian form (the form of a perfected body), and they will favor you with the body that completes your own, your proverbial other half—or so goes the logic of a marriage comedy. What this overlooks is that finding your other half would restore in you the very desire that led the first human beings to challenge the authority of Olympian rule. You would not be ending a long story; you would be reliving a very old one. The Genesis story incorporates an analogous logic of "no profit in return." Set aside for a moment thoughts of angels with flaming swords and Yahweh's anger. Suppose the man and woman are divinely restored to innocence and returned to Eden. They are still beings who carry the seed of knowledge—that is, the desire for it—within them. To prevent this seed from germinating, Yahweh would have to omit the tree, the woman, and the serpent. Those omissions don't leave much for the human being to be other than a mound of flesh fashioned from the clay of the earth. Hardly worth the bother.

Plato, I think, was well aware of the vicious circularity in the story of the circle people, where desire is forever chasing its own tail. Later in the *Symposium*, he has Diotima—who once versed Socrates in the art of love—preface her speech with an emendation of Aristophanes. Socrates reports her words as follows:

> "And there is a certain account," she said, "according to which those who seek their own halves are lovers. But my speech denies that eros is of a half or of a whole—unless, comrade, that half or whole can be presumed to be really good; for human beings are willing to have their own feet and hands cut off, if their opinion is that their own are no good. For I suspect that each does not cleave to his own (unless one calls the good one's own and belonging to oneself, and the bad alien to oneself) since there is nothing that human beings love other than the good."[12]

It may seem a fairly trivial emendation to qualify the desire for wholeness or one's other half with such a nondescript appeal to the good, but in fact Diotima adds to the myth of Aristophanes a whole new range of narrative possibility. Take her basic idea—that what is desired is always presumed to be good in some way—and apply it to the case of the sundered circle people. Can they reasonably presume that joining with their other half is a good thing? The answer to that is yes if they are aiming to restore the wholeness of their original desire, no if they are aiming to *satisfy* that desire. The latter kind of ambition assumes knowledge not yet in evidence. The circle people don't know what they would have come to know had they won their struggle against the gods; they cannot assume, then, that what satisfies half of their original desire would also satisfy the whole. If people who live out their desire by half presume to know the whole they are seeking, then they are guilty of a kind of hubris. They presume to see as the gods do and in so doing betray the needs of their own overlooked nature.

For the unemended Aristophanes the gulf between a divine and a human way of knowing is absolute. Human beings are forever locked into a losing battle with alien power; the best strategy for coping is to find wisdom in limits and solace in otherworldly piety. Diotima's emendation of Aristophanes offers the possibility of a different moral. Perhaps the gods we fight are alienated versions of ourselves. This is not to suggest that we create the gods, but that we are apt to settle the question of self-knowledge in the interests of something other than a desire to know—such as a desire to be whole (which is always a partial desire in Aristophanes, whether we emend him or not). Maybe at the end of inquiry the good will turn out to be what belongs to the self and nothing else; that will depend on just how

---

12. *Symposium* 205E–206A; Benardete (2001), p. 36.

generous a conception of self the desire to know permits. In the interim, it is self-defeating to insist on limits to knowing that are drawn in ignorance.

It is a point of honor in Kant, part of the dignity of practical reason, to keep to the human side of the difference between a divine and a human way of knowing. Keeping to the human side, not trying to know what is not given to a human being to know, is what leaves us with our moral integrity intact, and this is all the integrity that we can ever reasonably hope for. But this proves upon reflection to be no kind of integrity at all, not because the ideal of integrity is moral and morality is too hard, but because the ideal rests on an illusion—that human beings are in a position to draw an absolute limit to knowing in thought, thereby splitting a big thought, our biggest, in two. This act of self-splitting, rendered in the Aristophanes tale as a visitation of divine punishment, is in reality human hubris continued by other means. The gods, if they can't be conquered, are to be kept at bay, consigned to that part of ourselves we resolve not to know. Better to live without knowing than to surrender oneself to a god. One moral of the Genesis story is that it is too late for us not to want to know any part of ourselves and that it is furthermore something of a divine boon that it has been too late for us from the very beginning. Kant doesn't see this moral, perhaps because he can't afford to, and as a result he finds in Genesis matter for either a tragedy or a comedy and nothing to suggest that we aren't fated as human beings to live in the diaspora between nature and ideal—the space of the imperfect life.

For all their differences, Kant and Plato are crucially alike in the philosophical ambition that they bring to bear on their reading and retelling of stories. Neither of them is prepared to abandon the perfectionist impulse in moral philosophy, or the imperative to conform life to an ideal of life. Even if falling forever short of this ideal seems to be killing human happiness and hope, it does no good in response to try to love imperfection and celebrate the stories of people who do—at least not the imperfection that is the child of frustrated will. Plato celebrates and tries to make seductive the imperfection that comes of being released from the thought that we have nothing further to learn of the good and the beautiful. In the infinitely intricate pairings that shape and reshape human life, it is the delicate openness on both sides of the pairing to a further good that heals the split in human nature, makes our thoughts bigger, and directs us to a wholeness that is other than the sum of its parts. If the story that Plato has Aristophanes tell of human origins doesn't suggest this possibility to us, it may be because we look for wholeness where Aristophanes tempts us

Myth and Moral Philosophy

to look for it—in the perfection of the body. If Kant's take on the Yahwist makes Genesis seem similarly unpromising, perhaps that is because we look for wholeness where Kant tempts us to look for it—in the perfection of the will.

The temptation to look for perfection in all the wrong places is not entirely bad but is instead bound up with the knowledge of good and evil. This thought takes me to my final thoughts on the biggest myth in moral philosophy and on the resolute, albeit self-defeating, attempt of our biggest moral philosopher to demythologize it.

III. Exiting Eden

If moral philosophy is to be the arbiter of myth, then myth must always at some level be about the moral life and the struggle of imperfect beings to live it. This is not as far-fetched a presumption as it may at first sound. If a moral value is, as Kant believes, the supreme or overriding value of an ideally practical reasoner (someone who wants above all to act with right), then a story whose plot includes thinking beings with bodies eventually gets to the part about moral struggle. The body poses a problem for thought that only a law—a supremely practical one—can work out. Namely, how is thoughtful existence possible if an embodied being has to be preoccupied with obeying its hunger and thirst, seeking a mate, and fighting for its place in the hierarchy of the pack? It isn't possible unless there is somewhere in this being's consciousness a law that restrains desire. This has to be a law that gets its authority from having its legitimacy recognized and not from fear of punishment or death. If the law is obeyed only because the lawgiver is fearsome, then law-abiding behavior won't conform to any kind of value that can't be accounted for within an economy of competing bodily desires. So here is one way to end to circumvent the human story: the lawgiver threatens Adam; out of fear he abandons his partner to her separate fate; he lives on (and alone) in his Edenic prison.

The Yahwist myth in Genesis doesn't end on that kind of note because it is particularly good, in Kant's estimation, at representing the two fundamental truths of human moral development. One is that we have to move from servile fear of a lawgiver to self-rule in order to arrive at a moral conception of ourselves (which is for Kant the basis of any kind of self-conception); the other is that we will have violated the law of self-rule before we ever come to recognize its legitimacy.

Both of these truths seem paradoxically to put self-rule before self-conception. Can I either respect or violate a law I give to myself if I don't already have a conception of who the subject is here? I can well imagine having a *bad* conception of myself and acting in ways that either preserve or threaten the integrity of that conception, but in that case the good of self-rule is no longer unconditionally good, but a mixed blessing. I wouldn't want so to succeed as a self-ruler that the badness of my self-conception never occurs to me (the badness of being alone), and yet I wouldn't want so to fail that the work of reopening my self-conception seems pointless. The first human being in Kant's version of Genesis has a bad conception of himself—as being more of flesh than spirit—but the terrible irony of his situation is that he cannot revise this conception (via the knowledge of good and evil) with also violating the *authentic* law of his own nature. In effect Kant turns the story of the Yahwist into an Oedipal tragedy, though the tragic hero here—the fatally flawed Adam—is more akin to the Oedipus of Freud than of Sophocles.

The tragedy begins in the garden, where Adam seems to be living the ideal life. He has his material needs met (lots of nice fruit), he has a perfect mate (the woman), and his place in the order of things is well defined (Yahweh above, animals below). The source of his discontent is not that he is lacking some object of desire, but that he isn't. The part of him that is higher, that aims at self-conception, cannot emerge until he experiences lack. In forbidding him to eat from the tree of knowing good and evil, Yahweh helps his human son transform an inarticulate need for something to be lacking into a conscious desire to create something out of nothing—a new life. The intermediate stage is for Adam to be able to conceive of not wanting the life he has been given. This is what Yahweh's prohibition particularly enables. For the forbidden fruit is not just one among many objects of desire in the garden; it is the one object whose attainment represents the loss of everything else—except, of course, the woman. She is an ambiguous figure in Adam's mind. Before his defiance of his father, he calls her woman because he thinks of her as flesh of his flesh and bone of his bone (Gen 2:23), and afterwards he calls her Eve because she is to him the mother of all that lives (Gen 3:20). Both ways of describing her hint that she is as much mother as partner to the son who has chosen her. (For all sons except apparently the first, it is their mothers who are flesh of their flesh, bone of their bone.)

The Oedipal task of a son is to replace his father and wed his mother without actually having to replace his father or wed his mother. This is the

Myth and Moral Philosophy

way that a son moves from myth into history. The son as Kant conceives of him in the Yahwist myth is obsessively preoccupied with his relation to his father (the good and evil of it) and remarkably indifferent to his mother. Indifference is conservative; the son will not be able to conceive of becoming a progenitor of life, a father in his own right, without having to become *his own* father. "The human being," writes Kant, "must make or have made *himself* into whatever he is or should become in a moral sense, good or evil."[13] The ill-kept secret of *Religion* is that self-conception of this sort is impossible. Kant's Adam cannot find the motive to violate the law of his divine father without first conceiving of an antagonism between his father's interests and his own, but he cannot violate that law without coming to realize (too late) that his father's law is the law of his own nature.

In this tragedy of Freudian proportions, the son cannot forever remain under his father's protection without denying his own nature, and he cannot break from his father without breaking from himself and sacrificing his own integrity. He is, after all, his father's son. The result, far from an original self-conception, is an endlessly belabored attempt at redemption. Seeking to regain favor in his father's eyes, the son resolves to put his father's will above all of his other desires—a lifetime's offering of service to the law. What dogs this endeavor is the imperfection that motivates it; it was the father's will, Kant must suppose, for the son *never* to have violated his father's will. If stripped of an absolutist father to disobey, the son of Kant's imaging has no way to conceive of the flesh (his mother) as a distinct *object* of choice, and so he is forever doomed to confuse soul with body. If stuck, on the other hand, with an absolutist father to please, it will take longer than forever for the son to sort out this confusion to his father's satisfaction.

Kant's preferred way out of this apparent antinomy is to insist on the segregation of divine and human points of view. From my human point of view I have to assume that my quest for moral perfection never ends; I always fall short of the perfection that I rightfully expect of myself. From a divine point of view, my willingness to take on the endless labor of self-perfecting and not give into defeat and despair is what my father in heaven sees as a redeemed will. It is possible for me, then, to *live* the perfect life; only I will never *see* myself as living it. I lack my father's knowledge of good and evil. This split between knowing and living is characteristic of Adam's situation prior to his taste of forbidden fruit. Kant proposes to restore Eden in human nature by having us disown divine knowledge of

---

13. di Giovanni (1998), p. 65.

good and evil and live by the law of human freedom alone. This disowning is not, as Kant would have it, the innocent acknowledgment of a limit to knowing, but an attempt to draw the limit between human and divine knowing from the human side—an act of secession veiled as knowledge of one's place. It would be my own law, and not the father's, that would keep me from having sight of myself in my father's eyes. The moral I take from Kant is one that he never intended to offer: that it is harder to get out of Eden than get back. It is the former and not the latter task that puts my autonomy most at risk and compels me to find in a serpent's wisdom something other than a rejection of spirit—something, mythically speaking, that a divine father could love.

I can put this moral in demythologized terms. It is by resolving to live a morally perfect life that I run into the limits of my will to be perfect. Faced with these limits I have a choice: either will them as my own or be open to a revision in my self-conception (one I can't simply will to have). One way I can opt for the self-imposed limits is to reject as evil whatever subverts my will to perfection. But I should be careful here that I don't end up tyrannizing the very self I am so anxious to rule. Not everything that I may depend on for my value is evil. What I mean to suggest by all this is not that we should surrender ourselves blindly to chthonic forces whenever our efforts to do right fail, but that we shouldn't let our efforts to do right blind us to the generosity that comes of receiving.

John tells us that we love God because God loved us first (1 John 4:19). Only those of us who have forgotten the first thing about love are apt to find that a humiliating truth. The rest of us are released into a new perfection. And yet the rest of us is also, at any given time, none of us; love seems always to run the risk of having its offer of life construed as a way of binding the beloved's will or corrupting it. I don't think that this ambiguity is humanly controllable. (If it were, gardens would never have serpents.)

In his great essay on the question of gods—which is less about the many gods than the two different sides of divinity—John Wisdom issued this caveat about the way we tend to read the story of our origins: "We have eaten of the fruit of a garden we can't forget though we were never there, a garden we still look for though we can never find it. Maybe we look for too simple a likeness to what we dreamed."[14] If we cannot, as Wisdom suggests, escape the memory of a place we never inhabited, perhaps the problem is not that we cling to an image in a dream, but that our dreams have come to mean so little to us.

14. Wisdom (1945), p. 205.

11

The Original Sin
Sex and Christian Ethics

THERE IS LITTLE KNOWN about the life of the Christian monk Jovinian other than that he was getting himself into trouble in late fourth-century Rome. Jovinian kept insisting that a chaste life was simply no better, spiritually speaking, than a married one, and he would dare the consecrated virgins of his day to think themselves greater mortals than Abraham and Sarah and all the other revered husbands and wives of old. Although Jovinian was excommunicated and his views condemned in two separate Synods, one in Milan and the other in Rome, his dare had dampened the enthusiasm of many Roman Christians for a celibate life. The scholarly monk Jerome attempted to come to the rescue of holy virginity by writing two incendiary books against Jovinian, but Jerome did such a good job of trashing marriage that many in the Church felt some need of a rescue from the rescue. Around the year 401, the promising new bishop of Hippo, the man we now know as Saint Augustine, tried his hand at threading the needle: in one treatise he would argue for the goodness of marital sex; in another he would hold to the superiority of a sex-free life of devotion.

In what follows, I am not presupposing much of any antecedent knowledge of Jovinian, Jerome, or even Augustine, but you do not have to be a church historian to realize that there is a world of difference between an ethics of sexuality that takes sex to be a natural appetite and one that takes sex to be a veiled and perhaps perverse form of spiritual desire. Think of a spiritual desire as an enlightened desire for greater life—a vague conception, I concede, but good enough for now. Christian sexual ethics has tended to move sex into the realm of spirit, but not without generating anxiety about the precarious naturalness of a once purely carnal desire. The uneasy fit between the natural and spiritual sides of sex, epitomized by Augustine's halfhearted endorsement of marriage, is the theme of this chapter. I would love to be able to tailor the fit to make it all come out right, but I lack the wisdom for that. I speak from within the uneasiness and am prepared to offer you a few observations about what I see; I invite you to supplement and correct my vision.

I suspect that our friend Jovinian, who took a mundane view of sex, upset a good many Christians just because he was so deflationary about sex. Sex is just sex; if you want to give it up, knock yourself out, but sexual restraint is no more spiritually fraught, on this deflationary view, than is going on a diet to lose a few pounds. When Jerome exalts chastity and debases sexual satisfaction, he restores sublimity to the athleticism of sexual restraint. Such restraint is once again for the sake of something not debased, something grand. As a chaste person on Jerome's model of chastity, I await the end-of-time transfiguration of my frustrated sexual desire; to be blunt, I expect God on the day of judgment to accept my sexual frustration as desire for God. The problem with a view like Jerome's is its low expectation of any kind of transfiguration in this life; a sexual desire that stubbornly remains deaf and dumb to spirit does no better within a marriage context than outside of one. For his part, Augustine tries to be family friendly even as he is exulting the virtue of chastity, but it is far from obvious how he has found his way between the comic sexuality of a Jovinian and the tragic sexuality of a Jerome.

In his treatise on the good of marriage (*b. conjug.*), Augustine styles his sexual ethics as straightforwardly Pauline. In chapter 7 of his first letter to the Corinthians, Paul counsels widows and virgins to stay unmarried and married people to stay married. But everyone, whether married or not, would, he thinks, be better off not giving in to the highly distracting passions of a sexual life. Not better off is, in this case, not so bad. Paul certainly doesn't condemn the virgin who decides to marry or the widow who decides to remarry, but he does seem to regard the desire to start a new household as a mild kind of foolishness. Christ, he assumes, is due to return soon and is sure to replace a carnal with a spiritual order; further procreation in the flesh, given the imminence of a new order, is both bothersome and pointless. "I want you to be free from anxieties," Paul says to the Corinthians (1 Cor 7:32); family life is hardly anxiety-free. When Augustine takes over Paul's notion that marital sex is good as far as it goes, but chastity is better, he does so without sharing Paul's conviction that

Christ's return is imminent. Augustine refrains from making any kind of assumption about Christ's timetable, and in the absence of a clearly defined eschatological expectation, his appropriation of Paul proves to be less Pauline than it may at first seem.

In particular, Augustine has to worry more about a distinction that Paul makes but never labors. As any parent knows, there is a big difference between the distraction of sexual desire and the distraction of parenting. One tends to divert attention from the other. If it is a good thing, spiritually speaking, that parenting checks sexual desire, the implication is that sexual desire is more of a distraction from higher things than is parenting. In First Corinthians, Paul seems to be saying that sexual desire and parenting both distract from an ideal attention to divine matters, but given his belief in the imminent end of a carnal order, Paul is relatively uninterested in sorting out the difference between the two kinds of distraction. He simply condemns those who, failing chastity, fail also to seek the refuge of a marriage. Augustine cannot afford to be so blithely condemning. Unlike Paul he does not feel confident that a total revolution of spirit is just around the corner; he is therefore more inclined to take a hard look at the complexity of human motivation in this life, especially when it comes to sex. Although fixed in his intent to condemn any kind of sex outside of wedlock, Augustine is not so resolute in his condemnation of marital sex that is enjoyed, not simply endured. "It does not seem to me," Augustine writes in *De bono conjugali* 3.3, "that the good of a marriage lies solely in the procreation of children; there is also the partnership that is naturally expressed through sexual difference."

That last bit of the quote from Augustine, about the partnership, is hard to translate without paraphrasing. A more literal rendering of the Latin phrase *naturalem in diuerso sexu societatem* might read: "the partnering that is natural for a parted sex." Given this rendering, Augustine seems to be associating the good of marriage with the natural differentiation of the sexes that he finds described in chapter 2 of Genesis: a woman comes to be when a man is parted from a part of himself, and he awakens to find himself partnered with a being who is bone of his bone and flesh of his flesh; she is not simply a part of who he is, but nor is she alien to him. Augustine was an obsessive reader of Genesis, and so I find it hard to believe that he didn't intend the allusion to an original and idyllic form of sexual differentiation. He was, after all, just about the only church father ever to make sex one of the licit fruits of life in Eden: Adam and Eve, he imagines, would have enjoyed ideal sex with one another had they not sinned.[1] But it was also Augustine who was quick to insist that sex after Eden was a ruination: no heir to a lost paradise ever experiences sex innocently. This is Augustine's notorious doctrine of original sin; it prevents him from ever embracing the good of marital sex wholeheartedly: "Intercourse within a marriage," he writes (still *b. conjug.* 3.3), "makes something good out of the evil of sexual desire." It is, for Augustine, a limited and imperfect makeover. Marriage restrains sexual desire and redirects it towards a greater sociability, but it does not eliminate the root of the problem. Children, whether baptized or not, grow up to reinvent the sexual troubles of their parents. Augustine's best advice to married couples is to work towards a mutually agreed upon chastity.

I could say a great deal more about Augustine's ambivalence towards sexual desire, but were I to go on, I would still come to basically the same conclusion: that the message about sex from one of our greatest Christian luminaries has been equivocal. On the one hand sex is a mundane but generally unruly desire, best limited by what most naturally limits it: the gratifying but still burdensome business of childrearing. On the other hand, sex is a spiritually dangerous desire, one that inclines us to confuse something sublime with something mundane.

If we were to base our sexual ethics on the mundane view of sex, then moderation would be our cardinal rule. Let sex be moderated by sociability. If your desire for sex is keeping you from friends, family, and your most generous vision of a human community, then by all means try to be more moderate. Procreation supplies a natural context for sexual moderation only because procreation calls for child care. It is not having a child that is of primary ethical importance, but caring for one, and in even a minimally sociable society, the number of caregivers has to extend well beyond a grudgingly biological definition of a parent. If we were, by contrast, to base our sexual ethics on the spiritually dangerous view of sex, then everything I have just said about mundane sex and its regulation would have to be qualified. The ethical function of mundane sex, whether the sex is child-producing or not, is enhanced sociability; if enhanced sociability is not in fact the ultimate aim of spirit, if knowing God is something other than this, then a life of moderated sexuality is at best a second-best life. The best life would be one of sexual sublimation, a turn

---

1. Augustine's extended description of the nature of (hypothetical) sex in Eden can be found in *City of God* 14.23–24, 14.26; for intelligent commentary on these perplexing chapters, see Miles (2005) and Cavadini (2005).

to the higher that calls more for courage than it does for moderation. To repress a moderate carnal desire is to reserve for spirit only a small piece of your carnal involvement with the world; to repress an immoderate, self-aggrandizing carnal desire is to reserve for spirit your whole carnal world. The worst thing that you can do given the spiritual paradigm of sex is to surrender your flesh fully to the monster of sexual desire; if you cannot deny the monster everything, then at least deny it something and live the second-best life.

I wish at this point to make two points. One is that the two paradigms of sex—mundane and spiritual—are irrevocably two. They do not play well together, and when they are made to do so, the result is guilt, resentment, and internal conflict. My other point is that the temptation to confuse the two paradigms seems nearly irresistible. The Jovinian form of the confusion is to overvalue procreation and reduce the spiritual side of sex to an itch to reproduce; the Jerome form is to undervalue parenting and divest spiritualized sex of its natural basis. Augustine almost gives a spiritual value to mundane attraction when he values marital partnership for more than its procreative uses, but he is finally more negative about sex than he is positive about partnering.

Glum as this all seems, I don't want to leave you with the impression that a nearly irresistible confusion is necessarily unavoidable. The mundane and spiritual paradigms of sex are contrary and yet collapsible because they are contrary versions of the same failure: neither paradigm makes any real appeal to the sacramental character of marital sexuality. The mundane paradigm tells me that I ought to be in an exclusive, childbearing relationship because that is the best means I have at my disposal to moderate my sexual desire. Maybe it is, but the paradigm tells me nothing about what is good or holy about my desire for my partner. The spiritual paradigm tells me that if I repress my desire for my partner on earth, I will be better able to receive love from my partner in heaven. I find this hard to believe, but even supposing it were true, I have been given no clue as to why divine love seeks to fill the form of an abandoned marriage covenant. A sacramental view of martial sexuality suggests a correlation, not a competition, between the human image of an original partnership—male and female—and its divine exemplar. In Genesis 1:27 we are informed of this correlation in short but poetic order: "And God created the human in his image / in the image of God He created him / male and female he created them."[2]

2. For the translation of Genesis, I will be using Alter (1996).

Parting Knowledge

Before I move on to ponder the biblical image of sexual difference, the image that gets its best elaboration in the oldest story we have of creation, Genesis 2:4b—3:24, I feel a certain obligation at least to mention my awareness of our divisive national debate over the nature of a true marriage. It is the honest belief of many Christians, who for understandable reasons describe themselves as conservative, that sexual difference within a marriage is obviously the difference between a man and woman and that no other representation of this difference can possibly be given biblical warrant. I am not of this persuasion myself. As I will soon illustrate, I find the Genesis account of the first human partnering to be profoundly subtle and not given to a single interpretation. And while I have no objection to using such a rich text to inform an ethics of marriage and sexuality, my difficulty with a socially conservative reading of Genesis is that this kind of reading tends, or so it seems to me, to conserve the wrong thing. The basis of a sacramental marriage is not the human image but the divine exemplar. I am called to conserve, to the best of my limited abilities, the divine offering of sexual difference. In that way I secure a basis for my human variation of a divine theme. Will the variation have to take the form of a heterosexual marriage? The social conservative assures me that it will, but I cannot assign any religious value to that assurance until I also understand how heterosexual marriage is a paradigmatic image of God's inner life. If the social conservative is prepared to offer me *that* reading of Genesis, I am eager to listen. If not, then I am not so invested in the question of whether heterosexuality is the only way for a Christian reader of Genesis to interpret male-female differentiation. I begin, perhaps naively, with a more basic question: what is the biblical image of male and female in its original conjunction? I move then from Genesis 1:27 directly to the story that the redactor of the old texts offers as its gloss: the creation of male and female in Eden's garden.[3]

It will be my confident assumption that you are already familiar—perhaps overly so—with Adam, Eve, and the serpent. To spare you yet another recitation, I will restrict my exposition to the elements of the story that do most to inform the biblical notion of an original sexual difference. Let me begin by introducing *YHWH 'Elohim*. In classical Jewish piety it is a bad idea, an impiety in fact, to spell out the proper name of God or utter this name out loud in a public context. It is also part of Christian

---

[3]. I recognize that brief remarks on sexual difference in God fall well short of making the case for the sacramentality of same-sex marriage. I won't be making the case for this here, but for some insight into how the case can be made, see Rogers (1999) and the essays in Jordan (2006).

piety never to take the name of the Lord in vain. If your own sense of piety runs along these lines, I ask for your indulgence. When I speak or write of Yahweh, I am not calling upon the name of God; I am referring to a character in a story who, to my way of reading, best conveys the male image of a divine creator. I take Yahweh to be male because he does not create new life directly out of his own body; he infuses a part of himself into a prefigured earthen form, a body of clay, and comes up with an Adam—a creature whose name recalls the clay, *'adamah*, from which he was born.[4] Adam, for an Anglophone reader, is the proper name of a man. In Hebrew, *'adam* is a generic term for a human being; it is the Hebraic equivalent of the Greek word *anthrôpos*. You are an *anthrôpos* or an *'adam* in as much as you are a sentient being who is neither a god nor a beast, but something in between. The designation says nothing about the internal (or horizontal) articulation of your humanity, which is a function of sexual difference—your maleness and femaleness. The fact that Adam is, at one level, a nameless representative of an indeterminately sexed humanity does not mean that he isn't also a male character, and I will now begin to refer to him as such. But I would ask you nonetheless to keep the ambiguity in mind.

It is to Adam that Yahweh discloses the one rule of life in a garden sanctuary, where nothing wild is allowed to intrude: there will be no eating from the tree of knowledge. "On the day you eat from it," Yahweh tells Adam (Gen 2:17), "you are doomed to die." The Hebrew word for knowledge in this context, *da'at*, is like Greek *gnosis* or French *connaissance*: it is knowledge that banks on familiarity. Not all knowledge is like this. The knowledge we call objective puts the object of knowledge outside the home-life of the knower; such impersonal knowledge can often feel cold and alienating. If biblical knowledge has an alienating effect, it is not because the knowledge is foreign to the knower. Adam already knows what he is forbidden to know; he just doesn't know yet that he knows. We are told that knowledge taken from the tree of knowledge is both good and bad, that it hues our Adamic humanity with mortality; we are also told that *all* the fruit in Eden is lovely to look at and good to eat (Gen 2:9).

The creation of woman is set up as a test of Adam's self-knowledge. Yahweh wants Adam not to be alone, to have someone to sustain him throughout his days, but this someone has to be an intimate—as close to Adam as he is to himself. Adam dispatches all the false contenders, the birds of the air and beasts of the field, by giving them their names and a

---

4. For my sense of how specific Hebrew locutions shape the meaning of the unfolding narrative, I am much in debt to Alter (1996) and, even more so, to Trible (1978).

subordinate place in the order of things. When he awakens from a deep, Yahweh-induced sleep, Adam does not have to be told that he is face to face with his sustainer *('ezer)*[5]: he already knows that woman is flesh of his flesh and that he, as her human complement, is a man. The two of them are naked, Adam and his woman, and neither one feels shame. Significantly the text reverts in Genesis 2:25 to speaking of the woman's counterpart as *'adam*, the gender-inclusive concept, and as not as *ish*, the Hebrew word that specifically picks out a male.

Still we are told in just the previous verse that a man leaves his father and his mother, clings to his wife, and they become one flesh. Is this not a clear biblical warrant for a marriage between a man and a woman? I would say that a marriage between a man and a woman is taking its basis from the original pairing of Adam and his woman, but I don't think that this original pairing is itself a marriage. A man is flesh of his mother's flesh, bone of her bones. Adam is bound, in accord with the rhythms of life, to separate himself from his father, but his separation from his mother—a birthing—has to come first. Although it is possible to read Yahweh as both his father and mother in the Genesis text, I find that reading a real strain. When the woman offers Adam a taste of knowledge, she offers him a reminder of what all mortal sons and daughters know in their bones: that beings of breath and clay are all mother-born and, as such, have their deaths handed to them with their births. Our heavenly father may want, out of compassion, to keep us from digesting that knowledge too soon, but we do not stay children forever and an awareness of mortality, though it can feel both good and bad, is finally good.

But of course I have left out the part about original sin. Saint Paul sets the stage for a Christian theology when he describes Christ as the new and better Adam. The first Adam is bound to die; the second too will die, but only to rise up and renew a life manifestly greater than the one he was born to. We lovers of life had best surrender our lives, if Paul is right, to Christ's way of being human. But what manner of surrender is that? And where did the first Adam go so terribly wrong? The traditional answer to these questions, at least in the Augustinian tradition of theology—the tradition I know best—emphasizes the contrast between Adam's selfish disobedience to God and Christ's self-sacrificial vindication of fatherly rule. Both Adam and Christ choose to know a death that neither one need have known, but only Christ chooses his knowledge in accord with the

---

5. See Trible (1978), p. 90, for why "helper"—the traditional translation of *'ezer*—is so misleading.

will of his father. The disobedient Adam of Genesis is cast as a motherless man who is overly attached to a woman. From here it is not much of a leap to the conclusion that his sin has something essentially to do with his excessive attachment. His male heirs will be blamed for being overly sexed, his daughters blamed for eliciting that excess. This is the dreary picture of sexual inheritance that tempts an Augustine, despite his better angels, to demonize sex and that involves an entire tradition in the unlovely task of having to rein in a pathetic desire. If Christ is made to find his place within this picture, he emerges as the Adam who has no sexual desire at all.

I will end my gesticulating remarks about Genesis and sexual ethics with a radical suggestion. It is not my suggestion; it is Christianity's. The suggestion is that God too has a mother, and like all those mother-born, he invests his life's breath in a surrender of flesh. The first Adam had a mother too, but when he became aware of the terrifying burden of trust that a mortal life carries, he hid from his powerful father and disavowed knowing his mother: "The woman whom you gave by me," he tells Yahweh (Gen 3:12), "she gave me from the tree, and I ate." Adam's thinly veiled complaint against his father's justice can be rendered thus: "You left me alone with Mom, and she gave me something to eat; if you have a problem with that, take it up with her. You are the one, after all, who knows her best." Before Adam is forced out of Eden, he will name the woman "Eve" because, we are told (Gen 3:20), she was "the mother of all that lives." In spite of his explicit disavowal of her, Adam still retains some knowledge, perhaps mostly repressed, of his original mother. Outside of Eden, in the wilderness of his beginnings, he will come to know Eve as his wife, and together they will beget and raise children in the way that historical human beings now do. As Yahweh predicted, it won't go so easily for them—or for the rest of us.

Eve's abrupt changeover from original mother to sometime wife is, I think, the legacy of a fall from grace, but a fall that has little to do with human disobedience. Adam has to leave Eden not because he has disobeyed but because he is too likely, having tasted only the bitterness of knowledge, to want a taste from that other tree (Gen 3:22): "Now that the human has become like one of us, knowing good and evil, he may reach out as well from the tree of life and live forever." Yahweh prevents this from happening by sending Adam out to labor in the earth and by posting menacing angels to guard the way to the tree of life. If the gospel really is good news, then Yahweh does this not because he is a vindictive god, bent on diminishing an Adam's life, but because he is, as the other Adam insisted, a god of life (Mark 12:27).

I take it on faith that there is no way to eternal life except through the knowledge of birth, desire, and death. That knowledge is quite a labor. We have to work a lifetime to see and relate to one another apart from the resentments and false hopes that come of halfhearted knowledge. Jesus kindly reminds us that we don't know our father in heaven very well, certainly not as well as he does. Perhaps that is because we cling too hard to this father and so tend to project his protective image everywhere. In the short years of his recorded ministry, Jesus managed not to indulge in projections. He had a gift for seeing through to the original nakedness of those he met, and this revelation seemed to give them leave to love themselves realistically—a miracle of miracles. Towards the end, he was clearly worried about what would happen to those he left behind, but he did send us his Spirit, the Paraclete (John 14:16), which is our mother by another name. We don't know her very well either, though I suspect for different reasons.

It seems to me that the preeminent task of sexual ethics is to combat the illusions that alternatively trivialize and demonize sexual desire. When the illusions have lost some of their appeal, I trust that we will have left to us something like an original desire for knowledge. In anticipating this desire, we have the help of our teacher, Christ, the better Adam, who in life seemed largely uninterested in questions of sexuality. Perhaps this is because the illusions that hem us into a sexuality are not themselves especially sexual. I, for one, would take some consolation from that.

Dialogical Postscript

I wrote the essay "The Original Sin" conscious of the fact—even more so than usual—that I was writing over my head. In an effort to test and perhaps reframe the limits of my speculation, I enlisted the help of one of my best interlocutors over the years. Kathleen Skerrett, Dean of the Arts and Sciences at the University of Richmond and a philosopher of extraordinary finesse, read my essay, read some of my retrospection on my essay, and interposed her voice and perspective into my imperfect self-reflection. She has kindly consented to having a part of our exchange printed here.

Wetzel:

I don't think that this essay quite succeeds, but given the topic, I expected to fail. I am trying to gesture at something I really don't understand, and so I falter.

So much turns for me on Genesis 2:23:

> This one at last, bone of my bones
>   and flesh of my flesh,
> This one shall be called Woman
>   and from man was this one taken.

What is this an image of? A man inseminates a woman; within her womb, she turns a seed into a living being—flesh of his flesh and bone of his bone. (And while she does this, he is less involved in the process of begetting than she is, as if he were in "a deep slumber.") I sense a father fathering a daughter in this image, but the mother is veiled; she is not directly present.

Parting Knowledge

Skerrett:

Let me reflect back to you: The daughter is brought to her father. And he responds with wonder and a sense that she is of his own flesh. He understands himself as a sexuate being through the child. Before that he may not have understood the relation between inseminating and becoming a father. So he could not understand the relation he has to the creature he inseminates as a sexual relation to a woman or mother. It is retrospectively through the child that all of this becomes conceivably intelligible.

Wetzel:

Does the man want knowledge of his mother?

Skerrett:

He will need to know three things about himself: that he was born, that he is sexuate, and that he will die: all of these things are implications of sexual reproduction as the mode of procreation. He gets a bit of each of them as the story unfolds.

Wetzel:

When my daughter was born and I got to know her a bit, I was struck by the thought: *this* is how my mother knew me. A naked knowledge. What about the woman who is the man's wife—when does she enter the picture? Not directly, I think, until Genesis 4:1, when Adam knows Eve, and she gives birth to Cain. By then Adam has disavowed knowledge of his mother, and so he is fated (in a way that Freud got half right) to bind his wife to his repressed and originally imperfect knowledge.

Skerrett:

He knows that he is a sexuate being through the child; he knows that he is a mortal being through the wife. How does he learn that his is a natal being? He can't remember it. How can he find the mother to know if he cannot remember that he was once a small child? Perhaps he rebukes himself for not remembering a debt he cannot hope to repay.

Wetzel:

To repeat, to try (and flail) again, the "birthing" of the woman in Genesis 2:23 suggests two kinds of intimacy to me:

- a father's bond of flesh and bone with his daughter;
- a mother's bond of flesh and bone with her son.

We don't get an image of a perfect conjunction here. Parenting is an asymmetrical relation: the parent parents the child, but the child does not parent the parent. We get more of an intimation of a reciprocal relation if we move from a snapshot perspective into a broader conception of human interactions over time: the child can parent the parent later in life.

Skerrett:

Reciprocity need not imply equality, which is poorly predicated of human beings, anyway. But it could imply mutual regard, perception, and confusion—which fluctuate in intensity, maturity, and the obligations they entail toward the other.

Wetzel:

The tricky part about sex: *its misleading image of a perfect intimacy.*

Skerrett:

It is our souls that desire and sustain intimacy. We get inside each other by language, not by sex. I asked a biologist once to give me the most reductive account he could of what sex is, and he said, "friction"! So an image of perfect intimacy is covering over the friction of one person against another—an image doomed to mislead!

So what, then, miscues us over and over to seek personal intimacy by emptying consciousness toward that friction?

Wetzel:

In the biblical perspective, the procreative intimacies between male and female are introduced prior to any mention of a sexual coupling. When Adam knows Eve and Eve bears Cain, we have already been thrown into a situation of confusion and alienation. Women and men compete for creative authority; children do not understand.

Consider: we human beings can have many sexual partners, but we have only one mother, only one father.

Parting Knowledge

Skerrett:

Yes, and it seems crucial to look steadily at that fact, which we've stopped doing in the sex-is-socially-constructed heyday. The fact that we are generated of two differently sexed parents is central to the kinds of beings we are: natal beings, as well as sexuate and mortal beings.

Wetzel:

We often try, for moral, spiritual, and psychological reasons, to replicate or recall an original intimacy in our sexual partnerships. This, I suspect, has something to do with a fundamentally human desire to know and be known. But obviously the recollection of an original intimacy is not simply a matter of conjoining sexually to one particular man or woman: we will have to work to be open to the singularity of the other person, who, we can only hope, will be open to our own singularity.

Skerrett:

And, yet, don't we know our friends singularly and well and aren't we known likewise by them? And so what is this compulsion that fixes desire on *someone*? Further, erotic desire has a strange temporal quirk to it—one is always just a little too late to say no to its being fixed on someone. Desire does seem haunted by an origin that can nonetheless go ahead of the subject and entangle a future. It must have to do with language, I think, with our misconceptions about language too.

12

From Aphrodite to God the Father
A Question of Beauty

THE ASSOCIATION OF THE Greek goddess of beauty with sexual delight and the unruliness of erotic desire is well known to anyone with a cursory knowledge of the old stories. The progressive dissociation of the ancient god of Israel from sexuality, although not paternity, is also well known, this time to anyone with a cursory knowledge of Western philosophy. Freud thought that there had to be a connection between sex and beauty, but he admitted that psychoanalysis had little to say about it beyond the rather uninformative speculation that love of beauty must be "inhibited in its aim"[1]—it was love that wanted originally to be sexual in expression but ended up being something else. If the memory of the original eros were still operative in the sublimated love, as Freud assumed it would be, then a god of little or no sexuality would make for an unlikely beauty. Freud himself found nothing attractive in "the figure of an enormously exalted father," whose sole function was to secure otherworldly compensations for the battered and frightened children of this world. "The whole thing is so patently infantile," he famously writes, "so foreign to reality, that to anyone with a friendly attitude to humanity it is painful to think that the great majority of mortals will never be able to rise above this view of life."[2]

    I want to take up the question of the beauty of the Father in this chapter, and I begin with Freud principally for two reasons. First, I think that Freud is right to see in the notion of a divine father figure a personification

---

1. Freud (1961), p. 34.
2. Ibid., p. 22.

of a providential order. I do not mean to suggest by this that the idea of providence exhausts the idea of God's paternity (it seems obvious to me that it does not); my provisional suggestion is that the beauty of the Father, such as it is, comes through the physiognomy of the created order, the face that the material world, in its unfolding complexity, puts forward. This is not an uncontroversial view. It is possible to hold out for an independent experience of uncreated beauty, pure God as it were, in comparison to which material beauty is practically unreal. I do not understand this point of view well enough to say whether it is right or wrong; the proposed basis of comparison—the beauty that an immaterial God would share with his creation (albeit disproportionally)—is beyond my fathoming. So I am reduced to this, perhaps lesser, complexity: what beauty of this world is divinely fathered? Here Freud is helpful because his answer is so unsentimentally stark: the very idea of a providential order of paternal care is born not of perceptiveness, but of an infantile refusal to face facts.

The facts at issue are the familiar stuff of the problem of evil. We humans are vulnerable in the particularity of our affections; we suffer, we die, we add suffering to suffering, death to death. This is not our whole story, but it is a familiar part. It is not Freud's answer to the problem of evil, however, that interests me. His answer is clear. There is no father in heaven to query about the good; there is only the good that comes of a mortal struggle for knowledge without illusions. What interests me is the sort of illusion that Freud takes the father-god to be. If the desire that motivates the illusion is infantile, I have to wonder what the infant in the deluded adult is so desperately craving. Freud cannot think of any stronger childhood need than the need for a father's protection, and this need, he thinks, ousts union with the mother—the psychogenetic basis for a feeling of oneness with things ("the oceanic feeling")—from the foreground of human religious consciousness. I find it hard to imagine that Freud is right about the primacy of the need for protection, but I find it hard in any case to imagine an infant's point of view. As any parent knows, first-language acquisition involves a complex transformation of a child's self-consciousness and is far from a simple means for publicizing preexisting thoughts and desires. It is nevertheless perhaps fair to say that there is *something* about the infant's sense of being related to a world that gets expressed through an acquired language and so is there in some way prior to language.

I promise to be less vague about this something as this chapter proceeds, but for now I want to underscore that this is a something that parents do not necessarily want their children to outgrow; they may see it as very precious and essential to the person that the child is becoming. When Freud thinks of the infantile nature of religious need, he is thinking of a very fearful, almost paranoid, way of relating to the world. Apart from the father—whose love is not to be taken for granted—the child has no confidence that its happiness matters to anyone. There are, I suspect, children who express mostly the expectation of abuse and indifference in the way they use their words. That is a heartbreaking thought, but not a window into the nature of infant desire and its pathetic metamorphosis into religious need. If we allow ourselves the thought that infant desire—desire for the word—can be fundamentally trusting and not fearful, a different etiology of religious need suggests itself and the question of God's beauty, as I want to frame it, begins to emerge.

My sense of the question is much indebted to John Wisdom, who wrote his influential essay on gods with Freud's psychoanalytic caveats about infantile projections firmly in mind.[3] The gods are, from Wisdom's point of view, psychic forces, but this localization of their influence does nothing to diminish their power. They can, as studies of multiple personalities suggest, act like independent agents within a psyche. "One thing not sufficiently realized," he stresses, "is that some of the things shut within us are not bad but good."[4] I have come to realize, with Wisdom's help, that the infant within religious need is not always a bad influence; it is sometimes a source of beauty.

The burden of Wisdom's essay, which originated as a lecture to the Aristotelian Society, was to convince war-weary philosophers fascinated by logical positivism that a question of beauty could also be a matter of truth. While I concede the importance of such an endeavor, even for post-positivistic times, I construe the burden of my efforts here differently. Mainly I need to distinguish well between a question of beauty and a question about the good. In this undertaking I am going to turn to Plato for help. Plato may have envisioned the eventual convergence of the good and the beautiful, but for purposes of *paideia* (education, childrearing) he kept the two distinct. After taking my leave of Plato, I will suggest why the distinction matters to the question of the Father's beauty. Boethius will be of help here, with his ambiguous affirmation of providence. I conclude with a modest attempt to redeem an infant's point of view.

---

3. Wisdom (1945).
4. Ibid., p. 204.

Parting Knowledge

I. Ascending Darkness

Plato dramatizes the difference between wanting beauty and wanting the good in an exchange that Socrates reports having with the priestess Diotima, whom Socrates credits for having instructed him in the art of love.[5] Diotima asks Socrates what a lover of beautiful things wants when he wants beautiful things. Socrates offers—and how else could he have responded?—that the lover wants to have them. Diotima presses him further: "What will he have when the beautiful things become his?" Here Socrates is at a loss; he has no ready answer. Diotima shifts ground: "Suppose someone were to change the question, making it about the good rather than the beautiful. Tell me, Socrates, what about the lover of good things, what does he want?" Again Socrates appeals to the possessiveness of desire. The lover of good things wants to have good things, and in having them, Socrates is ready to say that this person is happy (*eudaimōn*).

In ethics the good sometimes competes with the right for primacy of place, but almost never with the beautiful. The good has a kind of gravitas to it, especially when it comes armed with a definite article, whereas beauty is apt to be flighty, superficial, and anesthetizing. To be beautiful is not necessarily to be good; to be good is to have some deeper sort of beauty, lost on those who value only looks and renown. The primacy of the good over the beautiful disposes philosophers to prefer a God of absolute goodness and mysterious inner beauty to a pack of good-looking gods who chase after mortal bodies. Plato often gets counted among these philosophers, despite his preference for monism (the good is all) over monotheism (the good is God).

In the exchange between Socrates and Diotima, it looks as if logos has firmly been allied with goodness. Socrates can *say* what it means to seek the good. It is to seek to be *eudaimōn*, not simply in the bland way that the happy are sometimes happy, but in the way that a wise person is well attuned to spirit, to the divine. If I become good, I end up not like an Olympian god, whose beauty is on the outside, but like Socrates, whose snub-nosed and aged frame houses his soul's invisible gold. If Socrates were to seek, as he was reputed to, the beauty of beautiful young men, he would not, so the story goes, be able to say what he would have by having the young men. Keep in mind that the *Symposium* is a dialogue that is preoccupied with the comedy of sexual desire—and also, although less overtly, with the tragedy of it. The problem is not with sexual desire per se,

---

5. *Symposium* 204D–205B; Dover (1980), pp. 34–35.

but with the ambitions that are put upon it. Imagine a man of great accomplishment, ripe with years, facing the waning of his powers; he becomes passionately enamored of a young man of great vitality and stunning looks. The older man is the lover (*erastēs*) that the dialogue alternately ridicules and tries to redeem. In the most obvious way, we of course do know, as do all the characters in the dialogue, what the lover would have were he to possess his beloved: he would have sexual delight. But to recall the question that stumped Freud: what does love of beauty have to do with sex? The beauty of the beloved is precisely what the lover cannot *have*. It is nontransferable. Sexual desire may pose a question of beauty, but it cannot answer the question that it poses.

In his first characterization of erotic desire, the one he convinces Agathon (whose name means "the good") to accept, Socrates claims that desire is always desire for what is lacking. If we sometimes seem to desire what we already have (health, say), that is only because we desire the *perpetuation* of our having it, the future having that is yet to be had. It is in light of this logic of desire that we can begin to see why Socrates was at a loss for words when Diotima asked him about the love of beautiful things. Certainly an older man can *desire* the beauty of a younger one, in that the younger man's beauty is lacking to him, but he cannot expect to make another's beauty his own. At best he can imitate that beauty. Perhaps he dyes his hair, dresses differently, or starts to work out regularly at the gymnasium. The point is that he can enjoy the beauty of someone else—in this case a younger man—only by attempting to master and manipulate the beauty of his own form. It is a dispiriting prospect, and matters are not much better when it comes to loving good things. If possession is really the form of all consummation, then what are the goods that I possess other than the ones that I quite literally consume? I possess the food that I eat when the food and I become one. This is hardly the kind of oneness that would incline me to pause between loving beauty and devouring the good. I experience the beautiful the way I experience the good—as a labor of self-preservation.

This is not where Plato leaves things, however, and he has his character Diotima further instruct Socrates in the fine art of loving beauty. Although there is an appetitive component to the love, in that we can feel ourselves always to crave a *further* beauty, the aim is not to consume beauty but to be in its presence. Diotima tells Socrates that those who earnestly pursue goodness seek "birthing in beauty—according to both body and soul."[6] He professes not to know what she means. He has, after all, been thinking of desire as an imperfection, a sign that something desirable is lacking in a person. Now he is being told that consummate goodness takes place in the presence of the beautiful (a non-consumable good) and that the consummation is not oneness but otherness. The good that I seek becomes other to me in the presence of real beauty; it also comes *from* me. I get to be other to myself, and that does not sound much like self-preservation, but more like parenting.

Diotima does go on to offer Socrates a fuller account of what it means to give birth in beauty, but she warns him that she is speaking of great mysteries and that, as a mere initiate, he may miss her meaning—especially at the end. The devoted lover, she tells him, begins in his youth to devote himself to the love of a beautiful body. As he grows older and more perceptive, he comes to see that the beauty of one body is much like the beauty of another, and so he cultivates his eye for a new kind of beauty, noticed at first in the enthusiasms of single soul. Again the lover is eventually able to abstract from a particular source of beauty to arrive at the unanchored idea. Near to the end of his journey, he finds himself immersed in a great open sea of ideas, a place conducive to contemplation and mental fecundity. There he may catch sight of beauty itself, unmixed with mortality, absolute in its offering. The effect of that sight in the seer is what Diotima calls "true virtue" (*aretē alēthē*).[7]

No doubt the absolute beauty of which Diotima speaks retains its element of mystery, as does the virtue that this beauty elicits, but her description of a real birthing in beauty is not without its telling particularities. She does not say, for instance, that seeing divine beauty causes a mortal or a mortal's offspring to become immortal. Her claim is that the effect of such seeing is to cause the lover of beauty to be particularly favored, loved even, by a god—a being who is naturally immortal. Since beauty is at issue, I will venture to speak of Aphrodite. The goddess loves the one who sees her in particular and therefore sees the absoluteness of her beauty; her love for this person is itself *particular*. I emphasize this last point because Plato is so often criticized for sacrificing the love of individuals on the altar of idealization.[8] Imagine that this is so. Now the goddess herself, having given her favor so particularly, will have to learn how to transcend both body

---

6. *Symposium* 206B; Dover (1980), p. 56.
7. Ibid. 212A; Dover (1980), p. 63.
8. See, for example, the very influential essay by Vlastos (1981), pp. 3-34.

and soul. Eventually she will meet up with herself and find the cathexis there unbearable, a pregnancy without end.

The ascent that would allow me as a lover of the good to transcend particular beauties is not, as Diotima has set it up, a progression of knowledge—for nothing is known yet—but a catharsis of desire. At the beginning of desire, I fit a particular beauty to my inarticulate sense of lacking it; when I conceptualize the lack, I release the particular from having to exist only to satisfy my desire. I begin by releasing bodies; I end by releasing souls. At the point where I am least possessive and most articulate about beauty's possibilities, it becomes possible for a particular beauty to release something in me—something good. Some other being, human or divine, may see the beauty in that goodness and so will not be tempted to consume it. Perhaps it will be the same being whose beauty elicited my goodness in the first place. Plato suggests, through his Diotima (his priestess persona), that it is always Aphrodite doing the eliciting. If so, then love's consummation is a divine mystery and one not much dispelled by speaking of Aphrodite as the Form of the Beautiful.

It is also a mundane mystery. I love my wife, but when I try to describe that love, I am compelled to use words that others have used to describe love and that I have used to describe other loves. I am tempted here to complain about the poverty of language, but Plato has led me to doubt the wisdom of such a complaint. If love of beauty has relieved my pursuit of the good from some of its infantile possessiveness, then why should I want my words to be possessive where my desire is not?

It is the very particularity of how I sometimes manage to love that reminds me of beauty's unavailability to possessive desire. And that is the reminder that releases my logos from jealously and other feelings of inadequacy and allows me to speak freely. I can see some truth in Diotima's claim (and I take it to be Plato's as well) that all beauty is one, but this is the oneness that intensifies the love of a particular beauty.

II. Motherless Aphrodite

The love of beauty articulates two aspects of desire for goodness: the desire to receive (to get what one lacks) and the desire to give (to offer what one has). Both these forms of desire suggest ways—apparently antithetical ones—of *becoming* good. It is fair to say that the way of acquisition has come in for more righteous disdain from just about every moralist under the sun than has the way of dispossession. Neither way, however, is very appealing when made into an independent norm. Apart from a tempering love of beauty, the desire to receive devolves into blind consumption, and the desire to give, its partner in ignorance, devolves into a blind willingness to be consumed.

Despite all the places in Plato where one can find disdain for bodily appetites and their incessant demands, he does not pit the contemplative enjoyment of beauty against appetitive desire. As I mentioned before, we owe to appetite our restlessness with too familiar a conception of beauty; appetite is always for what is lacking, in this case for new conception. This is not an insignificant debt. The ignorance that should worry the philosopher in us is not a lack of knowledge, but an inclination to be content with lack and live by a provincial wisdom. The voice of desire that is always saying to us "more, more, more" can be a check against this inclination. There is of course a catch. In order for appetite to be other than conservative ("more of the same, please"), it has to take in first an element of renunciation. This renunciation is not the release of goodness that Diotima associates with a vision of true beauty. That release is ecstatic and mysteriously fulfilling; this renunciation is irksome and difficult. It is like having to remove the sex from erotic desire, although sex is not the object of renunciation here. Simone Weil, who understood this side of Plato very well, characterized the requisite renunciation this way: "The beautiful is a carnal attraction which holds us at a distance and implies a renunciation. Understand here the most intimate kind of renunciation—that of the imagination."[9]

Plato and Weil would agree that human beings generally have a bad imagination for what makes them good. The figure of sport in the *Symposium*, that of the older lover, imagines that he will become better and more beautiful by keeping the company of a younger man. The symposiasts all agree that if the love of this lover is to be praised, its sexual expression has to be reined in or renounced altogether; if not, one is faced with the naked spectacle of an older man's indignity, and no one is prepared to eulogize that. The second speaker to try to beautify eros, the character Pausanias (Agathon's lover), introduces into the dialogue a dual genealogy for Aphrodite: motherless Aphrodite, the daughter of heaven, inspires lofty, sublimated love; pandemian Aphrodite, whose mother is Dione (an old earth goddess), inspires sexual desire.[10] Pausanias subordinates the younger, sexual Aphrodite to her older, patriarchal image. The moral he draws from such subordination is comically self-serving: as long as a younger man is

---

9. Weil (1988), p. 170.
10. *Symposium* 180E–181D; Dover (1980), pp. 26–27.

reasonably confident that his older suitor is well intentioned—intent, that is, on the younger man's education—the younger man is free to gratify his suitor in any way conceivable. The older man, being a true son of heaven, should have no interest in the chaotic pleasures of the flesh, but sublimation, as Freud suggests, is never without its element of self-deception.

For Freud the self-deception in sublimation has to do with wanting instinctual pleasures by other than instinctual means. It is as if we humans have a dual genealogy: the higher, paternal part of our psyche is parent to logos and law; the lower, maternal part is a source of antinomian beauty and pleasure. Freud would not have countenanced the idea of a motherless Aphrodite. In her place he puts an unlovely father who ignores his daughters and demands renunciation from his sons. They are to renounce their mother; they cannot, that is, allow themselves to recall through pleasure the intimacy of their original maternal connection. Freud has no sense of how beauty can be fathered. He has only his conviction that beauty and desire for the mother are somehow intimately connected. The missing element here is the renunciation that the experience of carnal beauty requires. It is, as Weil hints, a renunciation more intimate than that of sex.

The case of Boethius is instructive. He wrote his most important work, *The Consolation of Philosophy*, while awaiting execution. Boethius stood accused of treason against the Gothic emperor Theodoric, whom he had once served as a close adviser. Although the charges against him were politically motivated and based on dubious testimony, the verdict was a foregone conclusion. His few allies in the Roman Senate acquiesced to Theodoric, an aging and increasingly moody tyrant, and Boethius was tortured in prison and finally bludgeoned to death. His *Consolation* is an astonishing piece of self-reflection given the circumstances of its composition. He tries to convince himself there, using an adopted persona—that of Philosophy herself—that he is responsible for his own bondage. He has allowed himself to think that his great learning, his noble reputation, and his weighty responsibilities have made him the man he is. Now that all of this has come to nothing and he sits alone in a dark cell, the plaything of a tyrant, he finds himself on the edge of despair.

The *Consolation* describes a painful process of disillusionment, a renunciation of imagined worth. Boethius considers some of the artificial beauties he once enjoyed in life—the fine clothes and food that money can buy, the praise that reputation wins—and he has relatively little trouble heaping a philosopher's disdain upon these beauties. They are but trappings. What of natural beauty? Is his virtue as a person like the beauty of a countryside, or a calm sea, or a night sky? Boethius reminds himself that the beauties of the created order are not his to claim—nor can they be claimed: "Fortune can never make yours what nature has set apart from you."[11] So speaks Philosophy. Boethius is left with the thought of his own body, stripped of all alien impositions and reduced to its essential, original needs. Is his body, naked and unashamed, the one beauty that is truly his? If love of beauty is a love that resists possessing its object, Boethius will have to leave that judgment to someone else.

In his days of imagined worth, Boethius thought he could make Theodoric a better man. Theodoric, in turn, concluded he could make Boethius a man of no worth. The persistent fiction that the *Consolation* battles, whether it comes in benevolent or malign form, is that one person determines the worth of another. Not even God makes me good. God makes me who I am. It is up to me to accept the goodness of that and to others to see its beauty. When Boethius arrives at the notion of God that I have just evoked, he arrives at a notion of parenting that cuts through the usual human fascination with fortune and its manipulation. Here the beauty of the Father begins to insinuate itself.

III. The Beauty of the Father

Freud associated the exaltation of the father with an infantile need for protection, but he never said much about the sort of protection an infant would be seeking or why it would be bad for an adult to seek something similar. Most philosophers these days are convinced that consciousness is so bound to language that it would involve a category mistake to want to take up the idea of "infant consciousness." Perhaps. But infants are still very much a part of adult consciousness, especially when the adult is also a parent, and it is perfectly possible to describe this part. Here, for instance, is Augustine's attempt to meet up with the infant in himself (*conf.* 1.6.8):

> Little by little I was becoming aware of my surroundings, and I began to want to indicate my wants to those able to satisfy them. I wasn't able to do this, seeing that my wants were inside me and they were on the outside, lacking all sense for how to get into my soul. So I moved my limbs and used my voice, signing with my few signs, in the best way I could, what I wanted; but my signs did not really look like my wants. And when I wasn't getting what I wanted, either due to a lack of understanding or in order

---

11. *De consolatione philosophiae* 2.5, Boethius (1973), p. 202.

> to spare me harm, I grew resentful of the adults—free people, not slaves—who weren't being subdued, and I revenged myself upon them with a flood of tears. I have learned that infants are like this from infants I have been able to study, and they showed me that I was like this, more so than the nurses who, unlike them, knew me back then.

Augustine is not speaking of his own infancy from memory. He is identifying himself with the infants of his acquaintance, having in mind especially, I would think, what he remembers of his own son's first year or so of life.

As adults we are reduced to inferring what entrance into language must be like for human beginners. So how then do any of know us when we get the picture right? I think that this is the right question for a parent to ask, or someone with parental feelings, but a bad question to ask if the presupposition behind it is that there is nothing to get right. Parents attempt to respond to the needs of their children, and they cannot assume, without trading in their role as parents for something considerably darker, that children have no conception of their own needs if they lack words. Human beings are constantly trying to address one another's wordless needs, and in that regard we are all parents and infants to one another throughout our lives. Freud clearly lamented the perpetuation of infancy into adult life and found the whole idea of an eternally fathered humanity rather embarrassing. In this he betrayed his lack of feeling for infancy.

Consider the infant that Augustine describes. He is a bundle of desires. As he becomes aware of particular desires and the people whom he associates with their satisfaction, he increasingly uses gestures and sounds to convey what he wants. When he does not get what he wants, he throws a fit. Nothing surprising there. Augustine's infant is not just a response-mechanism to frustrated desire, however; he is a bit of an adult psychologist. He attributes *motives* to the adults who fail to respond to his infant gestures at communication. Either the adults fail to understand him, or they understand him just fine but realize that he is asking for something harmful. The basic assumption of this infant is that he is surrounded by people who care about his well-being and who are more than willing, consistent with that well-being, to satisfy his desires. It never occurs to him that he faces indifference or malice. His basic trust in life will encourage his interests in communication and dispose him to revise his desires when necessary. The motives that Augustine's infant attaches to adult non-responsiveness are precisely the motives that most parents *hope* their children will attribute to them when desires go unmet. Better our children think they have been misunderstood than abused; better still they look to a misunderstanding as an occasion for growth.

It hardly needs saying that parents are not perfect and that children, as they grow older, lose much of their original trust. The idea of an eternally fathered humanity puts an extraordinary burden on that trust, as it makes us all into siblings; if someone, who otherwise has no particular relation to me, seems indifferent to my well-being or positively disposed against it, I will have to take up that breach of sibling connection with my father in heaven. Without question the idea of an indefinitely extended family, housed under one father's roof, can be infantile. Suppose I look to my father in heaven to satisfy my current understanding of my happiness in an afterlife and to punish my bad brothers and sisters for frustrating it now. My idea is infantile because it is like an infant's idea of the world, minus the principle of growth. When Boethius looks to his father in heaven for solace, his idea of paternal care may be naïve, but it is certainly not infantile. He assumes that if his desires are not being met, then this is because he has something further to learn about his desires and which ones express him best. The hard corollary to his belief is that his enemy, Theodoric, is not just a means to his education, but a brother who has his own lessons to learn.

I suggested near the beginning of this essay, albeit provisionally, that the beauty of the Father comes through the face of creation. I can say now that when I refer to this face I do not mean the totality of things in their familial harmonies; I mean something that ages. I do not deny the possibility of the grand, synthetic vision; I simply admit that I do not have it. Nor am I sure that I have the heart to have it. I doubt whether I could say from a cross, "Father, forgive them, for they know not what they do" (Luke 23:34). It is even less clear to me that I would heed these words were they addressed to me. My love for my daughter is such that I fail to see how she could release me from the anger and grief I would feel over her suffering. But children sometimes do make this offering to their parents, and parents sometimes find the heart to receive it. There is a difficult beauty on both sides of this courage. It is not an infant's courage, but it is courage with an infant's possibilities.

13

Wittgenstein's Augustine
The Inauguration of the Later Philosophy

> "Truly I tell you, unless you change and become like children, you will never enter the kingdom of heaven."
>
> —MATTHEW 18:3

WITTGENSTEIN PERSONALLY ADMIRED AUGUSTINE and chose to open the *Philosophical Investigations* with an excerpt from book 1 of the *Confessions* (1.8.13)—the part where Augustine is describing his passage from infancy into a first language. It is clear from Wittgenstein's subsequent commentary that he is nevertheless critical of the picture of language that Augustine's self-description seems to presuppose. While many readers of Wittgenstein have been ready to endorse and elaborate his critique of that picture, few have given much thought to the confessional context of Augustine's offering and how that context may have informed Wittgenstein's reception of Augustine. In this essay, I join the small company of readers who have given sustained attention to this issue and propose that Wittgenstein's invocation of Augustine signals a new form of confessional writing.[1] It is

---

1. I am especially indebted to Stanley Cavell and to two other interpreters of Wittgenstein who are also astute readers of Cavell: Stephen Mulhall and Richard Eldridge. Cavell has shaped my basic sense of Wittgenstein's confessionalism, Mulhall has unearthed for me some of the theological content of that (peculiar) confessionalism, and Eldridge has helped me see why the unfinished business of Augustine's conversion is so important to Wittgenstein. See Cavell (1995 and 2002), Mulhall (2001 and 2005),

right to place the *Philosophical Investigations* in the genre of confession, but it is also true that its form of confession is novel, a transformation of the Augustinian paradigm.

I try to make good on my proposal by subjecting the inaugural passage of the *Investigations*—the excerpt from *Confessions* 1.8.13 and Wittgenstein's gloss in PI §1—to two closely related readings. In the first, I emphasize the peculiar nature of Augustine's recollection of his initiation into language. It is a problematic memory; strictly speaking, it is no memory at all. Augustine admits to being forgetful of his time as an infant, and so he clearly can have no recollection of what he was "thinking" before he could use words to convey his desires. None of this deters him, however, from inventing a memory of infancy based on what he has been able to infer from the testimony of nurses and from his own adult acquaintance with infant behavior. Augustine recasts his external access to infancy as a personal recollection, and in so doing he affects to have a more direct acquaintance with his original human desires than he in fact has. Since he admits to the pretense, he is obviously not trying to fool his readers into according him extraordinary powers of self-recollection. I take him to be dramatizing what his sense of himself *must have been like* at the time of his initiation into language. When Wittgenstein raises questions about Augustine's picture of first-language learning, he works to relieve his intended readers—all those tempted by what tempts Augustine—from having to buy into the necessity of Augustine's picture.

It is crucial to my reading of Wittgenstein that Augustine's memorial to his own infancy not be taken as a simple mistake about how any infant comes to acquire a first language. If it were a simple mistake, then we should be able to detach Augustine's theory of language learning from his memorialization of it and come up with a better theory. In the *Investigations*, Wittgenstein disavows having an interest in theorizing;[2] instead he seems bent on exposing some of the myriad ways that language use gets unhelpfully idealized and set in theoretical stone. It may seem that Augustine moves away from theory and into the form and flow of his own life when he trades in an inference for a personal memory, but his resulting self-conception, from Wittgenstein's perspective, remains hostage to a preconception about the work that words ideally do. In my second go at a reading of the inaugural passage, I emphasize this aspect of Wittgenstein's

---

Eldridge (1996 and 1997).

2. As in PI §128: "If someone were to advance *theses* in philosophy, it would never be possible to debate them, because everyone would agree to them." I will be using the revised fourth edition of the *Philosophical Investigations*, Wittgenstein (2009).

critique. It is not so much that Augustine will be shown by Wittgenstein to have misremembered his entry into language, as if there were something here to get over and be done with; the suggestion is more that Augustine's preconception of language use hinders him from recognizing the different forms that an initiation into language can take.

This preconception—that ideal language use assigns words to referents and does so without ambiguity—is no stupid prejudice; it is born of an innately human desire to be understood. The idea that we can speak with one another only if there is, in some ideality, a preconceived meaning for all the words we venture is nevertheless a tyrannical one. It encourages the notion—arguably infantile—that we are racing against one another in life to perfect the meaning of our words; the winner gets to be understood first. Wittgenstein associates the desire for idealized clarity with his favorite saint not to expose a weakness in Augustine's character but to underscore that a mind even as great as Augustine's can fall into this kind of temptation.[3]

The issue for me, however, is not whether Wittgenstein's critique of Augustine is admiring or respectful; it is whether his critique is invested enough in confession to be counted as confessional itself. If we stick to the root meaning of "confession" (*cum* + *fateor*)—an act of speech that seeks its completion in another's acknowledgment—then Wittgenstein's emphasis on the play of meaning *between* speakers can be read to be broadly confessional. Admittedly this reading seems a far cry from the Augustinian paradigm, where to confess is to address God and trade in sin for grace. "I resolve to recall my passed-over impurities and my soul's flesh-fixated corruptions, not," writes Augustine (*conf.* 2.1.1), "that I may love them again, but that I may love you, my God." His confession is indeed a communicative act that seeks acknowledgment from another (in the form of both judgment and forgiveness), but there is no possible substitute in his mind for God's acknowledgment. Suppose that we drop God from confession, devote all of our attention to human interlocution, and think of sin as a disposition, fed by fear and arrogance, to fix a meaning that is still up for social negotiation. The chatty notion of confession that is apt to follow

---

3. Norman Malcolm, a friend and student of Wittgenstein, wrote of Wittgenstein's intense admiration for Augustine. See Malcolm (2001), pp. 59–60: ". . . he revered the writings of St. Augustine. He told me he decided to begin his *Investigations* with a quotation from the latter's *Confessions*, not because he could not find the conception expressed in that quotation stated as well by other philosophers, but because the conception *must* be important if so great a mind held it."

from this would be a parody, not a transformation, of the Augustinian notion.

The reading that stands most in the way of catching Wittgenstein's confession is precisely the one that reads him as taking on Augustine without taking up Augustine's theological preoccupations with sin and grace. This pragmatic, unmystical Wittgenstein persistently redirects a long and venerable tradition of idealism in philosophy, one often given to devotion, away from supramundane revelations and towards the inescapably imperfect but fully human business of improving human understanding. Those attached to this kind of reading do not, of course, see Wittgenstein as reducing the notion of confession to parody; they see him as abandoning the idea altogether—at least when the context is philosophical.

Take, as illustration, the case of Miles Burnyeat, whose influential essay on Augustine's *De magistro* (*On the Teacher*) brings Augustine's thesis there about teaching to the scene of Wittgenstein's critique of *Confessions* 1.8.13.[4] In *De magistro*, a dialogue that comes some eight to ten years before the *Confessions*, Augustine defends the surprising thesis that no one ever teaches anyone anything; properly speaking, Christ, the inner teacher, is the only teacher. With regard to the negative part of the thesis, Burnyeat is prepared to tease out the affinities between Wittgenstein and Augustine, both of whom notice that no outward display of signs—words, gesticulations, pictures—can ever guarantee the delivery of an intended meaning. The effect of this notice is that both Wittgenstein and Augustine accord the first-person perspective an irreducible integrity: whether I grasp a meaning or not is in some primitive way, impossible to define further, about me. Burnyeat argues that Wittgenstein obscures this aspect of his kinship with Augustine by the way he chooses to excerpt *Confessions* 1.8.13; he leaves out the part where Augustine confesses to having learned language not from "adult speakers" (*maiores homines*) but by means of the mind that God gave him.[5] This is no simple case of inadvertence, thinks Burnyeat, but a decision on Wittgenstein's part to stay clear of Augustine's posit of an inner teacher, able to light up a mind from within. In Burnyeat's words: "To leave out God and the Platonic mind for the beginning of the *Philosophical Investigations* was to accept Augustine's problem as his own

---

4. Burnyeat (1987).

5. There are some translation issues that have made this part of *Confessions* 1.8.13 less than self-evidently about autodidactic linguistic ability. Since I happen to agree with Burnyeat about how the issues should be resolved, I will not go into them here; but see Burnyeat (1987), p. 2, n. 3.

and to declare that it must now be solved in naturalistic, purely human terms."[6]

Burnyeat's sense of the indeterminacy of ostensively defined meaning, the integrity of the first-person point of view, and Wittgenstein's revival, via Augustine, of "the ancient understanding of the complexity of understanding,"[7] is considerably more subtle than I have been able to convey above. In this case, however, I am less interested in the subtle side of Burnyeat than in his blunt confidence that his readers will find his contrast between Wittgenstein's naturalism and Augustine's reliance on God of obvious philosophical import. Although I am not one of those readers, I suspect that the implied import is that Wittgenstein is more philosophical than Augustine; both men may have had a genius for seeing where a philosophical perplexity lies, but only Wittgenstein, the story goes, solves his perplexities honestly, in "purely human terms." It strikes me, on the contrary, that a triumphant naturalism, when applied to Wittgenstein, ends up with little or nothing in the way of a triumph. Wittgenstein is just not very forthcoming with all those naturalistic solutions to philosophical problems. So he is either some kind of skeptical naturalist, a latter-day Hume, or he is not helpfully described as a naturalist.[8] And the problem with attributing a deus-ex-machina kind of supernaturalism to Augustine is that Augustine never asks his God for superhuman understanding or for a redemption that would exempt him from having to reckon with time.

It is not obvious to either Augustine or Wittgenstein that the problem of human understanding, when couched as the inability of one speaker to fix meanings in the head of another, is really a problem. If we take it to be a problem, then our real problem may be that we are moved to see a problem where there is none. The conception of philosophy that would attempt to address and undo a disposition to see a problem where there is none may be thought to liken a philosophical problem to a psychosomatic illness; the distress is real, but the source of the problem has been displaced by a fiction, a ghostly body double. As Augustine becomes aware of his sinfulness, he begins to notice his disposition to fictionalize himself. He has been inclined, in all kinds of subtle ways, to confuse the pain of his alienation from God and his own body with an aching desire to find himself complete in the eyes of someone else. Eventually he finds himself

6. Burnyeat (1987), p. 24.

7. Ibid., p. 23.

8. The most influential attempt to render Wittgenstein into a late modern skeptic has been that of Kripke (1982). For a dense but rewarding response to Kripke, see Cavell (1990), pp. 64–100.

able to take to heart this bit of Paul (Rom 13:14; *conf.* 8.12.29): "No more wild parties and drunken fits, bedroom antics and indecencies, rivalries and wrangling; just clothe yourself in Jesus Christ, your master, and don't look to lusts to care for your flesh."

It is fair to wonder whether the need that Augustine feels to adopt God's way of being human has anything to do with the "real need" (*unser eigentliches Bedürfnis*) that Wittgenstein invokes to free a philosophical investigation from a sublimed and, one might say, bodiless logic.[9] It is also fair to wonder whether Wittgenstein's fascination with words and his relation to them carries enough heart to move Wittgenstein into Augustine's neighborhood. When I question Burnyeat's confidence in Wittgenstein's naturalism (a widely shared confidence), I am not hoping to apply a salve of bland religiosity to an awkwardly denaturalized Wittgenstein. I am issuing a caveat: the naturalism that makes it easy for us to part Wittgenstein from Augustine's company is likely to be no more illuminating than the bland religiosity it displaces.

There is in fact a significant divergence between Augustine and Wittgenstein over confession, and it shows up in Wittgenstein's expropriation of Augustine's confessional voice. I will speak to that divergence as explicitly as I can in the concluding section of my essay. In the meantime, I will be working through my two readings of the inaugural passage, hoping to show how Wittgenstein's investment in his own initiation into a language is a form of confessing that he expropriates from Augustine. If someone still wants to call Wittgenstein's takeover a move into naturalism, I have no objection provided that the naturalism invoked is not preemptive and the nature of Wittgenstein's divergence from Augustine remains an open question.

Wittgenstein begins his *Investigations* by taking over a saint's troubled memory of his murky human beginnings. It is Augustine's memory; it is Wittgenstein's own; it is no one's. Much turns on the image of an unclaimed, perhaps abandoned, childhood.

I. An Uncertain Childhood: Augustine's Memory

Here is Augustine's memorial to his infancy as Wittgenstein has, by virtue of his excerpting, chosen to define it (PI §1; *conf.* 1.8.13):

---

9. PI §108, and cf. his remark in PI §36: "Where our language suggests a body and there is none: there, we should like to say, is a *spirit*."

When adults were calling something by name and doing so by moving their bodies in accord with an utterance, I would notice this and commit to mind the sound they were making when they wanted to point this thing out. That they wanted to do this was further apparent from their body language, the language that is, as it were, the natural speech of humankind: a change of countenance, a look, a gesticulation of limbs, a tone of voice that indicates an intent to seek and possess something, or reject and avoid it. Over time I made the right associations between words in sentences and sounds frequently used to point out objects, and once I had wrung the requisite sounds from my mouth, I used them from then on to announce my desires.

I have already indicated in my prefatory remarks what is tellingly selective about this excerpt. If Wittgenstein had begun his excerpt just a few lines prior to where he began it, we would know that Augustine remembers his boyhood (*pueritas*) but not his infancy (*infantia*) and that he discovered only later in life (later than his boyhood) the means by which he had first come to speak. In retrospect, he credits himself and God for bringing that means into some kind of fruition, but not the adults who were, as described above, modeling his words for him.

Left with what we have, Augustine is made out to be recalling his infant consciousness directly, and it turns out that his inner infant is remarkably given to soliloquy. He describes to himself his entry into language *before* he has ever acquired a public means of speaking. At first, Wittgenstein glosses over this striking aspect of Augustine's self-description. He simply tells us that Augustine's words put him in mind of "a particular picture of the essence of human language" (*ein bestimmtes Bild von dem Wesen der menschlichen Sprache*)—one where words name objects and sentences coordinate names. On the face of it, Wittgenstein is alluding to the theory of meaning he was attempting to elucidate in the *Tractatus Logico-Philosophicus*, the great work of his early career, but the logically simple objects of the *Tractatus* and the names that are of their essence are hardly the stuff of an infant's attention, even a preternaturally self-aware one.[10] Wittgenstein asks us to imagine, in conjunction with Augustine's picture, the following use of language (PI §1):

10. The *Tractatus* comes out of Wittgenstein's experience in the First World War. (He finished a draft a couple of months before his internment in an Italian POW camp.) I will be using the D. F. Pears and B. F. McGuinness edition, Wittgenstein (1961). For my purposes, I can forgo the nitty-gritty of Wittgenstein's picture-theory of meaning, but here is a small taste of the complexity surrounding his notion of a logically simple object (proposition 2.0123): "If I know an object I also know all its

> I send someone shopping. I give him a slip marked "five red apples." He takes the slip to the shopkeeper, who opens the drawer marked "apples"; then he looks up the word "red" in a table and finds a color sample opposite it; then he says the series of cardinal numbers—I assume that he knows them by heart—up to the word "five" and for each number he takes an apple of the same color as the sample out of the drawer.

Wittgenstein's shopkeeper is almost as odd as Augustine's infant. Perhaps he was that infant once, but now that he knows the rudiments of a public discourse, he is no longer quite so infantile. Still we need to assume—as if there were some question—that he can count to five on his own. It is hard to know what to do with this picture. I want to ask, how did this shopkeeper get to be this way? Wittgenstein's alter ego, the voice that craves definitiveness and perfect clarity, wants to know how the shopkeeper knows the meaning of his words.[11] It is not a question that Wittgenstein seems interested in answering: "Well, I assume," comes the response (PI §1), "that he *acts* as I have described. Explanations come to an end somewhere."

Augustine's description of his move out of infancy does invite at least a question or two about the mechanics of the move, about what *makes* it work. His inner infant knows what he desires and deems his desires significant: they can be assigned signs and then signified to those who are aware of having, or of having had, those very desires. But how does the infant ever know that his conception of the desire-sign conjunction is the same conception that the speaking members of his world have been assuming all along? A slip of paper with the words "five red apples" scribbled on it does not, after all, look much like an armful of red apples, and a cry of "milk!" is no naturally nearer to a desire for milk than a cry of "milch!" or "lac!" or a word intoned more like a question. I suppose that as long as the shopper keeps getting his desired number of apples and the infant his milk, the matter of how words like "five" and "milk" manage to have meaning need not come up. Hence Wittgenstein's curt dismissal of his alter ego's metaphysical anxiety over meaning (PI §1): "But what is the meaning of

---

possible occurrences in states of affairs. (Every one of these possibilities must be part of the nature of the object.) A new possibility cannot be discovered later."

11. Cavell notices the presence in Wittgenstein's text of two distinct voices: one he calls "the voice of temptation," the other "the voice of correctness." The tempter's voice asks for once-and-for-all clarity; the correcting voice undermines the motive for that request. See Cavell (2002), p. 71. For a more detailed discussion of Wittgenstein's use of dual, even multiple, voices in the *Philosophical Investigations*, see Stern (2004).

the word "five"?—No such thing was in question here, only how the word "five" is used."[12]

Just as I can imagine the shopper always getting his apples from the shopkeeper, I can also imagine, admittedly with some strain, that Augustine's infant always gets what he cries for. What I cannot imagine is that same infant entering into a language; for apart from having a desire go unmet, the infant has no motive to assign significance to any of his desires. At some point in a human life, memorable only after infancy, each of us faces a question of moment: am I being misunderstood, or is my desire being flatly refused? In the face of such a question, it would not be unnatural or even unusual for me to wonder whether I command the meaning of my words. Augustine reads his desire for command back into his infant awareness, apparently under the supposition that he once had, and perhaps still has, the ability to fix the meaning of his words on his own. If his memory is to be credited, then he knew what he meant by the words he used apart from having to participate in a prior practice of sign exchange (e.g., apples for a slip of paper that says "apples") and apart from having to take for granted the form of life that sustains the practice (e.g., the buying and selling of groceries).[13] One easy moral of Wittgenstein's shopping analogy is that Augustine has confused a question of meaning with a question of use; like every other infant on the planet, he learned how to use words before he ever knew or cared what they meant.

But like many easy morals this one too is misleading. It will incline us to think that Wittgenstein is idealizing language and reducing meaning

12. This exchange ends PI §1, the passage I have been calling "the inaugural passage." In his essay on "the child and the scapegoat" (Wittgenstein's myth of the fall), Mulhall (2005) plays out an inventive reading of the shopping analogy: he suggests that the shopper is Wittgenstein's stand-in for a child and that this stand-in is a far more promising representative of childhood than the child that Augustine portrays. The contrast seems less clear to me, but I am nevertheless indebted to the ingenuity and provocation of Mulhall's reading.

13. The concept of a *Lebensform* or "form of life" is a term of art in Wittgenstein and one whose significance is much contested. For some insight into that contestation, see Stern (2004), pp. 160–69. I am not trying to lay a fix on Wittgenstein's use of the term other than to suggest that a form of life is always *shared*. When Augustine writes about his initiation into language, he makes it seem as if he enters into his life with others only after he has inwardly established the significance of all his desires—established their coincidence, that is, with the signs that the adults around him were using to convey theirs. Note *conf.* 1.8.13, the line that immediately follows where Wittgenstein's excerpt leaves off: "So it was that I came to exchange tokens of vocalized desire [*voluntatum enuntiandarum signa*] with those around me and took my big step into the stormy sociability of human life, clinging all the while to my parent's authority and to the nod of other adults."

to a matter of word use. A first use of words, when idealized, gets accorded an extraordinary (I am tempted to say miraculous) power: it is able to contain all possible meanings within its own preexisting idiom. It becomes, in short, the mother of all meanings. Consider, along these lines, the sentiment that Wittgenstein expresses about Augustine in *Investigations* §32:

> Someone coming into a strange country will sometimes learn the language of the inhabitants from ostensive explanations [*hinweisende Erklärungen*] that they give him; and he will often have to *guess* how to interpret these explanations; and sometimes he will guess right, sometimes wrong.
>
> And now, I think, we can say: Augustine describes the learning of human language as if the child came into a strange country and did not understand the language of the country; that is, as if he already had a language, only not this one. Or again: as if the child could already *think*, only not yet speak. And "think" would here mean something like "talk to himself."

Assuming, as I think is the case, that Wittgenstein is offering a critique of Augustine, what is the critique? At the very least Augustine seems to have forgotten the difference between a speaking child and an infant.[14] The "infant" of *conf.* 1.8.13 already has a first language, albeit a private one, and he uses this language as a basis for acquiring a strange tongue—in this case the language into which he was born. However misguided it may be to think of one's birth language as foreign, I do not think that Wittgenstein's implied alternative is to publicize "infant" consciousness and exchange bad interiority for bad, perhaps worse, publicity. I hear his critique of Augustine hitting on the note of the child's estrangement: Augustine describes being born into a life where everyone is a stranger to him—not hostile necessarily, but strange in the way that people from different countries can be strange to one another.

From here, I see two ways to develop Wittgenstein's critique. In one we run with the notion that Augustine has illicitly shifted the focus of his memory. Let's not forget that he was father to a son whom he well loved and long outlived. Around the time of the *Confessions*, when Augustine was a few years past forty and Adeodatus nearly ten years gone, Augustine may still have remembered something about his son's infant efforts at first words. He would have remembered nothing, however, about his own

---

14. The German word for "infant"—*Säugling*—picks up on an infant's tie to the breast and not on a lack of language; even so, Wittgenstein is clearly struck by the prior literacy of Augustine's first-language learner, whom he refers to as "*das Kind.*"

efforts. No one—not Augustine, not Adeodatus—can remember his first entry into a language. When Augustine recasts his outside observer's point of view as a piece of introspection, he asserts a memory where there can be none. If this line of critique is reliable, then a theory in developmental psychology—that infants lack self-awareness—will have been verified by way of a thought experiment. Is it thinkable that we know the meaning of a word before we know how to use it? If not (and "not" is the presumption here), then self-awareness is quite unintelligible outside the context of socially regulated language use. Although I find this use of a thought experiment to be out of keeping with Wittgenstein and tending (again) towards the idealization of language, I have a simpler reason for rejecting the line of critique I have just adumbrated: it pays no attention to the specificity of Wittgenstein's critique. The child that Augustine describes cannot feel himself to be anything if he lacks self-awareness, but if that is Wittgenstein's point, then why does he suggest, more particularly, that the child is strangely made out to feel like a stranger?

In the alternative line of critique that I am about to follow, we need to entertain a more radical possibility about Augustine's fictionalized memory: that he does more than engage in a kind of sham introspection; he suppresses his memory of infancy altogether. The relevant memory is indeed wrapped up with Augustine's sensitivity to the infancy of others, but here we might be tempted to think that no amount of sensitivity can turn an inference into a personal memory. And of course if we mean by "personal memory" an inner viewing, originally (and perhaps permanently) private, then it is surely right to think that infancy is either observed or inferred but never remembered. On the other hand, it seems perverse to insist too strongly on parents having to observe the infancy of their children and never getting to experience it. The sober truth may be that I cannot have the experience of others, not even the ones I love intimately and raise from infancy, but the more supple realization is that a parented life is never unambiguously bounded. We tend to spill into our parents as they spill into us, all the way back to Adam and his father. When Augustine draws a boundary around his infancy and resolves the domain of inquiry into either inference or private memory, he makes infancy unconfessable—something that can never come between progenitor and child, for good or ill.

In his critique of Augustine, Wittgenstein aims to move Augustine back to confession, or more accurately (as we shall see), he corrects Augustine's confession in order to advance a confession of his own. He thereby honors one of Augustine's professed hopes: to be received and corrected by a confessional reader, a brother in spirit. "He is brother to me," writes Augustine (*conf.* 10.4.5), "who delights on my behalf when he approves of me and grieves for me when he does not, for he loves me all the same whether he approves or disproves. It is to him and his like that I reveal myself."

In my next section, I focus directly on the confessional aspect of Wittgenstein's reading of *Confessions* 1.8.13. For the remainder of this one, I hope to suggest where some inkling of Augustine's genuine memory of infancy can be found. Again this is not a matter of coming up with an alternative report of Augustine's mental state; it is a matter of finding what truth there is in his confession of infancy. To this end, I rely on the distinction that Wittgenstein makes in the sketchy addendum to the *Investigations*, the passage where he speaks to the nature of true confession (fragment xi, n. 319):

> The criteria for the truth of the *confession* that I thought such-and-such are not the criteria for a true *description* of a process. And the importance of the true confession does not reside in its being a correct and certain report of some process. It resides, rather, in the special consequences which can be drawn from a confession whose truth is guaranteed by the special criteria of *truthfulness*.

Wittgenstein is using the notion of confession (*Geständnis*) loosely and so not with an overtly religious or moral intonation. Stanley Cavell evokes a basic sense of confession when he writes, "In confessing, you do not explain or justify, but describe how it is with you."[15] Let's play out a bit what defeats or blocks confession at a basic level. You offer me some self-description and then tell me that I need, before presuming to understand you, to get into your head and note the meanings that you associate with your words. You are no longer confessing anything; you are mortgaging your words to a standard of correctness that neither you nor I can hope to meet. I cannot meet it because I cannot in fact get into your head. You cannot meet it because you cannot rely on your words to convey your intended meaning. When Augustine offers us his description of infancy in *Confessions* 1.8.13, he tempts us to get into an infant's head and note there the presence or absence of a world of meaning. If we resist this temptation, we are left having to draw conclusions from a truthfulness that rests on the application of "special criteria."

15. Cavell (2002), p. 71.

Wittgenstein says nothing about what those special criteria may be, but I suspect that nothing could be said about them in the abstract that would be other than vacuous. (And so why say anything?) When we turn to the specific case of Augustine's confession of infancy and its truthfulness, we clearly have to have more than *Confessions* 1.8.13 to work with. Otherwise we are left with a self-description that invites alienation from the condition of infancy, of the sort that Wittgenstein's describes in PI §32: the infant child, infancy itself, seems to belong to no one.

Tellingly we find more of what we need from Augustine in his description of his conversion. For most of book 8 of the *Confessions*, he recounts the anguish he once felt over his spiritual impotence, his inability to discard his old and discredited erotic fantasies and resolve upon a new life. We get to hear his agonized argument with himself in a garden retreat, to feel with him the futility of argument, and to wonder with Alypius, his friend and silent witness, whether Augustine has a way out of his private Gethsemane. In far less space than it took him to define the anguish, Augustine finally describes the moment of turning (*conf.* 8.12.29):

> Suddenly I hear a voice coming from a nearby house—hard to say whether it was a girl's or a boy's; it just kept chanting the words "pick up and read, pick up and read" (*tolle, lege*). Right away I felt more relaxed, and I began to think hard about whether children use a chant like that in some game they play. But I couldn't remember ever hearing it before. My tears now in check, I stood up, convinced that the chant was nothing else than a divine command to me to open my book and read the first verse that comes to view.

Augustine's book is a book of Paul's letters, and when he opens it he hits upon Romans 13:13–14. At that moment an imperative to pick up and read gives way in his mind to an imperative to clothe himself (*induite*) with Jesus Christ, his master, and junk the old erotic fantasies: they do the flesh no good. He reports having no need to read further; a "light of relief" (*lux securitatis*) fills his heart.

Augustine's reception of his new imperative is, I think, incomprehensible apart from the mediating voice of the child. It is a voice whose sexuality is latent (male or female, who can tell?) and whose offering to Augustine is to introduce him to a new, or perhaps just forgotten, form of play. Augustine takes that offering to be authoritative; he concludes that God is relating to him through a child's voice. Perhaps the child's voice just is God's voice; Augustine already believes, after all, that God was once a child—having been a child is an aspect of who God is. Perhaps the voice conveys what God remembers about being a child, a memory that Augustine is being prompted to share as he turns to the serious business of picking up a holy book and looking for himself in its pages. A spirit of play is not frivolity to a beginner in life, but a necessity, and the adult looking for a new start in life may well have to remember this before continuing on with too much serious business. If Augustine can still hear the child's voice in his divine call to a new humanity, then he is freed for a time from the oblivion that makes a child so strange to an adult.

The other way to read the force of the imperative, a reading I resist, is to accent Christ's persona as Augustine's lord and master and assume that Augustine is being given a divine gift of adult self-mastery—a gift that he is obliged over time, though perhaps a very long time, to accept. Whatever the merits of this reading, it tends to confuse self-mastery (which can't be a gift) with being released from a tyranny (which can be). And it is not always an act of will that brings about a person's liberation, but something more akin to a memory. A child's desire, in its remembered innocence, can sometimes get the better of adult lust and redeem aging flesh from the violence of unmet needs. When that happens, the adult is, in effect, trying on an original innocence.

Augustine believed, in keeping with his complex teaching about original sin, that only Jesus and Mary were originally innocent. The rest of us have to remember all the way back to Adam for some connection to an innocent beginning, and Adam's innocence did not, in any case, keep him from falling into sin. If adults and infants are equally defined by a history of disaffection, then infancy is simply disaffection looking for a name. But I do not think that this is Augustine's settled view of the matter. Yes, he sees some connection, a bloodline, between infant desire and adult disaffection, but he also has some inclination to put Christ into that same bloodline. Even when he relates to Christ more as a garment than as an extension of his own skin, the promise of a greater intimacy is always there for him. In confessing to conversion, he confesses to an innocence, distantly remembered, that checks his presumption to be speaking out of disaffection alone. Perhaps he has to unspeak the illusion of a language before he can speak at all. If so, then his conversion is his awareness that he is still learning a first language.[16]

16. When he speaks of Augustine's appeal to Wittgenstein, Eldridge emphasizes Augustine's awareness of the intimacy between conversion and language learning. I have taken a page (or two) from Eldridge and tried to develop his fundamental insight. See Eldridge (1997), pp. 121–28.

II. An Uncertain Childhood: Wittgenstein's Critique

I return now to Wittgenstein's critique of Augustine's picture of language, this time with a focus on its confessional aspect. Augustine confesses to sin, to a disposition to mistake his life's end and so also to misconceive his life's beginning. More than Augustine does, Wittgenstein sees misconception at work in *Confessions* 1.8.13, where Augustine describes his way into words. The language that Augustine imagines as his first—an affair of matching names to concrete objects of desire—rests on a picture of language that Wittgenstein considers to be, if not mistaken, then impoverished. Say that Wittgenstein is right. It is hardly a confessional critique to point out the mote in a brother's eye and not notice the beam in one's own. Does Wittgenstein ever confess to difficulties of his own? And are those difficulties of a piece with a saint's struggle to see through to the other side of a sinful disposition?

In the *Investigations*, Wittgenstein often gives voice to a disposition to expect the wrong kind of clarity in life. Here is one example (PI §101):

> We want to say that there can't be any vagueness in logic. The idea now absorbs us that the ideal *"must"* occur in reality. At the same time, one doesn't as yet see *how* it occurs there, and doesn't understand the nature of this "must." We think the ideal must be in reality; for we think we already see it there.

For Wittgenstein, the temptation to idealize language as logic and then expect reality to follow suit is neither trivial nor neatly intellectual, and it can operate in unexpected ways. In the preface to the *Tractatus*, the work of his most obsessed with clarity and yet given to nonsense, Wittgenstein tells us that the sense of his entire book comes down to this: "What can be said at all can be said clearly, and what we cannot talk about we must pass over in silence."[17] But, as it turns out, Wittgenstein cannot speak about what *makes* a sentence speakable without lapsing into nonsense.[18] This is because the narrator of the *Tractatus* finds himself in the same spot as the

---

17. Wittgenstein (1961), p. 3.

18. In 6.54, the penultimate proposition of the *Tractatus*, Wittgenstein makes his famous declaration about the nonsensical nature of all of his propositions: "My propositions serve as elucidations in the following way: anyone who understands me eventually recognizes them as nonsensical, when he has used them—as steps—to climb up beyond them." The proper interpretation of 6.54 has given rise to a controversial new school of Wittgenstein interpretation, one largely associated with the efforts of James Conant and Cora Diamond. For a class portrait of this school, see Crary and Read (2000).

infant in *Confessions* 1.8.13: he has to give words to the preconceptions of meaning that give words meaning—as if he were somehow able to speak ahead of himself. Wittgenstein hopes to make a virtue out of the irony: once the *Tractatus* gets us to see that there can be no special language of logic and that the logic of our language, of any language, has to be taken for granted, we will be less likely to indulge in unintended nonsense and more likely to speak correctly. We will speak, that is, only about objects of sense, as Augustine's child does, but with an adult's comprehension of the broader world of objects, basically the world of natural science.[19] More than this, we will have the good grace to honor logic, ethics, and aesthetics with a reverential silence. For now we know that there is no correct way to speak about what defies objectification.

In his preface to the *Investigations,* Wittgenstein encourages the notion that his new thoughts are all about his struggle to break from the grip of his old way of thinking:

> Four years ago I had occasion to re-read my first book (the *Tractatus Logico-Philosophicus*) and to explain its ideas to someone. It suddenly seemed to me that I should publish those old thoughts and the new ones together: that the latter could be seen in the right light only by contrast with and against the background of my old way of thinking.[20]

In the *Tractatus,* Wittgenstein counsels us to keep silent in the face what fails to admit of a correct description. In the *Investigations,* we are invited again and again to play with the idea that where the one correct description seems impossible or unutterable, there many descriptions may be usefully ventured. What we are given in the *Investigations* is not logic, but forms of life.[21] Wittgenstein tries to remind us there—and to remember himself—that what any of us begins with is a life and that this life can take a variety of forms.

Since it is not so easy to imagine having forgotten so mundane a truth, I can see why Wittgenstein would have wanted to bind his two ways of thinking—the old and the new—into a single book. We have to feel the force of a temptation before we can take much interest in the life that is free from its grip. A confession of grace can sound puerile when the fight

---

19. See TLP 6.53, where Wittgenstein identifies correct method in philosophy: "... to say nothing except what can be said, i.e., propositions of natural science."

20. PI, p. 10.

21. Ibid., fragment xi, n. 345: "What has to be accepted, the given, is—one might say—*forms of life.*"

against sin is removed from it and we are left only with a vision of child's play. Wittgenstein, as we know, never realizes his idea of publishing his two great works side by side, but he does bind his two ways of thinking together. In the *Investigations* the old way shows up as a voice of temptation, down but not out. If he were to have taken a more literal approach, setting his new thoughts against the letter of the *Tractatus*, he might have given us a more vivid sense of his self-scrutiny and struggle for catharsis. But I am more inclined to think that he would have succeeded mainly in making Augustine seem less interesting: Augustine makes the same mistake as the author of the *Tractatus*, but more crudely, like someone philosophically naive.

As the text of the *Investigations* now stands, Augustine holds a place of honor and authority. Wittgenstein allows Augustine to supply him with his most perspicuous picture of a subtle, but profound, temptation. In *Confessions* 1.8.13, Augustine writes as if the meaning of his words were given to him independently of his unfolding life in the flesh with others (a sin against the incarnation?); the result, as Wittgenstein shows us, is a picture of alienated childhood and a missing beginning to a life, a lost infancy. The moral for Wittgenstein is certainly not that Augustine is a clumsy philosopher, lacking in good grammatical sense (*of course* he knows that not all words are nouns); it is that Augustine's need to confess is so serious, so close to the bone of a human life, that even his slip at confession is illuminating. Augustine's slip in *Confessions* 1.8.13—the slip, that is, out of infancy and into something unconfessed—gives Wittgenstein a captivating insight into his old (and unconfessed) need for a "preconception of crystalline purity" (*das Vorurteil der Kristallreinheit*; PI §108).

The picture of language in the *Tractatus* is not a pictorial picture: it is a verbal prompt for the imageless form that a proposition and a state of affairs (real or possible) supposedly share in common. Apart from that form, no proposition would make sense (i.e., have a truth-value). The self that intuitively grasps logical form is what Wittgenstein calls "the philosophical self" (*das philosophische Ich*). His characterization of it in the *Tractatus* is largely by way of negation: "The philosophical self," he writes (TLP 5.641), "is not the human being, not the human body, or the human soul, with which psychology deals, but rather the metaphysical subject, the limit of the world—not a part of it." That may not sound like much of a self to be, but keep in mind that the alternative, the self that is of interest to psychologists, is for Wittgenstein a rather dingy affair. It fears death, wills to live inside a narrow point of view, and looks for happiness in altered circumstances. Meanwhile the properly philosophical self stays above all that: it lives at the limits of the world (TLP 6.43), regards with sublime indifference the world's particulars or the how of things (TLP 6.432), and, most beguiling of all, it never experiences death (TLP 6.4311). This is not a confessional self or any kind of self that looks at itself. If it were to write a book called *The World as I Found It*, then it would, Wittgenstein suggests (TLP 5.631), have to leave itself out of the account.

Augustine too is hoping not to identify himself with a dingy, grasping, puny self, but he seems to know better than Wittgenstein that it is possible to live at the limits of the world and still be that self. In *Confessions* 1.8.13, Augustine affects to speak at the limits of spoken language; both the affectation and the ambition make his infant persona seem philosophical in the Tractarian sense of that notion. In *Confessions* 1.6.8, in a passage closely allied to the one Wittgenstein excerpts from 1.8.13, Augustine accords his infant persona its infantile desires:

> Little by little I was becoming aware of my surroundings, and I began to want to indicate my wants to those able to satisfy them. I wasn't able to do this, seeing that my wants were inside me and they were on the outside, lacking all sense for how to get into my soul. So I moved my limbs and used my voice, signing with my few signs, in the best way I could, what I wanted; but my signs did not really look like my wants. And when I wasn't getting what I wanted, either due to a lack of understanding or in order to spare me harm, I grew resentful of the adults—free people, not slaves—who weren't being subdued, and I revenged myself upon them with a flood of tears. I have learned that infants are like this from infants I have been able to study, and they showed me that I was like this, more so than the nurses who, unlike them, knew me back then.

The last sentence makes it clear that Augustine is not claiming introspection as the source of his knowledge. He has no memory of his own infancy, but as I tried to show earlier, in keeping with a suggestion from Wittgenstein, the offer of a confession is not the self-report of a mental state. With that caveat in mind, notice what Augustine is offering us here. From his adult study of infants he claims to know what he must have been like as an infant. He paints his infant self as a narcissistic tyrant, bent wholly on getting his wants met.

Still his portrait is not simply of a tiny self-aggrandizer; there is as much pathos in what he depicts as aggression. The infant is angry and frustrated because he finds that his body language of desire is frequently breaking down. He tries to embody some desire of his, and the adults either miss his meaning or fail to respond to him for reasons he cannot yet comprehend, having little or no sense of harm. If he wants to recover an effective language of desire, he will need to study adult body language, which will include verbal gesticulating, and cue his desires to that. It will finally be someone else's body that will redefine for him the significance of his desires. We get the portrait of the infant-student attending to foreign bodies in *Confessions* 1.8.13. If we combine the student with the tyrant, we are left with someone who looks to lusts to care for his flesh (Rom 13:14) and forgets the significance of his own body; the portrait is of self-tyranny. Augustine has not reminded us of what it is like to be an infant; he has reminded us of what it means to remain an unconfessed sinner.

Now try to imagine the confession of the philosophical self. First hear this self speak about death and its freedom from death (TLP 6.4311):

> Death is not an event in life: we do not live to experience death.
> If we take eternity to mean not infinite temporal duration but timelessness, then eternal life belongs to those who live in the present.
> Our life has no end in just the way in which our visual field has no limits.

In Wittgenstein's German, the self that relates itself so to death is impersonal ("Den Tod erlebt *man* nicht") and, because an impersonal self is everyone's, it is also first-person plural ("*Unser* Leben ist ebenso endlos"). As I write about the passage above, I revert to the first-person singular, and I signal by this reversion the solipsistic perspective of the philosophical self, if one can still call a perspective the bare conceit of a perspective. Death is not an event in life: true, if my death is the only death that matters to me. Then I can claim, as if it were some kind of philosophical virtue, that I have no birth and no death: my recollection of the one is as inconceivable to me as my anticipation of the other. There is no "I" that comes to be and none that ceases: none, that is, until I recall that I may be someone in the eyes of someone else. My birth can be marked and celebrated; my death marked and mourned. Still I will not be able to claim the memories of my birth and death as my own; I can remember the limits of only the life that claims me from without—the one that enters my visual field and relieves me (for a time) of my timelessness. The memory of a limited life is always a confessional memory: it wrecks the integrity of the first-person point of view and puts us into one another's keeping.

Parting Knowledge

Having invited Augustine to open the *Investigations*, where the old philosophical self assumes a more recognizably human form, Wittgenstein does not then advance the argument—which would have been a rather ungrateful one—that Augustine's first try at words is, as he describes it, inconceivable. It is conceivable that Augustine could have come to believe that he needed to translate his body into another's or another's into his own in order to be understood at all, but no one who loves Augustine will want to think that this is how he entered his life with others or how he exited from it. Wittgenstein's loving tribute to Augustine is his playful insistence, carried throughout most of the *Investigations*, that Augustine's picture of language in *Confessions* 1.8.13 is simply unnecessary.

If he had claimed more than this, insisting in the style of the *Tractatus* on what is impossible to say, he would have usurped the power of logos that Augustine reserves for God. No longer the master of words, Wittgenstein is prepared to confess, in a voice never entirely his own, the darker possibilities of conception—the ones that orphan the soul and render the body a prison-house or a coffin. He is also open to the possibility of correction without self-torment.[22] I am tempted to say that Wittgenstein now writes out of humility, but I know too little about that peculiar virtue. It strikes me all the same that he begins the confession of his later philosophy when he looks without condemnation or approval at the unconfessed sin of someone he loves.

III. Sin and Grace: Reprise

Once it is granted that the Wittgenstein of the *Investigations* is a confessional writer, his preference for conceptual perplexity over prayerful agony ceases to be a simple matter of a naturalized outlook: it speaks to a shift that he effects *within* the idiom of a confession, one that suggests more than a few degrees of separation between him and Augustine. I am ready now to speak to that confessional shift of focus, and I begin with a bit of anecdotal information. In one on his informal remarks on religion, Wittgenstein has this to say about his grasp of divine election:

> In religion it must be the case that corresponding to every level of devoutness there is a form of expression that has no sense at a

---

22. Wittgenstein was well known for the severity of his self-judgments and his compulsive need to confess his shortcomings to friends and acquaintances. For a sensitive but unsparing portrait of this side of his personality, see Fania Pascal, "Wittgenstein: A Personal Memoir," in Luckhardt (1979), pp. 23–60.

> lower level. For those still at the lower level this doctrine, which means something at the higher level, is null and void; it can only be understood *wrongly*, and so these words are *not* valid for such a person.
>
> Paul's doctrine of election by grace, for instance, is at my level irreligious and ugly nonsense. So it is not meant for me since I can only apply wrongly the picture offered me. If it is a holy and good picture, then it is so for a quite different level, where it must be applied in life quite differently than I could apply it.[23]

Paul's doctrine of election by grace is usually taken to have these elements: (1) all of us, by virtue of original sin, are hell-bent on sticking with an unhealthy self-love; (2) some of us have nevertheless been predestined for a better love; and (3) those precious few, the elect, are in no position to resist God's "offer" of a better love.

The doctrine, thus parsed, is not Paul's but Augustine's. Augustine just happened to be very good at making the doctrine seem like Paul's.[24] It was from his reading of Romans 9 that he derived his doctrine of gratuitous and irresistible election, and with that doctrine in place he became ever more inclined to blame human beings for being Adam's heirs. Original sin developed in Augustine's mind into something between a fatal illness and a capital crime. If the trifecta of gratuitous election, irresistible grace, and original sin can be said to inform the *Confessions*—and it certainly would be hard to write out its influence altogether—then the Wittgenstein who finds ugly and irreligious nonsense in Paul is not likely to be reading Augustine at "the higher level."

Personally I have always found it profoundly unhelpful when reading Augustine to suppose that his doctrines have a life apart from the confessional context that supplies them with their application. It is crudely correct to say that Augustine holds to unmerited election, irresistible grace, and original sin. But I cannot, any more than Wittgenstein can, imagine those abstracted doctrines as *my* truths; they suggest to me a picture that I cannot apply but wrongly—a picture of willfulness and the abdication of love. On the other hand, I cannot remember having chosen to be born, I did not earn the love I was first offered, and I have been unable, try as I might, to refuse my need for unmerited love. My point is not that Augustine's doctrines, once confessionalized, become ordinary and livable.

---

23. Quoted from Wittgenstein (1998), p. 37e. The remark dates from late November 1937. I have slightly modified Peter Winch's translation.

24. For Augustine's reinvention of Paul, see two landmark essays: Stendahl (1963) and Fredriksen (1986).

Parting Knowledge

I mean something more along these lines: that we cannot fairly distance ourselves from the confession he models for us simply by gesturing to a supernaturalism that only he (deluded man or superman) can appreciate. When Wittgenstein is feeling less Kierkegaardian and more Augustinian about religion, he resists the lure of false sublimity very well.

In one respect, Wittgenstein resists it better than Augustine does, and here is where I would locate Wittgenstein's shift of confessional focus. He does not accept Augustine's notion that we are born into a world having to will, ever more desperately over time, the privacy of our desires. Where there is a tendency to forget how often a desire to live can be for another's desire to live, Augustine puts a darkly sublime will to preempt the exchange of desire that leads to mutual self-awareness. Too confidently he accuses himself of having pressed all his desires into the exclusive service of his own, original body—as if that determination were obvious. No wonder he discounts so easily the role his parents may have played in eliciting his first words. They are, to his infant self, just two more adults more or less disposed to guess at his desires. They have to guess at his desires just as he has to guess at theirs. The language that sets in between outsiders is a monument to alienation. There is no sign of an original parenting here, no nod to the responsiveness that comes before all the guesswork. When Wittgenstein contests the necessity of Augustine's account of language learning, he contests the idea that the world is naturally an orphanage. I cannot confess to having been born to such a world; there would be no one, not even God, to take my confession.

I can confess only to the sin that reminds me that I lack the synoptic view of my condition. Were I to see ahead of all the exits and entries of my shared life with others, I would be making yet another exit and falsely imagining it to be my grand entry. Here Wittgenstein reassures me that a language of timeless definitiveness and a perspective at the limits of my world is not in any case what I want: none of that would meet my "real need." Augustine warns me that I have taken my taste of the knowledge that is both disaffecting and full of promise and that now only God can help me. I do not think, despite how it may sound at first, that Wittgenstein and Augustine are speaking to very different forms of deliverance. The God who writes the synopsis of Augustine's life also remembers being an infant—a being whose power of logos lies in its need. Admittedly God's entry into infancy is only one expression of the power of God, but it is the one that defines the rest. That, at least, is what Wittgenstein calls us to believe.

Wittgenstein's Augustine

Here is Wittgenstein again, on Paul's religion (though really Augustine's):

> In the Gospels—as it seems to me—everything is *less pretentious*, humbler, simpler. There you find huts—with Paul a church. There all human beings are equal and God himself is a human being; with Paul there is already something like a hierarchy; honors and official positions.[25]

Doubtless Wittgenstein has a point to press against Augustine and his church, a serious claim of grievance. Still it is Augustine who describes his soul as a cramped lodging (*domus angusta*), a hut in need of repair (*ruinosa*).[26] And what is a church really but a village of such huts?

---

25. Wittgenstein (1998), p. 35e.

26. *conf.* 1.5.6: "Cramped is the place in my soul where you come to lodge: stretch it out, God, for it's a wreck."

14

What the Saints Know
Quasi-Epistemological Reflections

BEGIN WITH A SAINT's dilemma. The year is 1077. Anselm is not yet of Canterbury, not yet the great archbishop. He is still thinking his contemplative thoughts at the Benedictine monastery of Bec, where he is soon to become its abbot. Anselm tells us in the preface to the *Proslogion*, the work he is working on at the time, that he wants to find a single argument (*unum argumentum*), sufficiently potent to illuminate whatever he and his monks believe about God, but especially effective in three key areas: absolute existence, sovereign goodness, and the dependence of all creatures on the one absolutely existing sovereign God. He tries to think his way into his desired argument, to the point of exhaustion. It is only when he relaxes his intent and resolves to focus on other things that his guiding insight gets through, goading him (*cum importunitate*) to follow the path he has come to think impossible. He is to meditate on God as "the being greater than which none can be conceived" (*cogitari*). Famously Anselm turns his meditation into a proof of God's existence: a being that exists only in the mind of another is decidedly less great than a being that needs no other to exist; a truly self-subsisting being (and it turns out that there is only one of them) cannot be conceived not to exist. Less famously, but no less importantly, Anselm argues that God is inconceivable: a conceivable divinity, subject to someone else's conception, can hardly be self-subsisting. And herein lies Anselm's dilemma. If he is able to conceive of the God he reveres, then his God is not God; but if the God he reveres eludes his powers of conception, then his God is not his.[1]

One possible way out for Anselm is to lay claim to an experiential knowledge of God, or a largely nonconceptual sense of inconceivable greatness. I can't see where in the *Proslogion* Anselm does this, but imagine if he had. The knowing would have to have this much conceivability: that it is of God. An object-free knowing, feeling like nothing conceivable, is too inchoate to count as noetic; it knocks at the door of awareness but never enters the room. Meanwhile, the sensation of our current hypothetical interest floods a barely conceivable conception of God ("the being greater than which . . .") with rich but unutterable content. The hypothetical Anselm who has this sensation of God would be hyperconscious, or so far removed in his awareness from his normal habits of perception that he sees clearly the unbridgeable abyss between what he is experiencing—a veritable apotheosis of sensation—and what he will be able to convey to outsiders.

Consider one way of being at a loss for words. There are many things in my experience for which I lack a complete description: the love that allows me to love my daughter and son differently and yet without partiality; the justice that both individuates and unites; the pleasures of friendship; the beauty of play. I could go on. I lack words for these things, not because I can say nothing about them (I sometimes have much to say), but because I resist thinking that my knowledge of these things is ever complete. In this way, I aim to avoid the ignorance of which Diotima, the mysterious high priestess of Plato's *Symposium*, speaks. It is not lack of knowledge that starves and imprisons the soul, but rather, as Socrates hears from Diotima, the presumption to know where one still has need of understanding. "For it is precisely this," warns Diotima, "that makes the lack of understanding so difficult—that if a man is not beautiful and good, nor intelligent, he has the opinion that that is sufficient for him; consequently he who does not believe that he is in need does not desire that which he does not believe he

---

1. For the text and translation of Anselm's *Proslogion*, I am using Charlesworth (1965), but I prefer to translate *cogitari* as "conceived" rather than (more blandly) "thought." Conceiving connotes a creativity that mere thinking does not. It is when Anselm is still conceiving of God that he demonstrates God's existence. See *Proslogion*, chapters 2 and 3. This part of the *Proslogion* begins the history of the so-called ontological argument. I am not convinced that Anselm has an ontological argument to offer, not in anything like the modern sense, but I won't argue the point here. But see Marion (1999). Anselm first argues for God's inconceivability in *Proslogion* chapter 15 (a deceptively short chapter). After this come several chapters of chastened meditation on "inaccessible light" (*lux inaccessibilis*).

needs."[2] Also in keeping, I think, with wanting to avoid ignorance of this sort, I would disclaim knowing that I can *never* be free of the need for a transformed point of view. I take it on faith that in being ever desirous of better wisdom, I am not turning my back on what has been a definitive offering and wedding my desire to darkness.

Mine is not a faith without presumption, but consider the cost of a presumption-free faith, or another way of being at a loss for words. In this scenario, I would have, by way of ecstatic experience, definitive knowledge of the indescribable good; being *the* good, this good is also my good. Now what about all those other goods that I have been able, with my limited abilities, to describe? They may end up as severely limited goods, but if I am taking ineffability as a criterion of knowing the good, they lose even their limited status. Once I have a taste of the ineffable, I no longer need the illusion of other, articulable goods to sustain my desire. It does not follow from this, however, that such goods are no good at all. In losing their limited status, they fall squarely within the logic of ineffable goodness: I cannot say what makes distinctive goods good because I cannot say what makes God good. The catch is that I also cannot say what makes distinctive goods distinctive. Individuation has no foothold within a cloud of ineffability. I would need to use a language steeped in illusion even to describe the passing of the many varied goods into the one God, for, in retrospect, I see that there have been no goods but God, no goodness but unspeakable goodness. The faith required of me here has me continuing to use such a language for my worldly entanglements, confident that I will not thereby lapse into delusion myself.

Anselm's dilemma—roughly the disjuncture in ecstatic consciousness between empty conceptualization and inconceivable knowing—is a real dilemma, one that speaks to what I would call, somewhat diffidently, "the epistemology of mystical experience." And although I have certainly not said enough in my introductory remarks to rule out the possibility of an essentially inconceivable form of knowing, I am not going to pursue this possibility further. Supposing that there is this form of knowing, it would by definition fail to connect with even the thinnest of conceptualizations. This not only creates a gulf between mystics and their experientially challenged observers; it causes a fissure within the mystics themselves, who must, after their momentary ecstasies have passed, recollect what they have lost—a task of conceptualization. It is also doubtful whether such knowing has much, if any, relevance for saintliness. Anselm, after all, is

---

2. *Symposium* 204A; Benardete (2001), p. 34.

What the Saints Know

not aiming at a new and sublimely pleasurable sensation; he wants to have his life transformed, his heart made new. For this, he must resolve and not merely circumvent his dilemma. He must reunite knowing and conceiving in his knowledge of God—a task, broadly speaking, of incarnation. For the remaining two sections of this chapter, I will be speaking to resolution of this sort, though without restricting myself to Anselm's case.

But first I offer a brief reflection on the broad options for analysis that are evident in the philosophical literature on mysticism. When I opt out of the purely experiential approach to mysticism, where knowledge consorts with conceptually denuded sensation, I follow a modern rather than classical approach to mystical phenomena. The modern approach is well epitomized by two analytic studies: Wayne Proudfoot's anti-apologetic analysis of the logical grammar of experiential self-reports, and William Alston's tireless defense of the grounding role that experiential awareness plays in the formation of religious, and especially Christian, beliefs.[3] Proudfoot contends that a phrase like "the being greater than which none can be conceived" is less a description of some nonlinguistic entity that manifests itself in indescribable ways than it is a rule for the interpretation of experience. If Anselm believes that he has had a conceivable experience of beauty (e.g., being stirred by a plainchant), then he knows, by virtue of his regulating description of God, that his experience was mundane, not transcendent. His commitment to a preconception—in this case his preconception that God is beyond conceiving—can be said both to condition his experience and to place constraints on how he will later choose to explain it.[4] Although Alston sharply faults Proudfoot for seeming oblivious to the difference between what is required for the identification of an experience and what an experience makes manifest,[5] he, no less than Proudfoot, postulates an internal relation between conceptualization and experience. While practices of belief formulation do not, insists Alston, predetermine experience from the ground up, he does concede that there is no noncircular way for religious experience to ground religious belief. He just thinks that the circle is virtuous. I point out the conflict between Proudfoot and Alston not to adjudicate it (here is not the place to do so),[6]

---

3. Proudfoot (1985) and Alston (1991). For an illuminating summary and critique of Alton's intricate argument, see Gale (1994). For an approach to religious experience that gratefully takes up where Proudfoot leaves off, see Taves (2009), especially her chapter on explanation and attribution theory (chap. 3).

4. Proudfoot (1985), p. 119.

5. Alston (1991), pp. 16, 40–41.

6. I will say this much. I do not think, pace Alston, that Proudfoot's interest in

but to indicate that the analytic rejection of inconceivable knowledge, so characteristic of the modern take on mysticism, is in itself no embrace of naturalism.

William James is the most celebrated exponent of the classical approach, and by "classical" I mean "classically modern" and relative to the early twentieth-century emergence of a science of religion.[7] In the mysticism chapter of *The Varieties of Religious Experience*, the book that came out of his Gifford Lectures (1901–1902), James identifies mysticism with mystical states of consciousness and then famously distills a mystical state of mind into four elements: it has to be experienced to be known; it is itself revelatory; it doesn't last long; and to have it at all requires more surrender than resolve.[8] Only the first two elements are criterial. It is possible to have lasting, expertly engineered mystical ecstasies, but whether long or short, ruled or ruling, the experiences are always, as James dares to put it, "absolutely sensational in their epistemological quality."[9]

While I have vowed to leave behind the sensationalist epistemology that makes for a classical approach to mysticism, I am not going to abandon, at least not entirely, the troubled distinction in James between the saint who lives in response to an unseen order of goodness and the mystic who has had a taste of transcendent truth. Saints in James's story begin as sick-souled types, incapable of muddling their way through worldly virtues and pleasures that have come to seem either dismally empty or appallingly vulnerable. The evil that they see is real, but they are disposed to take what most of us consider a partial truth and render it absolute: self and world, to sick souls, are mutually defined by a pervasive and multifarious dearth of goodness.[10] The few of these souls who manage to escape

---

the conditioning effect of preconceptions commits him to the (ridiculous) view that experiences are always *of* concepts. He remains open to the possibility that mystical belief and practice are best explained by what mystics experience of God. But he does not believe that such a possibility is likely to be very illuminating. Proudfoot is more cognitive psychologist than theologian (hence Alston's animus).

7. I do not mean "classical" to refer to the ancient or premodern world. There is reason to believe that most premodern theologians lacked our modern obsession with the first-person perspective and so were not inclined to turn a theological logic of negation into a personal experience of absolute otherness. See Turner (1995), chapter 11, "From Mystical Theology to Mysticism," and also Louth (2007), the marvelous "Afterword."

8. James (2004), pp. 329–30.

9. Ibid., p. 367.

10. Ibid., pp. 130–31, 133 ff.

lives of melancholic resignation or worse undergo, psychologically speaking, death and rebirth: they have some sort of mystical experience.

It is hard to see how mysticism and saintliness can be pulled apart in James. Mystics without saintliness are just tripping, and saints without mystical insight are just wishful thinkers. Still James treats the saint and the mystic as if they were, analytically speaking, altogether different animals. Short of becoming mystics ourselves, we can never know, says James, what a mystical state of mind is truly like. And here ignorance has its privileges. James aims to reassure when he tells us that "mystics have no right to claim that we ought to accept the deliverance of their peculiar experiences, if we are ourselves outsiders and feel no private call thereto."[11] But when it comes to saintliness, many saints are, in his view, well equipped to infiltrate the security of our mundane points of view, particularly by way of their unnerving displays of charity—which may, or may not, qualify as wisdom. How would we know? James's astounding proposal is "to test saintliness by common sense, to use human standards to help us decide how far the religious life commends itself to an ideal form of human activity."[12] *Common* sense? The implication is that whereas mystical truth is a mystic's prerogative, saints and their handlers share a common world and a relevantly similar sense of goodness.

The postclassical question I am left with, once the mystic is no longer girded with a sensationalist epistemology, is this: what does it cost us to think that some people can know the truth without also having to seek and serve the greater good? Admittedly this is not a properly epistemological question. From either a classical or modern point of view, I ought to be asking how a person can come to know the good at all, goodness being one of truth's arguably many forms. I concede the point and venture from now on only quasi-epistemological reflections. They return me to Anselm's dilemma and a classic, and quite old, story.

I. Eden's Puzzle: Knowledge, Good and Evil

The story of the serpent in the garden and the loss of Eden—the Yahwist's folktale of humanity's emergence into labored life (Gen 2.4b—3:24)—is familiar enough.[13] It begins with Yahweh, the Lord God, fashioning a

11. Ibid., p. 367.
12. Ibid., p. 331.
13. For my translation of Genesis, I will again be using Alter (1996), whose running commentary on the text highlights the literary subtleties of the ancient Hebrew.

human from the humus of the soil and breathing the breath of life into his new creation: the *'adam*, the earthling, henceforth referred to as Adam.[14] Yahweh removes Adam from the soil of his origins and places him in a garden, Eden, where every tree is fruit-bearing and lovely to look at, including the two trees in the middle: the tree of life and the tree of knowledge, good and evil. Yahweh tells Adam that he can eat of every fruit save knowledge, "for on the day you eat from it, you are doomed to die" (Gen 2:17). Having issued this warning, Yahweh then resolves to make a partner for Adam, someone to sustain him, for "it is not good for the human to be alone" (Gen 2:18). When Adam emerges from an induced sleep, he recognizes right away that the creature crafted from one of his ribs is flesh of his flesh, bone of his bones: Adam and the woman face one another, naked and unashamed (Gen 2:25).

Now things get interesting. A talking serpent crashes the scene and suggests to the woman that knowledge is not the danger that Yahweh has been making it out to be. "You shall not be doomed to death," the serpent tells her (Gen 3:4–5), "for God knows that on the day you eat of it your eyes will be opened and you will become as gods knowing good and evil." The words have their effect. The tree of knowledge looks like sex on the vine to the woman, "a lust to the eyes" (Gen 3:6), and she eats. The man eats too, upon her offer, and the two of them quickly come to see what it is to be naked. They cover up (Gen 3:7). Yahweh acknowledges to his heavenly court that Adam (the *'adam*) has indeed become more godlike, knowing good and evil, and surmises that he will next want to eat from life and live forever. But before he can eat again, Yahweh drives Adam from Eden, "to till the soil from which he had been taken" (Gen 3:24), and posts an angelic guard to keep him from reaching the "other" forbidden tree—the one the woman seems already to have experienced in the form of (carnal) knowledge.[15] By now, Adam has named her Eve, "the mother of all that lives" (Gen 3:20), as if she were herself the tree of life.

The folktale, to say the least, abounds in symbolic possibilities. In typically Christian readings, where the dire nature of disobedience gets

---

14. Alter (1996), p. 8, n. 7, explains that "human/humus" is his rendering of the Hebrew pairing *'adam/'adamah*: the *'adam* is from the *'adamah*, the soil of the earth. When I revert to calling the human "Adam," I mean to keep the generic force of the name while also signaling a specific character.

15. The woman never clearly distinguishes between the two trees. When the serpent asks her whether Yahweh had forbidden her and her partner to eat from any of the trees, she replies that he was speaking only of the tree "in the midst of the garden" (Gen 3:3). Life and knowledge are both "in the midst" (Gen 2:9).

the emphasis, the serpent symbolizes Satan, the original agent of evil, here lying through his fangs to seduce human flesh and spirit into a place of irredeemable darkness. While not wishing to deny this kind of reading its due, I offer a different way into the symbolism. Start with what is, to my mind, the most dramatic but least elaborated turn in the story. The woman has taken her fateful bite; now she is offering to share her knowledge with her partner, the man. Consider his position. He breathes in Yahweh's breath, but it is she who completes his flesh. So which is it to be for him, the breath of his breath or the flesh of his flesh? Where I might be inclined to imagine a soliloquy worthy of a Hamlet, full of rueful indecision, the Yahwist seems to see only a ready response (Gen 3:6): "she also gave to her man, and he ate." But perhaps to call his participation in her knowledge "a response" is already to say too much. For when has Adam ever really been outside this knowledge? No one had to tell him that the woman was flesh of his flesh, bone of his bones; he just woke up to what he knew already. And as for her, notice that she does not fall into a dispirited knowledge of her own nakedness when she first takes from the forbidden tree and eats; it is only after Adam partakes that they both feel the urge to cover up their loins—perhaps to hide the sight from one another, but more likely to hide it from Yahweh, who sees death in the knowledge they have tasted. The real puzzle of Eden—and the key to its symbolism—is how a good knowledge becomes evil, becomes lacking, that is, in its own original goodness.

Some insight into this can be had by looking into the exchange between Yahweh and the newly disobedient human couple—the serpent is also there, but silent (Gen 3:8–19). Yahweh calls a frightened Adam out of hiding and asks him how he had come to learn of his nakedness. Who told him? Had he eaten from knowledge? Adam's words in reply are as veiling as his loincloth (Gen 3:12): "The woman whom you gave by me, she gave me from the tree, and I ate." What he says is both literally true and a lie of heart; under the guise of reporting two gifts, Adam has undone his gratitude, wed himself to a lonesome self-preservation, and offered up his partner (and even his God) to condemnation. When Yahweh turns his attention next to the woman, the bolder transgressor, she opts for self-effacement as her preferred mode of evasion: "The serpent beguiled me," she admits (Gen 3:13), "and I ate." The implication of beguilement is that she doesn't know her heart well enough to know the difference between what serves her life and what starves it. Perhaps that is true for the woman who suddenly finds herself partnered to her man's second thoughts, but not for Eve, the mother of all that lives.

Parting Knowledge

Eve knows that knowledge and life are fruits from one tree; she knows that when Yahweh, her partner in matters conceivable (Gen 4:1), forbids knowledge and warns of death, he is both offering his human children a safe haven from mortal travails and eliciting in them an independent desire to know life and leave the garden. (Yahweh, no less than the serpent, is a master of irony.) On the reading I am proposing here, the God who keeps all mother-born humans from returning to Eden has warned against a first taste of knowledge, a fall into mortality, and outrightly blocked a second, an undoing of birth. A birth, like a death, is indelible, and in a realm of mixed parentage, where flesh moves with and against spirit, there is never the one without the other. The two perspectives in Genesis on life's knowledge—heavenly and earthbound—are less antithetical than they have been made to seem.

But what about the apparent antithesis? In the broadly Augustinian tradition that includes the likes of Anselm, the antithesis is taken very seriously indeed, hardly as a mere appearance. The woman's trust of the serpent gets read as her (beguiled) complicity with Satan, the incorrigible subverter, and largely as a result of that complicity, the fleshly enfolding of one human beginning within another proves, in every case but one, to be a corrupting form of nurture. It is only through being in touch with Christ's blessedly innocent gestation in Mary (here the anti-Eve) that a few saints—I think of Augustine, Anselm, Teresa of Avila—are able to rise to an erotically charged experience of God and not incur the taint of sexualized sin.

For my quasi-epistemological purposes, the alleged disparity between Eve and Mary is less important than the epistemic distance between the Yahwist's Yahweh and the being greater than which none can be conceived. Is Yahweh even conceivably the sublime being that Anselm is seeking, with all his life's senses (*sensus animae*), to know? Take it for granted that Anselm is dogmatically committed to Yahweh's identity as the most high, Lord God, before whom there is no other. My question is not whether Yahweh is Anselm's God, but whether the Yahwist's characterization of Yahweh works against Anselm's kind of contemplative ascesis. There are two quite different ways in which it might be thought to do so.

In one, Yahweh's garden antics render him too conceivable a deity. He creates with mud, takes walks in the breeze, competes with a serpent for human attention, and loses his temper when he doesn't get his way. How is any of that sublime? To remain proper contemplatives, we would have to attribute Yahweh's anthropomorphic behavior to a symbolic or allegorical form of discourse. It is not that Yahweh, as God, ever truly gets angry or jealous, messy or whimsical; he just needs to be described that way until we have learned to recognize better the dispensable parts of ourselves: the imperfections, the vices, the immaturities. But as contemplative ascesis takes us deeper into what Anselm calls "inaccessible light," all symbolism becomes increasingly empty. An imperfect virtue never finds its perfect paradigm in the goodness that falls beyond conceiving, for there perfection is pointless (and there, of course, there is no "there"). At the hypothetical end of ascesis, Yahweh will have come to symbolize the inconceivable God no better and no worse than any other imagined alternative. We are back to wanting ineffably noetic sensations and hoping that saints like Anselm have had them.

But now consider the other way that the Yahwist, through Yahweh, offers us a symbol of divinity and not the full view. Here the Yahwist is in able control of the symbolism and stands in no need of outside allegorical intervention. Just read the story and notice how Yahweh begins to impersonate a lesser version of himself. The turning point comes when the two human characters, sobered by the separative power of knowledge, decide to hide from Yahweh rather than face him directly. They create in their imaginations a creator who is foreign to the power of conception, even hostile to it. Yahweh does not force them to imagine otherwise; he plays the part of the deity that they would have him be. This he does by sowing discord between the serpent and the woman's seed, multiplying the woman's pain in childbirth, and making Adam's labor in the soil wearisome and thorny (Gen 3:14–19). All told, the chastisements speak to an extraordinary (but not absolute) resistance to the life that comes from a conception of life, from a seed. The old belief that a seed has to die to give life (John 12:24; 1 Cor 15:36) hints at the knowledge, good and evil, that is struggling to regain its footing in human awareness. Yahweh has already done his part here, first by rendering the knowledge desirable (the command not to eat) and then by making the desire irresistible (the creation of the woman). In a later narrative tradition, though one largely in keeping with the Yahwist's sensibilities, even Yahweh doesn't resist the woman. Not only does he conceive a son with her; he identifies himself with that son. The years pass, and God incarnate grows up both to endure and to eradicate a human misconception: the one that has God hating a mortal life.

When I suggest that the Yahweh who disdains conception is less than the God that the saints want to know, I am not thinking of conception in sexual terms, or at least not in terms that confine sexuality to an affair of the flesh. I follow the Yahwist, who thinks of conception as the alchemy that binds spirit to flesh and renders flesh miraculously self-exceeding. The most spectacular illustration of this would be Christ's resurrection, but who among the living can claim to have seen that? Fortunately, there are more mundane examples to be had, lying closer to the bone of familiar flesh. Most parents tend to notice over time that their children, though like one or both of them in many ways, are not the sum of mother and father. Their personalities exceed what is given—or, it must be admitted, fall short of it. Some parents, though I would like to think most, meditate on their knowledge, good and not so good, of their children and look for the good that both honors what they know and reunites it with an original abundance: eternal, but never static, life. Meditation on the being greater than which none can be conceived is certainly a meditation on conceivability but also on what has been conceived already—parentally or otherwise.

I don't pretend to have resolved Anselm's dilemma. It is, in any case, less a dilemma to be resolved than taken to heart, where it pushes and pulls against the *rigor mortis* of a fixed point of view. The saint is always going to want to move the mystic out of the sanctuary of knowing and towards an unaccommodated goodness, ripe with new conception. To the extent that I am prepared, in my quasi-epistemological way, to speak of a mystical knowing, I am prepared to speak of a knowing dispossession. I do so next.

II. Knowledge Dispossessed: The Mystic's Ascent

Imagine a meditation on God much different from Anselm's. It doesn't begin with a prayer (though it might have ended with one); it begins in the naked solitude of a self-reflection. You are chagrined to think of the many falsehoods that you mistook for truth in your youth, and now you are wondering why you still trust yourself. What has changed for you, just your age? And why should that matter? What you have yet to confront in yourself is your willingness to be deceived, either because you lack discipline or because you have an active, if unacknowledged, desire not to know the truth. The only way to confront a lack of discipline is to engage in one, and that you are doing through mental effort. An unacknowledged desire is a more elusive foe, like a serpent in a garden. You decide to magnify the threat: life with a deceiver greater than which you cannot conceive. Your concocted Satan is you, of course, and it reflects the magnitude of your fear of being taken in—in this case by yourself. But if you can cleanly dissociate yourself from your inner deceiver, then you have some chance of being restored to an unself-conscious mode of knowing and the uncorrupted life that you have thus far been unable to recall. Only your discipline will tell.

The beauty of the meditation—and also its limitation—lies in its economized sense of discipline. Although you are your own deceiver, you ignore the side of you that invents simulacra of truth and you maintain a doubter's posture: your deceiver may be offering you (deceptively) the purest of truths; you refuse your assent nonetheless and thereby fashion, doubt by doubt, an impregnable sanctuary for knowledge. The ruling idea here is that no truth but your own is on the inside of your doubts, where knowledge never parts you from yourself and leaves you feeling vulnerable. Notice, above all, how blessedly powerless you are to carry out the sentence: I doubt that I exist. Here to doubt would be to disown the self that doubts, and having dissociated yourself from your demiurgic twin, the inventive deceiver, you have no other self to be. So here is your first and foundational truth: that you are undoubtedly the self that doubts. The God who stays within your sanctuary to offer you further truths will be defined by your doubts, and a doubting self is nothing if not security conscious.

Readers of Descartes will recognize that I have been rehearsing some of the private mythology of the first meditation, where a methodologically broody Descartes enters a waking dream and then faces off with "a malicious demon" (*malignus genius*). He plays doubter to his demon and aims at doubt's triumph—the cathartic first step towards secure knowledge. In one regard, however, I have altered his trajectory. When Descartes speaks of the risk of being deceived, he indicts the senses and never squarely addresses the possibility of self-deception. "Whatever I have up till now accepted as most true," he writes, "I have acquired either from the senses or through the senses. But from time to time I have found that the senses deceive, and it is prudent never to trust completely those who have deceived us even once."[16] The indictment takes in the usual tricks of perception—the bend of a partially submerged stick, the smallness of a distant object—and adds to that the possibility of wholesale sensory distortion, or life in a waking dream. Descartes argues for the dream possibility, thereby obscuring what is illusory about the indictment itself. He does not in fact get his sense of truth from his senses. He gets it from his mind's eye, the part of him able to see truth without having to consider a material context at all. (Think arithmetic equations, geometric symmetries.[17])

16. Descartes (1986), p. 12.
17. "For whether I am awake or asleep, two and three added together are five, and

It isn't his senses, then, that have caused him to be deceived, but his own habit-forming willingness to divert his attention from the one real source of truth and credit a wholly imagined alternative. The demon hypothesis might have become his occasion for venturing into the labyrinth of self-deception, where he is somehow both deceived and deceiver. But Descartes does remarkably little with the hypothesis. His doubting self is not very doubtful, after all, about the finality of mathematical truths and the God of his mind's eye. In the beginning of the third meditation, before he has replaced his deceiver with God, he is already prepared to declare that no deceiver can bring it about that he is nothing while he is thinking that he is something, "or bring it about that two and three added together are more or less than five."[18] And later on in the fifth meditation, where he considers God's existence a second time, we learn that God's existence is no less certain to him than a mathematical truth.

I pause to interject something of a Cartesian muse into my quasi-epistemological reflections for one principal reason: I want to signal how much a supposed paradigm of epistemology (nothing "quasi" or vaguely mystical about it) owes to a private mythology. The mythology is private inasmuch as its two main protagonists—the radical doubter and the demonic deceiver—are the twin birth of personal ingenuity. Descartes imagines the deceiver greater than which *he* cannot conceive; he does not imagine the deceiver greater than which *none* can be conceived.

Here are the words he uses to frame his mind's resolve: "I will suppose that not God, who is supremely good and the source of truth, but rather some malicious demon of the utmost power and cunning [*summe potentem et callidum*] has employed all of his energies in order to deceive me."[19] Descartes makes it sound as if he were making a choice between the divine deceiver and the demonic one, but his prior supposition has been that "everything said about God is a fiction."[20] The being deemed to be omnipotent and supremely good is, for present purposes, just someone's conception and nothing more (the assumption of Anselm's fool). But if there is no God, no source of truth, what can a deceiver do but lamely lean on the pseudo-truth that there is no truth and try to convince a doubter that truth exists? Descartes doesn't say anything about his deceiver's tech-

---

a square has no more than four sides. It seems impossible that such transparent truths should incur any suspicion of being false." Ibid., p. 14.

18. Ibid., p. 25.
19. Ibid., p. 15.
20. Ibid., p. 14.

nique, but it is easy enough to imagine a tedious parade of simple arithmetic and the dare, "Try not to believe that!" He never thinks to imagine that his inner deceiver has touched upon God only to reject that knowledge and chase after a fiction; he never imagines then that his deceiver is now bent on convincing its shadow—the halfhearted rebel, the doubter—of the fiction. But surely the greater deceiver is the one who knows the truth and turns from it and not the one who casts blindly into the dark and knows God no better than the doubter does. And if a fiction of God can somehow be made to seem more compelling than God, what greater power of deception can there be?

Perhaps none, but who would know? In the itinerary of saintliness, any knowledge of having become an ultimate deceiver, able to see past God and dress up a void, gets firmly dispossessed. Consider the case of Saint Augustine, looking back in book 7 of the *Confessions* (*conf.* 7.10.16 to 7.17.23) at what many have taken to be his first mystical experience.[21] He describes himself at the time as incapable of thinking of God other than in bodily terms—as lacking, that is, a notion of spirit—and as tormented by the problem of evil (*conf.* 7.3.5): "Is not my God not only good but also the good itself? How then," he asks in anguish, "do I come to want evil and not what is good?" Augustine gets both a revelation of spirit and a perplexing insight into his own self-described perversity when he begins reading in Platonist literature (most likely Plotinus). Soon after being exhorted to turn within and enter his own intimacies (*intima mea*), he feels himself being snatched away and taken up to a place he refers to as "a place of unlikeness" (*regio dissimilitudinis*; *conf.* 7.10.16). It is indeed an unlikely place. Above him, but far away, he hears God calling out to him, and the cry breaks through his heart's resistance to loving a beloved undefined by time or place. Below him, he surveys all the other things, the things not God, and he sees in their integration a virtual Eden—a place of divinely cultivated beauty, without evil (*conf.* 7.13.19). The most telling part of the vision is Augustine's lack of place within it. He is not at one with the God above; he is not an instrument of the beauty below. And since God and the created order exhaust for him all the possibilities of being, there is nothing for him to be or become in his assumed unlikeness. He has been trying to dwell in a place fit only for the leaving, and that, more than the sight of a still alien perfection, has been the real offering of his experience.

---

21. But there has been little consensus as to its significance. I have learned much from Kenney (2005). See also O'Donnell (1992), pp. xx–xxxii, for a masterful synopsis of a century of scholarship on the *Confessions*.

Parting Knowledge

Think again of this conjunction. On one side there is Augustine wanting to embrace evil and reject what is good; here he styles himself the serpent in his life's garden, the spoiler of an original perfection. This is the saint's confession. On the other side there is Augustine acknowledging his inability to conceive of life with God and clear his mind of a materialist's obsession; here he styles himself an unhappy Adam, hoping to cheat the dying part of knowledge and live his limited life forever. This is the mystic's lament. The saint, when conjoined to the mystic, must confess again: Augustine knows too little to claim a serpent's wisdom; his alienation from the good has not been his to will. The mystic, when conjoined to the saint, must seek a different kind of knowing: the way out of a materialist's obsession is through a materialist's clarity; Augustine has to take in the truth, voiced by Yahweh, that flesh is mortal.

If all of this made for an easy conjunction, I wouldn't be offering just quasi-epistemological reflections; I would be taking a saint's dictation. But there is still reason to hope, despite imperfect knowledge, that it is part of an eternal inspiration to be able to love a life that dies with both grief and gratitude. Augustine gets his best sense of *that* particular conjunction when he and his dying mother are taken up together into the third heaven, where "life is the wisdom through which all things—those that were and those that will be—are created" (*conf.* 9.10.23). There, in that alter Eden, there is no conflict between eternal wisdom and mortal life, and a son knows who his mother is. The hard part of knowledge, though still conjoined to its goodness, is to know that time, in God's embrace, is as much preserved as it is suspended. Monica dies less than a week after her mystical visit to paradise with her son, and Augustine feels the sharp pain of their parting (*conf.* 9.12.29).

The dispossession that releases a saint from a place of unlikeness and gives a mystic something to know is less the acceptance of death than surrender to self-limiting life. The God of Anselm's dilemma, the God both conceivable and not, has to be self-limiting or there is nothing for anyone to conceive. But doubtless it is tempting to forget that self-limitation in God is itself inconceivable. Descartes forgets this when he insists that God, following an imperative not to deceive, has deigned to become mathematics—a clear and distinct form of self-limitation. But this is just truncated mysticism. The saint's God is less apt to spare us the labor of becoming other to ourselves when we know. There is no conceivable knowledge of God that is not a self-offering. The inconceivable part is what we receive in return.

Works Cited

Adam, Charles, and Paul Tannery, editors (1996), *Oeuvres de Descartes*, vol. 7 (Paris: Vrin).
Agamben, Giorgio (1999), *The End of the Poem: Studies in Poetics*, translated by Daniel Heller-Roazen (Palo Alto: Stanford University Press).
Alston, William P. (1991), *Perceiving God: The Epistemology of Religious Experience* (Ithaca: Cornell University Press).
Alter, Robert (1996), *Genesis: Translation and Commentary* (New York: Norton).
Arendt, Hannah (1978), *Willing: The Life of the Mind*, vol. 2 (New York: Harcourt Brace Jovanovich).
Armstrong, Hillary, translator (1989), Plotinus: *Enneads*, vol. 1 (Cambridge: Harvard University Press).
Babcock, William (1988), "Augustine on Sin and Moral Agency," *Journal of Religious Ethics* 16, pp. 28–55.
Bair, Deirdre (1978), *Samuel Beckett: A Biography* (New York: Harcourt Brace Jovanovich).
Beckett, Samuel (1957), *Endgame: A Play in One Act* (New York: Grove Press).
Bedouelle, Guy, and Oliver Fatio, editors (1994), *Liberté chrétienne et libre arbitre* (Fribourg: Editions Universitaires).
Benardete, Seth, translator (2001), Plato: *Symposium*, with commentaries by Allan Bloom and Seth Benardete (Chicago: University of Chicago Press).
Bloom, Harold (1989), *Ruin the Sacred Truths: Poetry and Belief from the Bible to the Present* (Cambridge: Harvard University Press).
Boethius (1973), *De consolatione philosophiae*, Loeb 74 (Cambridge: Harvard University Press).
Brown, Peter (2000), *Augustine of Hippo: A Biography*, rev. ed. (Berkeley: University of California Press).
———. (1988), *The Body and Society: Men, Women, and Sexual Renunciation in Early Christianity*. (New York: Columbia University Press).
Burnaby, John (1938), *Amor Dei: A Study of the Religion of St. Augustine* (Eugene, OR: Wipf & Stock).
Burns, J. Patout (1980), *The Development of Augustine's Doctrine of Operative Grace* (Paris: Institut d'études augustiniennes).
Burnyeat, M. F. (1987), "Wittgenstein and Augustine *De Magistro*," *Proceedings of the Aristotelian Society*, Supplementary Volume 61, pp. 1–24.

Works Cited

Burrus, Virginia, Mark D. Jordan, and Karmen MacKendrick (2010), *Seducing Augustine: Bodies, Desires, Confessions* (New York: Fordham University Press).

Cary, Phillip (2008), *Outward Signs: The Powerlessness of External Things in Augustine's Thought* (Oxford: Oxford University Press).

Cavadini, John C. (1999), "Ambrose and Augustine *De bono mortis*," in *The Limits of Ancient Christianity*, edited by William E. Klingshirn and Mark Vessey (Ann Arbor: University of Michigan Press), pp. 232–49.

———. (2005), "Feeling Right: Augustine on the Passions and Sexual Desire," *Augustinian Studies* 36:1, pp. 195–217.

Cavell, Stanley (1990), *Conditions Handsome and Unhandsome: The Constitution of Emersonian Perfectionism* (Chicago: University of Chicago Press).

———. (1995), "Notes and Afterthoughts on the Opening of Wittgenstein's *Investigations*," in *Philosophical Passages: Wittgenstein, Emerson, Austin, Derrida* (Oxford: Blackwell), pp. 125–86.

———. (2002), "The Availability of Wittgenstein's Later Philosophy," in *Must We Mean What We Say? A Book of Essays*, updated ed. (Cambridge: Cambridge University Press), pp. 44–72.

Charlesworth, M. J. (1965), *St. Anselm's Proslogion*. Text, Translation, and Commentary (Notre Dame: University of Notre Dame Press).

Clark, Maudemarie, and Alan J. Swensen, translators (1998), Friedrich Nietzsche: *On the Genealogy of Morality* (Indianapolis: Hackett).

Cochrane, Charles Norris (1944), *Christianity and Classical Culture: A Study of Thought and Action from Augustus to Augustine*, rev. ed. (New York: Oxford University Press).

Colish, Marcia (1985), *The Stoic Tradition from Antiquity to the Early Middle Ages*, vol. 2 (Leiden: Brill).

Coyle, Kevin J. (1999), "Mani, Manicheism," in *Augustine through the Ages: An Encyclopedia*, edited by Allan D. Fitzgerald (Grand Rapids: Eerdmans), pp. 520–25.

Crary, Alice, and Rupert Read, editors (2000), *The New Wittgenstein* (London: Routledge).

Descartes, René (1986), *Meditations on First Philosophy*, translated by John Cottingham (Cambridge: Cambridge University Press).

di Giovanni, George, translator (1998), Kant: *Religion within the Boundaries of Mere Reason* (Cambridge: Cambridge University Press).

Dihle, Albrecht (1982), *The Theory of Will in Classical Antiquity* (Berkeley: University of California Press).

Dodaro, Robert (2004), *Christ and the Just Society in the Thought of Augustine* (Cambridge: Cambridge University Press).

Dover, Kenneth, editor (1980), Plato: *Symposium*, Cambridge Greek and Latin Classics (Cambridge: Cambridge University Press).

Eldridge, Richard (1996), "Wittgenstein, Augustine, Mind, and Morality," in *Wittgenstein and the Philosophy of Culture*, edited by Kjell Johannessen and Tore Nordenstam (Vienna: Hölder-Pichler-Tempsky), pp. 96–112.

———. (1997), *Leading a Human Life: Wittgenstein, Intentionality, and Romanticism* (Chicago: University of Chicago Press).

Eliot, T. S. (1943), *Four Quartets* (New York: Harcourt Brace Jovanovich).

Farnham, Willard, editor (1970), Shakespeare: *Hamlet* (New York: Penguin).

Works Cited

Flasch, Kurt (1980), *Augustin: Einführung in sein Denken* (Stuttgart: Reclam).
Freccero, John (1986), *Dante: The Poetics of Conversion* (Cambridge: Harvard University Press.)
Fredriksen, Paula (1986), "Paul and Augustine: Conversion Narratives, Orthodox Traditions, and the Retrospective Self," *Journal of Theological Studies*, n.s., 37:1, pp. 3-34.
Freud, Sigmund (1961), *Civilization and Its Discontents*, translated by James Strachey (New York: Norton).
Gale, Richard (1994), "The Overall Argument of Alston's *Perceiving God*," *Religious Studies* 30.2, pp. 135-49.
Gouhier, Henri (1978), *Cartésianisme et augustinisme au XVIIe siècle* (Paris: Vrin).
Graver, Margaret (2002), *Cicero on the Emotions: Tusculan Disputations 3 and 4*, Translation and Commentary (Chicago: University of Chicago Press).
Hampton, Jean, and Jeffrey Murphy (1988), *Forgiveness and Mercy* (Cambridge: Cambridge University Press).
Harrison, Carol (2000), *Augustine: Christian Truth and Fractured Humanity* (Oxford: Oxford University Press).
———. (2006), *Rethinking Augustine's Early Theology: An Argument for Continuity* (Oxford: Oxford University Press).
Harrison, Simon (2006), *Augustine's Way into the Will: The Theological and Philosophical Significance of* De Libero Arbitrio (Oxford: Oxford University Press).
Hick, John (1978), *Evil and the God of Love*, rev. ed. (New York: Harper & Row).
Hollander, Robert (2001), *Dante: A Life in Works* (New Haven: Yale University Press).
Horn, Christoph (1995), *Augustinus* (München: Beck).
Irwin, Terrence, translator (1985), Aristotle: *Nicomachean Ethics* (Indianapolis: Hackett).
James, William (2004/1902), *The Varieties of Religious Experience* (New York: Barnes & Noble).
Jordan, Mark D., editor (2006), *Authorizing Marriage? Canon, Tradition, and Critique in the Blessing of Same-Sex Unions* (Princeton: Princeton University Press).
Kaufmann, Walter, translator (1967), Nietzsche: *The Genealogy of Morals* (New York: Random House).
Kenney, John Peter (2005), *The Mysticism of Saint Augustine: Rereading the Confessions* (New York: Routledge).
Kolnai, Aurel (1973-74), "Forgiveness," *Proceedings of the Aristotelian Society*, n.s., 64, pp. 91-106.
Korsgaard, Christine M. (1996a), *The Sources of Normativity* (Cambridge: Cambridge University Press).
———. (1996b), *Creating the Kingdom of Ends* (Cambridge: Cambridge University Press).
Kripke, Saul (1982), *Wittgenstein: On Rules and Private Language* (Cambridge: Harvard University Press).
Kvanvig, Jonathan L. (1993), *The Problem of Hell* (Oxford: Oxford University Press).
Lauritzen, Paul (1987), "Forgiveness: Moral Prerogative or Religious Duty?" *Journal of Religious Ethics* 15.2, pp. 141-54.
Lebourlier, Jean (1955), "Essai sur la responsabilité du pécheur dans la réflexion de saint Augustin," in *Augustinus Magister*, vol. 3 (Paris: Institut d'études augustiniennes) pp. 287-300.

Works Cited

Le Guern, Michel, editor (2004), Pascal: *Pensées* (Paris: Éditions Gallimard).

Léon-Dufour, Xavier (1946), "Grâce et libre arbitre chez saint Augustin," *Recherches de science religieuse* 33, pp. 129–63.

Lombardo, Stanley, translator (2005), Virgil: *Aeneid* (Indianapolis: Hackett).

Louth, Andrew (2007), *The Origins of the Christian Mystical Tradition: From Plato to Denys*, 2nd ed. (Oxford: Oxford University Press).

Luckhardt, C. G., editor (1979), *Wittgenstein: Sources and Perspectives* (Ithaca: Cornell University Press).

MacDonald, Scott (1999), "Primal Sin," in *The Augustinian Tradition*, edited by Gareth Matthews (Berkeley: University of California Press), pp. 110–39.

Madec, Goulven (1999), note complémentaire 6, *Dialogues philosophiques* III, *Oeuvres de saint Augustin*, vol. 6, 3e éd. (Paris: Institut d'études augustiniennes)

———. (2001), *Lectures augustiniennes* (Paris: Institut d'études augustiniennes).

Malcolm, Norman (2001), *Wittgenstein: A Memoir*, 2nd ed. (Oxford: Clarendon).

Marion, Jean-Luc (1999), "Is the Argument Ontological? The Anselmian Proof and the Two Demonstrations of the Existence of God in the *Meditations*," in *Cartesian Questions: Method and Metaphysics* (Chicago: University of Chicago Press), pp. 139–60.

———. (2008), *Au lieu de soi: L'approche de Saint Augustin*, 2nd corrected ed. (Paris: Presses Universitaires de France).

Matthews, Gareth B. (1992), *Thought's Ego in Augustine and Descartes* (Ithaca: Cornell University Press).

Menn, Stephen (1998), *Descartes and Augustine* (Cambridge: Cambridge University Press).

Miles, Margaret R. (2005), "Sex and the City (of God): Is Sex Forfeited or Fulfilled in Augustine's Resurrection of the Body?" *Journal of the American Academy of Religion* 73.2, pp. 307–27.

Mulhall, Stephen (2001), *Inheritance and Originality: Wittgenstein, Heidegger, Kierkegaard* (Oxford: Clarendon).

———. (2005), "The Child and the Scapegoat," in *Philosophical Myths of the Fall* (Princeton: Princeton University Press), pp. 85–117.

Newman, Louis (1987), "The Quality of Mercy: On the Duty to Forgive in the Judaic Tradition," *Journal of Religious Ethics* 15.2, pp. 155–72.

Nussbaum, Martha (2001), *Upheavals of Thought: The Intelligence of Emotions* (Cambridge: Cambridge University Press).

O'Connell, Robert J. (1989), *St. Augustine's Confessions: The Odyssey of Soul* (New York: Fordham University Press).

O'Donnell, James J (1992), *Augustine: Confessions*, Text and Commentary, 3 vols. (Oxford: Clarendon).

———. (2005), *Augustine: A New Biography* (New York: HarperCollins).

Pinsky, Robert, translator (1994), Dante: *Inferno* (New York: Farrar, Straus & Giroux).

Proudfoot, Wayne (1985), *Religious Experience* (Berkeley: University of California Press).

Rist, John (1994), *Augustine: Ancient Thought Baptized* (Cambridge: Cambridge University Press).

Rogers, Eugene F., Jr. (1999), *Sexuality and the Christian Body: Their Way into the Triune God* (Oxford: Blackwell).

Works Cited

Ryan, Christopher (1993), "The Theology of Dante," in *The Cambridge Companion to Dante*, edited by Rachel Jacoff (Cambridge: Cambridge University Press), pp. 136–52.

Schmitt, Francis, editor (1946), Anselm: *Opera Omnia*, vols. 1 & 2 (Edinburgh: Thomas Nelson).

Shanzer, Danuta (2002), "*Avulsa a Latere Meo*: Augustine's Spare Rib: *Confessions* 6.15.25," *Journal of Roman Studies* 92, pp. 157–76.

Skerrett, Kathleen (2009), "*Consuetudo Carnalis* in Augustine's *Confessions*: Confessing Identity/Belonging to Difference," *Journal of Religious Ethics* 37.3, pp. 495–512.

Singleton, Charles S. (1957), *Commedia: Elements of Structure* (Cambridge: Harvard University Press).

Solignac, Aimé (1998), Note complémentaire 26, pp. 689–93 of *Oeuvres de saint Augustin*, vol. 13, 2e série (Paris: Institut d'études augustiniennes).

Sorabji, Richard (2000), *Emotion and Peace of Mind: From Stoic Agitation to Christian Temptation* (Oxford: Oxford University Press).

Starnes, Colin (1990), *Augustine's Conversion: A Guide to the Argument of Confessions I–IX* (Waterloo, ON: Wilfrid Laurier).

Stendahl, Krister (1963), "The Apostle Paul and the Introspective Conscience of the West," *Harvard Theological Review* 56, pp. 199–215.

Stern, David (2004), *Wittgenstein's Philosophical Investigations: An Introduction* (Cambridge: Cambridge University Press).

Stump, Eleonore (1986), "Dante's Hell, Aquinas's Moral Theory, and the Love of God," *Canadian Journal of Philosophy* 16.2, pp. 181–98.

Swinburne, Richard (1983), "A Theodicy of Heaven and Hell," in *The Existence and Nature of God*, edited by Alfred J. Freddoso (Notre Dame: University of Notre Dame Press).

Talbott, Thomas (1990), "The Doctrine of Everlasting Punishment," *Faith and Philosophy* 7.1, pp. 19–42.

Taves, Ann (2009), *Religious Experience Reconsidered: A Building Block Approach to the Study of Religion and Other Special Things* (Princeton: Princeton University Press).

Trible, Phyllis (1978), *God and the Rhetoric of Sexuality* (Philadelphia: Fortress).

Triolo, Alfred A. (1998), "Canto XI: Malice and Mad Bestiality," in *Lectura Dantis: Inferno*, edited by Allen Mandelbaum, Anthony Oldcorn, and Charles Ross (Berkeley: University of California Press), pp. 150–64.

Turner, Denys (1995), *The Darkness of God: Negativity in Christian Mysticism* (Cambridge: Cambridge University Press).

Verbeke, Gérard (1958), "Augustine et le stoïcisme," *Recherches augustiniennes* 1, pp. 67–89.

Vlastos, Gregory (1981), "The Individual as an Object of Love in Plato," in *Platonic Studies* (Princeton: Princeton University Press), pp. 3–34.

Walls, Jerry (1992), *Hell: The Logic of Damnation* (Notre Dame: University of Notre Dame Press).

Weil, Simone (1988/1947), *La pesanteur et la grâce* (Librarie Plon).

Wetzel, James (2000), "The Question of *Consuetudo Carnalis* in *Confessions* 7.17.23," *Augustinian Studies* 31:2, pp. 165–71.

———. (2002), "Will and Interiority in Augustine: Travels in an Unlikely Place," *Augustinian Studies* 33.2, pp. 139–60.

———.(2005), Review of O'Donnell (2005) in *Early Christian Studies* 13.4, pp. 528–30.

Works Cited

Williams, Rowan (2000), "Insubstantial Evil," in *Augustine and His Critics*, edited by R. Dodaro and G. Lawless (London: Routledge), pp. 105–23.

Wisdom, John (1945), "Gods," in *Proceedings of the Aristotelian Society*, n.s. 45, pp. 195–206.

Wittgenstein, Ludwig (1961), *Tractatus-Logico Philosophicus*, translated by D. F. Pears and B. F. McGuinness (London: Routledge & Kegan Paul).

———. (1998), *Culture and Value: A Selection from the Posthumous Remains*, edited by G. H. von Wright and revised by Alois Pichler (Oxford: Blackwell).

———. (2009), *Philosophical Investigations*, 4th ed., translated by G. E. M. Anscombe, revised by P. M. S. Hacker and Joachim Schulte (Oxford: Wiley-Blackwell).

Index

Citations to verses in the Old and New Testaments are listed under the headings "Old Testament" and "New Testament," divided by individual books. Citations to other publications are listed under the titles of the various works.

abandon (as emotional disturbance), 20
abandonment, 152
absence of God, 73–74
absolute beauty, 74–75
absolute time, 152–54
absolutized will, 13–14
acting rightly, 45, 182
Ad Simplicianum de diversis quaestionibus (*To Simplician—on various questions*, Augustine)
   1.1.14, 12
   1.2.10, 13
   1.2.13, 13
   1.2.16, 51
   1.2.20, 54
   1.2.22, 12, 49
   Madec on Flasch's reading of, 47
Adam
   apple, motives for eating of, 184
   Augustine's views of, 24, 95
   Christ, comparison with, 206–7
   counterfactual speculations on, 57
   creation of, 205
   dilemma of, 255
   disobedience to God, 23–25
   Eve, relationship to, 25, 196
   free choice and, 54–56
   life of the will and, 46, 47
   mother of, 207
   purified Platonist souls, similarity to, 22–23
   self-conception, 196
   self-knowledge, 205–6
   See also Adam and Eve
'*adam* (human), 180, 205, 254
Adam and Eve
   creation of, 180
   emotions of, prior to disobedience, 90–91
   first sin, roles in, 23–24, 54–55
   grief, role in establishment of, 89
   mortality, 91
   myth of will and, 22–26
   sexuality of, 17, 91, 201–2
   Yahweh, conversation with, 255–56
   see also Adam; Eve
'*adamah* (earth, clay), 180, 205, 254
Adamic freedom, 55
Adamic regime of grace, 46, 57
Adeodatus (Augustine's son), 15, 79, 110–11, 234–35
advantages, goods vs., 85–86, 93
aegritudo (grief), 89

Index

Aeneid (Virgil), 20–21
affect, 146
Against Julian—the unfinished work (*Contra Julianum opus imperfectum*, Augustine), 52
Against the Skeptics (*Contra Academicos*, Augustine), 123–24
Against two letters of the Pelagians (*Contra duas epistolas Pelagianorum*, Augustine), 51n8
aging, 258–59
akrasia (incontinence), 171
alienation from the good. *See* sin
allegory, 164–65
Alston, William, 251–52
Alypius, 15, 98
amoral desires, 186–87
anachronisms, 32. *See also* forgiveness, anachronism of
Anaximander, 121
angels, 25–26, 54, 92. *See also* gods
Anselm
    dilemma of, 248–49, 250–51, 258
    God, definition of, 248
    on God, contemplation of, 141–46
    God of, 256–57
anthrôpos (man), 205
anxiety (as emotional disturbance), 20
apatheia (freedom from passion), 86–87, 96
Aphrodite, 218–19, 220
appetite, 170, 171–72, 220. *See also* desire
Arendt, Hannah, 120n4
aretē alēthē (true virtue), 217–18
Aristophanes, 187–88, 189, 191, 192
Aristotelians, 85–86
Aristotle, 170
Arnauld, Antoine, 32n4, 34, 40, 41
arrogance, sin of, 177
ascesis, contemplative, 256–57
astrology, 70n9
attachment, 25
Attic Nights (Aulus), 85
attraction, 147
Au lieu de soi (Marion), 106
Augustine of Hippo, St.
    anti-Pelagian theology, 50, 51–52
    carnality, 11–12, 14–20, 43, 58, 99–100, 115
    celibacy, will to, 98
    childhood friend (*see* Augustine of Hippo, St., childhood friend, grief at loss of)
    confession, approach to, vs. Wittgenstein, 225–30
    confessions, twofold aspect of, 60
    conversion (*see* Augustine of Hippo, St., conversion)
    curse of his birth, 66
    doctrines (*see* Augustine of Hippo, St., doctrines)
    faithless love, habit of, 116
    family, 15 (*see also* Adeodatus; Monica)
    father, death of, 65
    as father, 109
    ideal self, search for, 76
    Korsgaard on, 119–20
    learning language, 108–10
    Manicheism, 19, 58–59, 63–64
    modernity, 121
    as mythologist of will, 10–14
    objects of desired knowledge, 81
    parents, and language, 246
    partner and, 15–16, 24
    as philosopher of God's will, 120
    philosophy, place in history of, 120–21
    presumption, lack of, 96
    as saint and mystic, 262
    self-conception, 113–14
    self-love, 84
    sexual fidelity, 16–17, 58
    sexual self-control, 18
    Stoicism, 83
    as teacher, 58–59
    theft of pears, 92–94
    as theorist, 27
    Wittgenstein, comparison with, 229–30
    see also *Confessionum libri XIII*; Manicheism; *specific individual concepts*
Augustine of Hippo, St., childhood friend, grief at loss of, 58–80

Index

Augustine, problem of addressing, 61
Augustine's guilt over friendship, 68–69
Augustine's madness and, 67, 68, 69–71, 74
consolations and, 67–68, 73–74
description of, 29, 65
falsity, 64
friend's baptism, 66–67, 70
friend's death, 59, 68
great question of, 75–76
introduction to, 58–66
language of grieving, redemption of, 66–74
pretense in, 68
and sin, aesthetics of, 74–78
summary, 78–80
Augustine of Hippo, St., conversion, 97–116
celibacy as basis for, 98–99
God and materiality and, 112–13
language and meaning and, 107–12
matter, nature of, 103–6
moment of, 237
nature of, 238
overview, 97–103
results of, 101–2
setting for, 98
summary of, 18–20
see also place like no other
Augustine of Hippo, St., doctrines
about, 245–46
of election, 245
of grace, 52
of gratuitous election, 11
of original sin, 4, 202
of predestination, 56
autonomy, 93, 120, 187, 191

bearers of a holy will (gods), 179, 183, 189, 193, 215
beasts encountered in hell, 163, 170, 171–72
beauty, 214–24
absolute vs. relative, 74–75, 77
desire for, vs. desire for goodness, 216–19

desire for goodness and, 219–22
of the father, 222–24
of God vs. human beings, 147–48
love and, 74, 213
sexual desire and, 217
sinning and, 26
Beckett, Samuel, 133, 152–53
beginning, as end, 133, 152–53
being, non-being vs., 39–40
being at a loss for words, 249–50
being greater than which none can be conceived. *See* God
being human, 149. *See also* human beings
being with God, being dead vs., 67–68
beings. *See* human beings
bestial persons, 170
biblical myths, of the Fall, 178
big thoughts (great thoughts), 189, 191
big truths, 75
birth, 243, 256
birthmarks, 5
Bloom, Harold, 168n20
body
bodily appetites, 28
body-mind relationship, 34, 42–43
desire for wholeness of, 188–95
doubt and, 42
exclusion from knowing, 35
of hell's sufferers, 165
knowledge of, 43
oneness, 122
otherness, 148
possibility of thoughtful existence and, 195
soul, separation from, 20–22
as source of human imperfection, 183–84
tyrranization of, 191–92
body language, 108, 109
body-mind relationship, 34, 42–43
Boethius, 221–22, 224
Boso (Anselm's interlocutor), 148
Brown, Peter, 15, 47
Burns, J. Patout, 49n4
Burnyeat, Miles, 228–29, 230

carnal will, 10

Index

carnality
  Adamic struggle with, Augustine's reading of, 20–26
  Augustine's, 58
  Augustine's carnal habit, 43, 115
  Augustine's habituation to, 11–12
  Augustine's preferred explanation of, 22
  Augustine's struggle with, 14–20
  Augustine's ties to, 99–100
  see also lust
Carthage, Augustine in, 59–60
causa deficiens. See deficient motives
causa efficiens (effective causes), 92
causes, 14, 121. *See also* deficient motives
Cavadini, John, 17
Cavell, Stanley, 236
celibacy, 15, 98, 199
certainty, 31
change, 190
chaste sexuality, 17
chastity, 15, 202
children, 214–15, 258. *See also* parenting
Christ
  Adam, comparison with, 206–7
  Augustine's dependence on, 125
  Augustine's description of, 73
  Augustine's experience of death and, 79
  divinity and humanity of, 3
  faith as virtue of, 13
  freedom in, 56–57
  freedom of, 49–50
  as God incarnate, 3
  grace of, vs. of God, 46n1
  humanity of, 56
  incarnation of, 151
  as Jesus of Nazareth, 3
  mystery of, 130
  questions of sexuality, lack of interest in, 208
  as teacher, 228
Christian moral values, 157
Christian sexual ethics, 199–212
  See also sex and sexuality
Christianity, radical claims of, 3
Christic regime of grace, 46, 57
Chrysippus (Stoic), 82
churches, huts as, 247
Cicero, 20, 82, 88–89
circle people in Plato's *Symposium* story, 188–89, 190–93
City of God. See De civitate Dei
classical value theorists, 119
classicism, 89, 118
comedy, 188
Commentary on Romans—select verses (*Expositio quarundam propositionum ex epistula Apostoli ad Romanos,* Augustine), 11, 12, 51
compensation, 146–47, 149, 150
compensatory will, 149, 150, 152
competition, 157
conception, 143–44, 257–58
conceptualization of experiences, 62, 251–52
concubines, 15–16
concupiscence, 53
condoning, 138–39
confession
  Augustine's, 239, 241
  basic imperative of, 60
  as philosophical genre, 43–44
  true, nature of, 236
  Wittgenstein's vs. Augustine's approach to, 225–30
  Wittgenstein's vs. Augustine's understanding of, 227
  see also Confessionum libri XIII (Augustine)
confessional readers of Augustine, 236
Confessionum libri XIII (Augustine)
  1.1.1, 28
  1.6.8, 222, 242
  1.7.12, 108
  1.8.13, 107–8, 225, 228, 230–31, 234, 236–37, 239–44
  1.8.13, Wittengstein's excerpt of, 225, 228–29, 231
  1.20.31, 78
  2.1.1, 44, 92
  2.2.1, 227
  2.5.11, 93
  2.6.12, 93

Index

2.6.13, 94
3.1.1, 60
3.4.7, 65
3.6.11, 40
4, 58–59, 59–62, 66, 78–79
4.1.1, 58
4.2.2, 15, 112
4.4.7, 59, 66, 68
4.4.8, 67
4.4.9, 60, 65
4.5.10, 68
4.6.11, 69
4.7.12, 29, 59, 60, 71
4.8.13, 29, 59, 71
4.9.14, 71
4.12.18, 72
4.12.19, 73
4.13.20, 74
4.15.24, 76, 77
4.16.28, 70
4.16.31, 75
6.15.25, 15, 16–17, 24, 112
7, 103, 112, 118, 126
7.1.1, 113
7.1.25, 39
7.3.5, 37, 113, 261
7.4.6, 37
7.10.16, 14, 18, 38, 39, 114, 127, 261
7.10.16–17.17.23, 261
7.11.17, 127
7.13.19, 39, 128, 261
7.17.23, 38, 43, 115, 126
7.18.23, 115
7.18.24, 129
7.20.26, 129
7.21.27, 125, 130
8, 48, 98, 102, 237
8.1.1, 14
8.1.2, 14, 99
8.3.7, 20, 25
8.5.10, 10
8.7.17, 99
8.10.22, 101
8.10.22–24, 19
8.11.21, 10
8.11.26, 11–12
8.11.27, 15
8.12.29, 10, 18, 96, 98, 126, 230, 237
8.12.30, 15, 101
8.17.17, 18
9.10.23, 262
9.12.29, 262
9.12.33, 77
10.4.5, 236
10.27.38, 76
10.29.40, 52
12.3.3, 104
12.6.6, 105
crisis, description of, 10
self-portraiture in, 11
consent, 83
The Consolation of Philosophy (Boethius), 221–22
consolations, 59, 67–68, 73–74
constantia (constancy), 89
contemplative ascesis, 256–57
contexts of application, 2
Contra Academicos (*Against the Skeptics*, Augustine), 123–24
Contra duas epistolas Pelagianorum (*Against two letters of the Pelagians*, Augustine), 51n8
Contra Julianum opus imperfectum (*Against Julian—the unfinished work*, Augustine), 52
conversion, 4, 103–4. *See also* Augustine of Hippo, St., conversion
courage, 167
craving (as emotional disturbance), 20
creation (created order)
  as beautiful to God, 127–28
  beauty of the Father and, 214
  cause of, 14
  ex nihilo, 14, 99, 128–29
  formation and, 112
  hell as original part of, 156
  materiality of, 104–5
  Platonism as doctrine of, 118–26
  possibilities of being and nonbeing in, 176
  as realm of privation, 127
  Yahwist's story of, 180–81
creative difference, 128–29
criminal disaffection, 93–94
crises, Augustinian vs. Cartesian, 31–32

Index

crisis in knowing, 28–44
  confession as philosophical genre, 43–44
  place like no other, 37–40
  radical doubt, 32–36
  sin and error, distance between, 40–43
crisis mentalities, 31
Cur deus homo (Anselm), 146–48

damnation, 53–54, 56. *See also* hell
Dante Alighieri
  ambivalence, Virgil and, 163
  hell, conception of, 175
  on hell, eternal motivation for, 160
  on hell, exit from, 166
  inner states, history of, 163
  midlife crisis, 162
  Nietzsche on blunder of, 156–57
  redemption of, vs. Virgil, 169
  retribution, attitude toward, 161, 165–66
  theological interest in, 161–62
  theology of hell, insight into, 176
  Virgil, relationship to, 163–64
  Virgil's leave-taking of, 176–77
daughters, 209–10
De bono conjugali (*On the good of marriage*, Augustine), 15, 200, 201–2
De civitate Dei (*City of God*, Augustine)
  8, 117, 118, 125
  8.3, 121, 123
  8.5, 118
  8.6, 118, 124, 125
  9.4, 85, 86, 87
  10.29, 125
  10.30, 21
  12:6–8, 92
  12:8, 92
  12.6, 26
  12.6–8, 14, 55n15
  12.7, 5
  13.1, 26
  14, 81–82, 87–88, 90–91
  14.5, 20, 21
  14.6, 82
  14.7, 84, 89
  14.10, 23, 91
  14.11, 24
  14.13, 23
  14.14, 25
  14.17–19, 17
  14.21–24, 17
  14.23, 17
  14.23–24, 91
  19.4, 88
  chaste sexual life, description of, 17
  Stoicism in, 88
De correptione et gratia (*On correction and grace, On admonition and grace*, Augustine), 46, 57
De dono perseverantiae (*On the gift of perseverance*, Augustine), 12
De duabus animabus (*On the two souls*, Augustine), 52
De finibus bonorum et malorum (*On Good Ends and Bad*, Cicero), 85–86
De Genesi ad litteram (*On Genesis—the literal commentary*, Augustine), 23, 27, 90
De Genesi adversus Manicheos (*On Genesis—the anti-Manichean commentary*, Augustine), 22, 23
De libero arbitrio (*On free choice*, Augustine)
  2.1.3, 45
  2.19.53, 45
  3.17.49, 14
  3.18.52, 54
  3.19.53, 56
  Augustine's absolute framing of will in, 14
  Augustine's concern about, 52
  on consent, 83
  on unfair punishments, 56
De magistro (*On the teacher*, Augustine), 110, 111, 228
De nuptiis et concupiscentia (*Marriage and sex*, Augustine), 51n8
De praedestinatione sanctorum (*On the predestination of saints*, Augustine), 56
De spiritu et littera (*On the spirit and the letter*, Augustine), 48

De Trinitate (*The Trinity,* Augustine), 28, 29, 40
death
　Augustine's experiences of, 79
　being with God vs., 67–68
　birth and, 243, 256
　first and second, 25–26
　love and, 29–30
　as outside of life, 243
　see also Augustine of Hippo, St., childhood friend, grief at loss of
debunking, demythologizing vs., 179
deceiving self (Descartes), 33–35
deficient motives (*causa deficiens*)
　as antithetical to presence in God's house, 25
　best explication of, 92–93
　evil will as, 94
　grace and, 5
　introduction of, 72
　of pride, 95
　for separation of soul from body, 22
　for sin, 55
demiurges, 129
demythologizing, 179–80
Descartes, René
　Arnauld, response to, 32n4, 34
　crisis, invention of, 31
　doubting vs deceiving self, 33–35
　on dream states, 33
　error and, 32–33, 35–36
　inner deceiver, 259–61
　on mind-body separation, 34
　on opinions, 32
　problem of error in, 36–38
　sin-error difference in meditations of, 40–42
　as thinking thing, 34
　on will, finite vs. infinite, 35–36
desire(s)
　amoral, 186–87
　of Augustine's infant self, 242–43
　comedy of human, 187–95
　conflict with will, sin and, 91
　dual, of human beings, 183
　erotic, 212
　expression of, 222–23
　to give and to receive, 219–20
　for God, sexual frustration as, 200
　for good/goodness, 5, 193, 219–22
　for hell, 157
　of hell-bound souls, 176
　hopeless justice and end of, 172–77
　infant, 215
　for knowledge, 191–92
　to lack goodness, 25–26
　language of, 243
　law restraining, 195
　movement of, and forgiveness, 146–52
　nature of, 1, 83
　perfection of, 53–54
　seeing and, 181
　sensation and, 144
　sex, relationship to, 18
　Socrates on, 217
　sources of, 21
　spiritual, 199–200
　theft in, 95
　for wholeness, 188–95
　see also will
despair, 20, 176
devil, conundrum of, 37
difference, Augustine's, from God, 128–29
diminishment, 145, 146, 152
Diotima (priestess in *Symposium*), 192–93, 216–19, 249–50
disaffection, 93–95, 134, 135, 238
discipline, 258–59
discontent, Adam's, 196
disobedience
　Adam's, 16, 25
　Adam's and Eve's, 54, 91–92
　as cause of Adam and Eve's mortality, 90
　Eve's, 23
dispossession, 261–62
dissent, 86
divine election, 51, 244–45. *See also* election
divine favor, 57
divine incarnation, 78–79
divine knowledge, quest for, 72
divine law, 181
divine love, 57, 106

Index

divine simplicity, 124
divine will, 160
divinity, 147–48, 181–82. *See also* God; gods
doctrine of creation (Augustine's), 118–26
doctrine of election (Augustine's), 245
doctrine of grace (Augustine's), 52
doctrine of gratuitous election (Augustine's), 11
doctrine of hell, 157–59
doctrine of original sin (Augustine's), 4, 202
doctrine of predestination (Augustine's), 56
doctrines, Augustine's, 245–46
doubting self (Descartes), 33–35
doubt(s), 35, 42, 259
dread lust, 21–22
dream states, 33
dreams, 198
dream-worlds, 33
duty to forgive, 139
dyads, 76

earth (*'adamah*), 180, 205, 254
earthly desires, 122
Eden
    exit from, 195–98
    expulsion from, 254
    puzzle of, 255
    sex in, 17
    story of, 180–81, 253–54
    symbolism of, 254–55
    Wisdom on, 198
    see also Adam and Eve; serpent
effective causes (*causa efficiens*), 92
election, 11, 51, 83, 244–45
Eliot, T. S., 133
emotional disturbances, 20
emotions, 21, 82, 96
emotions, Augustine's theology of, 81–96
    Adam and Eve and, 90–93
    disaffection, three degrees of, 93–95
    introduction to, 81–84
    Stoicism and, 84–89
    summary, 95–96

end, as beginning, 133, 152–53
Endgame (Beckett), 133, 152–53
epistemology of mystical experience, 250–51, 260
equality, 211
eros, 189
Eros, 188
erotic attachments (Augustine's), 14
erotic desire, 212, 217
error, 32–33, 35–36, 36–38, 40–43
Esau, 13
essence, 124
eternal life, path to, 208
eternal wisdom. *See* God
eternity, time vs., 38
eudaimōn (happy), 216
eupatheia (well-tempered passion), 89
Eve
    Adam's description of, 196
    creation of, 16, 181, 253
    Eve's knowledge, 255–56
    name of, 181
    role of, 207
    see also Adam and Eve
evil
    Augustine on, 113
    in creation, 128
    doing evil, self-knowledge and, 182
    evil disaffection, 94
    Freud on, 214
    good people doing, 53
    origins of, 184–85
    problem of, 37–40
evil will, 92, 94
Evodius (Augustine's interlocutor), 45
ex femina (from woman), 14, 20, 27, 99
ex nihilo creation, 14, 99, 128–29
existence
    being, non-being vs., 39–40
    doubt of, 259
    essence, difference from, in non-God beings, 124
    see also creation
existential judgments, 103
experiences, 62, 251–52
Expositio quarundam propositionum ex epistula Apostoli ad Romanos (Commentary on

Index

Romans—select verses, Augustine), 11, 12, 51
external goods, 88

faith, 12, 13, 78, 250
faithful people, 13
Fall (from grace)
  Kant's reading of, 181–82
  loss of wholeness and, 189
  moral of, 194
  as myth of moral philosophy, 178
  as tragedy, 196–97
  see also Adam and Eve; circle people; serpent
falsehood, 178–79
Father. *See* God the Father, beauty of
fatherhood, 210
father's protection, 214
father-son relationships, 107, 108–9, 110–11
faux materiality, 103
fear, sources of, 21
finite self, 36, 42
finitude, 77
first circle of hell, 169
first death, 25–26
first sin. *See* original sin
first woman. *See* Eve
Flasch, Kurt, 47
flesh, 22, 82, 116, 125
fools, 141–43
forgetting, about childhood, 109
forgiveness, anachronism of, 133–54
  absolute time and, 152–54
  Anselm's fool and, 141–46
  introduction to, 133–36
  as ironic, 152
  moralism and, 136–40
  movement of desire and, 146–52
  religious imagination and, 141
form, materiality and, 116
form of life (*Lebensform*), 233n13, 240
formation, creation and, 112
formlessness, 102
Four Quartets (Eliot), 133
Freccero, John, 161
free choice of the will (*liberum arbitrium*), 45–57
  Adam and, 54–56
  Augustine's terms concerning, 48–50
  Christ, freedom in, 56–57
  contextual development of Augustine's thinking about, 50–54
  divine will, relationship to, 160
  evil as expression of, 185
  God's grace vs., 12
free will. *See* free choice of the will
freedom
  Adamic, 55
  of Christ, 46, 49–50, 56–57
  human, nature of, 53
  ideal, 49
  laws of, 182
  libertarian view of, 158–59
  nature of desires and, 83
  from passion (*apatheia*), 86–87, 96
  to refuse grace, 47
  See also free choice of the will
Freud, Sigmund
  on connection between sex and beauty, 213
  on evil, 214
  on infancy, 223
  on religious need, 214–15
  on seeking protection, 222
  on sublimation, 221
  on unconditional love, 150–51
friend (Augustine's). *See* Augustine of Hippo, St., childhood friend, grief at loss of
friendships, 61, 71, 212
fruits, as seeds, 190
fundamental sounds, 153

Gaddo (child of Ugolino in *Inferno*), 175
Garden of Eden. *See* Eden
Gellius, Aulus, 85
The Genealogy of Morals (Nietzsche), 156–57
Genesis (Old Testament)
  Augustine's commentary on, 22, 23
  Augustine's counterfactual speculation on, 24
  Augustine's version of, 72

Index

Genesis (Old Testament) *(continued)*
  socially conservative reading of, 204
  sources of, 180
  story of (*see* Fall)
  see also Old Testament, Genesis *for specific verses*
genitals, placement of, 188, 189
gnosis (self-knowledge), 182, 210
God
  absence, 73–74
  Anselm on, 141–46, 248
  Augustine's conception of, 37
  Augustine's desire for love of, 44
  Augustine's differences from, 128–129
  Augustine's knowing of, 113–14
  Augustine's love for, 76, 125
  Augustine's Platonized, 117
  beauty of (*see* God the Father, beauty of)
  being other to, 147–48, 152
  Cartesian, 34
  as child, 237–38
  Christ as God incarnate, 3
  conceivability of, 144–45
  as creator of good and goodness, 222
  disaffection toward, 94–95
  existence of, 143
  fiction of, 260–61
  fools' denial of, 141–42
  formlessness, creator of, 102
  Freud on, 213–14
  grace of, vs. of Christ, 46n1
  as heart's rest, 28
  human knowledge of, 208
  humankind and, 3, 12, 13
  humanness of, 124
  infancy of, 246
  as judge and forgiver, 73
  knowing of, 120
  love by, 95
  love of, 72, 123, 198
  materiality and, 112–16, 127
  mother of, 207
  need for, 142
  as non-being, 125
  ontological argument for, 143
  peace of, 3
  Platonists' idea of, 118, 124–25
  prodigals, preference for, 20
  redemption and, 11
  self, basis for difference from, 42
  self-limitation, 262
  sexuality, dissociation from, 213
  as teacher, 110
  wholeness of, 77
  Yahweh as, 256–58
  YHWH 'Elohim, 204
  see also entries beginning "divine"; Yahweh
God, knowledge of, 248–62
  introduction, 248–53
  knowledge of good and evil and, 253–58
  self-reflection and, 258–62
God the Father, beauty of, 213–24
  desire for beauty and desire for good, differences between, 216–19
  good, ways of becoming, beauty and, 219–22
  introduction, 213–15
  nature of parenting and, 222–24
gods (bearers of a holy will), 179, 183, 189, 193, 215
good and goodness
  Augustine on desire for a, 5
  choosing, 11
  desire for, 1, 216–19, 219–22
  desire to lack, 25–26
  evil, conversion to, 255–56
  as exhausting the possibilities of being, 4
  found in darkness, 162–63
  God as creator of, 222
  highest good (*summum bonum*), 121–22, 123
  importance of idea of, 2
  indescribable, 250
  middling good, 45–46
  of obedience, inherited ignorance of, 50
  as object of desires, 193
  possessibility, 2
  problem of, 37

good people doing evil, 53
goods, 2, 77, 85–86, 93
grace
  aim of, 52
  Augustine's claims concerning his doctrine of, 52
  election by, 245
  emotions and, 96
  free will vs., 12
  freedom to refuse, 47
  of God vs. of Christ, 46n1
  nature of, 4–5
  regimes of, 46, 57
  transformation of desire and, 53–54
  will to break with God and, 10–11
gratuitous election, Augustine's doctrine of, 11
great thoughts (big thoughts), 189, 191
grief
  Augustine's rehabilitation of, 89
  Augustine's theology of, 61
  Cicero's vs. Augustine's terms for, 89
  as emotion worth avoiding, 88–89
  first form of, 89
  as God-bereft, 60
  Hamlet's, 64–65
  ideal of, 77
  revenge and, 175
  sin and, 62
  see also Augustine of Hippo, St., childhood friend, grief at loss of
Groundwork of the Metaphysics of Morals (Kant), 182
growing older, knowledge and, 258–59
habit, 19
Hamlet (Shakespeare), 64–65
Hamm (character in *Endgame*), 152–53
Hampton, Jean, 136, 138, 139, 140
happiness, 23, 86
happy (*eudaimōn*), 216
hate, 139, 157
heart
  effects of original sin on, 72
  God's keeping of, 60
  mind and, 28–29, 30
  mind-body relationship and, 42–43
  as transgressive, 28, 29
  See also emotions, Augustine's theology of
heaven, third, 262
hell, 155–77
  beasts encountered in, 163, 170, 171–72
  belief in, 155
  belief in doctrine of, 157–59
  Dante's conception of, 175
  despair and, 176
  exit from, 166
  first circle of, 169
  hopeless justice and end of desire and, 172–77
  inscription over gateway to, 156, 157, 165
  introduction, 155–56
  libertarian view of, 158–60
  motives for entering, 165–66
  motives for existence of, 157
  order in, 173
  organization of, 169–70
  as original part of creation, 156
  scandal of, 156–61
  theology of, Dante's insight into, 176
  tower of hunger in, 172
  Virgil in, 161–67
  Virgil's sin, 167–72
Helvius Vindicianus, 70n9
Hephaestus, 189
heteronomy, 120
Hierus (Roman orator), 76
highest good (*summum bonum*), 121–22, 123
hindsight, Augustine's, 72–73
hope, 138
hopeless desire, 171–72
hopelessness, 177
Hound of God, 174
hubris, 191, 193, 194
human beings
  body as source of imperfection, 183–84
  creation of, 180
  dual nature of, 183, 194–95
  God, breach with, 3
  God, differences from, 13
  initiative (*see* free choice of the will)

Index

human beings *(continued)*
  knowing of, 133–34
  moral development, 195–96
  personality of, and moral ideal, 179
  perversity and pure will of, 145–46
  Plato on kinds of, 188
  spirit, corruption of, 186
  wholeness, search for, 77
  see also body; desires; will
human desire, comedy of, 187–95
human understanding, 228, 229
humanity, divinely knowable, 147–48
humility, 129
hunger, 172–75
Hunger's Tower, 173
huts, churches as, 247

ideal freedom, 49
ideal(s)
  gods as, 179
  of grief, 77
  in reality, 239
ignorance, 50, 119, 249–50. *See also* knowing and knowledge
imagination, 143–44
immaterial spirit, 14
immoral law of freedom, 182
immortality, 30–31, 72
imperfect guides, 176–77
imperfections, 135, 183–84, 194
impressions, 85, 86–87, 88
incarnation
  Augustine's feel for, 100–101
  conversion as, 4
  divine, 78–79
  forgiveness and, 146–52
  of sin, irony of, 165
  surprise of, 117–18
  time and, 153–54
  see also materiality
incontinence (*akrasia*), 171
incontinent desire, 171–72
individuation, 250
the ineffable, 250
infancy
  Augustine's description of, 222–23
  Augustine's memory of, 226, 231, 235, 236–38, 242

  as disaffection, 238
  of God, 246
  lost, 241
infants
  Augustine's experience of, 108
  Augustine's portrait of, 242–43
  consciousness, 222
  needs, 214–15, 222–23
  self-awareness, 235
Inferno (Dante), 155–77
  3.19.5–6, 156
  canonical readings of, 160–61
  canto IV, 177
  canto XI, 169–70
  canto XXXII, 173
  hopeless justice and end of desire in, 172–77
  points of view in, 161, 162
  propheticism of, 165
  protagonist vs. narrator of, 161, 162
  sins, incarnations of, 164
  Virgil, sin of, 167–72
  Virgil in hell, 163–67
inspiration, 2
integrity, moral, 194
interior teachers, 111–12
internalized serpent, 185
intimacy, 210–11, 212
involuntary impressions (*phantasiae*), 85, 86
inwardness, 38–39
Ionian school of philosophy, 121
irresolute will, 45
ish (man), 206

Jacob, 12, 13, 51
James, William, 103–4, 252–53
Jerome (monk), 199, 200
Jesus of Nazareth
  Christ as, 3
  his way of seeing, 208
  source of merit of, 56–57
  tormentors, forgiveness of, 152
  will of, 150
  see also Christ
Job, 168
Jordan, Mark, 100–101
Jovinian (monk), 199, 200

280

Index

judgments, existential vs. spiritual, 103–4
Julian of Eclanum, 51, 52
justice, 158, 172–77
justification, 119

Kant, Immanuel
  on Adam, 196
  on amoral desires, 186–87
  on being a son, 197
  on the body, 183–84
  Eden, restoration of, in human nature, 197–98
  on evil, origin of, 184–85
  Fall, readings of, 181–82
  on Genesis, 26, 194
  Genesis story, demythologizing of, 179–80, 184–87
  on identifying value of myth, 179
  on immoral law, 182–83
  on moral values, 195
  Plato, similarities to, 194
knowing and knowledge
  in an idealized world, 120
  of beings, 133–34, 152
  desire for, 191–92
  desires for perfection vs., 187, 190
  dispossession of, 261–62
  doubt and, 259
  epistemology of mystical experience, 250–51
  of errors, 32–33
  goodness and, 2
  growing older and, 258–59
  human vs. divine way of, 193–94
  inspiration and, 2
  knowledge of good and evil, limits of, 186
  living, split with, 197–98
  nature of, 29
  objective knowledge, 205
  original knowledge, 2–3
  tree of knowledge, 23, 90, 180, 181, 205, 253
  types of, 134
  Yahweh's part in, 257
  see also crisis in knowing; God, knowledge of

Kolnai, Aurel, 136, 137, 138
Korsgaard, Christine, 118–19, 120, 121

language
  Augustine's picture of, 108, 228, 231
  Augustine's picture of, Wittgenstein's critique of, 225–27, 231–32, 234–35
  Augustine's picture of, Wittgenstein's confessional critique of, 227–28, 235–36, 239–44
  desires and, 212, 243
  expression of needs and, 223
  learning of, 108–10
  logic of, 239–40
  meaning of, 227, 232–33
  prayer and, 110–11
  teaching and learning and, 110
  Wittgenstein on, 106–7
  Wittgenstein on learning, 234
  Wittgenstein's example of use of, 232–33
Last Judgment, 165
law, 181, 182, 183, 195
learning, language and, 110
Lebensform (form of life), 233n13, 240
Lebourlier, Jean, 49n4
Léon-Dufour, Xavier, 48n4
leopard, in *Inferno*, 163, 170, 176
liberal studies, 75
libertarian view of hell, 158–59
liberum arbitrium. See free choice of the will
life, 18, 73, 162, 233n13, 240
light of security (*lux securitatis*), 96, 237
Limbo, 171
lion, in *Inferno*, 163, 170, 176
living, split with knowing, 197–98
logic, 239–40, 241–42
logic of desire, 217
logical paradox of forgiveness, 137
lost beginnings, 178
love
  Augustine's, for friends, 71
  Augustine's, for God, 76
  of beauty, 217–18

love *(continued)*
   blindness of, 28–29
   death and, 29–30
   failures of, 172
   by God, 95
   of God, 72, 123, 198
   hell's creation and, 156–57
   loving too much, 79
   mystery of consummation of, 219
   nature of, 49, 50, 74
   parental vs. sexual, 116
   pride vs., 95
   redemption from sin, 79–80
   unconditional, 150–51
   unity of, 71–72
   will, confusion with, 83–84
   will, distinction from, 150
lowest goods, 93
lust
   effects on body-soul tie, 27
   as pathologized privation, 17–18
   sense of own flesh, 116
   terrena cupiditas (earthly lust), 122
   will, opposition to, in paradise, 17
   See also carnality
lux securitatis (light of security), 96, 237

Madec, Goulven, 47–48
madness (Augustine's), in boyhood friendship, 67, 68, 69–71, 74
malignant genius (malicious demon, *malignus genius,* Descartes), 33–34, 35, 259–60
man and human
   'adam, 180, 205, 254
   anthrôpos, 205
   ish, 206
Mani (founder of Manicheism), 58n1
Manicheism
   about, 58n1
   Augustine on, as false religion, 63
   Augustine's, 19, 37, 58–59
   Augustine's, effects on his grief, 63–64, 68
   Augustine's divergence from, 52–53
   problematic aspects of, 69–70
Marion, Jean-Luc, 106

marital sexuality, 200–2, 203
marriage, 99, 199, 200–2
Marriage and sex (*De nuptiis et concupiscentia,* Augustine), 51n8
Mary (mother of Jesus), 256
material diversity, 121
materiality
   of conversion, 103–4
   of creation, 104–5
   of father-son receptivity, 107
   form and, 116
   God and, 112–16, 127
   good of, 97–98
   Wittgenstein on, 105–6
   see also Augustine of Hippo, St., conversion; incarnation
matter, 102, 103–6, 114, 129
meaning of language, 232–33
meditation, 258–59
Meditations on First Philosophy (Descartes), 31, 32, 41–42
middling good, 45–46
midlife crises, 162
mind-body relationship, 34, 42–43
mind(s), 28–29, 30, 102
mind's eye, 259
moderation of sexuality, 202–3
modern value theory, 119
monads, 76
Monica (Augustine's mother), 15, 77, 262
monism, 216
monotheism, 216
moral evil, 184–85
moral forgiveness, 136–40
moral idealization, 135–36, 179
moral integrity, 194
moral law, 181, 182, 183
moral life, 186
moral philosophy. *See* myth, moral philosophy and
moral values, 195
moral worth, 137
moralism, 141
mortality, 29–30, 90, 206, 210
mother, desire for, 214, 221
motherless Aphrodite, 220–21
multiple personalities, 215

282

mundane sex, 199, 200–2, 203
mutability, 105
mysticism, 251–53, 252
mystics, 250–51, 252–53, 262
myth, moral philosophy and, 178–98
   demythologizing, 179
   Eden, exit from, 195–98
   falsehood, connotations of, 178–79
   introduction, 178–80
   Kant and the serpent, mystery of, 180–87
   moral philosophy as arbiter of myth, 195
   Plato, comedy of human desire and, 187–95
myth of soul, Platonic, 21
myth of will, 9–27
   Adam's separation from Eve and, 22–26
   Augustine's conversion and, 14–20
   body-soul separation and, 20–22
   origins of, 10–14
mythology, private, 260

nakedness, 253, 255
naturalism, 229–30
needs
   religious, 214–15
   see also desire(s)
New Testament
   Matthew
      27:46, 151
   Mark
      12:27, 208
      15:34, 151
   Luke
      15:11–32, 92–93
      23:24, 151
      23:344, 224
   John
      12:24, 257
      14:16, 208
      19:30, 151
   Romans
      1:20, 114, 127
      7, 11–12, 51–52
      7:22, 110
      9, 11, 12, 13, 51
      9:10–29, 50–51
      13:13–14, 10, 98, 237
      13:14, 126, 230, 243
      14:1, 15
      31:13–14, 96
   1 Corinthians
      7:32, 200
      15:36, 257
   1 Timothy 2:14, 91
   1 John
      4:19, 198
Nicomachean Ethics (Aristotle), 170
Nietzsche, Friedrich, 100, 156–57
non-being, 39–40, 176
norms, 119
not being God, 13
nothing, love of, 95

obedience, 50
objective knowledge, 205
objects, knowing of, 133–34
oceanic feeling, 214
O'Donnell, James J., 59
Old Testament
   Genesis
      1:2, 104
      1:27, 203
      2, 201
      2:4b, 180
      2:4b–3:24, 90, 204, 253–54
      2:9, 205
      2:17, 180, 205, 254
      2:18, 254
      2:21–25, 16
      2:23, 196, 210
      2:25, 254
      3:4–5, 254
      3:6, 23, 181, 254, 255
      3:7, 254
      3:8–19, 255
      3:12, 25, 181, 207, 255
      3:13, 255
      3:14–19, 257
      3:20, 25, 196, 207, 254
      3:22, 207
      3:24, 180, 254
      4:1, 210, 256

Index

Exodus
   3:14, 114
Psalms
   14, 141
   18:6, 73
   53, 141
On admonition and grace (*De correptione et gratia,* Augustine), 46, 57
On beauty and aptness (*De pulchro et apto* Augustine), 74–75, 76
On correction and grace (*De correptione et gratia, On Admonition and Grace,* Augustine), 46, 57
On free choice (Augustine). See *De libero arbitrio*
On free will. See *De libero arbitrio*
On Genesis—the anti-Manichean commentary (*De Genesi adversus Manicheos,* Augustine), 22, 23
On Genesis—the literal commentary (*De Genesi ad litteram,* Augustine), 23, 27, 90
On the gift of perseverance (*De dono perseverantiae,* Augustine), 12
On good ends and bad (*De finibus bonorum et malorum,* Cicero), 85–86
On the good of marriage (*De bono conjugali,* Augustine), 15, 200, 201–2
On the predestination of saints (*De praedestinatione sanctorum,* Augustine), 56
On the spirit and the letter (*De spiritu et littera,* Augustine), 48
On the teacher (*De magistro,* Augustine), 110, 111, 228
On the two souls (*De duabus animabus,* Augustine), 52
oneness, of beauty, 218, 219
the ontological argument, 143
opinions, Decartes on, 32
original flesh, 22
original guilt, 54
original human love, 72
original innocence, 238
original intimacy, 212

original knowledge, 2–3
original sin
   Augustine's doctrine of, 4, 245
   human heart, effects on, 72
   Kant on, 26
   of midlife crisis, 162
   pride as cause of, 92
   roles of Adam and Eve in, 23–24, 54–55
   willing of subjection to corrupting influences as, 185
origins, causes vs., 14
otherness, 29, 120, 148–49, 235

pain and pain behavior, 105, 107
pandemian Aphrodite, 220
parables, of the prodigal son, 93
Paraclete, 208
paradise, lust and will in, 17. See also Eden
paradox, 106–7, 137
parental love, 116
parenting
   as asymmetrical relation, 211
   Augustine's language acquisition and, 246
   bad, 11
   children's desires and, 223–24
   parents' knowledge of children, 258
   sexual desire and, 201
   unbounded nature of, 235
Pascal, Blaise, 44
passion, 85, 86–87, 89. See also desire
Paul, Saint
   on Christ, 206
   conversion, 12
   flesh, captivity to, 51
   Letter to the Romans (*see* New Testament, Romans)
   on marriage, 99, 200–1
   on peace of God, 3
   Wittgenstein on, 247
Pausanias (character in *Symposium*), 220–21
peace of God, 3
pears, theft of, 92–94
Pelagianism, 50
Pelagius, 52

perfect faith, 78
perfected recollection, 3
perfection, desires for, vs. knowledge, 187, 190
personhood, 30
persons, 137. *See also* human beings
perturbatio (emotion), 88, 89
perversity, human, 145–46
Phaedo (Socrates), 121
phantasiae (involuntary impressions), 85, 86
philosophical genres, 44
Philosophical Investigations (Wittgenstein)
  §1, 226, 230–31, 231–32, 232–33
  §32, 237
  §101, 239
  §108, 241
  Augustine's place in, 241
  beginning of, 225
  as confessional, 226
  fragment xi, n. 319, 236
  on language use, 226
  on pain, 105
  preface to, 240
philosophical self, 241–42, 243
philosophy
  Augustine's place in history of, 120–21
  idealism in, 228
  as love of God, 123–24
  moral (*see* myth, moral philosophy and)
  pride as enemy of, 123
  see also Platonism; Platonists
philosophy, Augustine's history of, 117–26
  Augustine's return to self, 126–29
  introduction, 117–18
  Ionian school in, 121
  Korsgaard and, 119–21
  Plato in, 123–24
  Platonists in, 118–19, 124–26
  Pythagoreans in, 123
  Socrates in, 121–22
  summary, 129–30
place like no other (place of unlikeness, *regio dissimilitudinis*)

Augustine's experience of life from, 114, 115
impossibility of, 261
not part of creation, 127
readings of, 128–29
space of radical doubt, difference from, 38–39
Plato
  in Augustine's history of philosophy, 123–24
  as classical value theorist, 119
  comedy of human desire and, 187–95
  on desire for beauty and desire for good, difference between, 216–19
  on enjoyment of beauty and desire, 220
  Kant, similarities to, 194
  nature of art of, 188
  on the real, basis for, 120
Platonism
  Augustine's, 14, 114, 117–30
  Augustine's break with, 89
  Augustine's views of, 20–21
  autonomy in knowing and, 120
  as doctrine of creation, 118–26
  God, idea of, 124–25
  greatest puzzle of, 3
  without Christ, 129–30
Platonists, 2, 85, 118, 125
play, 238
Plotinus, 104n7, 114, 118, 125, 261
points of view, human vs. divine, 197–98
prayer, 12, 110–11
preconception of crystalline purity (*das Vorurteil der Kristallreinheit*), 241
predestination, 56
preemptive grace, 46
pride, 92, 95, 123
private mythology, 260
privation, 127
procreation, 202
procreative intimacies, 211
prodigals, 20, 93
propheticism, of *Inferno*, 165

285

Index

prophylactic grace, 46
proportionate harm, 158
Proslogion (Anselm), 141, 142–46, 248
protection, seeking, 222
Proudfoot, Wayne, 251–52
psychopathology, 170
punishments, vicarious, 56
Purgatorio (Dante), 176
purified souls, 21
Pythagoras of Samos, 123
Pythagoreans, 123

radical doubt, 31–32, 32–40, 38
reading Augustine, difficulties of, 63
reality, ideal in, 239
reason, 3, 43–44
reciprocity, 211
Reconsiderations (*Retractationes*, Augustine), 12, 22, 50, 52, 69
redemption, 11, 150
redemptive consent, 83–84
regio dissimilitudinis. *See* place like no other
reincarnation, 20
relative beauty, 74–75
religion. *See* Christ; God; gods; Jesus of Nazareth
Religion within the Boundaries of Mere Reason (Kant), 178, 182
religious forgiveness, 139
religious imagination, 141
renunciation, 220
res cogitans (thinking thing), 34
respect, of persons, 137
Retractationes (*Reconsiderations*, Augustine), 12, 22, 50, 52, 69
retributive justice (retribution), 157–58, 161, 165–66
revenge, 175
rewards, vicarious, 56
Ruggieri, Archbishop, 172–73

saints, 46, 252–53, 262
Satan, 5, 172
scandal, of hell, 156–61
science, 178–79
second death, 26

Seducing Augustine (Burrus, Jordan, and MacKendrick), 100
seeds, 190, 257
seeing, by Eve, 181
self
   Augustine's return to, 37–38, 126–29
   Descartes on, 42
   self-awareness, 235
   self-blinding reason, 3
   self-conception, 196, 197
   self-control, 99–100
   self-deception, 221, 258–61
   self-definition, 94, 137
   self-determination, 160
   self-diminishment, 145, 146
   self-disclosure, 161
   self-escape, 67–68
   selfish desires, 5
   self-knowledge (*gnosis*), 182, 210
   self-limitation, of God, 262
   self-love, 29, 84
   self-mastery, 238
   self-reflection, 258–62
   self-rule, 195–96
   self-tyrrany, 243
   who is not yet, 38–39
   Wittgenstein's philosophical self, 241–42
sense of value, 86
senses and sensing, 143–44, 259
separation, in attachment, 25
serpent (in Garden of Eden)
   Adam's vs. Eve's belief in, 54, 92
   autonomy and, 187
   Eve's belief in, 23
   evil of, 26–27
   Genesis story of, 90
   internalized, 185
   Kant's demythologized reading of, 184–87
   lies of, 181, 254
   source of evil of, 185
   symbolism of, 181–82, 190, 255
sex and sexuality, 199–212
   desire, relationship to, 18
   dissociation of God from, 213
   Jovianian on, 200

Index

in marriage, 200–2
moderation of, 202–3
natural (mundane) side of, 199, 200–2, 203
original goodness of, 17
recognition of, through fatherhood, 210
sexual continence (*see* celibacy)
sexual desire, 43, 201, 212, 217
sexual difference, 181, 201, 204, 205–6, 212
sexual ethics, 200, 208
sexual fidelity, 16–17
sexual frustration as desire for God, 200
sexual identities, 188–89
sexual love vs. parental love, 116
sexual pleasure, Augustine on, 201
sexual restraint, Jerome on, 200
spiritual side of, 199, 202–3
true marriage, debate over, 204, 206
see also carnality
sexism, 24
Shanzer, Danuta, 16
sharpness, context for, 2
she-wolf, in *Inferno*, 163, 170, 171–72, 174, 176
Simplician, 11–12, 83
sin (alienation from the good)
  abandonment, temporal relationship to, 152
  aesthetics of, 74–78
  of arrogance, 177
  Augustine on, 5
  Augustine's, own characterization of, 78
  beauty, relationship to, 26
  capacity to, as humanness, 149
  and conflict between will and desire, 91
  deficient cause of, 5, 55
  desire for absolute antithesis between God and humanity as, 78–79
  early definition of, 52
  error, differences from, 40–43
  facing, 172
  first, roles of Adam and Eve in, 23–24
  in grief, 62, 77–78
  hierarchy of, 170–71
  human responsibility for, 25–26
  insensibility of God and, 145
  irony of incarnation of, 165
  Jesus' knowledge of, 152
  as love of nothing, 95
  place like no other and, 39, 128
  power of, 60–61
  pride as cause of, 92
  psychology of, in *Inferno*, 170
  redemption of love from, 79–80
  selfish desires and, 5
  sinners, separation from, 138–39, 140
  Virgil's, 167–72
  as will of rational beings, 4
  will to, freedom and, 160
  see also original sin
sinners, sin, separation from, 138–39, 140
skepticism, 134, 137, 139, 140
Skerrett, Kathleen, 116n22, 209–12
Socrates, 121–22, 216–18
Socratic disputation, 123
Soliloquies (*Soliloquia*, Augustine), 81
solipsism, 36
sons, 196–97. *See also* father-son relationships
Sorabji, Richard, 84–85
soul(s)
  body, separation from, 20–22 (*see also* death)
  cardinal movements of, 88
  desire for God, 53
  emotions and, 21, 88
  hell-bound, desire of, 176
  intimacy and, 211
  monads vs. dyads, 76
  purified Platonist, Adam's similarity to, 22–23
  rebirth, wish for, 25
  see also spirit
speaking French, 1–2
speaking significantly, 142–43

287

Index

spirit
  Augustine on, 114–15
  Augustine's conversion to, 19
  Augustine's identification with, 101–2
  flesh vs., 10, 14, 25, 27, 82, 256, 258
  God as, 75, 98, 113, 118, 151, 261
  good, temptation and, 185
  Kant on, 186
  love and, 116
  rule by, 82
  sin and, 55
  spiritual desire, 199–200, 202–3
  spiritual judgments, 103–4
  spiritual will, 10
  wise persons and, 216
  see also soul(s)
stability, Augustine's desire for, 14, 19, 20
Starnes, Colin, 62
Stoicism
  Augustine's construct of, 95
  Augustine's rejection of, 84, 89
  on emotional disturbances, 20
  and emotions, Augustine's theology of, 84–89
  on freedom, 50
  Sorabji on, 84–85
  on wise persons' experience of passion, 85
struggle of will, 10
sublimation, 221
suicide, 88
summum bonum (highest good), 121–22, 123
Symposium (Plato), 187, 188, 216–17

Talbott, Thomas, 159
teaching, 110, 111, 228
temporal relationships. *See* forgiveness, anachronism of
temptations, 184, 185–86, 186–87
terrena cupiditas (earthly lust), 122
Thagaste episode (Augustine), 59–60
Thales of Miletus, 121
theism, 125
theodicy, 36, 128
Theodoric, 221–22, 224

theological allegory, 164n12
things, causes of, 121
  See also materiality
thinking, negative aspects to, 107
thinking thing (*res cogitans*), 34
third heaven, 262
Thomas Aquinas, 125
time
  absolute, and forgiveness, 152–54
  endings and beginnings and, 153
  eternity vs., 38
  incarnation and, 153–54
  Wittgenstein on timelessness, 243
  See also forgiveness, anachronism of
time-tested affection. *See* human beings
To Simplician—on various questions. See Ad Simplicianum de diversis quaestionibus
tower of hunger, 172
Tractatus Logico-Philosophicus (Wittgenstein), 240
  2.0123, 231n10–232n10
  5.631, 242
  5.641, 241
  6.43, 242
  6.54, 239n18
  6.432, 242
  6.4311, 242, 243
  picture of language in, 241
  preface to, 239
  theory of meaning in, 231
tragedy, 188, 196–97
tree of knowledge, 23, 90, 180, 181, 205, 253
tree of life, 90, 180, 181, 207–8, 253
The Trinity (*De Trinitate*, Augustine), 28, 29, 40
Triolo, Alfred A., 171n23
tristitia (grief), 89
true confession, 236
true marriage, 204, 206
true virtue (*aretē alēthē*), 217–18
trust, of children for parents, 223–24
truth, as problem of articulation, 64
Tusculan Disputations (Cicero), 20, 82, 88–89
tyranny, 191, 243

Index

Ugolino, Count (in *Inferno*), 172–75
unconditional love, 150–51
understanding, 228, 229, 236
unfair punishments, 56
unity of love, 71–72
unwilling acts, 48

value, nature of, 119
value-neutral material world, 121
values, moral, 195
The Varieties of Religious Experience (William), 103–4, 252
vicarious punishment and rewards, 56
vicious persons, 170
Virgil
　Dante's relationship to, 163–64
　as deus ex machina, 163
　fate of, 176–77
　in hell, 163–67
　infernal, case against, 169–70
　Job, comparison with, 168
　on motive for entering hell, 166
　Oedipal reading of, 168
　as Platonist, 21
　prophecy of Hound of God, 173
　sin of, 167–72
　tragic vs. allegorical readings of, 163–65
virtue(s), 11, 12, 13, 86
voice of the child, Augustine's conversion and, 114, 116, 237–38
das Vorurteil der Kristallreinheit (preconception of crystalline purity), 241
vulnerable beauty, 77

wanting. *See* desire
Weil, Simone, 220, 221
well-tempered passion (*eupatheia*), 89
Wetzel, James
　Augustine, debt to, 3–4
　Augustine, readings of, 4
　Augustine, relationship to, 101
　on Augustine's doctrine of original sin, 4
　daughter, relationship to, 224
　difficulty of reading *Confessions* 4, 61–62
　on goodness, wanting for, 2
　on goods, wanting for, 1–2
　Platonism, unease with, 2–3
　son, language learning and, 108–9
　as teacher, 4
wholeness, 77, 188–95
will
　absolutized human, 13–14
　affect and, 146
　Augustine's emphasis on, 9
　Augustine's notion of, 49, 55, 96
　Augustine's struggle of, 10
　to be moral, 183
　to be other to God, 39–40
　to choose ignorance, 14
　compensatory, 149, 152
　conflict with desire, sin and, 91
　dissociative, 57
　election of, 12
　evil, 92, 94, 185
　finite vs. infinite, 35–36
　of God, 120, 149–50
　greatest conceivable, 145
　incarnate, 151
　irresolute, 45
　libertarian view of hell and, 159–60
　life of, forms of, 46
　love vs., 83–84, 150
　lust, opposition to, in paradise, 17
　as middling good, 45–46
　opposition to, 183
　otherness of, 148–49
　power of, 36
　pure, human perversity and, 145–46
　quality of, emotions and, 82
　spiritual vs. carnal, 10
　unwilling acts and, 48
　see also desire(s); free choice of the will; myth of will
willful forgetting, 21
wisdom, 49
Wisdom, John, 198, 215
wise persons, 85
Wittgenstein, Ludwig, 225–47
　Augustine, admiration for, 227n3

289

Index

Wittgenstein, Ludwig *(continued)*
    Augustine, comparison with, 229–30
    Augustine, tribute to, 244
    Augustine's childhood memories and, 108, 230–38
    Augustine's picture of language, critique of, 225–27, 231–32, 234–35
    Augustine's picture of language, confessional critique of, 227–28, 235–36, 239–44
    confession, approach to, vs. Augustine's, 225–30
    confessional shift of focus, 244–47
    on matter, 105–6
    naturalism, 229–30
    on paradox, 106–7
    on true confession, 236
    two ways of thinking, 240–41
woman, first. *See* Eve
women, Augustine's desire for, 14
words, 232–33, 233–34, 249–50. *See also* language

Yahweh
    about, 204–5
    Adam and Eve and, 90, 205–6, 253–54, 255–56
    Adam's self-conception and, 196
    autonomy and, 187
    as God, 256–58
    as the one God, 91
    son, conception of, 257
    tree of life, protection of, 207–8
    see also God
Yahwist (Genesis author), 180, 184, 185
YHWH 'Elohim, 204

Zeus, 189

www.ingramcontent.com/pod-product-compliance
Lightning Source LLC
Chambersburg PA
CBHW021652230426
43668CB00008B/599